The Best, Worst, Weird Movies Of the 1990s

MARK MCPHERSON

Copyright © 2017 Mark McPherson

All rights reserved.

ISBN-13: 978-1977719430
ISBN-10: 1977719430

CLASSIFICATIONS

BEST: These movie are absolute must-sees of the decade, the ones that every lover of film should consider mandatory viewing. *Examples: Beauty and the Beast, Fargo, Pulp Fiction.*

WORST: Treat these like the plague. These are the movies so ill thought and horrendously produced they're not worth your time. *Examples: Godzilla, North, Wild Wild West*

WEIRD: The weird movies are the ones that are either so odd, peculiar or of the era they must be seen to be believed. *Examples: Addams Family Values, Home Alone, Space Jam.*

12 MONKEYS

DIRECTOR: Terry Gilliam | SCREENWRITER: David Peoples, Janet Peoples | CAST: Bruce Willis, Madeleine Stowe, Brad Pitt, Christopher Plummer | GENRE: Science Fiction | RUNNING TIME: 129 min | MPAA RATING: R

CLASSIFICATION: WEIRD

Based on the French short film *La Jetée*, Terry Gilliam's *12 Monkeys* (1995) may be the director's most grounded work, despite its somewhat tricky scenario. The future of 2035 is one where humans have been forced underground after a virus spread by a terrorist group has wiped out five billion people. In the cold and industrial underground, built with material that is rusted and leaking, prisoners are tasked by the remaining ruling class for solving the crisis.

Cole (Bruce Willis) is the lucky or unlucky prisoner assigned with traveling back in time to figure out what caused the initial spread of the virus that began in 1996. But since nothing in the dark future appears to be working at 100%, Cole is instead sent back to 1990. He arrives bloody and sweaty, only to be quickly arrested and sent to a mental institution. Just a few minutes into the movie and Willis is already as dirty and battered as he was by the end of the *Die Hard* pictures. During his brief stay before being sent back to the future, he meets the crazed mental patient Jeff Goines, played with frantic insanity by an energetic Brad Pitt. Cole is additionally diagnosed by Doctor Kathryn Railly (Madeleine Stowe) as crazy for stating his mission as a time-traveler. He'll meet them both in the future when he is transported back and sent to 1996.

Cole's mission begins to come together when he discovers Jeff is an animal rights activist and that Jeff's father (Christopher Plummer) works in the lab carrying the plague-like virus. But it's ultimately Cole himself that becomes the most intoxicating element of this story. A vast departure from Willis' cocky hero roles, Cole always feels confused, abandoned and emotionally drained. His mind is plagued with all sorts of deja-vu and disorientation for every space he occupies, fearful of what he'll discover next in his investigation. This helplessness makes him unique as a man who is not only unsure of what will be his next move but who he even is.

Per usual for Gilliam, his shooting sets are as massive and detailed as his story ideas. I loved the look of the underground future which seems devoid of color, warmth and in desperate need of a good polish. Even the way Gilliam shoots a mental institution or a graffiti-covered street of the 1990s always makes the viewer feel as uneasy as Willis. Gilliam has always had a knack for shooting his films with a great of deal care, but *12 Monkeys* stands out in that there is an engine of strong characters and plot pulling his big ideas about memories, technology and time paradoxes.

12 Monkeys came about at a tough time for Universal Studios as they were very reluctant to approve the project. Even with Bruce Willis and Brad Pitt attatched, the studio was already spending a fortune on the sci-fi action picture Waterworld, leading to *12 Monkeys* receiving a smaller budget and forcing Willis to take a pay cut. But thanks to both the principal cast and Gilliam's stellar direction, the film ended up being a box office success and garnered several award nominations, including a Best Supporting Actor Academy Award nomination for Brad Pitt. It's a rather remarkable picture as it finally brings some direction and understanding to Gilliam's usual depictions of insanity and surrealness, which are far more scattershot in his previous movies. *12 Monkeys* slows down just enough to decipher his genius without sacrificing any of his directorial charms.

ACE VENTURA: PET DETECTIVE

DIRECTOR: Tom Shadyac | SCREENWRITER: Jack Bernstein, Tom Shadyac, Jim Carrey | CAST: Jim Carrey, Sean Young, Courteney Cox, Dan Marino | GENRE: Comedy | RUNNING TIME: 86 min | MPAA RATING: PG-13

CLASSIFICATION: WORST

On television, Jim Carrey was known as the multi-purpose white guy of the black skit show *In Living Color*, where he perfected such characters as the ineptly dangerous Fire Marshall Bill. In movies, he made his name known as an eccentrically maniacal detective obsessed with animal cases. His character's signature comedic move: speaking through his ass by pulling apart his butt cheeks and putting on a silly voice. His catchphrase: *"All-righty then!"* Not much of a phrase, but Carrey's delivery still made it stick in his annoying way.

It's strange to think that *Ace Ventura: Pet Detective* (1994) launched the career of Carey with such a baffling concept. Ventura (Carrey), dressed in a Hawaiian shirt with curved-up hair, is a private investigator so obsessed with animals he secretly hordes various species within his apartment. His odd brand of detective skills makes him the perfect candidate for solving the case of the Miami Dolphins' missing mascot, an actual bottlenose dolphin. Who could be behind such a strange kidnapping? The same people who end up kidnapping Dan Marino as well.

Aside from his love of animals, the Pet Detective's skills don't appear all that different from a regular detective. Most of Ventura's investigation is spent on questioning suspects, seeking physical clues and discovering motivations. When he's not doing real detective work, however, he's doing his best to act as a sugared-up clown, desperate for a laugh in any scene. Any chance he has to embarrass the local police force by proving them wrong, he does so with annoying voices, flailing limbs, and a smug smirk. Every action comes with extreme exaggeration, as when Carrey discovers he's kissed a man, which results in him vomiting and setting his clothes on fire. He's apparently superhuman as well the way he can catch a bullet in his teeth while driving a car. He is the adult equal of the kid on the playground who can't decide who he wants to pretend to be, smushing all these juvenile traits into a Frankenstein's monster of an aggravating joker.

The success of *Ace Ventura* launched not only Carrey's movie career of the 1990s but also the character of the Pet Detective. A sequel promptly followed, *Ace Ventura: When Nature Calls* (1995), which found the actor in Africa with a more animal-related adventure, but the same old arm-flailing and butt-talking gags. An animated series also followed in 1995, a commercial tie-in that repeated for Carrey's success on *Dumb and Dumber* and *The Mask*. Even a spin-off picture was commissioned for home video, *Ace Ventura Jr.: Pet Detective* (2009) sans Jim Carrey and Ace Ventura, with the character's son taking over the detective business.

For being his debut movie role, Jim Carrey comes off as a comedian at the bottom of the barrel, despite his film career just starting to blossom. He parades about the screen as a maniacal mental patient that is impossible to comprehend or sympathize. I hate to make judgments about the audience for this movie, but let's put it this way: Carrey's performance was nominated for Worst New Star at the Razzie Awards and Best Comedic Performance at the MTV Movie Awards. Take from that what you will. Or just enjoy the comedic brilliance of a talking butt.

ADDAMS FAMILY VALUES

DIRECTOR: Barry Sonnenfeld | SCREENWRITER: Paul Rudnick | CAST: Anjelica Huston, Raúl Juliá, Christopher Lloyd, Joan Cusack, Christina Ricci | GENRE: Comedy | RUNNING TIME: 94 min | MPAA RATING: PG

CLASSIFICATION: WEIRD

Barry Sonnenfeld's 1991 film adaptation of *The Addams Family* had all of the style, but not much of a drive. Sticking close to the original TV series, the movie presented the peculiar family in nuggets of grim and weird humor amid a not-so-impressive plot of someone trying to swindle the easily duped clan out of their fortune. It's a premise that retains much of the appeal of the original TV show but doesn't tie much of the bits together for a complete story. It was a picture more funny in small bursts than being all-around hilarious with jokes about death and homicide.

But Sonnenfeld's 1993 sequel, *Addams Family Values*, finds plenty for the family to do besides a few one-scene skits. The always vibrant Gomez Addams (Raúl Juliá) and his seductive wife Morticia (Anjelica Huston) are glowing over the arrival of their third child Pubert, born with Gomez's trademark mustache. A nanny is required to look after Pubert which leads to them hiring Debbie (Joan Cusack), another deceiving villain that once more desires the fortune of the Addams. Her methods are different from the swindlers of the previous movie, however, as Debbie aims to seduce the feeble Uncle Fester (Christopher Lloyd) out of his money.

While Fester is quickly smitten by Debbie's demands for marriage, the children of Wednesday and Pugsly are sent off to summer camp. Faced with smile-drunk camp counselors and condescending waspy campers, the two find themselves cornered and fearful that their usual dark antics will not be enough to scare them off. Aided by Joel (David Krumholtz), a nerdy camper who fancies Wednesday's oddness, they stage their revenge against the elite campers during a Thanksgiving festival play that turns into a massacre of sorts.

The gags of the Addams family work far better in this scenario as there are multiple plots in play to keep the jokes fitting and hilarious. When Fester marries Debbie, there's a bachelor party held in his honor where Lurch accidentally puts a stripper in a cake before he bakes it. When Wednesday tries to escape summer camp, she is horrified that the campers prevent her exit with an upbeat sing-along. Debbie's attempt at killing Fester leads to amusing scenes where the murderous bride can't seem to knock off her husband, be it with electricity in the bathtub or dynamite in the house. And baby Pubert finds all sorts of ways to get into trouble, especially with Wednesday and Pugsly continually trying to kill off their baby brother with no productive results.

With most characters on their adventures, there's finally a chance to admire the bizarre relationship of Gomez and Morticia. Far grander than mere whispers of French, Raúl Juliá and Angelica Houston have real chemistry in their giddy displays of disturbing love. They embrace, dance and revel in sharing an experience in electrically-charged chairs. No danger of couples counseling in this marriage as one can hardly imagine what could bring them apart.

A few comical cameos help make the world outside the Addams' household a little more strange and exciting. Peter Graves plays the stern host of the television program America's Most Disgusting Unsolved Crimes. David Hyde Pierce plays the doctor reacting to the uncommon delivery of Pubert. Nathan Lane plays a smug police sergeant who is entirely disinterested in the plight of the Addams (Lane would later portray Gomez in a musical stage production of The Addams Family). Even Barry Sonnenfeld gets into the act as Joel's nervous dad.

So much of *Addams Family Values* works with its contrasting forces of the enthusiastically twisted Addams and the uneasy yuppie culture. The returning cast is in top form, their gags are hilarious, and the plot is exceptionally paced where the bits never linger past their big punchlines. The only thing that doesn't work is the attached song, a version of Tag Team's infamous "Whoop!" rewritten to reference the movie by inserting the words *"Addams Family movie"* into the lyrics. So bad was this song that it was nominated for the Golden Raspberry Award for Worst Original Song, making the previous movie's silly use of MC Hammer for "The Addams Family Groove" far more enjoyable.

ALADDIN

DIRECTOR: Ron Clements, John Musker | SCREENWRITER: Ron Clements, John Musker, Ted Elliott, Terry Rossio | CAST: Scott Weinger, Robin Williams, Linda Larkin, Jonathan Freeman, Gilbert Gottfried, Frank Welker | GENRE: Fantasy (Animated) | RUNNING TIME: 90 min | MPAA RATING: G

CLASSIFICATION: BEST

Disney's animated films were becoming famous and revered in the 1990s for their groundbreaking animation and musical numbers that refuse to leave the ears. *Aladdin* (1992) was no exception, but it was the first time that one of the voice actors dominated the movie. Few people know the voices of Ariel from *The Little Mermaid* or Beast from *Beauty and the Beast*, but everyone remembers the voice of the Genie. When Robin Williams was brought on for the supporting role of Genie, all his manic comic energy was accurately transferred into animation. Williams was born for animation roles, and Aladdin thankfully takes full advantage of his rapid-fire comedy.

Before Williams pops up to own the picture, however, there's enough of a colorful setting with memorable music to get in the mood. The evil vizier Jafar seeks to acquire a magical lamp that contains a genie from the Cave of Sorrows, but the only person that can enter without facing a grim fate is one that is referred to as a *"diamond in the rough."* That diamond happens to be the plucky thief Aladdin, hungry enough to steal bread from the market, but with a golden enough heart to share it with needy children. He is mesmerized by the lovely Princess Jasmine, but figures he doesn't have a chance as a street rat. It's not until Jafar kicks him into the cursed cave to discover the lamp that the poor kid finds a friend in the charismatic Genie. Aladdin's prospects of impressing the princess significantly increase with a three-wish genie of phenomenal cosmic power.

As Genie aids Aladdin in his quest to seek the heart of the woman he loves, Williams' pulls out all the stops with an unforgettable comic performance. When explaining the rules of wishing, an endless array of impersonations are made, from Groucho Marx for *"no refunds"* to Peter Lorre for refusing to raise the dead. The Disney animators were able to match Williams' style as they inserted their references of Genie imitating the extended nose of Pinocchio and having his finger snapped by Sebastian, the crab from

The Little Mermaid. If the constant references by Williams go over much of the kids' heads, they'll at least grasp the satire of previous Disney pictures.

The only actor that was able to stand out as much as Williams was the always-loud and punctuating Gilbert Gottfried as Jafar's parrot pal Iago. Gottfried's delivery of blaring sarcasm and constant anger for pretending to be a mindless parrot makes him the perfect sidekick for the sinisterly refined Jafar. Initially, the personalities of Iago and Jafar were swapped, but the change is much more fitting for Gottfried's style and made him just as memorable as Williams.

Some of the supporting cast can stand out without any discernable voices at all. Aladdin's monkey pal Abu (Frank Welker) displays a range of character without much of any recognizable dialogue in his monkey sounds, ripe with inflection and emotion. The magic carpet, a character with no voice or facial features, conveys a wide range of emotions for being a piece of fabric with tassels. It's a testament to the Disney animators that could invoke character in just about anything, living or fabric.

The musical numbers are an instant joy, if not easy to sing. "A Whole New World" is a memorably sweet melody, but Williams' "Prince Ali" has such a manic pace I'm surprised the chorus could keep up with him. Upon repeat viewings, the songs become more natural to memorize and sing along. Credit for these classic songs should be given to Howard Ashman and Alan Menken, especially since Menken died before completion of the film.

While *Aladdin* received much glowing praise, it had equally as much controversy. The film came under fire for its peculiarly white leads, questionable lyrics that were edited later, the suggestive language in muffled dialogue, Robin Williams being stiffed on his contract and claims of stealing content from the animated film *The Thief and the Cobbler* which had been in development long before *Aladdin* was conceived. Despite all these faults, *Aladdin* remains an unforgettable work of quality animation, grand adventure, great music and the most expressive of characters. To this day, it still wins me over with music that never fails to tap a toe and Williams' performance that never fails to crack a smile.

ALIEN 3

DIRECTOR: David Fincher | SCREENWRITER: David Giler, Walter Hill, Larry Ferguson | CAST: Sigourney Weaver, Charles Dance, Charles S. Dutton, Lance Henriksen | GENRE: Science Fiction | RUNNING TIME: 114 min | MPAA RATING: R

CLASSIFICATION: WEIRD

The *Alien* franchise had gone through a rollercoaster of different movies. With Ridley Scott's original film, *Alien* (1979), it was a horror picture with no way out of a space station infested with the vicious xenomorphs. In James Cameron's sequel picture, *Aliens* (1986), the horror aspect is replaced with the bloody action of space marines firing machine guns at the acid-spitting creatures. Not to be outdone or appear as a pale imitator, director David Fincher puts his unique mark on the third *Alien* picture as his directorial debut. Despite the movie being a box office failure and despised by many, including Fincher himself, *Alien 3* (1992) remains a distinct and alternative entry in this movie series of aliens that skitter through vents, lay eggs in your stomach and rip your guts out for dinner.

But before the movie can proceed down its new path, a bit of housecleaning is in order. Many of the surviving characters from the previous film are killed off-screen during their flight home from an alien-infested installation. The sole survivor is naturally the lead character of Ripley, reprised once more by the tough-as-nails Sigourney Weaver, who is ejected from the spaceship and crash-lands at a penal colony/foundry. The inmates of this prison are not only all men but men with a double-Y chromosome syndrome that makes them antisocial, violent and more prone to rape. It's a setting that's made all the more uninviting when a xenomorph alien arrives, scuttling through vents and shredding up the inmates.

The look of this new setting is not as sterile as *Alien* or industrial as *Aliens*, relying more on gothic structures with rusted surfaces. Everything feels large and daunting with plenty of low shots looking up at the characters and the giant structure they inhabit. With lots of dirty rooms, vast pits of fire and towering cranes on a wasteland of a planet, it honestly feels as though Ripley has descended into hell. She has no one left to rely on or protect in a prison where she is not only raped by the inmates but a xenomorph alien as well. There's an alien baby brewing in her body, and wants it out, even at the cost of her life. It's not every day you see a dark sci-fi picture where a woman wants an abortion as she battles aliens.

While the movie succeeds in atmosphere and cinematography, it's a bit of a shame that it falls apart when delving into the action aspect. The one xenomorph attacking the prison is spawned from a dog, taking on dog-like tendencies as it rampages on all four legs with a long tail. The director's cut featured the alien spawning initially from an ox, so I guess it could be ox-like as well. The alien appears awkward, produced with the special effects of a rod-puppet composited into the footage, a technique usually favored over stop-motion. He sticks out like a sore thumb when the composition appears off in an enclosed space with lots of smoke and dilapidated interiors clashing with the metallic puppet. The snarling creature is far more efficient in the few close-up shots when he is a practical effect of costumed animatronics. He is also not a terrifying presence in that his methods for killing humans is predictable with some overused cliches of the series, almost as if the monster were an afterthought to this production.

Alien 3 deserves some credit for one of the most memorable shots in the entire series. Ripley sits in a panic state on the floor of the prison medical bay, her face distressed and turned to the side with her eyes closed. The xenomorph comes right up to her face in a close-up shot where it opens its drooling mouth to reveal a second mouth that hisses at her. It's a fantastic shot for featuring the hero and villain in the same frame, making for the most fitting and telling of memories of the *Alien* saga.

While being the dourest of *Alien* movies with its cold and depressing story, it's a solid end to the series as an acceptance of death and sacrifice with all its religious iconography and stark representations of a rusted hell. Or at least it would have been if not for the 1997 sequel, *Alien: Resurrection*, which revives Ripley in the form of a clone. I would say that's in poor taste, but *Alien 3* does begin by wiping out nearly all characters and traits from the previous movie. Fair is fair, I suppose.

AMERICAN BEAUTY

DIRECTOR: Sam Mendes | SCREENWRITER: Bruce Cohen, Dan Jinks | CAST: Kevin Spacey, Annette Bening, Thora Birch | GENRE: Drama | RUNNING TIME: 122 min | MPAA RATING: R

CLASSIFICATION: BEST

American Beauty (1999) is as much a tragic drama as it is an absurd comedy of suburban life. Kevin Spacey plays Lester, a middle-aged loser husband, and father that seeks more out of his life that he knows is circling the drain. He decides to go on the offensive with his cynical nature and ultimate desires. He hates working at his corrupt company and decides to blackmail them into paying him a year's salary to leave. He hates his prim and controlling wife that he defies her by buying a Pontiac Firebird without consulting her. He realizes that he is despised and has snapped to a point where he no longer cares what others think of him or his actions. If he can't please others, he can at least satisfy himself in more ways than one.

The movie asks us not to root for Lester's kamikaze lifestyle shift, but rather sympathize with his reasons to pursue a more selfish life. His wife Carolyn (Annette Bening) appears to care about her couch more than her husband, fearing he'll spill beer on it when he attempts to come on to her. By the time he discovers that Carolyn has been having an affair, he's so far down his crisis hole that he feels nothing. The only person who seems to display any genuine interest in him is his daughter's friend Angela, a teenage girl he has sexual fantasies about during her cheerleader halftime performance. It is this attraction which leads him down the path of attempting to recapture his youth by working out, smoking pot and flipping burgers for a living.

Observed from within the comfy confines of a materialistic society, it's easy enough to write off Lester as a madman. It's not until we witness those around him crumble how refreshing his blunt honesty can be. Carolyn is consumed by her glamorous lifestyle, desperate to find more in an affair. The neighbor Ricky (Wes Bentley) has grown so bored that he sees a bizarre fascination in filming everything from a paper bag caught in the wind to Lester working out in the nude. Ricky's father (Chris Cooper) is a repressed mess of a former Marine, continually testing his boy for drugs and trying hopelessly to deny his homosexual urges.

This is not a movie about who is in the right or wrong for the disaster that transpires when all these emotional arcs merge. It is a movie about loneliness and the odd behaviors it instills within American society. Sometimes it's tragic, and other times it's darkly comedic. It's easy enough to laugh at Carolyn's waspy lifestyle as much as it is to find some somber relation in her struggle to feel something more. Ricky's video of a paper bag could be seen as either a sad reflection of life's frailties or hilarious for a pretentious teenager making a pretentious video.

The film's most iconic shot of Angela naked and surrounded by roses, seen in Lester's fantasy, represents the fervent desire of indulgence that is traditionally closed. Lester ends up more or less victorious for taking the road more taboo, obliterating the usual barriers of cozy suburban life. He regards life as beautiful - too beautiful to be worried about what he might never do. *American Beauty* is a cathartic view on this lifestyle, celebrated for all its wonder, weirdness, darkness, passion and plastic bags.

AMERICAN PIE

DIRECTOR: Paul Weitz, Chris Weitz | SCREENWRITER: Adam Herz | CAST: Jason Biggs, Shannon Elizabeth, Alyson Hannigan, Chris Klein, Tara Reid, Seann William Scott, Eugene Levy | GENRE: Comedy | RUNNING TIME: 95 min | MPAA RATING: R

CLASSIFICATION: WEIRD

"We'll just tell your mother that, uh, we ate it all."

This is the awkward solution between a father and his teenage son after the son has been caught fornicating with a pie. He placed his genitals inside the baked dessert as he'd heard tell from his friends that the sensation of a vagina is equal to that of warm apple pie. That is the length the teenagers of *American Pie* (1999) are willing to go for sexual release: the molestation of baked goods.

The movie's title gimmick aside, there's more to offer in the raunchy teen sex comedy than copulation of confectionaries. It's a simple tale of four teenagers attempting to lose their virginity before the high school year is over. It's not exactly the most far-reaching of high school goals, but a goal well within their power to complete. It's not going to be easy, however, given that most of them are awkward nerds. Not the thick-glasses, pocket-protector stereotype nerds of previous Hollywood pictures, but typical teens who are not quite sure of themselves yet.

The most awkward amongst the horny collective is Jim (Jason Biggs). You may remember him from the pie scene. He becomes the butt of many jokes with the bad luck of an intruding father (Eugene Levy) and accidentally left his webcam on when he unsuccessfully attempts to have sex. His pals face their share of embarrassment as they stumble towards losing their virginity, but none so publically humiliating as Jim prematurely ejaculating over the internet for the whole school to see. One can only imagine how much more damaging it would be if it went viral worldwide.

While the movie is undeniably raunchy and gross as most teen sex comedies go, *American Pie* redeems itself slightly by taking a less cruel approach to the subject of teenage boys attempting to get laid. The prospect of sex leads the boys to discover that being intimate requires more understanding and listening rather than just learning the best moves in bed. The women they pursue have more dimension in their personalities than their breasts, including band nerd Michelle

(Alyson Hannigan) who is somewhat sincere beneath her geeky exterior. The antagonizers of the virgins, the jocular Stifler (Seann William Scott) and dorky briber Chuck (Chris Owen), receive their comeuppance for their smugness. Everything seems to turn out fine for the underdogs as they all find themselves accomplishing their goals, one of which with Stifler's slutty mother.

American Pie is a bit of a throwback to the classic teen sex comedies of the 1980s, but the better ones with characters worth caring about rather than just being a meaningless series of titillating acts and gross-out gags. On the level of *Animal House* or *Fast Times at Ridgemont High*, the movie is compelling at weaving a raunchy picture for teens to giggle about while watching. It is worth a watch if not for Jason Biggs' comic nature of a nervous teen then for Eugene Levy's awkward talks about sex with his son. Or perhaps Biggs placing his penis in a pie is enough of a draw.

THE AMERICAN PRESIDENT

DIRECTOR: Rob Reiner | SCREENWRITER: Aaron Sorkin | CAST: Michael Douglas, Annette Bening, Martin Sheen, David Paymer, Samantha Mathis, Michael J. Fox | GENRE: Comedy | RUNNING TIME: 114 min | MPAA RATING: PG-13

CLASSIFICATION: BEST

The American President (1995) sounds like a fable that shouldn't work for its combined elements of romantic comedy and thoughtful politics, but it plays out brilliantly thanks to a tight and intelligent script. A single President of the United States wants to date an environmental lobbyist he has become infatuated with. *"The President can't just go out on a date,"* scoffs the Chief of Staff (Martin Sheen) upon hearing this proposal. The President (Michael Douglas) cites how Jefferson and Wilson have done so in the past during their terms. It's not just a strange phenomenon to him, and the movie not only makes the audience believe in this romance amid politics but also accept the world around their courtship.

Michael Douglas perfectly plays President Andrew Shepherd with a witty charm, a smart mind and admirable stumbling around non-presidential activities. His life is a busy one for walking meetings, the constant back and forth on issues and trying to wedge in just enough time for his daughter. But when the day is done, and he bids a goodnight to his staff, the loneliness of having lost his wife three years ago takes its toll. He decides to take a gamble when speaking with the highly-vocal and fresh-faced environmental lobbyist Sydney Wade (Annette Bening) and attempts to ask her out. It's a risk in that Shepherd has not only been out of the dating game for so long, but his calculative mindset of a president makes it much more difficult to woo. He asks an aide what Sydney might think if he asked her out to a state dinner, only to receive the suggestion of a pollster gathering some data for such a scenario. He tries to order flowers for her, but cannot do so on his own as his credit cards are in holding.

There's a disconnect between the two, but it plays out hilariously in the scene where Shepherd calls her up for a date. Sydney believes the call to be a prank as she has just moved in with her sister and hasn't given out her new phone number. Sydney hangs up, he calls back, and she's still not buying that the President of the United States is calling her. It isn't until Shepherd tells her to call the White House and ask for him that she feels embarrassed for speaking to the President in such a way. Shepherd is slightly ashamed that he had to prove himself, making him all the more anxious to ask her out and fall back on his state dinner strategy to land himself a date. It's a scene that could have made for bad comedy but is genuinely sweet for its likable and witty characters.

Naturally, their relationship becomes a big deal. The press hounds their developing romance with watchful eyes of the latest headlines. Shepherd's conservative opponent (Richard Dreyfuss) uses this love as a chance to influence the election year. Sydney's boss (John Mahoney) is anxious about how this type of relationship will affect her severe political career. And the White House staff (Michael J. Fox, Anna Deavere Smith, David Paymer) becomes increasingly nervous at how such a public perception will hurt their crime bill.

Nothing feels generic in this romantic comedy that refuses to water down any of its elements to make the relationship easier to digest. When Shepherd is discussing his political strategies, he has the tact and collective nature of a man who knows what he's talking about. The tactics of his political opponent with the campaign of family values is a believable situation to stir up controversy in the public eye. When Shepherd awkwardly approaches the subject of physical intimacy, it's a playfully charming and romantic scene the way Sydney takes a quick liking towards jumping in the sack with him. All of this could have been sitcom fodder, but never settle for anything of the sort.

Aaron Sorkin's script was so apt and snappy with character and politics that much of his unused content for the picture was used in the creation of the White House TV drama, *The West Wing*. Sorkin would write almost all the episode scripts for four seasons where Martin Sheen would reprise his role as White House Chief of Staff. There was so much to admire and explore in Sorkin's world of politics and passion that it couldn't be contained to one movie. But director Rob Reiner still does a remarkable job at keeping such a simple story with complex themes as entertaining as it is biting.

ANACONDA

DIRECTOR: Luis Llosa | SCREENWRITER: Hans Bauer, Jim Cash, Jack Epps Jr. | CAST: Jon Voight, Ice Cube, Jennifer Lopez, Eric Stoltz, Owen Wilson | GENRE: Horror | RUNNING TIME: 89 min | MPAA RATING: PG-13

CLASSIFICATION: WEIRD

Anaconda (1997) is a creature feature that delivers big time on the titular monster. You will see the giant anaconda that attacks humans. You will see it eat a man whole. And you will see that anaconda regurgitate its prey. All of this is hilariously presented in a high-energy horror presentation of great camp and cheesy special effects.

The cast is damn near perfect for such a ludicrous production. Jennifer Lopez plays documentarian Terri shooting a film on the Amazon River, appearing mostly in tank tops and tight pants (insert joke about how anacondas don't want none unless they got buns, hun). Her boat, filled with a filming crew and scientists, runs across local snake hunter Paul Sarone, played by a dazed and crazed Jon Voight. Sarone knows the area and can help the crew find the tribe they are seeking to film, but will eventually take over their boat and force them into helping him find and kill a legendary giant anaconda. It isn't long before both Voight and the anaconda are fighting to be the cheesiest villain of the picture. It's almost romantic when these two forces meet.

The supporting cast, existing mostly to be eaten by the snake, have their moments. Ice Cube plays the cameraman, Danny, remarking on how ridiculous their journey has become. Owen Wilson plays the easily-persuaded sound engineer, Gary, who sides with Sarone to keep the plot on schedule and makes such goofy statements as asking if the jungle makes you horny. Eric Stoltz plays the required scientist man and Jonathan Hyde plays the British narrator, both fulfilling the essential functions of monster movie characters. And Danny Trejo is perfectly cast as the unlucky guy who decides to shoot himself in the head at the beginning of the movie.

Those expecting to see a lot of the creature will not be disappointed. And those hoping for some delightfully dated special effects for the anaconda will not be disappointed either. Given the scale, speed and actions of this creature, computer graphics were used for most of the shots when the snake is on the offensive. The technology for the creature, composed of animatronics and computer animation, may not have been as reliable to make the sight of an anaconda swallowing a man whole not look silly, but you can't help admiring the filmmakers for being so ambitious.

If the movie isn't as terrifying with its star attraction, it's at least stuffed to the gills with creativity. We witness the POV inside the walls of the anaconda's mouth before he attempts to eat another human. The anaconda snatches a human mid-air and coils around him quickly before taking a bite. There are even some unique non-anaconda attacks where a scuba diver swallows a wasp that stings his throat. Jon Voight will also kill a woman with his legs. And the atmosphere of the jungle is correctly sold with the humid and alluring cinematography. Maybe the jungle does make you horny.

As with most creature features, *Anaconda* would spawn a series of lesser sequels, as well as a crossover picture of *Lake Placid vs. Anaconda*, much cheaper and very light on camp value. Try as they might, those follow-up films will never be able to duplicate the tender moment when Jon Voight is swallowed whole by a giant anaconda, his feet dangling out of the mouth. That type of movie cheese is magnifique.

APOLLO 13

DIRECTOR: Ron Howard | SCREENWRITER: William Broyles, Jr., Al Reinert | CAST: Tom Hanks, Kevin Bacon, Bill Paxton, Gary Sinise, Ed Harris, Kathleen Quinlan | GENRE: Drama | RUNNING TIME: 140 min | MPAA RATING: PG

CLASSIFICATION: BEST

Apollo 13 (1995) is not just an American story of survival in space, but a unique tale of how such limited technology saved a space shuttle from turning into a floating coffin for the unlucky astronauts. It's a most profound picture for its sobering look back at an age that didn't have as fast computers, strong alloys or reliable engines, despite being the most expensive of materials assembled by the greatest minds of the era. But it's also a celebration of the space program that was so bold, courageous and resourceful during the most nail-biting of moments in American history. No extra subplots or cheesy characters are present for melodrama. A shuttle mission gone awry is drama enough, and director Ron Howard maintains focus.

True to the story, the tension centers on the 13th Apollo mission to the moon with astronauts Jim Lovell, Fred Haise and Jack Swigert piloting the shuttle. On the journey, an oxygen tank explodes. This event turns their mission dire as a host of problems are presented. The leaking of the oxygen means they could not only run out of air soon, but also suffer carbon monoxide poisoning. They need to make it back to Earth, but need to come in at just the right angle. If it's not precise, they could incinerate on reentry or launch out of Earth's orbit.

Director Ron Howard puts an awful lot of effort into making sure his production has all the allure of a blockbuster, but does away with nearly all the fat. Tom Hanks, Gary Sinise, and Kevin Bacon perfectly play the roles of three American astronauts without extra subplots or scene-stealing moments. The special effects of selling the Apollo launch and weightlessness of space are amazingly believable, but never overtake as a spectacle. There is a laser focus on the mission at hand, and it is worth telling without some more in-depth examination of the characters.

We do, however, understand enough about the characters to like them and hope they make it out alive. We get to know about them, their families and their training before they hop on the shuttle and find themselves in a desperate situation. While they float above with their fates uncertain, the smoking and sweating scientists are monitoring the mission on the ground, led by Kranz (Ed Harris), desperately seek to find a means of saving the astronauts. They form ideas about how to get the capsule heading back to Earth while the astronauts struggle to stay alive long enough to implement the plan. The pressure can be felt on all sides from the chain-smoking scientists to the freezing astronauts to the families watching the television reports at home.

It's clear that Ron Howard put more effort into nailing the story and atmosphere than anything else and it works to the benefit of keeping the movie exciting. Any director could aim for the drama of Lovell's wife agonizingly watching the television for her husband to return from space, but it takes a meticulous director with excellent insight to detail the specifics of the astronauts creating a tool to clean the air supply. All eyes are on this mission, and Howard rarely pulls us away from a second of its tension. It's the perfect movie for the viewer that desires more attention to technical details than the perspective drama to be provoked. There's no time for melodrama when Apollo reports to Houston that they have a problem.

ARMAGEDDON

DIRECTOR: Michael Bay | SCREENWRITER: Jonathan Hensleigh, Tony Gilroy, Shane Salerno, J. J. Abrams | CAST: Bruce Willis, Ben Affleck, Billy Bob Thornton, Liv Tyler, Will Patton, Steve Buscemi, Peter Stormare, Keith David | GENRE: Action | RUNNING TIME: 150 min | MPAA RATING: PG-13

CLASSIFICATION: WORST

Armageddon (1998) isn't so much a movie as it is an exercise in loud! It's an experiment by Michael Bay to see how far he could blow up every scene to absurd proportions. Every action scene is shot with extreme camera motion and earth-shaking sound. Every moment of melodrama, heroism and comedy is played up with the most laughably surreal of dialogue and insipid of emotional manipulation. Even the editing is chaotic in how the movie cuts from scene to scene more as though it were the world's longest movie trailer. This is a movie so wrought with frenetic and uncontrollable action that it's the most greasy and fatty of blockbuster junk food.

Earth is under attack from a giant asteroid the size of Texas, making its path known as early meteors slam into New York City causing massive explosions in typical Michael Bay fashion. I recalled a premise from the novel The Dig in which astronauts were sent to stop a gigantic asteroid by detonating charges in specific areas to shift the trajectory away from Earth. Such logic is too dull for Michael Bay's action-packed direction, which requires his astronauts to blow up the whole damn asteroid! Don't worry - the explosion is written off as splitting the asteroid in two, both pieces missing the Earth with stray fragments being vaporized in the atmosphere. It makes no sense, but little does in this blaring farce.

For such a dangerous mission, NASA decides to hire a ragtag group of capable men up to the task. One of those men is Harry Stamper (Bruce Willis), a deep-sea oil driller that NASA believes will be best for drilling into the asteroid to set the explosive charge. He makes a comical list of demands and convinces other drillers to join him on his mission, including his daughter's boyfriend A.J. (Ben Affleck), though they'll all have to be trained to be astronauts first. Affleck asked Michael Bay why he didn't make these characters astronauts that had to prepare to be drillers as that would be easier. Bay's response: *"Shut the fuck up!"*

The movie is loaded to the brim with cliches of every

blockbuster to make it the most far-pleasing of popcorn action. Due to the popularity of *Titanic*, a romantic subplot was added in between A.J. and Harry's daughter Grace (Liv Tyler), but is laughably portrayed with them sensually touching each other with animal crackers. The drillers-turned-astronauts march towards the shuttle as the whole world watches with a swelling score and bubbling patriotism. To ramp up the tension of the mission, a character must sacrifice their life to blow up the asteroid as the digital clock is ticking down to the remaining seconds before Earth is destroyed. And when this character makes that sacrifice, his life must quickly flash before his eyes with epic orchestral music.

At 150 minutes, *Armageddon* is overkill for thrill. New York blows up, a space shuttle blows up, a space station blows up, another shuttle blows up and more explosions are to be had on the asteroid. Bodies can be seen falling from collapsing skyscrapers and flying out of smashed space shuttles. Characters speak loudly and proudly with such nothing lines as *"We're not leaving them behind!"* and *"The clock is ticking!"*. Coffee cups are dropped and shattered as time runs out on the digital clock counting down to doomsday. This movie is a rollercoaster ride where the mechanisms have malfunctioned and you're forced to sit through another four rounds of speeding fury, begging for the trip to stop as you grow nauseous and tired of it all.

Michael Bay would later admit to *Armageddon* being his worst film for only having 16 weeks to shoot. If he had the chance, he said he would go back and redo the entire third act. Whether he'd include more or fewer explosions is up for debate.

ARMY OF DARKNESS

DIRECTOR: Sam Raimi | SCREENWRITER: Sam Raimi, Ivan Raimi | CAST: Bruce Campbell, Embeth Davidtz | GENRE: Comedy | RUNNING TIME: 81 min | MPAA RATING: R

CLASSIFICATION: WEIRD

Army of Darkness (1992) is the third and final chapter of Sam Raimi's *Evil Dead* saga, but it's vastly different from its predecessors. There's more action than horror and more slapstick than gore. Gone are the grotesque demons, replaced by hordes of sword-wielding skeletons. Gone was the giddy insanity with buckets of blood, replaced by the silly satire of medieval fantasy. It's very fitting that this picture doesn't carry the title of *Evil Dead III*, even though it was only titled as such because Sam Raimi could not use the subtitle The Medieval Dead.

Despite taking a different approach, *Army of Darkness* has its moments of action-oriented fun and solidifies Bruce Campbell's character of Ash as a quotable horror icon. Picking up directly from where *Evil Dead II* left off, Ash finds himself sucked through a portal into the Middle Ages. Armed with his shotgun (or "boomstick" as he calls it) and his hand that was replaced with a chainsaw, he frightens the peasants of a peaceful kingdom into favoring him as their hero.

The only way to make it back to his own time is through that nasty book of the dead, the Necronomicon. All Ash has to do is speak the sacred words in front of the book, a coded phrase lifted directly from *The Day the Earth Stood Still*. He must have never seen that movie as he says the words incorrectly and ends up summoning the undead to attack the living. It's now up to this movie-illiterate hero to save a kingdom from being overrun by the undead.

The undead, however, doesn't seem as hard to confront given that they're skeletons, animated with absurd puppetry. How could one not laugh at the sight of skeletons playing drums or blowing flutes as they march into combat? I didn't know skeletons could play the flute without lungs. Must be all that demonic energy and what-have-you. These evil forces are led by an evil reflection of Ash, dubbed as Evil Ash, with less skin than regular Ash, but more skin than the skeletons. Ash is most likely not as afraid of doing battle with his evil doppelganger, considering he meets one earlier with skin and has no problem blasting him in the nose with a shotgun. He must also do battle with the love interest Sophie that has been transformed into a flying demon as well, making her *"real ugly"* when possessed.

Campbell finds himself in more of a hero role this time as he trains armies to do battle with the dead, dashingly combats bad guys with swords on castle walls and convinces the women he saves to kiss him. He doesn't appear as frightened or frantic as he was in the previous *Evil Dead* movies, much wittier and cavalier with his actions. Skeletons and clones are probably a piece of cake after having battled an undead force that possessed and killed all his friends. He also seems to be having more fun in battle than the previous movies when he has the opportunity to drive a contraption built for chopping up skeletons. He's become so used to such violence that the usual scenes of chopping off limbs and geysers of blood are routine to the point of being comical. The movie must realize it can't one-up *Evil Dead II* in the graphic horror department, which explains the more epic treatment of such carnage with an adventurous score by Danny Elfman.

Though seemingly much different in tone, *Army of Darkness* provides a fittingly silly end to the *Evil Dead* series, leaving Ash as the undead-slaughtering hero of his own time. It may have been a little too happy considering the original ending featured Ash traveling too far in time to when the world had ended. Director Sam Raimi preferred the original ending as he always found Ash to be a fool, considering his misfortunes in dealing with the undead. No matter the conclusion, Ash remains an iconic horror king worth hailing towards, even if he can't remember the most simple of instructions.

AS GOOD AS IT GETS

DIRECTOR: James L. Brooks | SCREENWRITER: Mark Andrus, James L. Brooks | CAST: Jack Nicholson, Helen Hunt, Greg Kinnear | GENRE: Comedy | RUNNING TIME: 139 min | MPAA RATING: PG-13

CLASSIFICATION: WEIRD

Few roles were so perfect for Jack Nicholson than that of the curmudgeon writer Melvin in *As Good As It Gets* (1997). He plays such a smug man that desires silence and despises any human contact distracting him from writing inside his lonely apartment. Not content with merely telling his gay neighbors to refrain from knocking on his door, he bursts into a cackle of an aggressive rant with that devilishly iconic grin.

"Not if there's a fire, not even if you hear the sound of a thud from my home, and one week later there's a smell coming from there that can only be a decaying human body and you have to hold a hanky to your face because the stench is so thick that you think you're going to faint. Even then, don't come knocking."

Only Nicholson could deliver such a line with the crass of a misanthrope with charm. Despite Jack eating up the scenery, his co-stars do an admirable job keeping in step. Helen Hunt plays waitress Carol, a single mother who happens to be the only woman that can tolerate Melvin's attitude at the diner. She's kind, but also quite paranoid of Melvin's intentions the way he favors her service more than other waitresses, to the point that he's willing to pay for her to stay. She's aware of her authority, however, as when she makes him take back the slander he slings about her asthmatic son. Melvin bitterly backs down as he can't stand to eat anywhere else or be serviced by any other woman.

A chance for gaining more of her attention comes when Melvin is saddled with babysitting the dog of his gay neighbor Simon (Greg Kinnear). He warms up to the dog so much that returning him spurns sorrowful emotions he feels ridiculous about having for a stupid dog. There's something oddly sweet and hysterical to watch Nicholson have an emotional breakdown over a pet that he previously favored tossing down his building's garbage chute.

The script by James L. Brooks (*Broadcast News*) and Mark Andrus (*Life as a House*) proceeds down a familiar route of sentimentality, but has enough surprises to avoid the sitcom pitfalls narrowly. It's as if

Brooks and Andrus took on the challenge of reworking a standard romantic comedy script into something more without changing the overall plot.

Yes, Jack Nicholson's character must eventually learn to accept others, but not without plenty of room to be a curmudgeon with his usually excellent Nicholson-isms. Nearly every interaction he has ends with an insult. A female fan of his writings asks how he can write women so well; *"I think of a man and I take away reason and accountability."* Nothing is off limits for his politically incorrect character where gay people, black people, and dogs all become targets. I half-expected him to perform some rendition of the chicken salad scene from *Five Easy Pieces*, but Helen Hunt's emotional determination seems to prevent that level of insult.

As Good As It Gets never really takes off with its emotional progression that falls back on a relatively smooth resolve, but there are enough great performances and quotable lines to make its relatively breezy story enjoyable. Nicholson, Hunt, and Kinnear are all in top form, as are the likes of the supporting cast of Cuba Gooding Jr., Harold Ramis, and Skeet Ulrich. Nicholson and Hunt both won an Academy Award for their performances, but it wasn't so much a surprise for Nicholson. He was already an acting legend for much better roles that also won him Oscars. Jack accepted the award with many thanks, but it would have been far more entertaining if he put on more of the crass for receiving yet another award. Since he already had his hands full with two Oscars, maybe he could have asked someone to hold it where he told them to shove the chicken salad.

AUDITION

DIRECTOR: Takashi Miike | SCREENWRITER: Daisuke Tengan | CAST: Ryo Ishibashi, Eihi Shiina, Renji Ishibashi | GENRE: Horror | RUNNING TIME: 115 min | MPAA RATING: R

CLASSIFICATION: BEST

In the many Japanese horror pictures I've come across, none creep me out more than Takashi Miike's profoundly unsettling *Audition* (1999). It features one of the most chilling and disturbing of torture scenes in which a woman slowly places needles into a man's eye and then cuts off his foot with wire. The squirms and moans of the victim coupled with the childlike cooing of the female killer make the scene profoundly and unforgettably disturbing.

The plot centers on Shigeharu Aoyama (Ryo Ishibashi), a middle-aged man who lost his wife many years ago. His teenage son Shigehiko (Tetsu Sawaki) encourages him to find a new woman and his co-worker Yasuhisa (Jun Kunimura) has just the plan. Yasuhisa stages a fake audition for female actresses to play the "role" of Aoyama's wife. The top candidate is Asami (Eihi Shiina), a shy and mysterious woman with references that cannot be reached. Aoyama phones her for a date where she is surprised that he decided to call. What he doesn't know is that Asami has been waiting on his call for days, sitting next to the phone while someone trapped inside a sack struggles to escape in the background. She has something sinister in store for Aoyama as her romantic facade quickly entraps him for the most gruesome of climaxes. The two are virtually auditioning each other for their ends, both selfish and immoral to such disturbing degrees.

What makes Asami's bloody third act all the more terrifying is how it comes almost out of left field. Most of the build-up comes in the form of melodrama with sterile settings and lucid hallucinations of time passing. The film plays out like a light dream before the nightmare quickly descends like a ton of bricks towards the gritty finale. Miike has always been a master of blindsiding the viewer by delivering the most unexpected of endings, almost to the point of trolling his audience's expectations. *Audition* is perhaps his most genius of tonal shifts that transforms from romantic drama to odd thriller to savage horror within the span of a few scenes.

The film has often been the subject of considerable debate in whether or not it is feminist or misogynist for its treatment of women. The first half seems to swing towards the misogynist side the way Aoyama auditions women to be his wife. He films them as they stare directly ahead, answering whatever questions he asks and some taking off their clothes to prove they can do nudity. Aoyama is fearful and sometimes loathful of women, as in a scene at the bar when he is irritated by some businesswomen making noise in the background. But when the second act reveals the horrific truth of Asami's intentions, the revenge nature suggests a stronger theme of feminism. There's a conflict of gender conduct in this film that swings the pendulum back and forth before eventually severing a limb.

Miike's *Audition*, for being as biting and gory as it was, has been labeled as one of the biggest inspirations for the horror subgenre of torture porn, a format that favors more horror of the body than the mind. Director Eli Roth admits that the film was a huge inspiration for his brutal and bloody picture *Hostel* (2006), to the point that he gave Miike a role in the movie as one of the torturers. Unlike its imitators, however, *Audition* stands firmly unique for its hard themes of gender norms and not being as reliant on easy money shots of gore. It's far more terrifying to imagine Asami's bloody act of amputation than to witness all its gory details, present though they may be. That cutesy cooing she delivers while sawing is pure nightmare fuel.

AUSTIN POWERS: INTERNATIONAL MAN OF MYSTERY

DIRECTOR: Jay Roach | SCREENWRITER: Mike Myers | CAST: Mike Myers, Elizabeth Hurley, Michael York, Mimi Rogers | GENRE: Comedy | RUNNING TIME: 94 min | MPAA RATING: PG-13

CLASSIFICATION: WEIRD

Mike Myers wrote the script for his spy comedy *Austin Powers: International Man of Mystery* (1997) in only three weeks. It's clear from the result that he not only has a firm grasp on what is most amusing about spy movies, but also the perfect characters for this spoof. He writes himself as characters that embody familiar tropes, but has the creative delivery and acting to make them characters all his own.

Austin Powers (Myers) appears in the 1960s as a British spy and sex symbol, a colorful James Bond with a more amused obsession with shagging. With his loud suits, thick glasses, and bad teeth, he's desirable to women and despised by his enemies. His top rival is the villainous Doctor Evil (also Myers), an instantly recognizable parody of James Bond nemesis Ernst Blofeld. Both of Myers' characters embody the appearance of Bond and Blofeld, but have hilarious traits and mannerisms to make them comically distinct. With Doctor Evil's gray suit and white shoes, along with his stiff arms and odd gate, he shares more in common with Pee Wee Herman in his mannerisms.

The plot shifts from the psychedelic 1960s to the modern 1990s when Doctor Evil freezes himself in space with Powers following in suspended animation as well. They awaken to an era where their ways must be altered to be the heroes and villains they so desperately want to be.

Doctor Evil discovers that most of his evil schemes for causing stirs in the Royal Family and puncturing the Ozone layer have already been done. This leads him to wing his evil plans with capturing some nuclear warheads and holding the world for ransom, an amount he must also tweak as a million dollars isn't as significant for a corporation to fork over. He also discovers that he has a teenage son (Seth Green), which forces him to take an awkward stab at fatherhood and the Macarena.

Austin, however, comes to the most shocking of revelations in a world that isn't so accepting of his sexually adventurous antics. Reactivated by the British Ministry of Defense, his old female sidekick Mrs. Kensington (Mimi Rogers) has grown too aged to carry on the fight and passed the torch to her daughter Vanessa (Elizabeth Hurley). Austin tries to woo her with the usual giggling and questioning of horniness, which shocks Vanessa more than turns her on. He soon comes to realize that his style has become a bit of a joke as others laugh at his dorky threads and lack of knowledge about the Cold War. The 60s era spy must evolve into the 90s era spy, embracing such technology as compact discs and condoms.

Aside from making plenty of amusing homages to several *James Bond* pictures, the bulk of the comedy derives more from the era-challenged ignorance of these characters and their weird personalities in general. Doctor Evil attends a parenting group where he reveals his twisted childhood of his prostitute mother, insane father and a ritualistic shaving of testicles. Austin attempts to sound cool while seeking a lead at a blackjack table, but comes off as a goof who doesn't know how to play blackjack. Even the *Bond* references themselves are amusing for the uninitiated. You don't need to be aware of *Bond* villain Odd Job to appreciate the ridiculousness of his parody figure, Random Task, throwing shoes to kill people; *"Who throws a shoe? Honestly!"*

The strength of *Austin Powers'* generation-crossing comedy made the characters of Powers and Doctor Evil the most iconic of movie figures. Such simple lines as *"Yeah, baby!"* and *"One million dollars!"* became as memorable as any classic *Bond* banter. The variety of gags that ranged in everything from numerous *Bond* references to silly lines to the sight gag of hiding the sausage with a literal sausage, proving that there was enough creativity in *Austin Powers* for at least two sequels. It'd be easy to scoff at the movie's ridiculous amount of hype that followed, but I still can't help cracking a smile at Myers' sly satire and character. As Austin so liberally quotes from *Beyond the Valley of the Dolls*, *"It's my happening, and it freaks me out!"*

AUSTIN POWERS: THE SPY WHO SHAGGED ME

DIRECTOR: Jay Roach | SCREENWRITER: Mike Myers, Michael McCullers | CAST: Mike Myers, Heather Graham, Michael York, Robert Wagner, Seth Green, Elizabeth Hurley | GENRE: Comedy | RUNNING TIME: 96 min | MPAA RATING: PG-13

CLASSIFICATION: WEIRD

Mike Myers and Jay Roach had such a hit on their hands with *Austin Powers* that they had to follow it up while the groovy iron was hot and the character was just starting to become an annoying figure to replicate. This story is not as robust as the first picture nor are the gags as clever this time around. The premise of time travel is also a pretty lazy device for easy jokes that don't make too much sense within the world of *Austin Powers*. But when Austin (Myers) questions this logic, he's told by his superior Basil to not think about those things and just enjoy yourself. He then turns to the camera and informs the audience to do the same.

The Spy Who Shagged Me (1999) never seems to take itself too seriously, as in the opening wiping of the slate where it turns out his new wife Vanessa was a robot trying to kill him. Austin subdues her and is dismayed for all but a few seconds before celebrating being single again with a naked strut around a hotel. But there's no time to celebrate as Doctor Evil has broken out of prison, acquired a time machine and traveled back to the 1960s to steal Austin's "mojo," his apparently mystical chemical that gives him super sexual powers. Stricken with an inability to shag, Austin pursues his nemesis into the past, aided by 1960s agent Felicity Shagwell (Heather Graham). As her name would imply, she digs on Austin's philosophy of constant shagging, making his need to reacquire his mojo a top priority.

Myers managed to write two more iconic and quotable characters in this sequel. Doctor Evil clones himself a pint-sized version of himself he dubs Mini-Me (Verne Troyer), wearing matching attire and speaking only in baby-like grunts and squeals. Like any baby, most of his comedy derives from his stature and his miniature accessories for replicating Doctor Evil, from tiny chairs to tiny pianos. For the second original character, Myers puts on pounds of makeup to turn himself into Fat Bastard, the overly tubby and easily flatulent assassin who would prefer Mini-Me be inside his belly. He's a crudely amusing figure, even if his funniest line is repeating a jingle from an Applebee's commercial.

The film doubles up on the references and comedy, for better and worse. More *James Bond* movies are parodied for the inclusion of a laser cannon (*Diamonds Are Forever*), a secret volcano base (*You Only Live Twice*), an outer space setting (*Moonraker*) and, of course, Mini-Me (*The Man with the Golden Gun*). Austin will once more stop the movie to introduce a musical number by Burt Bacharach, this time paired up with Elvis Costello. The returning character of Mustafa (Will Ferrell) will once more pop up to suffer another death that he drags out with rambling dialogue. Most of the comedy derives from more misunderstandings, including a play on shadows where henchmen believe Felicity is pulling all sorts of items out of Austin's butt.

While *The Spy Who Shagged Me* doesn't have the same freshness of spy satire that its predecessor boasted so well, there's enough funny sequences and comedic energy to warrant one more round of shagadelic antics. The playfulness with the *James Bond* material leads to some amusing bits, the fourth-wall breaking script has its moments (*"Funny how England looks in no way like Southern California"*), and the modern jabs at the 1960s are pretty bright. The scene where Austin mistakes a stool sample for coffee, however, is not so amusing and proof that the comedy was starting to run out of gas, despite how much of it is released in the film by Fat Bastard.

THE AVENGERS

DIRECTOR: Jeremiah S. Chechik | SCREENWRITER: Don Macpherson | CAST: Ralph Fiennes, Uma Thurman, Sean Connery, Jim Broadbent, Fiona Shaw, Eddie Izzard | GENRE: Action | RUNNING TIME: 89 min | MPAA RATING: PG-13

CLASSIFICATION: WORST

Sean Connery announced his retirement from acting in 2006, but I'm surprised he didn't announce it sooner after playing the villain in *The Avengers* (1998). He'd already had to endure the embarrassment of being dressed in a diaper and braids in *Zardoz*, but he shouldn't have had to continue his suffering by dressing up in a bear costume in this movie. Sure, the script rationalizes this decision as a means of concealing identities in a secret organization, but let's not mince words here: Sean Connery, who ten years earlier won an Academy Award, had to wear a goofy looking bear suit in a meeting room with others dressed in similarly colorful bear suits.

Based on the iconic 60s British spy TV series, *The Avengers* does its best to present an action picture that is distant from both the series' fans and viewers coming in cold. The cast is strong enough with the likes of Ralph Fiennes as secret agent John Steed and Uma Thurman as his companion Emma Peel. Both are excellent actors, but don't mesh well with the script requiring a romance to form between them, a relationship that was never present in the TV series.

There are plenty of opportunities for a romance to develop, but these scenes never amount to much. Emma first meets John by visiting him in a sauna where he is reading the newspaper in the nude, his bowler hat to his left. It could be a kinky scene, but it's surprisingly dull aside from some forgettably suggestive puns. Several scenes have just as much potential squandered, as when they engage in fencing or play chess while discussing their mission. They seem more interested in one-upping each other with one-liners than they are genuinely attracted to each other.

Their mission is to stop ex-ministry agent Sir August De Wynter (Connery) and his *James Bond*-style weather machine. His plan is so by the book it's tedious: control the weather and demand world leaders pay him not to have their countries pounded by a blizzard or a hurricane. But he also appears to be involved in cloning as Emma finds herself squaring off against a duplicate of herself. And he apparently has mechanical bees (yes, mechanical bees) to stop intruders approaching his mansion. The movie can't decide on an exact character for the villain and even resorts to dressing Connery in Scottish attire when making his demands.

The Avengers adheres to nearly every spy movie cliche to the point of handholding the audience through every scene. For example, Connery addresses his room of cohorts and asks who wants out, assuring them that he'll accept resignations with a monetary severance package. He says this in a shot where poisonous darts are visible on his suit. Is it supposed to be shocking that he then uses those darts on the unlucky few that raise their hands to leave? One would think that by now henchmen would realize there's no such thing as an acceptable resignation from an evil organization.

The film was a disaster before it even premiered. Warner Bros. had faith in the director Jeremiah S. Chechik (*Diabolique*) and the stars attached, but regretted their trust when a test screening went poorly. The studio forced Chechik to edit down the picture to a shorter length, leading to some confusing story progression. There was no second test screening, and no premiere was held. When released into theaters August of 1998, it was a major bomb that Warner Bros. attempted to wash their hands of the production after a painful release. Even when Chechik offered to produce the director's cut for home video free of charge, the studio declined.

Nothing about *The Avengers* feels as flashy, sexy or exciting as the *James Bond* pictures it was trying to emulate. There's hardly any sexual tension between Fiennes and Thurman, no bright action scenes and plenty of laughably bad British spy tech that includes human-sized hamster balls and cars that dispense tea and milk. It's such a ridiculous misfire of an American perception of British spy movies that I'm surprised Fiennes' bowler hat didn't make crumpets.

BABE

DIRECTOR: Chris Noonan | SCREENWRITER: George Miller, Chris Noonan | CAST: James Cromwell, Roscoe Lee Browne, Christine Cavanaugh, Hugo Weaving | GENRE: Comedy | RUNNING TIME: 92 min | MPAA RATING: G

CLASSIFICATION: BEST

Babe (1995) is a talking animal picture that is more enduring, sweet and exceptionally written than I ever expected for a movie about a pig. What separates it from the competition is how much character and story is placed within the barnyard animals and less on the human characters. Such storytelling is best suited for animated films, but the special effects of staging talking animals had advanced to such a point where a talking pig could be technically sound and not hinder a smart and intelligent story.

The film's titular pig protagonist (voiced by Christine Cavanaugh) is chosen by Australian Farmer Arthur Hoggett (James Cromwell) and spared the one-way ticket to Pig Paradise, as Babe calls it. Saddened to be orphaned, Babe is taken in by the farmhouse dog Fly and her pack of puppies. While on the farm, he gets to meet all the residing animals and understand their simple and entertaining stories. The duck Ferdinand believes himself to be a pig and is terrified of the genuine prospect about being eaten for dinner. The male collie of Rex has hearing problems and bitterness towards sheep. A choir of mice provides musical interludes between scenes that come off more oddly sweet than annoyingly necessary to lighten some of the film's mildly dark subjects about being eaten.

The little pig discovers he has a natural ability to herd sheep. Coached by his foster mother dog, Babe puts his best hoof forward in trying to be the top sheepherder among the scoffing dogs and sheep. One tip he receives is that if the sheep don't listen, a little bite will get them moving. He's not malicious though, as he apologizes to the sheep that will tell him to ask next time if he wanted them to hustle.

A pig sheepherder may at first seem odd to Farmer Hoggett, but he's very accepting of this pig since the beginning, thinking of their meeting as some sort of destiny. As Babe continues to astound Hoggett, he starts to go with the flow and accept that his pig is a genius. He'll even resort to dancing a jig if only to pick up the pig's spirits. The movie ends with Babe competing in the National Sheep

Dog Trials, where the pig proves that species need not bind the competition. Does he win? Let's just say he does enough to make Cromwell remark the film's most quotable line; *"That'll do, pig."*

Babe is a rare bit of family entertainment that manages to be innocently cute without the annoying baggage of frantic action to keep kids watching or adult jokes to keep the parents interested. There is a sweetness here that won't give you a toothache, created from real character development and honest lessons about life. Even when it was released next to another pig movie the same year by the name of *Gordy*, nobody could forget the cute little pig that could, earning a nomination for the Academy Award for Best Picture. It's not every year you see a movie with talking animals nominated for such an accolade. Yes, that will indeed do, pig.

BABY GENIUSES

DIRECTOR: Bob Clark | SCREENWRITER: Bob Clark, Greg Michael | CAST: Kathleen Turner, Christopher Lloyd, Kim Cattrall, Peter MacNicol, Ruby Dee | GENRE: Comedy | RUNNING TIME: 95 min | MPAA RATING: PG

CLASSIFICATION: WORST

If there were an award for the worst movie premise of the 1990s, the winner is without question *Baby Geniuses* (1999). Here is a picture so mind-numbingly convoluted and dumb that it redefines the definition of what makes a bad movie. It mistakenly entertains the idea that if babies are already adorable, they'd be even more lovable as talking geniuses. This sounds like a story better suited for a cartoon that would find more exciting things to do with talking babies than bland banter and karate kicks.

Just try to follow this plot if you can. Ellen (Kathleen Turner) is funding a laboratory to study her theory that babies can speak to one another through a secret language, believing that there is some hidden message in baby babble. The lead scientist (Christopher Lloyd) finds that everything babies do contain some level of hidden genius. A baby smashes random keys on a piano keyboard, only for some computer technobabble to reason that the baby is playing an elaborate symphony. I smell science grant fraud.

To fund this ludicrous study, Ellen opens a theme park to generate income, but loads it up with far too many animatronics and theatrics to ever be profitable. Namely, she builds a giant robotic baby that is automated to walk around the park, talk to kids in a creepy low voice and pick them up to give them hugs. Nobody in the park seems to find the idea of a giant mechanical baby that physically touches you to be the least bit frightening. It's not until later when the robot malfunctions does it indeed become a terror, along with a host of other animatronics gone awry.

Of the genius babies studied in the lab, the test subject of Sly organizes an escape and stages a revolt of the wee ones. He communicates to the other babies in language that is more knowing, but by no means smart. Most of that brain power must have gone into Sly's ability to perform karate kicks, fling adults into the air and disco dance to "Staying Alive." The babies must also have the power of absorbing pop culture psychically for being so young and able to make references to *Saturday Night Fever* and *Austin Powers*.

The manner in which the babies talk comes off creepy and unconvincing for compositing talking lips over toddlers. It's a method that is reminiscent of the Synchro-Vox technique used in the old cartoon *Clutch Cargo*, where live-action lips were edited on top of illustrated characters. It was a cheap and creepy effect when used in the late 1950s, and it's still just as bizarre when used on babies in 1999.

What's most baffling about this picture is that it was helmed by Bob Clark, the director of the classic comedy *A Christmas Story* (1983) that everyone in the family could relate. I don't know who among the family could connect to something as surreal and misguided as this film. One could reason that babies and toddlers would find the most to love in the picture, but I'd like to believe they have better taste. If we're to believe the philosophy that babies possess universal truth until they begin to speak actual words, something as tired and tedious as *Baby Geniuses* would suck out any enlightening intelligence before word one.

BABY'S DAY OUT

DIRECTOR: Patrick Read Johnson | SCREENWRITER: John Hughes | CAST: Joe Mantegna, Lara Flynn Boyle, Joe Pantoliano | GENRE: Comedy | RUNNING TIME: 99 min | MPAA RATING: PG

CLASSIFICATION: WORST

Baby's Day Out (1994) contains many physical gags of bumbling kidnappers trying to catch a baby that manages to escape both their clutches and certain death. The kidnappers are comically beaten in classic slapstick fashion as the baby crawls his way innocently out of any situation. In a cartoon, this could be very amusing. But in the form of live-action, this farce is too terrifying, contrived and cartoonish to find funny.

Baby Bink is scheduled by his wealthy and neglectful parents to have his photo taken for the newspaper. Three bumbling criminals, led by Joe Mantegna, decide to kidnap Bink during the photo shoot and hold him for ransom. But that pesky baby always manages to find a way to escape these criminals that quickly lose track of him. It's a familiar premise for cartoons in which an unwitting protector is run through a violent series of physical gags as the innocent protectee wanders through dangerous obstacles with ease. Such comedy is amusing because it's fun to watch cartoon characters flattened like pancakes and smashed into the pavement, as they'll regain shape in the next shot.

But watching Baby Bink wander through traffic, crawl along a construction site and wander into a gorilla cage is unfunny for what will happen to the criminals and more frightening for what will happen to the baby. Change the music for the scene where Bink narrowly avoids being hit by cars, and you have more of a horror picture than a family comedy. Even the slapstick elements fall flat as the laughs rely entirely on how amusing it is to watch a man be hit in the face with a hammer or have his crotch set on fire. Bless Joe Mantegna, but he just can't provide the right comical reactions for a man trying to suppress his cries of pain as his genitals are set aflame.

Believe it or not, there is a plot to this ridiculous series of baby-chasing antics. Bink isn't just randomly crawling from place to place, but is, in fact, travelling to familiar spots he remembers from a book his nanny read him. This is the nanny's warped and correct logic in deciphering where Bink will be found at the end of the day. Not only is the audience expected to buy into the idea of a baby narrowly avoiding death and three bad guys surviving the most bone-breaking of tortures, but we're now supposed to believe that a baby has an instinctive memory of where to go when he is lost in the city. Bink might as well be talking at this point, ala *Look Who's Talking*.

Baby's Day Out was written by John Hughes, having previously written the *Home Alone* movies in which another youngster bests bumbling bad guys with cartoon violence. But the *Home Alone* movies were at least more engaging as the boy defending his home was smart enough to form traps and outwit such inept burglars. Baby Bink seems to only have luck on his side when fighting off his kidnappers, despite a scene where he firmly grabs Joe Mantegna's crotch and twists his testicles. The only saving grace of the movie and the most prominent excuse for dismissing its shortcomings is that an adorably cute kid plays baby Bink himself. You know, the type of kid you wouldn't want to watch crawl into busy city streets and be run over by traffic.

BACK TO THE FUTURE PART III

DIRECTOR: Robert Zemeckis | SCREENWRITER: Bob Gale | CAST: Michael J. Fox, Christopher Lloyd, Mary Steenburgen, Thomas F. Wilson, Lea Thompson | GENRE: Adventure | RUNNING TIME: 99 min | MPAA RATING: PG

CLASSIFICATION: WEIRD

The final chapter of *Back to the Future* doesn't carry the same amount of zippy pluck as the first movie or the fantastic special effects of the future in the *Part II*. *Back to the Future Part III* (1990) is played more or less as a western and not a particularly great one at that. But where the movie does succeed is in bringing the arcs of Marty McFly (Michael J. Fox) and Doc Brown (Christopher Lloyd) to a satisfying conclusion.

When we last left Doc and Marty, the Marty of 1985 finds himself stuck in 1955 with the Doc of 1985 now trapped in the past. After some research with 1955 Doc, Marty is dismayed to discover that 1985 Doc was gunned down in 1885 by Mad Dog Tannen (Thomas F. Wilson), the ancestor of Marty's long-time nemesis Biff. Thankfully, the Doc trapped in 1885 has hidden the DeLorean time machine for a hundred years so that Marty could go back and save him. It's a perplexing setup to get Marty back to the old west, but it's slightly less convoluted than the alternate timeline future skipping in the previous picture.

The plot is mostly a repeat of the original *Back to the Future* in Hollywood western garb. Marty goes back in time to save Doc from his demise, runs across his bloodline in an embarrassing moment, must best the Tannen lineage and also make it back to his own time with limited resources of the era. What's more interesting this time around is Doc Brown and his chance at finding love in the old west. He rescues and befriends the lovely Clara (Mary Steenburgen), but fears he cannot make their relationship work as a time traveler. This dynamic creates some surprisingly fun scenes for Christopher Lloyd in which he shares a kiss with Steenburgen and goes on the ultimate bender at the bar.

This is very much a tradeoff movie in which Doc steals most of the show and even Marty's catchphrase; *"This is heavy."* Director Robert Zemeckis had stated that he felt he'd done everything he could to Marty's family, thus the shift in focus. Even though Marty ultimately gets to face off against Tannen, Doc is the ultimate driving force for many of the events and not just the crazy scientist of tricks and exposition. He develops a loud and massive machine he has built for the sole purpose of making ice cubes. His scheme of sending Marty back to 1985 by pushing the DeLorean with a locomotive is as intelligent as it is exciting, especially when the train is headed straight off a cliff. Doc assures Marty the bridge will be there in the future and you'll just have to take his word on that.

Part III was a bit of a rushed production in that it was filmed back-to-back with *Part II*; the second film was being edited while the third movie was shooting. Even so, there's still some cleverness in both the writing and direction that pays homage to westerns. As Marty prepares in 1955 to enter the old west, he mentions Clint Eastwood to Doc, who says he's never heard of him. It's amusing in that Eastwood didn't become an icon of westerns until the 1960s, but also clever as the shot features movie posters for *Revenge of the Creature* and *Tarantula*, both featuring an early Eastwood. Though Eastwood never appears in the film, a few western cameos pop up in the form of Bill McKinney (*The Outlaw Josey Wales*) and Matt Clark (*Wales* again). Ronald Reagan was approached for the role of the old west mayor, but turned it down.

While *Part III* doesn't have the most originality in how it repeats the expectations of the previous films (including the obligatory moment where Tannen must be covered in manure), it still has enough spirit and character to bring the trilogy to a fitting close. There isn't any new aspect of time travel divulged, but how much more is there to say about it after two movies of messing up timelines? This is more or less a victory lap for the lovable characters, the energized direction of Zemeckis, the witty writing of Bob Gale and the most iconic time machine in movie history.

BAD LIEUTENANT

DIRECTOR: Robert Zemeckis | SCREENWRITER: Bob Gale | CAST: Michael J. Fox, Christopher Lloyd, Mary Steenburgen, Thomas F. Wilson, Lea Thompson | GENRE: Adventure | RUNNING TIME: 99 min | MPAA RATING: PG

CLASSIFICATION: BEST

Harvey Keitel plays a dirty cop in *Bad Lieutenant* (1992) so deep in the mud he does not appear to exist as a person and more of an out of control machine driven by desire and fear. He is drowning in alcohol, drugs, sex and is gambling his way into debt. He is so short-fused he'll shoot his radio if he's furious with the score of the baseball game. This is a horrible person, and the saddest part is that he realizes this, drudging hopelessly from one sin to another in hopes that he'll feel something before his life comes to an end that will be coming very soon.

Keitel's character is never once referred to by name, as he is less of a human and more of a blurry mess of bad decisions. While on the job trying to resolve a shoplifting situation, he shoots a bullet over the ears of the accused shoplifters and pockets the money they stole. While another cop questions those involved, Keitel takes some food from the shop.

When off the clock, he is snorting cocaine, injecting drugs into his veins and having sex with two hookers at a time. The sensation of drugs and sex have long since departed his husk of a body.

We don't know too much about this character outside of his major issues. He is married, but staggers home in the middle of the night and wakes up to the kids watching television without a word from himself or his family. This kind of neglectful behavior has become the uncomfortable norm. While he does speak with his kids in the car as he drops them off at school, it's nothing talk about bathroom times and being a man. His banter with his fellow cops is of similarly distant subjects, focused more on placing bets on the next ball game and arguing about the odds.

When some men violently rape a nun, Keitel takes on the case and is frustrated with the cooperation of the victim. The nun knew her attackers, but chooses not to identify them as she has already forgiven them. Forgiveness is something that seems almost foreign to Keitel in his world, but is something he hopes he can find as all other pleasures have failed him. Inside a church, his character has a vision of Jesus Christ that reduces him to tears and anger, struggling to understand and maybe attain redemption. It is a virtue so distant that turns him into a blithering mess as he hopelessly reaches toward it.

New York director Abel Ferrara gives his film a raw and dirty edge that few directors would dare walk for fear of being too ugly. The camera holds on several of Keitel's most uncomfortable of scenes that paint him as a dirty cop. When he pulls over two girls, he agrees to let them off if they can arouse him while he masturbates. He visits his regular drug dealer for another shot in his veins, sending his mind into a void where euphoria left long ago. After sleeping with two prostitutes, he stumbles around naked in a daze with his face a blank mess of aimlessness. These scenes are long and painful to watch, but perfectly portray the conflicting inner struggle of a cop who has lost all control of his sense of self.

For such an unconventional and daring role, *Bad Lieutenant* deserves to be recognized as Keitel's strongest of performances and not just the NC-17 movie where he flashed his penis that wasn't *The Piano*.

BATMAN AND ROBIN

DIRECTOR: Joel Schumacher | SCREENWRITER: Peter MacGregor-Scott | CAST: **George Clooney, Arnold Schwarzenegger, Chris O'Donnell, Uma Thurman, Alicia Silverstone** | GENRE: Action | RUNNING TIME: 125 min | MPAA RATING: PG-13

CLASSIFICATION: WORST

After the success of *Batman Forever* (1995), Warner Brothers' demanded a quick follow up of *Batman and Robin* (1997), a rushed job of grander production values and goofier writing. The movie was, as star Chris O'Donnell described it, a toy commercial. It certainly looked like one to be sure.

Batman, played this time by a snide George Clooney, dons a costume more blue than black with breathing room for his pronounced nipples. His partner Robin (O'Donnell) wears a similar outfit with a brighter red and a glued-on mask. Every member of the Bat banner pilots either the stylishly colorful Batmobile or sleek motorcycles with the Bat insignia. There are additionally jets, snowmobiles, and snowboards for the caped crusader and company to surf through the sky. Batman even comes armed with the Bat Credit Card, which raises all sorts of questions, even for being a one-off joke device.

Batman and Robin find themselves foiling the villainous Mr. Freeze, played by Arnold Schwarzenegger under pounds of shining armor that encases his snowy white skin. He's stealing a diamond that he can use to freeze all of Gotham City while at the same time seeking a cure for his ill wife, currently being held in suspended animation. The wife backstory was absorbed from *Batman: The Animated Series*, but Freeze's demeanor is entirely derived from the 1960s *Batman* TV series. Every ice, snow and cold pun is lobbed out of his mouth in this script to the point where any joke that could be made about such a character has been exhausted.

In his quest to freeze Gotham, Freeze teams up with the cartoonishly seductive Poison Ivy, a botanist-gone-mad played with an embarrassing level of camp by Uma Thurman. She has developed a particular pheromone that makes her irresistible to men, leading to Batman and Robin fighting over her. The research she's performed before putting on the flower-power costume was used against her will on a prisoner to create a supervillain dubbed as Bane (Robert Jeep

Swenson). This villain was a reasonably intelligent muscle-bound character from the comics, but this movie reduces Bane to a muscle so dumb he can only speak in growls behind a mask. There's no room for clever dialogue in this pun-filled script with action sequences big on scale and low on IQ.

As if the screen wasn't already crowded with goofy characters, Batgirl is also introduced as Barbara Wilson (Alicia Silverstone), the niece of Wayne's butler Alfred. She's been living in England her entire life, but somehow hasn't formed an English accent. She arrives just as Alfred is suffering from a rare disease and only Mr. Freeze has the cure. Not content with sitting on the sidelines, she jumps into another tight leather suit and joins the fight for Gotham. Alfred had apparently been anticipating her arrival as he created an introduction video and a special Batsuit for when Barbara discovers the Batcave. It makes one wonder if Alfred should have put less time into making Barbara a suit and more effort into improving his health. I can only imagine what he has in store for when an uncle drops by.

To keep the direction light and comical, Schumacher would announce over a megaphone to his cast and crew on set *"remember, everyone, this is a cartoon"* before each take. But when so much money was spent on such elaborate effects and intricate costumes, the question arises: Why not just make a cartoon? He would later apologize in interviews and commentaries that he was aiming for something much different than what *Batman* fans wanted. And they certainly didn't want a plethora of ice puns or nipples on Batman's costume.

BATMAN FOREVER

DIRECTOR: Joel Schumacher | SCREENWRITER: Lee Batchler, Janet Scott Batchler, Akiva Goldsman | CAST: Val Kilmer, Tommy Lee Jones, Jim Carrey, Nicole Kidman, Chris O'Donnell | GENRE: Action | RUNNING TIME: 122 min | MPAA RATING: PG-13

CLASSIFICATION: WEIRD

After the dreariness of Tim Burton's *Batman Returns*, Warner Bros. attempted to restructure *Batman* for a lighter tone. Less Frank Miller, more Adam West. Joel Schumacher took over directing duties and delivered a far glossier version in *Batman Forever* (1995). It was more operatic, action-driven and goofier than the raw and dark themes of *Returns*. It's a palette cleanser of sorts to remind the audience that a superhero who dresses up like a bat doesn't have to be taken too seriously. He didn't have to be this ridiculous either for retreating to the style of the 1960s campy TV series.

Batman has been recast for this picture with Val Kilmer replacing Michael Keaton. It's not much a shift considering how boring the character of Batman is in the movies. As Bruce Wayne, Kilmer is a predictably docile and dull billionaire. As Batman, well…he has the chin. I guess that's enough for the love interest of Dr. Chase Meridian (Nicole Kidman), who would much prefer the leather-bound Batman as opposed to the boring Bruce Wayne. If only she could recognize chins to discover that Batman has less personality than she initially thought.

While attending a circus, Bruce decides to take in the orphaned acrobat Dick Grayson (Chris O'Donnell) after his family is killed in a criminal plot. Grayson is rebellious at first, but will soon decide to change his ways when discovers Bruce Wayne is Batman and that maybe he could be Robin. Wayne's impressive collection of motorcycles doesn't hurt either.

The villains are two cacklers vying to outlaugh each other. Tommy Lee Jones plays Two-Face, a district attorney turned maniacal criminal after half his face was disfigured by acid that must have been neon to give his skin that purple color. Two-Face's gimmick of a split personality is meant to provide a theme of duality to his crimes, but there doesn't seem to be another personality present. Either both personalities are insane or that second identity is so deeply buried it doesn't appear in this picture.

Two-Face teams up with The Riddler (Jim Carrey), a lunatic scientist that wants to use his brain-draining invention on Gotham to increase his IQ. That's a believable scheme for the mad genius that values mind over matter. What's not as believable is Carrey's goofy performance, dancing around in orange hair with green pajamas. He seems to be channeling more of the manic nature of The Joker than the calculative insanity of The Riddler.

Despite a welcome change in color and tone, *Batman Forever* still suffers from the same problems as Burton's films. Batman is still a bore, more notable for the costume than the character. The villains are just as underdeveloped, despite having the most fun in the strangest of outfits. The environment is so bombastic and lavishly designed that the film loses sight of its players within Gotham. It all feels so uneven and overwhelming, but has some charm with the likes of the snarky Chris O'Donnell and the dry wit of Michael Gough as Bruce's butler Alfred. But when a *Batman* picture has to rely on Robin and Alfred to carry the charisma, there's something very wrong when the campy dialogue and sets are more fun than the caped crusader himself.

BATMAN: MASK OF THE PHANTASM

DIRECTOR: Eric Radomski, Bruce Timm | SCREENWRITER: Alan Burnett, Paul Dini, Martin Pasko, Michael Reaves | CAST: Kevin Conroy, Mark Hamill, Dana Delany, Hart Bochner, Abe Vigoda | GENRE: Action (Animated) | RUNNING TIME: 76 min | MPAA RATING: PG

CLASSIFICATION: BEST

Mask of the Phantasm (1993) is the most underrated of theatrical *Batman* movies, often forgotten, but fondly looked back on. Produced by the same team behind the acclaimed *Batman: The Animated Series*, they knew the *Batman* comics, understood them, adored them and were perfectly aware of how to translate them to screens big or small. It was a stark contrast to the more grim and goofy *Batman* movies of Tim Burton and Joel Schumacher, as Bruce Timm and his band of writers and directors found a perfect balance of detective noir and comic book camp.

As opposed to taking over the city of Gotham, the villain of the mysterious Phantasm, appearing as a hooded grim reaper with a mechanical arm weapon, simply wants to knock off a few mobsters for revenge. Batman, voiced by a gruff and sincere Kevin Conroy, tracks down this murderer, but finds himself being accused of these crimes, launching a heavier police assault against the caped crusader. The added wild card of The Joker (Mark Hamill) makes his situation all the more intense.

While Batman attempts to unmask the Phantasm and solve the pattern of murders, he must also come to terms with a lost love that returns to Gotham City. Andrea (Dana Delany) is revealed through flashbacks as an old girlfriend of Bruce Wayne from his pre-Batman days. Bruce fell easily for this woman, but became tearfully frustrated about whether to settle down with her or continue his sorrowful vigilantism. There's an extremely emotional moment for him when he visits his parents' grave and pleads with them for forgiveness, attempting to rationalize that he has done enough to avenge their deaths. Broken and tearful, he admits to them, "*I didn't count on being happy*" as he is anxious and uneasy about a simpler life he denies himself. It is his last temptation before donning the cowl and becoming Batman.

The film is oddly adult for an animated superhero picture, more than just another skirmish of heroes and villains. After Andrea abruptly leaves Bruce in the old days, the two meet again in the present with deep bitterness towards each other. The case of the Phantasm unfolds as a grim mystery of murder most foul and tragedy most grim. Even the climax inside a dilapidated theme park of the future comes across more thrilling than goofy, despite a miniature city scene as a retro homage to the older *Batman* comics with giant props.

Selling the serious nature of the story was a genuine voice cast that didn't attempt to do the usual cartoon voices. Kevin Conroy sells Batman as a gritty and brooding figure while also capturing the gentle and frustrated side of Bruce Wayne. Mark Hamill voices The Joker with the perfect amount of bravado and sinisterness, performing a unique balancing act between clown and killer. Conroy and Hamill both became so iconic in these roles that they reprised their characters numerous times in animated series, movies and video games.

The supporting voice cast also bodes well, cast by legendary voice director Andrea Romano, to sound more real than cartoon. Abe Vigoda and Dick Miller slip perfectly into the roles of aged mobsters. Stacy Keach brings his deep and smooth voice to the role of the mysterious Phantom. Dana Delany portrays the tragic love interest of Andrea with the right amount of smarts and regret. She would later fulfill the staple role of Lois Lane on *Superman: The Animated Series*.

Mask of the Phantasm was originally intended to be a direct-to-video movie, but was abruptly decided on by Warner Bros. to receive a theatrical release. The screen format was changed, the animation received a slightly larger budget and the film was rushed out into theaters Christmas of 1993. Due to the quick and odd scheduling, *Phantasm* went unnoticed by many audiences and critics upon its release, only receiving overwhelming praise after being released on home video in 1994.

For being so under the radar, *Mask of the Phantasm* is more of a sleeper hit. I often bring it up as one of my all-time favorite *Batman* movies which usually makes others scratch their heads about which movie I'm talking about. I then mention it's the animated one from 1993 and their eyes go wide with realization, all the fond memories flooding back of a *Batman* picture that was less cartoonish than the live-action pictures, despite being a cartoon itself.

BATMAN RETURNS

DIRECTOR: Tim Burton | SCREENWRITER: Daniel Waters | CAST: Michael Keaton, Danny DeVito, Michelle Pfeiffer, Christopher Walken | GENRE: Action | RUNNING TIME: 126 min; MPAA RATING: PG-13

CLASSIFICATION: WEIRD

Of the many Batman movies released in the 1990s, *Batman Returns* (1992) is by far the darkest. Needlessly dark, in fact. It's as if Tim Burton was so embarrassed to be making a movie about a man who fights crime in a bat costume that he was determined to put a bafflingly macabre and odd coat of darkness on this superhero franchise. He may have achieved his goal of distancing himself from the usual *Batman* hype, considering that McDonald's pulled their Happy Meal tie-in deal.

The movie begins with perhaps the most depressing of openings in any *Batman* movie: The abandonment of an ugly infant child into the river. Due to an incident with their baby attacking a cat, the Cobblepot family decide that the only sane thing to do is literally send their child downriver. I can only imagine how they would respond if their toddler tortured the dog. The unlucky baby Oswald ends up at an abandoned zoo where penguins raise him, hence his villain name of The Penguin (Danny DeVito). He grows into a bitter, dirty and hate-filled human with penguin-like features that desires revenge on a city that shunned his ugliness. He also somehow has some colorfully dressed henchmen to do his bidding.

Before you can shed a tear for Penguin's plight, the movie leaves his pathos and steers us towards another villain. The white-haired Max Shreck (Christopher Walken) wants to control an energy monopoly on Gotham City. Blackmailed by Penguin, Shrek devotes his resources to making Penguin socially acceptable and eventually a mayoral candidate. If Penguin can make his way into office, Max will be able to build his energy factory without interference from the current mayor. It's rather easy to run for mayor of Gotham considering Penguin's lack of political experience, his shadowy past and his short temper which leads to biting off noses.

And then there's the third addition of Catwoman (Michelle Pfeiffer). Her origin is perhaps the most confusing of all as Selina Kyle, a secretary of Max who was tossed out a window for knowing too much. When she lands on the cold pavement, she is somehow nursed back to health by a swarm of cats. Animals sure do a lot of parenting in this picture. The cats have apparently endowed Selina with nine lives, a spell they must have cast amid trying to eat her body. One room-destroying mental breakdown and S&M outfit later, she is ready to play the role of Catwoman and get revenge on Max. Or just go crazy as she runs rampant in a department store for no reason, whipping the heads off mannequins and making the building explode.

Where is Batman in all this? Once more played by Michael Keaton, the titular character is more aloof than he was in the previous picture. He doesn't have much to do aside from punching a few henchmen and stopping Max's evil scheme. But he isn't much of a hero in how his Batmobile is easily sabotaged by henchmen and even fails to save a woman from being murdered by bats. There's a romance that develops between Batman and Catwoman, but it never reaches the erotic tension that is greatly implied. How sexual can two characters be when they spend all of their romantic moments dressed up as a tire and a suitcase?

Batman Returns thankfully has a strong cast and unique visual style in an attempt to cover up its murky tone and muddled story. But Burton's trademark style of Gotham City, with its gothic design and costumed henchmen, can only go so far to make one overlook the shortcomings of the characters. I didn't feel anything for Penguin's sob story, Catwoman's sexiness, Max's desire for power or Batman's mysteriousness. The movie attempts to be dark and noirish, but features surreal moments of comedy as when Batman adds record scratches to Penguin's audio admission of public manipulation. The lack of maintaining a consistent tone or narrative gives this aimless production a stylishly bitter nihilism - something that feels out of place for a *Batman* movie.

BEAUTY AND THE BEAST

DIRECTOR: Gary Trousdale, Kirk Wise | SCREENWRITER: Linda Woolverton | CAST: Paige O'Hara, Robby Benson, Richard White, Jerry Orbach, David Ogden Stiers, Angela Lansbury | GENRE: Fantasy (Animated) | RUNNING TIME: 84 min | MPAA RATING: PG

CLASSIFICATION: BEST

After *The Little Mermaid* (1989) launched the Disney Renaissance of breathtaking animation and unmatched musical numbers, it was *Beauty and the Beast* (1991) that defined the new wave of Disney animated classics for the 1990s. It was a film that represented everything that made the studio great: gorgeously colorful animation, a fantastical castle setting, a magical curse, a brave heroine and some of the most memorable melodies in movie history. There's a magic present that can make the viewer forget they're watching an animated film, as with the Academy Awards voters that nominated it for Best Picture, marking a massive turning point in animation history.

The story follows Belle (Paige O'Hara), a French girl who is too lost in her books to take much notice of her prudential town. It's a busy and charming town of bakers and barbers that find Belle odd for having her nose constantly in a book and her father continually tinkering on new inventions. One man who hopes to change her ways is the muscular and smug Gaston, the town's prettiest and strongest man that aims to make Belle his wife, whether she likes him or not. As she states in the song "This Prudential Life," she desperately hopes there's more out there for her than what it is presented to her in town.

When her father becomes lost in the woods, she discovers he is being held captive in a magical castle by the prince now cursed as the titular Beast (Robby Benson). The prince is both terrifying and expressive for appearing a cross between a buffalo, a bear, a wolf and a gorilla. He is cursed to this form until he can find true love before the pedals of a magical rose all fall, cursing him as a beast forever. Belle could be that true love, but the Beast will have to find his way into her heart and make her see past all his hair and teeth.

While Belle stays in the Beast's tower initially as a prisoner, she is treated to a spectacular dinner display by the castle servants cursed as household items. Lumière, a valet, turned candlestick, entertains her with a late-night dinner show of the charming number "Be Our

Guest." Cogsworth, a servant, turned clock, does his best to keep the castle secure and on schedule, but can't enforce it much with his small stature. Mrs. Potts is a teapot that brews tea for Belle, served up by her son-turned-teacup Chip.

The production on this film is astounding, to say the least. The scene in a massive golden ballroom where Belle and Beast share dance over the film's dreamlike theme song is one of the most vividly romantic and technologically impressive moments in all of Disney animation, using a stunning combination of 2D and computer graphics. The music written by Howard Ashman and composed by Alan Menken has gone down in history for featuring some of the most catchy and enjoyable songs of any Disney movie. Also worth noting is the script by first-time screenwriter Linda Woolverton, who wrote the story before storyboarding had begun, going against the usual flow of Disney assembling animated features.

Beauty and the Beast received much acclaim, but I still feel its most impressive achievement was being nominated for the Oscar of Best Picture. There's a theory that the Academy Awards created the Best Animated Movie category in 2001 to keep animation out of the Best Picture nominations. If true, they failed when Pixar's *Up* (2009) was nominated for Best Picture as well as *Toy Story 3* (2010) the following year, proving that great animated films can be as grand, epic and thoughtful as live-action. The best-animated films transcend their medium to the point where you don't feel as though you are watching a cartoon. And *Beauty and the Beast* was no mere cartoon.cartoon.

BEAVIS & BUTT-HEAD DO AMERICA

DIRECTOR: Mike Judge | SCREENWRITER: Mike Judge, Joe Stillman | CAST: Mike Judge, Demi Moore, Bruce Willis, Robert Stack, Cloris Leachman | GENRE: Comedy | RUNNING TIME: 81 min | MPAA RATING: PG-13

CLASSIFICATION: WEIRD

To just label the immature antics of *Beavis & Butt-head* as stupid would do a great injustice to these animated icons. Created by animator Mike Judge, the two teenagers were the ultimate satire of brain-dead American youth, minds rotted by MTV with humor most juvenile. Crudely drawn with big heads and skinny bodies, their laughter of "huh-huh" and "heh-heh" became the infectious cry of idiocy.

For their theatrical debut in *Beavis & Butthead Do America* (1995), the audience is invited to laugh at not only the titular dolts, but also the world that can't recognize them as idiots. In their small world, *Beavis and Butt-head* (both voiced by Mike Judge) have the singular goal of retrieving their television that was stolen from them. Their inept detective skills lead them to a cheap motel where they are mistaken by sleazy criminal Muddy Grimes (Bruce Willis) as hitmen hired to "do" his ex-wife, Dallas Grimes (Demi Moore).

Muddy is inferring they will kill her, but Beavis and Butt-head translate his slang as sex. Their limited attention now drawn to "scoring" with Dallas, they accept his offer to fly to Las Vegas and do the misinterpreted deed. A counter-offer is made by Dallas when they first meet, taking advantage of the boys' childish desires. She tells them to meet her in Washington D.C. for sex while they unwittingly carry her biological warfare device inside their pants.

The bulk of the comedy comes from Beavis and Butt-head being almost entirely unaware of the plot. Though their active goal seems to be scoring with Dallas, they become easily distracted by anything they come across in their travels. They visit the Hoover Dam and find themselves drawn to security station monitors, smashing buttons until the dam releases and floods a nearby camping site. They attend a church and mistake the confessional booths for restrooms, later taking on the roles of priests when church-goers ask for forgiveness. Even something as simple as the automatic flush of bathroom urinals can engross them for hours. Their limited IQ makes America a haven for entertainment, as everything from petrified wood to suggestive town names is a giggling riot.

As they travel to their destination, they are hounded by both a distraught Muddy and ATF Agent Flemming (Robert Stack), a strict man with an unhealthy obsession for cavity searches. Muddy thinks these two teenagers are double-crossing him. Flemming believes they are terrorists bent on destroying America. Butt-head believes he is going to score with "the lady with the big boobs." Beavis thinks he wants "tee-pee" for his "ca-ca" after downing a dozen cups of coffee and donning the identity of Cornholio.

The animation, though still as crudely designed as Mike Judge had intended, receives a noticeable upgrade from television quality, especially during many of the movie's musical interludes. When Beavis and Butt-head first arrive in Las Vegas, they hit the disco dance floor with their brand of awkward dancing while the camera swoops around in a shot similar to the ballroom scene of *Beauty and the Beast*. The two of them later have a hallucination in the desert where Beavis has a chaotic vision of a heavy metal hell over Rob Zombie's "Ratfinks, Suicide Tanks and Cannibal Girls."

The only intelligent force at play in this farce is the director, hopelessly attempting to help the duo find clues to the whereabouts of their stolen television. The soundtrack tries to bring some emotional resonance to the retrieval of their stolen TV with a powerfully uplifting score. This is the most tender of moments for the duo, basking in the glow of finding their beloved television, discussing if they'll score in the future and insulting each other with labels of "butt dumpling" and "dillhole." Such is the poetry of the immature teenager, brilliantly lampooned for all their humanity and stupidity in cartoon form. They'd probably laugh at that sentence as I said "poon."

BEING JOHN MALKOVICH

DIRECTOR: Spike Jonze | SCREENWRITER: Charlie Kaufman | CAST: John Cusack, Cameron Diaz, Catherine Keener, Orson Bean, Mary Kay Place, John Malkovich | GENRE: Comedy | RUNNING TIME: 112 min | MPAA RATING: R

CLASSIFICATION: BEST

Spike Jonze and Charlie Kaufman made their big debut with *Being John Malkovich* (1999), proving that both the director and writer were overflowing with inventive ideas. They have the creativity to conceive dreamlike worlds of distortion and oddities, but make them grounded enough in reality where relatable and flawed characters can live within the weird walls. It's a film that never gets lost in its whimsy by filling its story with characters that are just as interesting so that the background can remain the background. This helps keep a rather bizarre and twisty little premise from veering off course, always feeling calculative and smart for a film of tiny offices, mind invasion and teleportation.

Craig (John Cusack) is a street puppeteer with puppets too weird to make for pleasing street entertainment. His home is crowded by animal boarders, the result of his drab wife Lotte (Cameron Diaz) running a pet store. Times are tough and Craig seeks out a desk job, but in the strangest of places. The office he works at is located on the 7½ floor of a New York building, making the offices half the height of the other floors, where employees shuffle with hunches through their tiny work environments like giants. In this odd place, Craig starts becoming romantically infatuated with his co-worker Maxine (Catherine Keener). The entire film could have just been about Craig's affair while working in such a strange workplace that can only be accessed by rigging the elevator and prying open the doors with a crowbar. But there's so much more the movie has to offer.

Inside the office is a hidden doorway that Craig discovers and opens to reveal a long tunnel. He crawls through it to find out that this passageway lets him inside the mind of John Malkovich (played by himself). Craig can experience what it's like to be this man for about 15 minutes before he is launched out of Malkovich's mind and dropped next to the New Jersey Turnpike. Quite the find in the office. He shares this discovery with Maxine who recommends they turn this gateway to the mind into a business opportunity, charging others for the chance to be Malkovich.

There are so many points with a weird plot such as this where the film could have lost its steam and fell back on all its weirdness it had already built up. But Jonze and Kaufman never make the movie that easy. There are many more twists that result from this portal. One character turns transgender and begins to find herself attracted to Maxine. Malkovich himself enters the entrance and encounters a glitch of a world that could either be the dream or nightmare of someone with a massive ego. Messy relationships mount when character start entering Malkovich's mind while he is having sex. And that's only within the first half of the picture as the second half gets even crazier with sordid affairs and mind puppetry.

Being John Malkovich is one of those rare original films that holds no firm comparison and is often tough to describe with its surreal brilliance. As you can imagine, it was not an easy sell. New Line Cinema dropped the picture after the chairman asked: *"Why the fuck can't it be Being Tom Cruise?".* It was a gamble of a role for Malkovich considering the actor could be doomed to forever being associated with a box office bomb or only being known for one character. Though the film wasn't a significant financial success, it was nominated the Academy Award for Best Director, launched the careers of Jonze and Kaufman, became a critical favorite of the year and Malkovich would go on to be known for more than that weird movie where people crawled inside his head.

BIG DADDY

DIRECTOR: Dennis Dugan | SCREENWRITER: Steve Franks, Tim Herlihy, Adam Sandler | CAST: Adam Sandler, Joey Lauren Adams, Jon Stewart, Rob Schneider, Cole Sprouse, Dylan Sprouse, Leslie Mann, Steve Buscemi | GENRE: Comedy | RUNNING TIME: 93 min | MPAA RATING: PG-13

CLASSIFICATION: WORST

Adam Sandler graduated from giving kids bad advice in *Billy Madison* (1993) to raising a kid with bad advice in *Big Daddy* (1999). His immature behavior was at least semi-understandable in *Billy Madison* as he was attempting to blend in with elementary school students. But now he's saddled with being a parent, and his usual bits of public urination and manipulation of easily duped people are not as amusing when staged as fatherly advice. Any son raised on such values is doomed, but the movie still wants us to feel bad when social services want to take the child away.

The movie begins by establishing Sandler as the unlikable slacker Sonny Koufax, a slob of a 30-something with no direction in his life. Into his apartment strolls Julian, a five-year-old boy abandoned by his mother. Julian should be present to inspire Sonny to get off his butt and act his age, but not in Adam Sandler's twisted world of comedy. Sonny, as the adult role model, teaches little Julian how to be an antisocial kid with such activities as throwing tree branches at inline skaters and peeing on the wall of a McDonald's because they won't let you use the restroom. He has an amazing amount of hostility for such a lazy guy.

Remember, we're supposed to root for Sonny to obtain custody of the kid. And when social services come to take Julian away, we're supposed to weep. Why? I guess it would be heartbreaking if Sonny never had the chance to fatherly bond over teaching Julian how to leave an upper-decker in the toilet or throw bricks into traffic.

Sonny's antics could be forgivable if there were some form of redemption for recognizing the error of his ways. But the movie wants the audience to not only consistently laugh at his mean-spirited actions, but celebrate his ineptitude rather than pity it. Sonny feels no guilt for his attacks on women, the elderly, the homeless and pigeons. He also has no shame as he's willing to throw his body into oncoming traffic just to make Julian smile. I'm surprised Sonny even bothers trying to censor himself in front of the kid.

His actions make the courtroom case of the third act incredibly preposterous, as witness after witness is called on to testify that Sonny is a good parent worthy of Julian. This is where the movie attempts to be overly sentimental and make the case that a 30-something with no direction in his lazy lifestyle and a hatred for society is a suitable guardian. While he does try to reform himself during the second half of the picture, so much time has been spent on making Sonny so vile and hateful that it's hard to believe he'd make such a quick transition. It's too little too late for this script, especially when it tumbles with the insertion of a gay lawyer duo that are so stereotypical they may as well be cartoon characters.

Sandler's attempt at merging sentimentality and raunch go together about as well as peanut butter and salsa. He wants to make a raunchy comedy where a child can do and say inappropriate things, but also wants a drama about adoption and family. Either one could make for a great picture, but this script refuses to do any of the hard work to make it gel. Several movies have tried similar plots of unconventionally raising a kid, but they worked because there was some genuine sincerity in the hearts of the odd adoptive parents. Whatever sweetness may be in Sonny's heart is artificial amid the festering bile of his character.

THE BIG LEBOWSKI

DIRECTOR: Joel Coen | SCREENWRITER: Ethan Coen, Joel Coen | CAST: Jeff Bridges, John Goodman, Julianne Moore, Steve Buscemi, David Huddleston, John Turturro | GENRE: Comedy | RUNNING TIME: 117 min | MPAA RATING: R

CLASSIFICATION: BEST

The Big Lebowski (1998) is best remembered in moments as opposed to its plot of madness. I initially didn't recall much about why hired goons pissed on the rug of The Dude (Jeff Bridges), but I can nearly recite the following conversation with his bowling buddies about how the rug tied the room together. I can't remember much about how Walter (John Goodman) tracked down a lead of a school student, but I vividly remember Walter's outburst during negotiations when he destroys a car in his rage. What was the point of John Turturro's character as the rival bowler Jesus? Who cares - we get to see him lick a bowling ball and tell his foes that *"nobody fucks with the Jesus."*

The Dude, also known as Lebowski, is a bearded and long-haired slacker that prefers to wear shorts and sandals for all occasions. He doesn't aspire to much outside of bowling with his friends and taking it easy, which makes him confused when he's targeted by porn king/loanshark Jackie for money he owes. It turns out The Dude has been confused with the wrong Lebowski, but he is still steamed that his rug has been urinated on by the extorting goons. The Dude has very little interest in who this other Lebowski (David Huddleston) is or why he owes Jackie money. He only seeks him out to be compensated for his ruined rug and be done with it.

His disinterest doesn't mean much to everyone else who views him as a pawn that can be used for dropping off ransoms. But as long as he can be paid in cash and White Russians, he's willing to go through with whatever crazy scheme is afoot. And there are plenty of absurd plots going on as he finds himself running across a German nihilist bandleader (Peter Stormare), a horny redheaded artist (Julianne Moore) and a missing girl with a missing toe.

It's almost pointless to decipher the plot; it's a fool's errand for anyone seeking to enjoy this strange and easy-going comedy. It's the characters and their scenes which become glued to the mind. How could anyone forget the peculiar sequence when the wealthy Lebowski's daughter Bunny (Tara Reid) propositions The Dude for sex, only for the overhearing assistant (Philip Seymour Hoffman) to laugh loudly and uneasily? Or the moment when the nihilists visit The Dude in his bathtub to drop a ferret in the water? What of poor Donny (Steve Buscemi), the third wheel of The Dude's circle of friends that is always interrupted by Walter telling him to shut up? And what about The Dude's dream of a giant bowling alley and the German nihilists chasing him with giant scissors? These are moments that stick with the viewer long after, even if we can't quickly put them in sequential order with the twisty story.

While the plot may be complicated to piece together, its overall philosophy and tone are as clear as day. It all comes back to the easygoing Dude who approaches each moment as it happens, always looking at the big picture even if it appears small to everyone else. He's content enough to spend an evening at home, sipping his drink as he enjoys the company of his rug. He's in the moment and just goes with the flow of whatever strange route life presents him. That still doesn't mean he's completely content as he is known to explode at anyone from an improper dispersal of human ashes to The Eagles playing on the radio. For the most part, however, he takes life one White Russian at a time.

For featuring such unforgettable characters and scenes, *The Big Lebowski* has rightfully become a cult picture, spawning Lebowski Fest as a convention for screening the movie and having bowling parties. One could spend all day trying to analyze The Dude's strange dreams and the overarching themes of its curvy plot, but it's best just to accept its weirdness and appreciate the hilarity of it all. The narrating Sam Elliot reveals a few more details about what happens to The Dude, after all, is said and done, but he's satisfied taking comfort in his simple words: *"The Dude abides."*

BILL AND TED'S BOGUS JOURNEY

DIRECTOR: Pete Hewitt | SCREENWRITER: Chris Matheson, Ed Solomon | CAST: Keanu Reeves, Alex Winter, William Sadler, Joss Ackland, George Carlin | GENRE: Comedy | RUNNING TIME: 93 min | MPAA RATING: PG-13

CLASSIFICATION: WEIRD

The "dude" duo of Bill and Ted were fun to laugh at in *Bill and Ted's Excellent Adventure* (1989) because of their ignorance of history and their "bodacious" ideas of what to do with historical figures. But the pair is a little more relatable in the sequel as they venture into the afterlife, a realm most are about as knowledgeable about as Bill and Ted. I could only shrug at their stupidity this time and rock along on their journey through heaven and hell to the tune of Megadeth's "Go To Hell."

Bogus Journey (1991) goes straight to the highest heights of absurdity, posing that the duo was so grand with their music that they created a utopian society of rocking out. But not for the evil Chuck De Nomolos (Joss Ackland) who wants to rewrite history by sending robot versions of Bill and Ted into the past to assassinate the rock legends that changed the world. The 1990s Bill S. Preston (Alex Winter) and Ted "Theodore" Logan (Keanu Reeves), despite growing a little wiser from their time travel adventure, are easily killed by these robotic clones. While the robot Bill and Ted proceed to tarnish their reputations, the souls of the real Bill and Ted must find their way out of hell, best the Grim Reaper (William Sadler) into bringing them back to life, find a means of defeating their mechanical doppelgangers and win the Battle of the Bands.

The movie manages to find something original, creative and hilarious in every scene. While the Grim Reaper is essentially a parody of the figure that appears in Ingmar Bergman's *The Seventh Seal* in both design and premise, the game for the ownership of souls has replaced chess with rounds of Battleship, Clue, electronic football, and Twister. When Bill and Ted are trapped in hell, they're confronted with their worst nightmares of a demonic Easter Bunny and grandma seeking a smooch. The duo seeks the aid of heaven's greatest scientists to assemble good robots of themselves, only to discover the smartest scientist is a pair of hairy alien creatures known collectively as Station.

William Sadler follows the boys in their journey after being beaten by them and is a tremendous comedic talent. He quickly shifts from a spiritual icon of quiet dignity to a guy trying hopelessly to be cool around these two kids. In one of his funniest segments, he helps the hairy aliens by pushing a shopping cart through a hardware store, passing by a smoker that he mentions he'll be seeing soon on the other side. His dialogue also matches his comedic appearances, trying to explain to God that Bill and Ted gave him a Melvin with his underwear.

The production values are pretty amazing for Bill and Ted's adventures. The cramped corridors of hell with skewed doors and distorting perspectives, making the underworld appear more like a stylish Tim Burton set. The depiction of heaven is more than clouds and winged angels, existing as an elaborate album cover of Yes. The good robots created by the alien scientist are uniquely clunky and stiff, behaving just a tad more believable than bad robots. That being said, the evil robot dudes of the future, perfectly replicating the mannerisms of Bill and Ted, do have their moments of creative insanity, as when they play basketball with their heads that can be easily removed and reattached.

There are so many other elements that the movie crams into its ambitious script with great fun. George Carlin reprises his role as time-traveler Rufus, serving as a bookending overseer in the goofiest of future clothing. Jim Martin of Faith No More appears in the future as a music teacher who looks hilariously out of place. Cartoon voice actor Frank Welker does triple duty voicing the special effects of Station, Satan, and a demonic Easter Bunny, all of which come with his trademark gravelly growls. This all contributes to making Bill & Ted's second outing weirdly worthy of its air guitars of excellence.

BIO-DOME

DIRECTOR: Jason Bloom | SCREENWRITER: Kip Koenig, Scott Marcano | CAST: Pauly Shore, Stephen Baldwin, William Atherton, Joey Lauren Adams, Teresa Hill, Rose McGowan | GENRE: Comedy | RUNNING TIME: 95 min | MPAA RATING: PG-13

CLASSIFICATION: WORST

As the last gasp of Pauly Shore's MTV days, *Bio-Dome* (1995) was a premise that most would favor for Shore: Enclosing him within a geosphere, isolated from the rest of the world. But it quickly turns into a wish gone wrong, as a collective of scientists and the audience are forced to occupy the same space with Shore and his equally inept partner played by Stephen Baldwin. The scientists are stuck with them for about a year and the audience 95 minutes, though it might feel as though it's a year with how the movie slogs through its tired and overused dude humor.

It's amazing how the opening credits and music find a way to be just as annoying, loud and unfocused as Shore's usual brand of comedy. The introductory animation sequence is loaded with blaring sound effects, shot with chaotic imagery and played to a generically incoherent rock song. Let this serve as a warning for any who enter unwittingly: Abandon all smiles ye who enter here.

Pauly Shore works hard to make this one of his worst movies yet. The first scene finds him smashing Baldwin in the head with a book so they can get out of volunteering with their girlfriends. The following scene features Shore forcing Baldwin to chew on his toenails. The next scene they throw a firecracker at an animal. During all of these scenes, the two of them are spouting off some of the lamest dialogue that even the most brain-dead of slackers would find offensive to their vernacular.

Shore and Baldwin, known as Squirrel and Stubs respectively, mistakenly wander into the environmental experiment of a Bio-Dome as they believe it to be a mall where they can relieve themselves. They are sealed inside with scientists that have committed an entire year of their lives to being locked inside the dome. The girlfriends of Squirrel and Stubs are so committed to environmentalism that they believe such a sacrifice of their time is a noble devotion to science. Maybe the boys can learn something about the world and gain a new perspective on saving the planet. NOT!

What follows is a cavalcade of crude and aggravating gags designed to make Shore and Baldwin the most unlikable characters in the picture. They consistently pester the scientists by destroying their precious experiments without a hint of guilt, laughing with stupid glee at all the misfortune they cause. I kept waiting for that moment for them to win me over, but it comes far too late in the picture after the destructive duo raid the dome's food supply while getting high on laughing gas and later holding a party within the dome where outsiders are invited inside.

To call *Bio-Dome* the worst movie of Pauly Shore's 1990s film career would imply that there was a high for him somewhere in that decade. This film is on par with other Shore-lead movies for making the usual lame jokes, laughing with that familiar annoying voice and pulling off some unimpressive slapstick. He once again won a Razzie award for Worst Actor, sharing his 1995 award with Tom Arnold, and once more his film underperformed at the box office. Bio-Dome didn't exactly destroy Shore's career; his audience had just grown tired of his antics and probably didn't want to be considered his "buuuddy" anymore. All good things must come to an end. I'm not sure what good thing Shore had to offer, but it certainly came to a close with this picture.

THE BIRDCAGE

DIRECTOR: Mike Nichols | SCREENWRITER: Elaine May | CAST: Robin Williams, Gene Hackman, Nathan Lane, Dianne Wiest | GENRE: Comedy | RUNNING TIME: 118 min | MPAA RATING: R

CLASSIFICATION: WEIRD

The premise of *The Birdcage* (1996) seems like something out of a cosmopolitan sitcom that could have easily been an endless stream of tired gags. True, it is based on the more sophisticated Franco-Italian film *La Cage aux Folles* (1978), but doesn't succumb to the easiest of laughs as most American translations tend to favor. Thanks to some smart casting, a knowing script by Elaine May and perfectly timed direction by Mike Nichols, the film manages to elevate past the usual barriers of screwball comedies and does away with lazy stereotypes it could have easily fallen back on.

Robin Williams plays Armand Goldman, the gay owner of a drag club in Florida. He lives above the club with his lover and drag star Albert, played by Nathan Lane. For such notable comedians playing gay characters, they're surprisingly refined as the story tries to establish them more like a couple that's been together for twenty years. Lane still has a lot of fun as a gay man that's so insecure about his age he relies on his flamboyant houseboy Agador (Hank Azaria) to supply him with tranquilizers that are aspirin. Armand is in need of the aspirin for putting up with Albert's paranoia and trying to run a club, as Williams plays the role with a more contained snark than his usual exploding personality allows.

A problem occurs when Armand's son Val (Dan Futterman) decides to bring over his fiance and her family to meet him. Val doesn't want the girl's parents to meet Albert, however, as her father is a conservative senator (Gene Hackman) that certainly wouldn't approve of the gay lifestyle. But Armand is determined to stick it out for his son and manages to convince the boy's one-night-stand mother (Christine Baranski) to pretend to be his wife for an evening.

The film could essentially write itself at this point with the expected bits of dashing in and out of the kitchen while Albert crashes the party as a drag queen that easily fools the senator. But neither the script nor the actors go on autopilot for this comedy. I loved how serious Williams takes the drag show philosophy, encouraging his extra dancers to embrace the styles of Fosse or

Madonna, but keep it inside. Williams briefly breaks into his frenetic nature during this scene, but still pulls himself back with remarkable restraint. It helps that he is given some funny lines to work with; *"So you're going to a cemetery with your toothbrush. How Egyptian."*

Nathan Lane performs his comfy persona of an over the top and dramatic gay man, but it suits him well. He doesn't exactly sell the role of being Val's mother well enough that a senator would buy him as a woman, but he's having so much fun in the role that I was willing to go along with it as much as the senator's wife (Dianne Wiest) who catches on early. Hackman, too, seems to be having a blast as a senator hoping that Armand and his wife can help promote the family values he stands for.

The climactic end to the dinner can be seen coming a mile away, but that's not the point of such a comedy. What matters is that the cast can sell their roles so well and elevate telegraphed humor for such a plot. Williams and Lane play off each other so well that the familiar scene of undergoing training to act straight comes off more hilarious than routine. I cracked up pretty hard when Lane attempts to walk like John Wayne with a stagger. Williams responds that it's perfect; *"I just never realized John Wayne walked like that."*

BLADE

DIRECTOR: Daniel Myrick, Eduardo Sánchez | SCREENWRITER: Daniel Myrick, Eduardo Sánchez | CAST: Heather Donahue, Michael C. Williams, Joshua Leonard | GENRE: Horror | RUNNING TIME: 81 min | MPAA RATING: R

CLASSIFICATION: WEIRD

At a time when DC Comics was touting *Batman* as a PG-13 blockbuster, Marvel took a wild and bloody stab at an R-rated superhero picture with *Blade* (1998). New Line Cinema had initially wanted the film to be a lighter spoof, but screenwriter David S. Goyer knew this was the wrong route to take for the half-vampiric hero that hunts down vampires. If you're going to hunt bloodsuckers with a sword, you better show some blood, and you better make it look cool.

The character of Blade has an interesting story even if the character itself doesn't have much of a personality. His pregnant mother was attacked by a vampire during birth, having a boy that was half human and half vampire. He grew up on the streets until vampire hunter Whistler (Kris Kristofferson) takes him under his wing to give him a future in the secretive world of vampire killing. By the time he's an adult, Blade is a master of swords, guns, leather outfits and sunglasses in his crusade against the vampire underground. Oh, and a sharp boomerang that he seems to have the most fun using against the undead.

Blade is on the hunt for another half-human, half-vampire by the name of Deacon Frost (Stephen Dorff), a villain aiming for nothing less than to have vampires take control of the world. He convinces the vampire elders to go ahead with a war against humans after slaughtering one of them to prove his point. Half-vampires have to work a little harder up the chain in the stuffy world of vampire politics. He plans to resurrect a vampire blood god to aid in the battle of bloodsuckers versus non-bloodsuckers.

Sometimes serious and sometimes dropping character for insults and smiles, Blade replicates the persona of Burton's Batman by embodying a character more interesting for his world than his role. He is at his best when he embraces the comic book format of bounding over rooftops, slicing up bad guys with glee and rescuing a doctor (N'Bushe Wright) from being transformed into a vampire. The potential cure: liquid garlic. Blade, too, takes a similar serum to keep him more human than vampiric, but Whistler needs to make a stronger batch as the vampire hunter is building up a resistance. I didn't expect goofy science in a vampire hunting movie, but it surprisingly fits for the comic book movie genre.

The special effects have aged as well as milk. While computer graphics were making great strides in the late 1990s, they perhaps weren't ready to handle the scale demanded by *Blade*. The climax of the film features a circle of vampires transforming into winged skeletons that crawl out of their mouths and shatter their bodies. Even worse is the immortality effect of Frost where he can recover quickly from being sliced in half with a tornado of blood that magnetically snaps his body back into shape. Kudos to director Stephen Norrington for at least being ambitious with his comic book movie with computer graphics that couldn't properly portray his wild vision.

The film is more interesting for the trail it blazed. Snipes would reprise Blade for a superior sequel directed by Guillermo del Toro of *Hellboy* fame. The success of *Blade* convinced Marvel to go ahead with developing the first *X-Men* movie for theaters two years later. One year later, the Wachowskis would capitalize on the leather trenchcoat outfits and techno music with *The Matrix* (1999). And to think it all started with a film where Snipes pranced around in a leather outfit while slicing Stephen Dorff into a terrible computer animated effect.

THE BLAIR WITCH PROJECT

DIRECTOR: Daniel Myrick, Eduardo Sánchez | SCREENWRITER: Daniel Myrick, Eduardo Sánchez | CAST: Heather Donahue, Michael C. Williams, Joshua Leonard | GENRE: Horror | RUNNING TIME: 81 min | MPAA RATING: R

CLASSIFICATION: WEIRD

The most unlikely of independent hits, *The Blair Witch Project* (1999) was surprisingly engaging and unique for being a minimalist horror picture where no boogieman is seen, and no bloody money shot is present. Shot in eight days, the movie was made for under a million dollars (some reports claim it was as low as $20,000), and the filmmakers were hopeful that their picture would play on cable television. They did not expect it to play in theaters for a wide release where it would gross over $200 million. Who could?

Three filmmakers by the names of Heather, Mike and Josh (all using their real names) venture into the woods with two cameras (one black-and-white 16mm camera, one color camcorder) and sound equipment to seek out the legend of a witch that slaughtered children in the woods near Burkittsville. Before their camping trip, they stop to interview some of the local townsfolk which give them fair warning about venturing into those woods, not as grave foreboding but semi-serious joking. The trio finds this talk more exciting than ominous.

The movie relies on the most straightforward techniques in the most believable of scenarios to scare the audience. The first major problem is that they've lost their way in the woods, causing them to walk around in circles for days. They start finding stick figures made out of twigs are left on the ground, taunting the filmmakers as if someone is playing a practical joke. But if it is a joke, then who is behind it? And if it is the witch, what does she want? The mysteries keep mounting as the filmmakers begin to disappear and panic sets in. It isn't long before Heather makes her tearful and snot-dripping farewell to the camera as she fears her last moments on Earth are approaching.

The Blair Witch favors a highly realistic tone for its mockumentary style to make the audience believe that maybe there is a witch out in those woods. What helped stir up interest and box office in such a movie was the brilliant and relatively cheap use of generating hype. It was one of the first films to utilize an elaborate internet campaign to generate buzz with a website full of fake news reports based on the events of the film. At the Sundance Film Festival, flyers were passed out that asked if anyone had seen the characters that went missing in the movie. Even a faux documentary on the fictional Blair Witch was released on the Sci-Fi Channel before the movie's release. Every marketing step was taken to ensure that the public bought into the film as an actual found-footage film, short of staging a literal disappearance of the actors.

With so much hype around the picture, it may lead an outsider to view the picture with a "that's it?" attitude. There's no witch, no blood and no familiar scares of most contemporary horror. But the key to its success was that less was more. It's more frightening thinking about what might be out in the woods than showing what's in the woods. If the picture had decided to show a witch based on its budget, it'd most likely be some old woman in a cloak. She could be scary, but it's a figure far more terrifying in the realm of the imagination than that of a low-budget horror. The filmmakers have enough faith in themselves and the audience to tap deeper into our fears more than any special effects ever could.

THE BODYGUARD

DIRECTOR: Mick Jackson | SCREENWRITER: Lawrence Kasdan | CAST: Kevin Costner, Whitney Houston, Gary Kemp, Bill Cobbs, Ralph Waite | GENRE: Drama | RUNNING TIME: 129 min | MPAA RATING: R

CLASSIFICATION: WEIRD

The Bodyguard (1992) was promoted as a romance between celebrity and bodyguard, but is more of a unique clash of two worlds. This makes the movie a bit of a tease for those that came in expecting a genuine love story between Whitney Houston and Kevin Costner only to discover there's a chasm of chemistry between them that prevents an early embrace. They still become romantically involved, but not without some feuding talk and dangerous death threats.

Whitney Houston is perfectly cast as pop music sensation Rachel Marron singing Whitney Houston songs. She is being stalked and sent death threat, one of them acted on when an exploding doll is sent to her dressing room. Her manager (Bill Cobbs) hires bodyguard Frank Farmer (Kevin Costner) as protection. He's a good protector for having been trained as a Secret Service agent, despite that one time he didn't prevent a bullet from hitting Ronald Reagan. He vows never to get involved with his clients, but will he fall for the lovely Rachel?

Well, not at first. They have a predictable feuding where Rachel despises having restricted freedom while Frank can't stand her uncooperative nature of the spoiled diva. It isn't until a riot at Rachel's concert does she grow close enough to her bodyguard to sleep with him. But Farmer pushes her away to remain professional and get in some more action-packed moments as Rachel's protector. Costner's exciting scenes range from the simplistic of taking a bullet to the absurd of chasing after a stalker's van on foot.

Lawrence Kasdan's script attempts to mix celebrity egotism with thriller elements. Houston does a solid job portraying a pop star's strange sense of invulnerability that will be torn down when she is threatened. Director Mick Jackson doesn't water down the danger of the situation where Rachel is targeted with personal death threats over the phones and multiple bombs sent towards her. It's unfortunate, however, that the film succumbs to weak dialogue and an obvious red herring.

But, of course, the biggest selling point of the picture was Whitney Houston and her accompanying music. The inclusion of her unforgettable hit singles of "I Will Always Love You" and "I'm Every Woman" propelled the film's soundtrack to be the best-selling of all time, selling over 17 million copies in the US alone. The film would additionally be nominated for the Academy Award for Best Original Song for two of the five songs Houston sang.

Let's face it: *The Bodyguard* was a Whitney Houston vehicle and little else. It's the only possible way the film could have grossed $400 million worldwide. It indeed wasn't for Kevin Costner's performance, which was decent in its right, but doesn't generate a real spark when paired with Houston. The film itself is also pretty egotistical for a climax that takes place at the Academy Awards where her character wins the Oscar for Best Actress. Houston wouldn't be nominated for Best Actress, but did receive a Golden Raspberry nomination for Worst Actress.

For being as ludicrous with its plot and blatant with its Houston touting, the film has often become the subject of parody with "I Will Always Love You" being the most iconic aspect of the movie. And aside from the shot where Costner rushes Houston to safety in his arms, there wasn't much of anything memorable from the film. It's a film that's worth a watch for the endless parodies it created and as a snapshot of Whitney Houston's career when she was a big name at both the box office and the Academy Awards, brief though it was.

BOOGIE NIGHTS

DIRECTOR: Paul Thomas Anderson | SCREENWRITER: Paul Thomas Anderson | CAST: Mark Wahlberg, Julianne Moore, Burt Reynolds, Don Cheadle, John C. Reilly, William H. Macy, Heather Graham, Nicole Parker, Philip Seymour Hoffman | GENRE: Drama | RUNNING TIME: 155 min | MPAA RATING: R

CLASSIFICATION: BEST

Paul Thomas Anderson's *Boogie Nights* (1997) is a film about the pornography industry, but not from the simple perspectives of forced eroticism or juvenile giggling. It is more of a classic tale of fame, taking place in the late 1970s when porn was shot on film and still shown in theaters. It was a golden age of experimentation with the hope that maybe films with graphic sex could be cinematic and artistic. Those dreams would be shattered when the industry moved to home video in the 1980s.

Before the industry would fall from grace, pornography was a thriving business in 1977 that Eddie Adams (Mark Wahlberg) could ditch his job as a dishwasher at a Hollywood nightclub and become a prolific star of porn films. He is picked for the job by Jack Horner (Burt Reynolds), a pornographer that believes there is something beautiful behind those jeans. Jack is so impressed by Eddie's sexual audition on Rollergirl (Heather Graham), an actress that keeps her skates on during sex, that he hires him for his porn films under the name Dirk Diggler.

What follows is a story about the messy world of eroticism without being very erotic. Sex begins to lose its allure and passion if it's your day job. Horner no longer watches the act that plays out in front of his cameras with any titillation. He can't see past the $25,000+ it costs him to fund these productions and potential income that awaits him. While he views pornography as a business, Eddie treats it as stardom. He buys a new house, a new car, a fancy wardrobe and deals in cocaine. He is so revered for his gift of a large penis he has no problem whipping it out for the curious film financier Colonel James (Robert Ridgely).

Except for the final shot that showcases Dirk's penis, the film doesn't feature much nudity. This is a smart move for the picture as it builds up the allure of Dirk's genitals rather than revealing it early on for an easy visual gag. Anderson teases the audience with this essential body part of the industry that by the time it is finally revealed we understand why Horner refers to it as Mr. Torpedo Area and why the Colonel seems so amused by its sight.

As with a lot of Paul Thomas Anderson productions, this is an ensemble picture that better portrays the various ins and outs of the industry. William H. Macy plays assistant director Little Bill; he is aggravated to discover his porn star wife is having sex with a collective of men in the driveway, only for her to tell him to shut up for embarrassing her. Ricky Jay plays a cameraman that is somehow under the idea that every film he works on is unique with its style. John C. Reilly plays Dirk's friend Reed that begins to form a crush on him. Other names worth noting are Don Cheadle as a secondary porn actor, Luis Guzman as a club manager aspiring to star in adult movies and Philip Baker Hall as the boss of Colonel Jake, making the miraculous discovery of the potential of videotape.

Anderson had stated that he wanted his film to be rated NC-17, most likely for an abundance of sex and nudity, but he settled on an R rating. It suits him for a movie that is more about being disillusioned by sex rather than reveling in its prolific age of porn. He doesn't want to arouse our sexuality so much as question our appetites for being turned on and the work that goes into turning out such content. It's a world coated in money, drugs, custody battles, prostitution and murder amid all the frustrations of trying to maintain an erection for a scene. Anderson's film paints a portrait of a business that may not have been better off being doomed to home video where porno was valued more like the product that it was than whatever artistic merit it might have had. Whatever art was present, it wasn't worth its weight in blood and blow that transformed acts love to another day at the office.

BOUND

DIRECTOR: The Wachowskis | SCREENWRITER: The Wachowskis | CAST: Jennifer Tilly, Gina Gershon, Joe Pantoliano | GENRE: Drama | RUNNING TIME: 108 min | MPAA RATING: R

CLASSIFICATION: BEST

Before the Wachowskis were redefining action and science fiction with *The Matrix* (1999), they were taking a whack at noir thrillers with their directorial debut of *Bound* (1996). Their film set out to shatter many of the stereotypes of cinema by portraying the main character as a lesbian. Some studios recommended that they change the lesbian into a male character to increase interest, but the Wachowskis declined as they wanted to be trendsetters and not just go with the Hollywood flow. The result was a film that was tough to make, but would ultimately define the fresh style of the Wachowskis for years to come.

Gina Gershon plays Corky, a lesbian fresh off a five-year prison sentence that moves into a new apartment as a handy woman with tools and paint. Her first visitor is her next-door neighbor Violet (Jennifer Tilly), a woman married to mobster Caesar (Joe Pantoliano) who is not very discreet in cheating on his wife. Violet is more interested in Corky, however, as sparks fly quickly between the two over a cup of coffee and later when Violet needs help getting her ring out of the kitchen sink. This tactic is usually portrayed by women to lure men over to their place for sex, but it seems to work just as well for women seducing women.

While their steamy affair continues with plenty of passionate sex, a mafia plot of money laundering and violence looms behind closed doors that were not closed all the way. Violet's desire to run away with Corky becomes all the more tantalizing and urgent with the increasing mob activity that Caesar brings home with him. A mobster is drug into Caesar's bathroom and has his fingers cut off with garden shears. He returns home one night a bloody mess while carrying laundered money that will literally have to be laundered to remove the blood. The secret lovers decide to steal the money and run with an elaborate scheme that twists and turns with plenty of deception, sex and violence.

For a story where plans go awry, *Bound* is uniquely crafted with precision direction for its many shifts in genre tones. When Corky and Violet share their first kiss and sexual embrace, it's played out slowly with eroticism that builds rather than quickly cutting to them naked in bed. When they discuss their game plan for swiping the money, they treat it with an earnest seriousness that has natural bursts of amusement. It goes dark with its mixing of noir and caper elements, but takes care never to go too macabre with its bloody money tale. So trim is this script that it finds just the right moments to make a perfectly timed joke, as when one gangster begs not to be shot after having already been shot multiple time before he falls to the floor.

The Wachowskis are unapologetic in this film for their love of genre and devotion to lesbian romance. They asked Pantoliano to study Bogart and Gershon to study Brando to match what they believed to be the best acting for a story of crime and passion. The visual style perfected by cinematographer Bill Pope is a respectful nod to classic noir, but also adheres to the Wachowskis' inspiration of Frank Miller's *Sin City* comic books. Great care was taken in making sure that the sex scenes felt genuine that the duo consulted feminist and sex educator Susie Bright to make sure the film's critical lesbian moment didn't come off as false.

Bound made a lot of people sit up and take note of these two filmmakers before they would be better known for the *Matrix* franchise. The movie won many festival awards, and the Wachowskis were compared to the likes of the Coens and Hitchcock. From a small budget restricted to a few apartment interiors, they were able to craft a film that is sexy, dangerous, bloody and intelligent with exquisite craftsmanship. It's also a remarkable recovery for Gershon who felt wasted with her sexiness in *Showgirls*, a film that cost $45 million to sell sex at its most artificial of titillation. The Wachowskis were able to deliver more eroticism on a budget of $6 million. Now that's a bargain!

BOYS DON'T CRY

DIRECTOR: Kimberly Peirce | SCREENWRITER: Andy Bienen, Kimberly Peirce | CAST: Hilary Swank, Chloë Sevigny, Peter Sarsgaard | GENRE: Drama | RUNNING TIME: 118 min | MPAA RATING: R

CLASSIFICATION: BEST

Brandon Teena (Hilary Swank) could be put under a microscope for being a trans man in Nebraska, but *Boys Don't Cry* (1999) doesn't want to turn him into a case study. Formerly Teena Renae Brandon, he doesn't view the shifting of gender as some grand move for acceptance or empowerment. He doesn't wish to carry any other identity than that of being a boy, a gender she favors with her short hair and stuffing of jeans. If Brandon looks the part and being a boy in the south is so much fun, why not live it up?

Based on true events, more factually presented in the documentary *The Brandon Teena Story*, the film follows Brandon on her tragic love story. Despite getting into a few fights, Brandon is a nice enough guy to attract the heart of Lana (Chloe Sevigny) who has never met a man more sweet. When surrounded by the violent men in her life of John (Peter Sarsgaard) and Tom (Brendan Sexton 3rd) in her rundown Nebraska community, Lana is astounded that a man would be sweet and willing enough to run away with her to Memphis if she wanted to pursue a singing career. Of course, she'll also be surprised to discover Brandon doesn't have a penis. But Lana sticks with Brandon for the long haul, accepting that he was born a woman and that he has a bitter past that is still catching up with him.

Brandon doesn't spend much time lamenting on the deeper social aspects of the identity he has chosen. A loud and proud gender swapper doesn't have much of a place in the simple southern states of beer drinking, trucking, TV lounging and karaoke. Part of Brandon likes the simplicity of it all, where he can hang out with a bunch of guys at the bar without the slightest hint of tension for him being anything other than a dude.

Not to sound too insulting of her looks, but Hilary Swank does an exceptional job at looking the part of a man that is a woman behind the underwear and socks. Her performance is a genuine surprise as she takes a very tough role and finds just the right notes, never veering off course in the concealment of her gender. Equally strong is Chloe Sevigny as the love interest that goes through probably the biggest shift in the story. She is amazing to watch and decipher when she figures out Brandon is a woman and when she finally accepts it. Her flirtation, naivete and confidence define her as a simple southern girl that will soon develop thoughts and emotions that are not so simple.

Director Kimberly Peirce put an astounding amount of effort into making this picture. It took nearly five years of research to write the script and three years to cast. Peirce wanted the film to feel as authentic as possible and lifted dialogue directly from documentary footage. The result was a fantastically tragic romance of Shakespearean quality that garnered multiple awards (Hilary Swank won the Academy Award for Best Actress) and has been endlessly analyzed for its themes of gender, identity, homophobia and midwestern social classes. It is far more than merely a meticulous observation, but a living and breathing story of characters bound by nature, trapped by society and desperate for any ounce of happiness they can find in the countryside. The film lets us get deep enough into its world that by the time the story reaches its bloody and tragic conclusion, we feel every blow. And *Boys Don't Cry* will give you quite the pummelling.

BOYS N THE HOOD

DIRECTOR: John Singleton | SCREENWRITER: John Singleton | CAST: Ice Cube, Cuba Gooding Jr., Morris Chestnut, Larry Fishburne | GENRE: Drama | RUNNING TIME: 112 min | MPAA RATING: R

CLASSIFICATION: BEST

John Singleton made history for being the youngest man to be nominated for the Academy Award for Best Director for his film *Boyz n the Hood* (1991), and it's easy enough to see why he earned such a nomination. Having made the movie in his 20s, he proved that he had an ear and an eye for the black youth of Los Angeles. Singleton also has the unique gift to look ahead to all the potential a young black man can have in his future if he can survive living in a neighborhood of drugs and violence. All the grades and morality he builds up won't mean a thing when gun-toting gangsters roam the streets.

Tre Styles is bright enough to be a scholar, but also ill-tempered enough to be a hoodlum. He is sent to live with his father Furious (Laurence Fishburne) in the Crenshaw neighborhood of Los Angeles in hopes that he'll learn some discipline. His dad is smart enough to know the ghetto and lays down the essential rules Tre will need to succeed in life. Even when armed with all this advice, he has so much more to learn on the streets. While living in Crenshaw under his father's strict and fearful rules, Tre is reunited with his old friends of Doughboy, his brother Ricky and Chris their friend. They've been lucky enough to survive childhood, but some quickly descend that path of drugs, alcohol, and guns. Parents can only protect these kids from these dangers for so long as children and even less so when they become teenagers.

Doughboy (Ice Cube) grows up to join the Crips gang and celebrates his release from prison with a barbecue. Ricky (Morris Chestnut) is a promising high school football star, but also has an infant son to deal with. Chris is now wheelchair-bound after being paralyzed by a gunshot. Tre (Cuba Gooding Jr.) has somehow managed to avoid most of these pitfalls of youth by maintaining his grades, taking an honest part-time job and holding a healthy relationship with his girlfriend, Brandi (Nia Long). He could make it to college, but, again, there are no guarantees in his neighborhood.

Singleton is unflinching in his portrayal of his characters to make them both detailed and flawed. Doughboy makes terrible decisions, but is not merely a bad person. He wants to look out for Tre, but can only briefly surface from the inky depths of gangster vices that have shaped his consistent anger at the world. There's an emotional scene where Doughboy sympathizes with Tre's desire to leave the gang before violence erupts, but without an overly dramatic speech. A man such as Doughboy is not a poet, but does his best to show some maturity as much as anybody that has grown up in the ghetto. Singleton's script lets us understand nearly every character's motivations and backgrounds and not simply indulge in melodramatic gang violence where we'd care more about the bullets than the boys.

The film feels so real for being based on Singleton's childhood, still fresh and vivid when he penned the script at an early age. He was incredibly protective of his writing that he felt the need to direct his own story with his style for his directorial debut. You can see his shooting style evolve over the course of the film as everything was shot in sequence while he was trying to find his footing. And though he didn't win the Academy Award for Best Director, Singleton did win multiple awards from the Image Awards, New York Film Critics Circle Award and Young Artist Awards. He became a notable name in Hollywood after his debut and would continue to direct several black films including *Poetic Justice* (1993), *Higher Learning* (1995) and even the remake of *Shaft* (2000).

And to think just a few years before *Boyz* he was an intern on *The Arsenio Hall Show*.

THE BRADY BUNCH MOVIE

DIRECTOR: Betty Thomas | SCREENWRITER: Laurice Elehwany, Rick Copp, Bonnie Turner, Terry Turner | CAST: Shelley Long, Gary Cole, Michael McKean | GENRE: Comedy | RUNNING TIME: 90 min | MPAA RATING: PG-13

CLASSIFICATION: WEIRD

While other TV-to-movie adaptations struggled to make classic series more contemporary for the 1990s, *The Brady Bunch Movie* (1995) thrives on its dated concept. The movie takes place in the 90s, but for the Brady family, they're still in their little bubble of the sitcom world of the 1970s. It is a simple household of six children where the regular problems of the household are Peter worrying about his cracking voice and Jan being jealous of Marcia's attention. It's unclear if their house was transported into the future or if the sliding timeline of television slid them all the way up to 1995. Whatever the reason, this family is trapped in the comfy and goofy 70s of perms and bellbottoms.

The outside comes knocking when real estate developer Larry Dittmeyer (Michael McKean) seeks to foreclose on their property to build a mall. He can't wait to get rid of them as he has lived next to them for years and can't stand their goofy and chipper spirits. In particular, Cindy drives him nuts with her cute smile and toothy lisp; *"Why don't you hop back on the Swiss Miss package where you belong, huh?"*

He won't have to wait long, however, as the family owes $20,000 in taxes. For the parents of Mike (Gary Cole) and Carol (Shelley Long), they do their best to keep it under their hats, but Cindy overhears and relays this information to her siblings. While Mike struggles to land an architect contract to acquire the funds, the kids go about raising the money in their ways. The fate of their house seems like an urgent issue, but the family approaches this situation as they would any other hardship with smiles and understanding. They take life's struggles easy because they realize they're the Brady Bunch and that everything will work itself out by the end as it would in any other episode of the show, especially with the familiar soundtrack and scene transitions straight out of the 70s. You didn't think they were going to lose a talent competition with the prize of $20,000, did you? That just wouldn't be good for ratings.

The film relies almost entirely on the one joke of the 70s family misunderstanding the go-go 90s. Mike doesn't seem to grasp how dated his architectural designs appear, mistaking out of time for timeless. Marcia's dates come with different definitions: protection means sweater, third base is holding hands, french kisses are accidents, and lesbian flirtation goes unnoticed. The outside world can do little more than gawk at their exploits, though this modern 90s environment appears just as dated now with such lines as *"she's harder to get into than a Pearl Jam concert."*

The Brady Bunch Movie is more amusing to decipher on how this TV family can exist and thrive with such a clash of culture. People think they're weird, but few call them out for being old-fashioned. Their neighborhood finds them strange, but eventually admit that they're a little envious of such a life where a slightly stern moral message can resolve any issue. It's not normal for a family to take financial woes so quickly and pick up their spirits with a potato sack race, but damned if I wouldn't want life to be that simple. This style and tone treat *The Brady Bunch* with both a satirical jab at their personalities, but also an affectionate homage to their warmth.

The most frightening trait of the family is Jan's inner voice for her growing jealousy of Marcia. It turns out there's more than one voice inside that head, and one of them wants to rob a bank. Even scarier is that the voices can apparently be passed down to each generation and can only be vanquished by the words of former Carol Brady star Florence Henderson, cameoing in the film as Grandma Brady. But, wait, if Henderson is playing the elder Brady, would that mean the current Brady family is another generation? *Brady Bunch* lore is weird. Very, very weird.

BRAM STOKER'S DRACULA

DIRECTOR: Francis Ford Coppola | SCREENWRITER: Francis Ford Coppola, Fred Fuchs, Charles Mulvehill | CAST: Gary Oldman, Winona Ryder, Anthony Hopkins, Keanu Reeves | GENRE: Horror | RUNNING TIME: 128 min | MPAA RATING: R

CLASSIFICATION: WEIRD

The most positive and negative thing to say about *Bram Stoker's Dracula* (1992) is that director Francis Ford Coppola aimed to make the titular vampire a more original figure. He doesn't want to duplicate the classic look of Bela Lugosi with the slick black hair and cape. His Dracula, played by Gary Oldman, is in one instance portrayed as a ghostly figure in a red robe with a giant bubble hairdo. It's a silly costume, but it's hard to deny that it's stylistically distinct from previous Draculas and certainly the most memorable of the lot. Perhaps not for the reasons Coppola intended, but still memorable.

The film begins suitably with Vlad the Impaler (Gary Oldman looking less goofy in red armor) fighting in the Crusades that are beautifully portrayed with slaughtering shadows against the orange evening sky. He returns home to discover his wife has killed herself and is enraged that all the work he did in the name of God still led to his wife's death. One way to interpret this is that God is testing Dracula's faith. If so, he fails spectacularly as he renounces his religion and switches sides for the powers of Satan. Dracula wastes no time embracing vampirism as he promptly stabs a cross and drinks the blood that spews forth. He must have hit a major artery as the red fluid begins to flood the chapel.

That was in 1462. Skip ahead to 1897 and Count Dracula is looking a little older and with a questionable hairstyle, but still hanging in there for the return of his wife. His latest visitor to his creepy Transylvanian castle is the young attorney Jonathan Harker, confusingly played by Keanu Reeves fresh off Bill & Ted's Bogus Journey. Dracula witnesses in a photo the face of Jonathan's fiancee, Mina Murray (Winona Ryder), and is convinced she's the woman he has been waiting over 400 years to return.

Dracula dresses himself up as a younger and more dapper man for his journey to London to make this union true and creepy, but runs into roadblocks in his quest. Mina is more eager to marry Jonathan after Dracula fails to kill him and the two are reunited.

Vampire hunter Van Helsing (Anthony Hopkins) becomes alerted of Dracula's presence and is hot on his trail. The old vampire still takes some time to hypnotize and nibble on Mina's unlucky friend Lucy (Sadie Frost) that is soon transformed into a vampire, proving he hasn't lost his bite after all this time.

The story shifts back and forth between London and Transylvania to the point of lacking coherence in its almost random flow of events. The acting is all over the place from Oldman's natural grace of creepiness to Reeves' awkward personality that feels out of place for the era. It's very evident from these shortfalls that Coppola was far more interested in the presentation of Dracula's world than the characters that occupy it. His sets are grand and operatic with huge attention to detail in everything from the gaslight lamps of London to Vlad's muscle-like armor of the Crusades. The film was so atmospheric and gorgeous that the actors have to fight to stay relevant when crowded by fancy costumes and decadent cinematography.

The title of *Bram Stoker's Dracula* feels slightly inappropriate, given that the choice of using the author's name came about more for filming rights than any faithfulness towards the novel. But what Coppola lacks in storytelling, he nearly makes up for with one of the most alternative visions of the classic vampire story. His version evokes an eeriness, sexiness and otherworldly vibe, even if little of that comes from the characters. Except for Reeves, I can't blame the actors; how intimidating can Gary Oldman be as Dracula when it looks like his hair requires a bra?

BRAVEHEART

DIRECTOR: Mel Gibson | SCREENWRITER: Randall Wallace | CAST: Mel Gibson, Sophie Marceau, Patrick McGoohan, Catherine McCormack | GENRE: Action | RUNNING TIME: 178 min | MPAA RATING: R

CLASSIFICATION: BEST

Mel Gibson could act in action pictures, but who knew he could direct such an epic war movie? Gibson's take on the legendary Scotsman William Wallace, who he also plays, is a gritty, violent and grand portrayal on his fight against the English. It's not exactly the most accurate of historical pictures for being based on a classic poem of Wallace's exploits and ignoring certain aspects of Scottish history to allow for kilts. But Gibson's film works for focusing more on the brutal war of the 13th century than adhering to its specifics. He also looks pretty good in a kilt.

Braveheart (1995) is bubbling with enough pure emotion and bone-breaking action to make even the most jaded of viewers who are bored by historical pictures to sit up for all of its three hours. The story begins with Wallace as a boy who grows up witnessing the atrocities of the English on his homeland. He is terrified when he discovers a barn full of Scottish corpses dangling from the ceiling and faces nightmares when his father is killed in combat. Wallace tries to find peace by becoming a simple farmer and marrying his childhood sweetheart, but the English just couldn't let him be. The kingdom invokes primae noctis against the Scots, where the English must have sex with any recently wed Scottish maidens on their wedding night, in the strange hope of breeding the Scots out of their land. When Wallace's wife refuses to be raped and is killed in a struggle, he can stay silent no longer; he picks up a sword, dons the blue war paint and leads armies into a battle for freedom.

As Wallace's name becomes widely known, so do the stories of his campaign that start to exaggerate him into a mythical legend. Rumors start spreading of how many men he killed and how tall he is. This exaggeration fits in perfectly with the story Gibson is weaving that is built more for the heart than the brain. He plays Wallace as a heroic leader that can deliver inspiring messages on the battlefield and cry out for freedom with his dying breath. Patrick McGoohan plays the villain of King Edward Longshanks as nothing less than a cunning and sinister ruler. His prince son (Peter Hanly) is a sniveling and gangly wimp that cowers in the corner until he can be king and father an heir. The princess (Sophie Marceau) doesn't care for her husband and is more easily wooed by the blue eyes of Wallace. These are not exactly the deepest of characters, but never boring for being given dialogue as blunt as the action.

Gibson certainly didn't skimp on the action scenes that are frequent, long and heavy on the blood and carnage. Limbs are hacked off, guts are penetrated, heads decapitated and skulls crushed. Wallace stages several clever assaults against the English where he launches sneak attacks of secondary forces and archers hidden in the distance. In one of the film's best battles, the English on horseback charge towards Wallace's forces, only to face the Scots' perfectly timed pikes when it is too late to pull back. Gibson made the smart call of removing most of the music from these scenes to let us hear all the violence. He also shoots these war scenes beautifully, allowing the viewer to fully absorb the gorgeous green battlefields that are as vivid as the blood spilled on it.

Braveheart boasted strong direction by Gibson as his picture would win the Academy Awards for Best Cinematography, Best Director, and Best Picture. It also defined his style for his future films of graphic violence, from the gruesome tortures of *The Passion of the Christ* (2004) to the horrors of war in *Hacksaw Ridge* (2016). But what's most surprising about *Braveheart* is how Gibson was able to successfully turn a Scottish tale of war into a red-blooded and patriotic film with traditional heroism and red-blooded patriotism. Not many actors could pull off such a balancing act of producer, director, and star of their picture, but Gibson proves that he's just as much of an ambitious leader on this project as the character he portrays.

A BRONX TALE

DIRECTOR: Robert De Niro | SCREENWRITER: Chazz Palminteri | CAST: Robert De Niro, Chazz Palminteri | GENRE: Drama | RUNNING TIME: 120 min | MPAA RATING: R

CLASSIFICATION: BEST

Robert De Niro's *A Bronx Tale* (1993) finds the young Calogero continually asking the question of how he wants to be viewed. Is it better to be loved or feared? His father Lorenzo (De Niro) tries to instill in him that it's tougher to be liked, but safer to live for staying sincere and hard-working. Calogero's neighborhood mafia boss Sonny (Chazz Palminteri) will make the case that being feared can lead to a more comfortable life of money, but a constant lack of trust. Cal won't figure this out so quickly at the age of nine; he'll have to grow up and learn these lessons the hard way to make them genuinely stick.

At age nine, Calogero is played by Francis Capra with an adventurous view of his Brooklyn neighborhood. His friends watch the local mobsters with such admiration that they mimic them as they would comic book heroes. His dad, saddled with a bus driving job, stresses that he shouldn't be hanging around them as they're bad news. Lorenzo is smart enough to know not to take dirty money for secure jobs from Sonny, but his son isn't as strong. All Calogero can see is the cash he can attain quickly and easily for the simplest of tasks around the local mafia hangout of a bar.

The kids of the neighborhood already have questionable moralities with how they throw rocks at the blacks and harass the local food cart merchant, but Calogero begins to degrade when he witnesses a mafia murder and refuses to finger Sonny as the one who pulled the trigger. Guilt doesn't eat him up in such an environment. When he admits this sin to the local priest, he thinks nothing of God's higher power in judgment; *"Your guy may be bigger than my guy up there, but my guy is bigger than your guy down here."* The priest agrees.

Calogero won't know the real terrors of such a life until he is a teenager (Lillo Brancato, Jr.) and more active in Sonny's mob to experience all its nastiness. He learns the violence that comes with the job when called upon to beat up some biker punks that amble into the bar. He discovers that the war against the blacks his friends rage in their spare time doesn't seem as fun when there is a black girl he fancies. But the most fearful lesson he learns is the lack of trust from such a life, as when a paranoid and violent Sonny begins to assault Cal for something going wrong with his car. If he continues down this path, Cal could find himself just as crazy, continually looking over his shoulder for the next bullet with his name on it.

The story was based on a one-person show by Chazz Palminteri, based on his real life. This explains how much intelligence and detail he gives every character, including his role as Sonny. Any writer can stage a mafia leader to be a bad guy, but this script provides us with a perspective on why he chose the life of crime, reasoning that if nobody cares about you that you better make them fear you. Lorenzo is seen as a man who struggles with money, but has no fear of his morality, arguing that Sonny is more of a wimp for pulling a trigger rather than holding a job. Both of these figures give Cal sound advice; there's a sweet moment where Cal is convinced the black girl likes him after Sonny explains to him about the tell of a girl based on how they enter a car.

A Bronx Tale was a collaboration between Palminteri and De Niro, only after Palminteri had refused a million dollars for the rights to his story. With Palminteri writing and De Niro directing, they have crafted a story that is uniquely rich with value, atmosphere, and character. There are just as many moments of pure bliss between pals and neighbors as there are brutal encounters of gang violence. Calogero's story is a stellar one for the lessons he learned, the love he found and the neighborhood he understood in more ways than one. To him, however, it's just another Bronx Tale.

BULWORTH

DIRECTOR: Warren Beatty | SCREENWRITER: Warren Beatty, Pieter Jan Brugge | CAST: Sean Astin, Warren Beatty, Graham Beckel, Halle Berry, Don Cheadle, Nora Dunn, Jackie Gayle, Ariyan Johnson, Joshua Malina, Michele Morgan, Oliver Platt | GENRE: Comedy | RUNNING TIME: 111 min | MPAA RATING: R

CLASSIFICATION: BEST

Warren Beatty's *Bulworth* (1998) is a ruthless political comedy built on the solid premise of what would happen if a politician stopped talking safe. Beatty plays California Senator Bulworth during an election season where he has become disenchanted by the whole political game. Fed up with his life, he takes out a massive life insurance policy, hires a hitman to kill him over the weekend and proceeds to kamikaze his way through his campaign with nothing to lose. And what better way to go nuts with your political career than to start rapping at a rally?

The movie goes straight for the political jugular in how Bulworth is first seen studying his campaign commercials, finding himself depressed and frustrated that he's sold out his views for the comfy seating as a conservative taking corporate donation. Something has to change and who wouldn't want to see a senator savagely attack a rally of wealthy contributors with a smile on his face? No longer worried about the future of his career or his life, he plunges headfirst into any situation where he can spout some truth and rattle some cages. He strolls into a rally at a black church where he whips up the crowd about how blacks will never have power unless they buy it from the rich people. He stuffs his face at a dinner for Jewish movie moguls, commenting how they're a bunch of rich bastards that make mostly crap. The C-Span reporters that were expecting a relatively routine campaign are caught off guard.

Each blunt speech he delivers leaves him energized and hopeful, as his chief of staff Dennis (Oliver Platt) sweats bullets in the corner, eager to stage any distraction for his senator going off the script. Even more frustrating for Dennis is when Bulworth decides to divert his campaign trail into an underground nightclub where he proceeds to smoke weed and dance the night away. Dennis tries to rationalize all of the senator's behavior as just blowing off some steam, but even his spin control won't be enough to undo the damage Bulworth is prepared to deal. His new air of honesty has given him enough energy to party in the club long after the younger folks have gone to bed.

He instantly falls for Nina (Halle Berry), a black activist who he gleefully invites into his limo at first glance. After making a scene in a televised debate where he drinks on the air, he follows Nina home and decides to lay low from, well, everyone. The paparazzi find him irresistible; his campaign managers are furious with him, the public can't get enough of him and, oh yeah, that assassin he hired is still out to kill him. While in her ghetto neighborhood, he gets a firsthand experience of the drug dealing that goes on in the street and the corrupt police officers that profile. This experience fills him more with raw rage than political strategy, especially when he goes on television to state his solution; *"Everybody just gotta keep fuckin' everybody 'til they're all the same color."*

Much like its protagonist, *Bulworth* is a gamble of political, social and racial commentary. Sometimes it's ripe with hilarious satire when the senator begins to freestyle an insulting rap about health insurance companies at a rally where the industry representatives are present. Some of it's lacking as when Bulworth talks down police in a manner that plays out more cartoonish than insightful. And some of it's just weird; a wise black man floats around Bulworth to lay some philosophy on how he should be a spirit and not a ghost. Get it?

The film works best as a window into the cage-rattling of 1990s politics that was present in such pictures as *Wag the Dog* (1998). If *Bulworth* isn't the aptest in how it twists and turns in it's savage and satirical ranting; it is at least the loudest and ruthless for demanding the American public to wake up and take a more critical view of government. There may never be a politician so ruthlessly daring and sobering as Bulworth, but it's still amusing to believe there may be a senator out there who is one tragedy away from throwing the public relations rulebook out the window, giving a big middle finger to political correctness to say fuck on national television. Some senators do this by mistake; *Bulworth* does it to feel human, a form that most political figures are rarely seen as.

THE CABLE GUY

DIRECTOR: Ben Stiller | SCREENWRITER: Judd Apatow | CAST: Jim Carrey, Matthew Broderick, Leslie Mann, Jack Black, George Segal | GENRE: Comedy | RUNNING TIME: 96 min | MPAA RATING: PG-13

CLASSIFICATION: WEIRD

The Cable Guy (1996) is a comedy more amusing to examine than it is to laugh along. Jim Carrey usually played likable goofs in the 1990s, but here he is playing cable repairman Chip as a genuine creep of a nerdy antagonist that is nowhere near as funny as the movie would want us to believe. He's an obnoxious, TV-obsessed, lisp-speaking, unhinged stalker that would not be fun to hang around. But the film has an odd intoxication just for testing the limits of how far Carrey can go with his zaniness until it turns vile. If *Dumb and Dumber* was an exercise in his innocent ignorance, *The Cable Guy* reveals his sinister side of playing an idiot.

Chip's target to obsess over is Steven (Matthew Broderick), a man who is living alone after his girlfriend turned down a marriage proposal. Arriving late to install the cable for Stephen's apartment, Chip becomes determined to turn his latest customer into his most recent friend, but by the most inappropriate of means. Friendship isn't exactly off to a good start when you call your customer a jerk-off and start sexually feeling up the walls for where to install the cable. But with the prospect of free cable, Steven makes a deal with the slapstick devil by agreeing to be Chip's friend. No amount of free TV and movies could ever be worth such an uncomfortable friendship, even with HBO and Cinemax.

The film strangely has no exciting or insightful commentary on Chip being a socially inept freak, grown from a consistent and unhealthy diet of television. He is staged more like a clown for his media references, as when he stages a fight reminiscent of the *Star Trek* episode Amok Time to do battle with Steven. That event, as you may recall, found Captain Kirk and Spock fighting to the death in Vulcan tradition. It'd be interesting to examine if Chip considers this an act of proving loyalty or a means of testing survival, but the scene isn't worth much past its pure physical humor.

Carrey will try the patience of the audience for how far his comedy will go. There's a scene where he stalls a basketball game for some pre-game warm-up that involves him dashing back and forth across the court. I doubt even the most accomplished of comedic actors could make such a scene funny, appearing to only be humorous for his boundless energy. All Broderick can do is look scared and terrified while he stands aside for Carrey's antics, especially once a line is crossed in their relationship which turns from awkward to insane quickly.

The movie does have little nuggets of comedy that takes advantage of TV's ridiculousness and Carrey's adoption of its teaching into his life. There's an amusing ode to *Silence of the Lambs* with fried chicken, a running gag of a Hollywood court trial featuring the film's director Ben Stiller and a TV movie based on the trial starring Eric Roberts. While these scenes are amusing on their own, they come with the baggage of being saddled with a story where Carrey will brutally beat a man in a bathroom, hold Steven's girlfriend hostage in mid-air and try to drown Steven in a pool of water.

The Cable Guy isn't so much funny as it is fascinating to study for both Jim Carrey's character and Carrey himself. For as insufferable as his role was at times, it was interesting to see him venture out of his usually likable comfort zone. The darker aspect of his comedy makes him a truly terrifying figure, especially in a nightmare sequence where he bursts through a door with demonic eyes, viciously chasing after his human prey like a crazed panther. After this film, he would take on the more dramatic roles as the lead of *The Truman Show* (1998) and *Man on the Moon* (1999). He proved in those movies that he could play a more human and flawed character that could evoke laughs without pressing his nipple seductively against the glass or forcing Owen Wilson to suck on the exhaust nozzle of a hand dryer.

CAPE FEAR

DIRECTOR: Martin Scorsese | SCREENWRITER: Wesley Strick | CAST: Robert De Niro, Nick Nolte, Jessica Lange, Joe Don Baker, Robert Mitchum, Gregory Peck | GENRE: Drama | RUNNING TIME: 128 min | MPAA RATING: R

CLASSIFICATION: WEIRD

There's one unforgettable Robert De Niro scene in Scorsese's remake of *Cape Fear* (1991) that makes the movie classic and defines its style separate from the original. While stalking the Bowden family, De Niro's character of Max Cady follows them into a movie theater where he proceeds to smoke a cigar and laugh maniacally at the screen. It's a true moment of insanity the way De Niro indirectly mocks the Bowden family with an unforgettable cackle. It's also bizarre to watch a grown man laugh so hard at *Problem Child*.

De Niro is the key to this picture about how evil pollutes all that it touches, including the victims. This is a remarkable shift from the 1962 original film in which Sam Bowden, originally played by Gregory Peck, played the heroic lawyer that defends his family against the evil Max Cady (Robert Mitchum) who stalks his family. Scorsese's version doesn't boil the Bowden family down to such simple characters.

Nick Nolte now plays Sam as a man who has just as many problems with his family as he does the sinister Max, a former client of Sam who was found guilty and recently released. He's been through counseling with his wife Leigh (Jessica Lange) for an affair he once had, along with a fresh one on the horizon. His teenage daughter Danielle (Juliette Lewis) despises her family for the many fights of mom and dad that she tries to drown out with television. Life is already hell for Sam and Max hasn't even entered the picture yet.

When Max finally does show his face as a tattooed ex-convict that lawyered his way out of prison, he looms over Sam's light as a taunting presence that fans the flames of the family's troubles. Max has grown wise enough to know that Sam concealed evidence, but also astute enough to understand the legal boundary that he can dance around. Sam pleads with the cops to have Max arrested, but there's nothing they can legally do.

Max's plan is somewhat genius in how he doesn't merely want revenge, but to evoke a madness out of Sam's guilt by poisoning everything in his already toxic life, including the family dog who he poisons. Sam's current love affair interest (Illeana Douglas) becomes a target that is brutalized and raped by Max, but doesn't press charges out of shame. He will later set his sights on Danielle by impersonating a drama teacher at her school, and she'll fall for him. Sam starts to get desperate and hires some goons to rough him up, but this backfires on him as well. The twisted game continues until the brutal showdown on a houseboat.

The performances of De Niro and Nolte are stellar as they are both playing characters of great sin. Max is indeed a villain of frightening terror, but also a wronged man with a reason to torture Mr. Bowden. His calculative and twisted methods make him a memorable movie villain. Some of his most notable scenes include calling out a hiding Sam after beating up some hired muscle and rising from the lake after his face has been charred. While De Niro was nominated for an Academy Award for his performance, Nolte shouldn't be discounted either for efficiently playing a man with worry in his eyes for the rough waters he weathers in dealing with his family and his stalker. There is also a surprisingly good performance by Joe Don Baker as a private investigator and some cameos by the previous films stars of Gregory Peck, Martin Balsam, and Robert Mitchum.

Steven Spielberg was originally going to develop this film, but found it too violent and decided to hand it off to Martin Scorsese. It was a smart move as Scorsese was able to see more character in creating such a brutal story, more for the sake of understanding the terror than rationalizing it. The film is probably the director's most ambitious of productions at the time for being a remake of a classic and working with one of the most massive budgets at that point in his career. And while this isn't Scorsese at his best, it's a movie that proved he can take a classic film and find something more past the black-and-white of both the visuals and the story. Heroes don't come so merely packaged in his pictures, and they rarely succeed without suffering at the hands of a horrific antagonizer.

CHASING AMY

DIRECTOR: Kevin Smith | SCREENWRITER: Kevin Smith | CAST: Ben Affleck, Joey Lauren, Adams Jason, Lee Dwight Ewell, Jason Mewes, Kevin Smith | GENRE: Comedy | RUNNING TIME: 113 min | MPAA RATING: R

CLASSIFICATION: BEST

Kevin Smith is a geek that knows how to write authentic and hilarious geeky dialogue. Take the opening scene of *Chasing Amy* (1997) where comic book artists Holden (Ben Affleck) and Banky (Jason Lee) are promoting their comic book at a convention. While at an autograph table, Banky gets into a fight with someone who claims that comic book inkers are little more than tracers. Banky will then stage a convincing argument with comic book artist Hooper (Dwight Ewell) about racism in *Star Wars* and later a genuinely heated debate about whether or not Archie and Jughead were gay. These are not conventional topics, but, then again, this isn't a traditional romantic comedy.

Holden finds himself attracted to Alyssa (Joey Lauren Adams), another comic book artist that can match his wit. They seem as though they should be a couple, but one hangup prevents them from being together; Alyssa is a lesbian. This could have been a record-scratch moment in the plot where the movie goes into ignorant rom-com mode of easy laughs, but Smith never makes his story so simplistic. Most of the dialogue after this discovery revolves around sex with an open and honest air. Banky is so intrigued by meeting a lesbian that he quickly starts up a conversation with her about trading battle scars from sex. Holden will later talk about how he wishes girls had a frankness during sex to instruct like CNN or the Weather Channel by providing updates.

These are all funny scenes, but they carry real weight to them because the characters feel relatable and not just vehicles for dirty jokes. Smith writes his script with geeky and sexual humor, but also a serious nature for love between the players. By the time Holden finally confesses his love for Alyssa, the film takes a startling turn into how complicated and uncomfortable a relationship can be. Alyssa is torn about trying to find herself when she falls for a man. Holden finds himself conflicted with her past while trying to deal with Banky's jealousy. This leads to several awkward arguments, one of which is beautifully punctuated with the action of a hockey game.

There are plenty of psychological surprises abound as the film progresses, but it never feels out of place or random, even when the characters abandon their silly discussions as the story becomes darker with revelations and issues. There's a bit of intelligence and eloquence to these people. One of the most interesting side characters is Hooper for playing an artist that's all about black power in public, but is a smirkingly wise gay man among friends. He seems like a one-off joke at first, but remains in the story as an example of how his fans would instead accept an angry black man than a gay one.

As the third film of his career, Smith once more connects his characters with the View Askewniverse. Stoners Jay (Jason Mewes) and Silent Bob (Kevin Smith) appear in the film to collect their checks for the rights to Holden drawing them as the comic book superheroes Bluntman & Chronic. As they did in *Clerks*, the two drop into the story to deliver some philosophy on relationships with Jay's vulgar vernacular and Silent Bob breaking his silence for intelligent observation. View Askew regulars of Brian O'Halloran and Scott Mosier appear in small roles, as well as a brief appearance by an early Matt Damon. Many of the characters and events, namely the Bluntman & Chronic comic book, would resurface in Smith's *Jay and Silent Bob Strikes Back* (2001).

Chasing Amy is a suitably chaotic view on relationships that amount to tough questions of sexual identity, making for Smith's most relatable and dramatic of comedies. He paints his characters as complex figures that are never so simple as most movies would portray young people in love. Sometimes they're sweetly emotional with confessing their true feelings and refusing to let them bottle up inside. Sometimes they're frustrated when they can't come to terms with sexual histories and love triangles. And sometimes they just have to find some comic books to prove that Archie was seeking a three-way with Betty and Veronica.

CHILD'S PLAY 2

DIRECTOR: John Lafia | SCREENWRITER: Don Mancini | CAST: Alex Vincent, Jenny Agutter, Gerrit Graham, Christine Elise, Grace Zabriskie, Brad Dourif | GENRE: Horror | RUNNING TIME: 84 min | MPAA RATING: R

CLASSIFICATION: WEIRD

While *Child's Play* had a legitimately frightening premise of the Chucky doll being a living being that secretly murders others, the sequel doesn't have the same luxury of ambiguousness or surprise. A killer doll isn't too scary if you think about it. They're small enough to kick, light enough to throw and are most likely made out of cheap material. For such limitations, *Child's Play 2* (1990) concocts the strangest of scenarios to bring Chucky back to life, have him kill again and suffer a demise that is ridiculously elaborate.

In the previous film, the murderous soul of Chucky possessed a Good Guy doll and terrorized young Andy Barclay (Alex Vincent). While Andy is sent into foster care for nobody believing his mother's story about a killer doll, the PlayPal company tries to clear its name by recreating the Good Guy dolls to prove they do not become possessed by the souls of killers. They were wrong as Chucky is rebuilt and back for revenge on Andy. Perhaps the company should have had an exorcist to make sure the dolls were free of possession.

The film continues with the premise of the previous movie that children form imaginations attached to their toys that nobody believes. Andy's foster family and surrounding community are quietly killed by Chucky in the shadows, leading others to think it is Andy who is the killer. Unlike other horror movies, however, Andy is not as helpless or convinced that he's gone insane. Nobody can sway him from believing that Chucky is out to kill him. If the adults don't believe or help him in his plight, he'll go on the offensive himself. When he realizes Chucky is hiding in the basement, Andy ventures down with an electric knife and is smart enough to know that if the doll is hiding in the dryer that you should stab the clothes before checking them first.

Chucky is a much more versatile doll than he was in the previous movie. Thanks to improved special effects, the toy can now walk more convincingly, brandish weapons in full-body shots and has a face far more terrifying with expressions. In his most highly technical scene, Chucky stabs Andy's teacher with an air pump and proceeds to beat her to death with a ruler. When he stabs her, he screams with fury with a matching face of rage. When he marches towards her with the ruler, his eyes look demonic when paired with his devilish smile. As far as killer dolls go, none are more intimidating than Chucky.

The climax of the film goes for the most audacious of showdown locations: a doll factory. There are just as many ways to kill Chucky on this production floor as there are for Chucky to get rid of Andy. Machines that insert the doll eyeballs can be used to puncture eye sockets. Rows upon rows of Good Guy Dolls provide the perfect cover for Chucky. Vats of boiling plastic can make for an easy means of melting down Chucky while also giving him a hideously grotesque sendoff.

While most horror franchises tend to be handed off to other writers to concoct crazier stories, the *Child's Play* series was consistently written by Don Mancini. He would continue the *Child's Play* saga by bringing Chucky to an army camp (*Child's Play 3*), giving him a bride (*Bride of Chucky*) and having him deal with fatherhood (*Seed of Chucky*). And while these films predictably turned the horror icon more comical, the demonic doll had proven himself in this movie to be a competent horror villain to stand among the modern greats of Freddy Krueger and Jason Vorhees, even if he needs a ladder to match their height.

CHUNGKING EXPRESS

DIRECTOR: Wong Kar-wai | SCREENWRITER: Wong Kar-wai | CAST: Brigitte Lin Chin-Hsia, Takeshi Kaneshiro, Tony Leung Chiu-Wai, Faye Wong | GENRE: Drama | RUNNING TIME: 98 min | MPAA RATING: PG-13

CLASSIFICATION: BEST

Chungking Express (1994) is a wonderful portrayal of quirky, confused and complicated people in the crowded corners of Hong Kong. A young cop faces a quarter-life crisis as he approaches his 25th birthday. A mysterious blonde-wigged woman becomes a mess as her underground drug operations go south. A restaurant employee plays "California Dreamin'" loudly at the counter to avoid thinking. Another cop laments about the recent breakup of his girlfriend by treating all his inanimate objects like human beings, from stuffed animals to washcloths. Some of these characters collide, and some don't. Some of their stories have an ending and others ambiguously fade away.

Qiwu, the quarter-life crisis cop, has an unhealthy obsession with expiring food, seeking out canned fruits and meats one day before they expire, more out of principle than penny-pinching. He spends his evenings at a takeout restaurant, desperately calling up girls from his past, hoping to find love during the midnight hours. He consistently jogs, hoping his body will use up the tears either out of loneliness or for comprehending his limited time on this planet.

He later runs across a woman in a blonde wig and sunglasses. She spends her nights running a drug trade, hiring Indian immigrants to smuggle narcotics out of the country, but Qiwu will never learn this about her. He bumps into her once on the street and then again at a bar where they share drinks before sharing a hotel room. You might assume from this meeting that the two form an odd relationship of cop and drug dealer. You may even think Qiwu hooks up with the unusual new addition of the peculiar Faye at his usual takeout joint. And you'd be wrong.

When the movie appears to become predictable towards the middle, the story veers off course and shifts to a new cop character, referred to only as Cop 663. This story still has Faye, but now takes place during the day and is a far lighter story of love lost and found. Faye takes an interest in the cop after reading a note left by his flight attendant lover that started days ago. She sneaks into his apartment during the day and playfully begins to toy with the environment, changing food labels and adding pictures to his walls, hoping that the cop will notice something different in his usual routine. There's a happy ending to this tale, but, again, not as predictable in character or tone.

Director Wong Kar-wai has a very casual and engaging approach, due partially to going into production with a script not finished and with a limited amount of time to shoot. He takes the time to focus on the little aspects of these characters while not revealing too much information. Qiwu becomes an interesting puzzle for his obsession with both time and distance, thinking about how close he will get towards people and how long before he will meet them or part ways.

When the story shifts focus to the blonde-wigged woman, the camera breezily pokes around the corners of her cramped operations, from where the drugs are hidden to where the immigrants will eat. Sometimes the framerate will drop for a thrilling chase through the streets and sometimes the camera will zoom close onto something arbitrary, be it the expiration date on a can or the jukebox of a nightclub. There's always something to see and someone to follow in Kar-wai's constantly moving portrayal of Hong Kong.

The Chinese title for *Chungking Express* translates to Chungking Forest or concrete jungle. The English title of adding in Express better emphasizes the connection of the restaurant where Faye works and where the cops usually stop by to order coffee or confess their woes. It's a location that plays a more prominent role in their lives, more than just out of routine, and Kar-wai lets us in on the simplistic beauty of such a typical city sight. It's one of many beautiful scenes in a picture that paints loneliness in the city with a strange and sometimes indescribable joy.

THE CITY OF LOST CHILDREN

DIRECTOR: Marc Caro, Jean-Pierre Jeunet | SCREENWRITER: Gilles Adrien, Jean-Pierre Jeunet | CAST: Ron Perlman, Daniel Emilfork, Judith Vittet, Dominique Pinon, Jean-Claude Dreyfus | GENRE: Science Fiction | RUNNING TIME: 112 min | MPAA RATING: R

CLASSIFICATION: WEIRD

The City of Lost Children (1995) is the most lavish dystopian fantasy Terry Gilliam never made. It is a dark tale that takes place in a twisted and rustic society of thieving children, cybernetic cyclops people and morbid adults. The visuals are striking as a steampunk painting come to life, and the practical and computer-generated effects create a surreal appeal. But just as with Gilliam's movies, the symbolism and the world overtake the characters who are lost in its rust and fog.

The villain of the picture is the bald and short-fused Krank (Daniel Emilfork). High atop his oil-rig laboratory, he has kidnapped children throughout the land to aid in his dream experiment. Krank cannot dream, and it has apparently caused him to age prematurely. He figures that if he can extract the dreams of children with a clunky bit of headgear and scientific doodads, he can return to his childlike state. Aiding him in his mad experiment is a gaggle of dopey clones, a dwarf scientist lady and a brain that floats in an aquarium, speaks through a gramophone and can see through an old camera lens.

Kidnapping the children for Krank is a secret army of cyclops men. Initially blind and deaf, they work for Krank in exchange for whirring eye-pieces and hearing aid guns to help them see and hear. Their latest capture is Denree, a little boy we don't know much about except that he likes to eat and burp. His big brother is a carnival strongman by the name of One (Ron Perlman), determined to rescue Denree at any cost. He eventually teams up with the thieving orphan Miette to track down the Cyclops cult and find out where all the missing children have gone.

Such a description makes the film sound like a whimsical adventure. While it has its moments of wonder, the film is very depressing, dark and violent with its world. The little children that Krank captures are subjected to experiments and nightmares where they appear genuinely afraid. The orphan children are forced to steal for The Octopus, an evil pair of Siamese twins who are more than willing to kill anyone that steps out of line. The circus performer Marcello (Jean-Claude Dreyfus) uses trained fleas to poison victims with a serum that transforms them into bloodthirsty beasts, leading to a very unpleasant scene where Perlman smacks and chokes a little girl while under the powerful spell. The waterfront streets are filled with thieves, murderers, seductresses, and cruelty at every turn, while the oil-rig lab has so much tension the childish clones can't help but scream and cry as much as the children they imprison.

But for as overly dark as the script is played out, the visuals are a vibrant display of great creativity and effects. Every shot appears detailed and distorted in this grimy world that it looks uniquely beautiful while still being dirty and drab. The cyclops henchmen are a brilliant design of steampunk tech where they can only see through a monochrome lens. There's an unforgettable sequence where one of the cyclops men, hypnotized by Marcello, chokes another cyclops to death with the unlucky victim's eyepiece output connected to the killer, forcing the cyclops to watch himself be murdered. The dream sequences feature some remarkable camera effects that contort the settings into a moving distortion akin to a lava lamp. In one of the film's grandest of effects showcases, Krank becomes trapped in a dream where he slowly ages downward while a woman grows older, seamlessly transitioning the characters in height and wrinkles.

The City of Lost Children features such a stylish and surreal world that it's a shame there isn't much of a narrative to match its visual brilliance. The journey of One isn't all that deep or intricate, finding more appeal in Perlman's buff body and long face than any charisma he might have. While Krank's scheme is an elaborately clever one, his character is more fun to decipher than he is to follow. The film is still a notable landmark of visual storytelling for directors Marc Caro and Jean-Pierre Jeunet. They have an eye for detail, even if it's more focused on where to place the character within the frame rather than how to stage them with personality.

CLERKS

DIRECTOR: Kevin Smith | SCREENWRITER: Kevin Smith | CAST: Brian O'Halloran, Jeff Anderson, Marilyn Ghigliotti, Jason Mewes, Lisa Spoonhauer | GENRE: Comedy | RUNNING TIME: 92 min | MPAA RATING: R

CLASSIFICATION: BEST

Though the plot of *Clerks* (1994) finds itself trying to concoct crazy scenarios in a one-wild-day movie, there's a surprising amount of relatable mundanity and malaise to working at a convenience store. Dante (Brian O'Halloran) arrives early to start the coffee brewing. He's short on newspapers and decides to swipe a few from a corner dispenser. The metal shutter locks have been gummed up with chewing gum, forcing Dante to create a sign with a bedsheet and shoe polish to assure patrons the store is open. He finishes opening the store, shaking his head and burying it in the counter for wasting another day peddling cigarettes and beef jerky. The worst part: *"I'm not even supposed to be here today."*

He's not alone, however, as his eccentrically foul-mouthed friend Randal (Jeff Anderson) mans the video store next to him. With a complete disregard for workplace etiquette, he frequently closes the shop to hang out with Dante and discuss topics such as the innocent lives of the construction contractors on the second Death Star. There will occasionally be a customer to chime in with something interesting to say, as with a roofer that enlightens the boys on the politics of contract jobs, but most customers seem to be annoyed by these two and their work ethics. At their worst, the customers will start a riot about cigarettes or threaten to beat them to a pulp. In one instance that almost ends in violence, Randal spits his drink at an annoying customer to prove his point that title does not dictate behavior and that people who recite tabloid headlines are insufferable.

Dante is too distressed about his current love life to be worried about cleaning up after all of Randal's messes. His relationship with Veronica is on rocky ground with her lying about her sexual partners and Dante overreacting (*"37!?"*). Further complicating Dante's status is the return of Caitlin, an old high school flame that he recently learned is about to be engaged.

While Dante grapples with which girl to hook up with, Randal continues to enter the picture and deliver some smart-ass philosophy, posed in the vernacular of a 20-something. He's a chaotic force in how he encourages Dante to close the store frequently, but Randal is still a friend; he confesses to Caitlin that he won't forgive her if he breaks Dante's heart again. He makes this admission, however, while watching hermaphroditic pornography at the Quick Stop counter. In the background, standing just outside the Quick Stop, is the drug-dealing duo Jay (Jason Mewes) and Silent Bob (Kevin Smith). They rarely have much to add to the lives of Dante and Randal, aside from heckling certain scenes, but were such memorable characters that became a staple of Smith's future films.

Director Kevin Smith loads his picture up with meaty dialogue, but never keeps the movie as simple as two employees talking away the hours. Realizing he can't leave work to play his street hockey game, Dante decides to play his match on the roof of the store. When discovering that an old friend from high school recently passed away, Dante and Randal close the shops and take off briefly for the funeral. When Dante becomes furious with Randal for ruining his love life, a violent fight breaks out where every bit of junk food in the store becomes a weapon. For spending all day at work, the two of them spend an awful lot of time not doing their jobs. It's hard to blame them when they're insulted by customers, paid poor wages and probably live off the worst possible food the Quick Stop has to offer.

Clerks was shot on such a tiny budget of roughly $27,000 that Smith became creative with shooting. He wrote in the bit about the shudders being jammed to prevent the windows from displaying the outside, allowing him to shoot day scenes at night. Smith used any money he could find to finish his indie film, from maxed out credit cards to insurance money to selling his comic book collection. The risk paid off as Smith's picture was met with overwhelming praise and led to him directing his next film *Mallrats* (1995) on a budget of $6 million. Though Smith's career in comedy films has its hills and valleys, including the lesser sequel *Clerks 2* (2006), never forget that it all started at the Quick Stop with amusingly genuine arguments about workplace behavior, romantic affairs, nudie booths and *Star Wars*.

CLIFFORD

DIRECTOR: Paul Flaherty | SCREENWRITER: Jay Dee Rock, Bobby Von Hayes | CAST: Martin Short, Charles Grodin, Mary Steenburgen, Dabney Coleman | GENRE: Comedy | RUNNING TIME: 90 min | MPAA RATING: PG

CLASSIFICATION: WEIRD

Clifford (1994) is an unfunny comedy so strange and otherworldly in its assembling that it begs for further examination. Not much is known about how such a film came to be. From what little information I could dig up, the original writers were so ashamed of the film that they had their names replaced with pseudonyms. It was initially filmed in 1990, but shelved until 1994 due to financial issues with Orion Pictures. There have been theories it was shelved for so long due to poor press screenings, but this was never proven.

The film begins in the year 2050 where Martin Short plays a wise old priest who talks with a rebellious young kid about how he was once a troublesome little boy himself. There's no reason for this staging as the film transitions into the 1990s. Actually, no, there is a reason: To showcase Martin Short as an old man. The film's director seems to be under the impression that Short is a versatile enough actor that can fit any role. For the rest of the film, Short plays the part of the bratty 10-year-old Clifford. There are more tricks with filming than makeup to sell this image as Short wears little more than a wig and little suits. The rest of the adult actors stood on boxes to appear larger and make Short seem more believable as a child. Short is a small guy, but not that small. And even with all these tricks, he still looks like a goofy adult.

Clifford is a brat of the worst variety. When on a flight to Hawaii with his parents, he desperately wants to go to Los Angeles and visit a dinosaur-themed amusement park. His means of getting there involves entering the cockpit and shutting off the engines. He will go on to play mean jokes, act like a spoiled brat and continue to annoy with the most obnoxious of voices that I doubt any 10-year-old could match. It's as if Short is trying to outshine the bratty lead of Problem Child.

The boy is taken in for a week by his uncle Martin (Charles Grodin) to show off to his girlfriend (Mary Steenburgen) that he's good with kids. And Clifford makes it his mission to push every single one of his buttons like a pensive kid in an elevator. This is a kid who will not stop with the threats until he gets what he wants. So you can imagine how well he'd take it when Martin informs the boy that he can't take him to the dinosaur amusement park because of work. The dinosaur park is no longer his desire; Clifford now wants to destroy Martin's life. These pranks range from putting hot sauce in Martin's drink to mocking his boss to getting him arrested by calling in a bomb threat.

Does this sound like a little kid? No, wait, forget the kid part; does this resemble a human being? Martin will at one point sit Clifford down and scream at him "Can't you just act like a human boy for a second here?" Wouldn't it be a fascinating twist if Clifford wasn't a little boy and an escaped convict masquerading as a little boy? It's a bit farfetched, but so is Short's portrayal of a kid. It appears as though Martin is the only one who can see that this is an evil child capable of real harm to others. He's a manipulative devil that will sabotage people's careers and records so that he can go to that stupid dinosaur park.

Eventually, Clifford will make it to the park, and this is when the movie goes off the rails into the realm of madness. After having lost his job because of the boy, Martin loses his sanity and whisks Clifford away to the park after hours, where he proceeds to torture the boy by speeding up a ride to dangerous speeds. The park itself is a massively elaborate set that has surprisingly no funny aspects to it and exists entirely to malfunction and be destroyed by Martin's revenge scheme to kill this kid. The only positive point of this climax is that it doesn't end with Martin finally learning to accept the brat. Who could? Anything less than calling this kid an inhuman monster would be a grave injustice. It is for this reason that the movie's only stellar actor is Charles Grodin for putting on his best displays of manic frustration and sinister insanity.

The only reason I haven't classified *Clifford* as one of the worst movies of the 1990s is that further study is needed. There's so little known about this film's mysterious existence with so many questions left unanswered. What went down behind the scenes that led to the writers wanting nothing to do with the film? What were producers Larry Brezner and Pieter Jan Brugge aiming for with this project? It is such an odd little film of comedic misfires that make it feel as though it's from another planet of unknown origins. Very few bad movies are ever this fascinating.

CON AIR

DIRECTOR: Simon West | SCREENWRITER: Scott Rosenberg | CAST: Nicolas Cage, John Cusack, John Malkovich, Steve Buscemi, Danny Trejo, Ving Rhames | GENRE: Action | RUNNING TIME: 115 min | MPAA RATING: R

CLASSIFICATION: WEIRD

Simon West's *Con Air* (1997) assembles the craziest bunch of criminals to hijack a plane. John Malkovich plays Cyrus the Virus, the criminally insane leader of the hijackers. Ving Rhames is Diamond Dog, a right-hand man of Cyrus just itching to slice his way up the food chain. Danny Trejo is Johnny 23, named after his 23 convictions for rape, though he suggests Johnny 600 would be a more accurate title. Steve Buscemi is Garland Greene, a serial killer who comes dressed in his own Hannibal Lecter costume of restraints. And at the center of it all is Nicholas Cage, made up in his weirdest of long hair, as the discharged Army Ranger Cameron Poe. With such wild characters, West embraces more of a knowing action silliness. It was a smart call as you can't exactly take a movie seriously where Cage tries to sound menacing with a line like *"Put the bunny in the box."*

The hijackers are all prisoners on a massive transport flight to a maximum security prison. Poe is particularly pissed about this event as he is on this plane after having finished serving his sentence, fulfilling the old tropes of a hero being pulled back into the fold one day before freedom and having a wife and child waiting for him back home. Cyrus' master plan is to fool authorities by landing the plane at Carson Airport for another pickup of prisoners and then take off to a non-extradition country. Meanwhile, on the ground, John Cusack plays a US Marshall that tries to bring the plane down peacefully, while the hot-headed DEA agent played by Colm Meany wants to blow it out of the sky. What follows is lots of shouting, explosions, gunfights and a hard crash-landing on the Las Vegas strip.

This is a film of big action and base dialogue, where characters shout such familiar nothings of *"That's my fuckin' plane!"* and *"I'm not gonna STAND HERE and LISTEN to THIS SHIT!"* while bodies pile up and explosions occur. What makes the film work is the earnest nature of the actors putting their all into a simple script. Cage takes the material serious enough that he's not just a cartoon character for the script, but he's almost playing it too seriously as a simple man of simple desires with a distractingly terrible voice that seems to be channeling Elvis.

Buscemi takes care not to go too crazy with his psychotic character, reserving himself to be more natural for a guy in restraints. Cusack, bless him, is doing his best to stand out for a role where he's mostly shouting over the phone. But it's ultimately Malkovich who steals the show as a dry villain that can sound earnestly evil and committed to his plan, but with remarkable charisma for being so devoted to such a laughable story.

And, of course, the visual effects do their job to stage some fantastic action sequences. Highlights include Cage outrunning a fireball, a car being drug along by the plane until it slams into a fort and a destructive landing in Las Vegas that results in substantial levels of property destruction. The Las Vegas landing, in particular, has an extra level of camp for an accompanying soundtrack of electric guitars which echoes shades of *Top Gun*.

Director Simon West has an admirable fearlessness for such a picture. His pacing is exceptional for always keeping the film moving quickly before we have enough time to question any of its plots. He keeps his actors intense, his action big and his soundtrack cranked up high. West isn't aiming to make a smart film, but a film that will never bore. And for featuring scenes where Buscemi sings a song with a little girl, the guitar of the Hard Rock Cafe gets demolished, and Nicolas Cage brushes off a bullet to the arm like a bee sting, I was never bored. The film more than earns its brainless glee to feature "Sweet Home Alabama" over the credits of the smiling convicts.

CONGO

DIRECTOR: Frank Marshall | SCREENWRITER: John Patrick Shanley | CAST: Laura Linney, Dylan Walsh, Ernie Hudson, Grant Heslov, Joe Don Baker, Tim Curry, Bruce Campbell | GENRE: Action | RUNNING TIME: 109 min | MPAA RATING: PG-13

CLASSIFICATION: WEIRD

Bruce Campbell once addressed a crowd at the Alamo Drafthouse about how bad movies are made. He asked the audience to play a studio executive as he pitched them a movie. It would be directed by Frank Marshall, the man who produced all of Steven Spielberg's movies. The script is based on a book by Michael Crichton, the screenplay is written by Oscar-winner John Patrick Shanley and cinematography would be done by Allen Daviau of *E.T.* fame.

"Will you make this movie?" he asked the crowd.

A few agreed.

"Well, congratulations! You just made Congo*!"*

Credentials mean little when working with a story such as *Congo* (1995), retooling most of the original novel's flimsy premise to create something even more farcical. Joe Don Baker, in all his chunky and overacting glory, plays a greedy tycoon that seeks a rare African diamond to use in a laser system for his communications industry. He seems to have found this diamond, thanks to his son Charlie tracking it down, but not before some killer gorillas attack Charlie and disrupt the satellite transmission. What happened to Charlie? Who cares - Baker is more concerned about those diamonds!

Baker sends in an odd team for the rescue/pilfer mission. There's Baker's female assistant Karen, played with an out-of-place humanity by Laura Linney. There's the Romanian philanthropist Homolka with a sinister hidden agenda, represented by the always-likable villain Tim Curry. A primatologist (Dylan Walsh) stages the preposterous expedition and brings along his gorilla pal Amy, a special effects creation which speaks through a machine which spits out a ridiculously childish girl voice. Either the filmmakers made this choice in voice for Amy to sound like a creepy kid when stating the dangers of the jungle or they thought to give a female ape an innocuous child voice was hilarious. It's the latter for me.

Their journey through the jungle is a hilarious one, both

intentionally and unintentionally, worthy of the old television adventure serials where wild animals were portrayed as being so terrifying that the explorers pumped them full of bullets. But since machine guns seem a little old-fashioned, Congo features a laser gun that will slice off the arms of evil gorillas. The gorillas that assault the adventuring party will additionally be consumed by lava that burns them into crispy bits of Congo Fried Gorilla.

Before all the ape cooking, however, there are plenty of fun scenes with the amusing cast. Amy gets to sit with the humans on the plane ride over and has a martini to calm down, making for the hilarious single shot of the ape sipping a hard drink. Homolka pisses off a militia leader with his presence, prompting the irritated Captain Wanta to scream at him; *"Stop eating my sesame cake!"* Ernie Hudson plays Monroe, a guide that describes himself as a white hunter that happens to be black, trying to remain brave and serious in this ridiculous story. The expedition leads to the lost city of Zinge, where a corpse hand clutching a diamond signals a warning of killer apes. Amy fights back against the apes with her synthesized voice calling them ugly.

Despite being an enjoyable bit of pulp, not everybody seemed to enjoy the spectacle. Michael Crichton, in particular, was not happy with what director Frank Marshall did with his material. The movie was nominated for several Razzie awards, including Worst New Star and Worst Supporting Actress for Amy the Talking Gorilla. Whether the nominations belong to the gorilla or the gorilla's voice is up for debate. It's hard to say if the film would have been viewed better if it fulfilled Crichton's original wish of using a real gorilla for the role of Amy. I can't imagine animal rights activists would be all that pleased with a real gorilla drinking booze; that's just too wild.

CONTACT

DIRECTOR: Robert Zemeckis | SCREENWRITER: John Patrick Shanley | CAST: Jodie Foster Matthew McConaughey, James Woods, John Hurt, Tom Skerritt, Angela Bassett | GENRE: Science Fiction | RUNNING TIME: 149 min | MPAA RATING: PG

CLASSIFICATION: BEST

While Robert Zemeckis was pushing the boundaries of special effects with his daring films of the 1990s, his sci-fi drama *Contact* (1997) is his most ambitious of projects more for its story than its visuals. Here is a movie about an alien contact that comes packaged with heavy themes of science, faith, politics, language and philosophies of the unexplored corners of the universe. There were plenty of movies about humans making contact with aliens in the 1990s, but this film stood out as one of the best for being more interested in how aliens would speak to us rather than what color their death rays would be.

Jodie Foster plays Dr. Ellie Arroway, an astronomer patiently listening to outer space for possible signs of life. She is almost entirely alone in her commitment as everyone else seems to hear her with ears that are either apathetic, economic or morally opposed to the project of SETI (Search for Extraterrestrial Intelligence). Despite the dwindling funds of what many deem a pointless endeavor, Arroway's persistence pays off when she picks up a signal 26 light-years away in the Vega system. The signal first comes in the form of sound, a pattern of violin-like rumbles, and then later in the form of a video which, when enhanced, is revealed to be that of Hitler's televised broadcast during the Olympic games. Naturally, the American government becomes very uneasy with such a discovery.

Peeling the message back further reveals information on building a particular machine that can transport one person through space to meet those that sent the signal. The transport is constructed, but the biggest question is determining who will take the trip. Foster's character volunteers, but is subjected to a harsh screening of panelists where her faith comes into question. Christian philosopher and old flame Palmer Joss (Matthew McConaughey) calls attention to her atheism, asking if she believes in God before the panel. Religion shouldn't play a role in such a mission and yet it does when a religious fanatic (Jake Busey) suicide bombs the project.

Much of the dialogue is rather direct, almost to the point of reflecting a cringy sci-fi B-movie. What helps sell the story more for its ideas than its talk is the exceptional acting. Foster and McConaughey have a complicated relationship where they form a romance over their intelligent arguments on religion and science. John Hurt plays an eccentric billionaire that keeps pushing Foster's arc with his secret discoveries and gracious contributions. Tom Skerritt is a competing scientist with mustache and sunglasses, eager and smart enough to take credit for Foster's work. James Woods and Angela Bassett do a fantastic job as presidential advisors who quickly fear the alien message as a threat. All of them make the movie much more intriguing than the underwhelming climax of what lies at the other end of the wormhole.

Contact was based on a novel by Carl Sagan who envisioned a more realistic depiction of what the first contact with aliens might appear as and how it would be handled. His story went through a long and agonizing road to making it to the screen, passed between many screenwriters and directors. When Zemeckis was initially offered the chance to direct, he declined as he didn't want to film a script that ended with angelic aliens and a light show in the sky. He would eventually be given full artistic control and rightfully so. His direction of a tireless Foster weathering the storms of ignorance, scrutiny and personal beliefs for the unknown rings true with a timeless quality for such weighty concepts of existence. For a movie about aliens, *Contact* is brimming with more humanity and soul than explosions and starships.

COOL AS ICE

DIRECTOR: David Kellogg | SCREENWRITER: David Stenn | CAST: Vanilla Ice, Kristin Minter, Michael Gross | GENRE: Comedy | RUNNING TIME: 91 min | MPAA RATING: PG-13

CLASSIFICATION: WORST

Cool As Ice (1991) is such a tremendously bad and indicative 1990s film that it makes me want to lie about my age to be disassociated with the decade. This is not a movie; it is a vehicle for pop star Vanilla Ice to grace the big screen with all his music and sell more records. For a celebrity that once held major endorsement deals, dated Madonna and had a cameo role and song featured in *Teenage Ninja Turtles 2: The Secret of the Ooze*, it's amazing that his first big role in a film built specially for him looks so cheap and sloppy.

Most celebrities do well to play themselves in a movie, but Ice comes off too artificial and egotistical in the role of rapper Johnny Van Owen. After an extended concert, in what looks like a fan factory, he takes off to the next town with his rapping cohorts on motorcycles. While en route, he jumps a fence with his bikes and spooks horse rider Kathy (Kristin Minter) who isn't impressed with his ability to frighten horses. She doesn't like him, but she'll soon come around to dump her current boyfriend and start dating Johnny. This will not happen out of any change in character he'll have to make, but through his musical abilities to sweep her off her feet. After all, Vanilla Ice shouldn't have to change himself for some girl, not when he's already the perfect rapper on the planet in this movie that every kid idolizes, and every adult despises.

If you can look past the frenetic cinematography better suited for music videos, the plot involves Kathy's family in a witness protection program with some goons that are after her father. If Johnny can best the bad guys, maybe Kathy will finally love him, and her father will let them date.

This is not only a mediocre star vehicle, but a baffling one as well for its random design and execution. When Johnny and his crew visit a repair shop to have their bikes fixed, it looks less like a mechanic's home and more as the vacation home of Pee Wee Herman for its wacky and colorful interior. The mechanic is a bumbling fool played by Sydney Lassick, a long ways away from his more dignified role in *One Flew Over The Cuckoo's Nest*. When introducing Kathy's family home, the camera whips all around the house with music and sound effects, leaving the viewer unsure if this is supposed to be a music video or an introduction of what the Winslow family usually does around the house.

Scenes which attempt to showcase Johnny and Kathy as having romantic chemistry are awkwardly off and just plain wrong at times. How sexy can a date to a construction site possibly be? Ice's dialogue ranges from the most childish of banter to embarrassing slinging of 90s lingo. Lame pickup lines of *"Drop that zero and get with the hero"* are easy enough to groan at, but how does one interpret a line like *"I'm gonna go across the street and, uh, schling a schlong"*?

Cool as Ice was exceptionally awful in more ways than one. The theatrical release spanned a pitiful 393 theaters and earned only $1.2 million in its run. The soundtrack, featuring four new songs from Vanilla Ice, just came in at #89 on the Billboard 200. Critics predictably brutalized the picture for its nonsensical commercialism of the hip-hop artist. It swept the Razzie nominations in nearly every category from Worst Picture to Worst Song ("Cool as Ice") to Worst New Star, which Vanilla Ice won. As such, Ice wouldn't appear in another movie for at least a decade, and his future roles were almost entirely mockeries of his former celebrity status. David Kellogg disowned the picture and went back to his bread and butter of working on music videos.

There was one person who came out of the film unscathed. Janusz Kamiński, the director of photography, would go on to be a cinematographer for Steven Spielberg, working as the cinematographer on such pictures as *Schindler's List*, *Saving Private Ryan*, and *Minority Report*. That's a far more exciting story than watching Vanilla Ice pop a wheelie and get the girl he doesn't deserve.

COOL WORLD
DIRECTOR: Ralph Bakshi | SCREENWRITER: Michael Grais, Mark Victor | CAST: Kim Basinger, Brad Pitt, Gabriel Byrne | GENRE: Comedy | RUNNING TIME: 102 min | MPAA RATING: PG-13

CLASSIFICATION: WORST

Director Ralph Bakshi was best known for his adult animated movies of the 1970s, but his unique style of irreverent and biting animation didn't seem to have a place in the 1990s. As his first animated feature in nearly a decade, Bakshi wanted to make a horror movie of what happens when animated and live-action characters have sex. Though Paramount initially gobbled up the idea with a spoon, studio meddling with the script turned *Cool World* (1992) into the least Bakshi of any Ralph Bakshi film.

The rules of Cool World are very odd and convoluted to follow for a cartoon dimension that exists on top of our world. It can be entered from either the scientific advancement of cartoon character Dr. Whiskers or the magically inviting hands of a sexually drawn woman. Prisoner/cartoonist Jack Deebs (Gabriel Byrne) has illustrated a comic book of this world, but it's apparently existed since before he was born as Frank Harris (Brad Pitt) fell into this world in the 1940s. Finally released from prison, Jack finds himself sucked into this cartoon world where 2D figures occupy matte paintings and flat sets. Bakshi wanted the sets of *Cool World* to resemble walking through a living painting, but it looks more like a world of cardboard.

One rule of Cool World made semi-clear by Frank Harris, now acting as the world's law enforcement, is that humans and cartoons cannot have sex. If they do, cartoons can be transformed into humans and escape Cool World, which is dangerous for some reason. Despite being warned by Frank, who himself has a cartoon girlfriend, Jack can't help himself as the sexually depicted cartoon character Holli (Kim Basinger) quickly leads him back to her place. Basinger's performance was rotoscoped over with drawings which allowed for the only moments that seamlessly mesh animation and live-action.

After some PG-13 sex, Basinger begins to become human and leaves her world behind. And by this point, the plot has become so muddy and confusing with the conflict between the two worlds that the movie spirals out of control into a smear of aimless animation doodled onto the screen.

Bakshi was furious about how much control had been taken away from him on this project. Paramount threatened him with a lawsuit if he didn't finish the PG-13, horror-free version of *Cool World*. The only aspect he seemed to have control of was the hand-drawn animation layered on top of the live-action footage. He used this artistic arena to have fun with the animators he had hired on for the project by turning them loose without the script.

Rather than make the animators stick close to the shots of the story, Bakshi told them to *"do a scene that's funny, whatever you want."* This freestyle sense of direction can be felt through the animation that appears more as sketches on top of the live-action footage rather than meshing with third-dimension interaction. The few times where a live-action character touches a cartoon character feels very awkward, as you can quickly sense the actors working against nothing.

Halfway through the production, Kim Basinger attempted to rewrite the script, stating that she'd really like this to be a film she could show to sick children in hospitals. Bakshi told her, *"Kim, I think that's wonderful, but you got the wrong guy to do that with."* Indeed, Bakshi is not the type of director you phone in to make an animated picture that succumbs to the whim of market data or buckles under the pressures to be more kid-friendly. I can only imagine how hard he grits his teeth through this production, eventually giving up on Hollywood studios altogether for messing with his vision. And given how incoherent *Cool World* turned out to be, it's hard not to be as bitter as Bakshi for what could have been a satisfying dose of counter-culture during the Disney Renaissance.

THE CRAFT

DIRECTOR: Andrew Fleming | SCREENWRITER: Andrew Fleming, Peter Filardi | CAST: Fairuza Balk, Robin Tunney, Neve Campbell, Rachel True | GENRE: Horror | RUNNING TIME: 101 min | MPAA RATING: R

CLASSIFICATION: WEIRD

The Craft (1996) stood firmly apart from the pack of teen movies of the 1990s for focusing on the true outsiders of high school. The lead teens are not the prim and proper teenagers with bright skin and fashion styles ripped straight out of a department store catalog. These girls are goths who find themselves fascinated by the occult and witchcraft. And their lives become all the more exciting and complicated when it turns out the magic is real and within their grasp.

The film plays almost like an after-school special about the dangers of witchcraft, but played up to an absurd degree that they missed the message and made dabbling in the dark arts seem cool. Sarah Bailey (Robin Tunney) is the new girl in Catholic school and finds herself attracted to the bad crowd rumored to be witches. They're fittingly dubbed The Bitches of Eastwick, and I have to wonder if this was the alternative title for the picture. The collective of Bonnie (Neve Campbell), Nancy (Fairuza Balk) and Rochelle (Rachel True) find themselves drawn to Sarah as well when they discover she has some supernatural power that will make their witch powers stronger by completing the coven. They chant spells, hold blood rituals and perform such feats as levitation. The latter is an everyday activity that most girls perform at sleepovers, but these girls go the extra mile by making their friend float with magic.

The foursome thankfully finds better uses for their witchcraft once they realize how powerful they really are. Bonnie cures her burn scars with a spell that clears up her skin. Rochelle gets revenge on a racist blonde girl by making her hair fall out. Sarah can finally make the mean boy at school she fancies, Chris (Skeet Ulrich), stop spreading vicious rumors about her and turn him into her love slave.

Nancy goes darker by casting a spell that kills her stepfather and allows her her mother to cash in a hefty insurance policy to move into a better home. Of course, they will go too far with their power and become corrupted by their abilities. This leads to depression, narcissism and the girls fighting over their men by casting transformation spells to pose as each other and have sex with their friends' boyfriends. Witchcraft is one hell of a drug!

With so much nastiness in the lives of these young witches, a question arises: Why not use these powers for something bigger besides getting even? If they were reasonable witches, sure. But when you're a teenager, and the whole world seems to be against you, angst can make you do selfish and destructive things to lash out violently. Thankfully, these girls seem to reserve their wrath to their Los Angeles community of smug attitudes and nasty talk. And they look rather attractive doing so in goth outfits that appeared more alternative and outsider in the 1990s.

The film has fittingly gained a cult status over the years for touching on so many topics that most teen films shy away from including. The plights of poverty, racism, self-esteem, and suicide are addressed with a surprising earnest for a film with magic, revenge, and sex. It's as much a violent horror movie as it is a coming-of-age film for teenage girls struggling with everything from their sexuality to their social status. During a time of witch-related teen TV series such as *Charmed* and *Sabrina the Teenage Witch*, there was something more authentically entertaining about *The Craft*, where teen witches used their powers to kill their stepparents rather than turn them into toads.

THE CROW

DIRECTOR: Alex Proyas | SCREENWRITER: David J. Schow, John Shirley | CAST: Brandon Lee, Ernie Hudson, Michael Wincott | GENRE: Action | RUNNING TIME: 102 min | MPAA RATING: R

CLASSIFICATION: BEST

It's a little depressing that Alex Proyas' *The Crow* (1994) comes with the bitter aftertaste of the unfortunate and the eerie. This is one of Brandon Lee's most iconic and powerful performances as an avenging hero with a dark theme. It is also Lee's last performance after an error was made with the guns on set, leading to his demise during production. It seems a little strange that his last picture would be that of playing a character who rises from the dead and maybe a little poor in taste to debut so soon after his passing. Still, Lee's family wanted the movie to be released and it deserved to be seen as one of the most stylish comic book movies from an era when the genre was more campy than gritty.

Eric Draven (Lee) was a rock star that was murdered just before he was about to be married. His wife died as well, but Eric isn't ready for the grave just yet. According to the opening narration, crows escort souls to the next world, but will bring them back if the soul is unhappy. And there's not a lot for Eric to be happy about, despite the painted smile of black on his pale white face when he returns to the mortal world. He's out for revenge on the evil kingpin and all his minions that targeted his apartment and ruined his wedding, aided by a crow that acts as a scout of sorts.

What follows is a series of violent and stylish executions by Eric, peppered with distorted flashbacks of the night of the murder. He targets the criminals who killed him one by one as he corners them in alleyways, intrudes on them in bed and sends them speeding off in burning cars that topple and explode. Eric also delivers some fitting banter during his hunt; he breaks into a shop of one of the gangsters while quoting Edgar Allen Poe's *The Raven*. Crows and ravens are different birds, but I doubt the cowering gangster would point that out to a resurrected man who can't be killed with bullets. In between killings, Eric rocks out with a guitar on the roof. I suppose his revenge can take a breather if he can bust out some sick riffs to blow off some steam.

On his journey for anti-hero style justice, he makes a few allies.

Sarah (Rochelle Davis) is a little girl whose drug-addicted mother doesn't love her, but a visit from Eric and some supernatural squeezing out of heroin turns that life around. Police Sergeant Albrecht (Ernie Hudson) is a beat cop always under the thumb of his superiors, but committed to helping both Sarah and Eric who will aid him in the final battle.

But Michael Wincott steals the show almost as much as Lee for playing the long-haired and sinister kingpin, Top Dollar. His slurring and snarling of such lines as *"Aw, this is already boring the shit out of me. Kill 'im!"* make him a darkly fun villain. He's also ruthless in his murders. It's not enough that he stabs his messenger fatally with a sword; he has to shoot a couple of rounds into him as well, never patient enough to let his victims slowly bleed to death.

The Crow was based on a comic book by James O'Barr and director Alex Proyas does his best to make the film pop as a darkly gorgeous comic book movie. The dark and rainy exteriors of the city look amazing as the camera swings and hurdles around for the most striking shots of this urban hell. It's as visually stunning for its size and flare as far as Tim Burton's version of Gotham City in *Batman* or Ridley Scott's vision of a futuristic Los Angeles in *Blade Runner*. The action scenes are expertly shot with heaps of playful perspectives and great use of shadows, especially when Eric lays waste to an entire room of goons with the overhead lights swinging. This soundtrack, featuring tracks by The Cure and Joy Division, was so intense that even an interrogation scene with a brooding orchestral score still features rock music playing in the background, as the villain's lair seems to have a concert going every night.

The film is bittersweet to watch for all the potential Lee had as a rising star. Yes, he's terrific in the film's many explosive action scenes and wears that makeup well, but it's impressive how he also maintains a certain attention-grabbing charisma with his personality. Whether he's mocking his targets with a smile or tearfully retelling his story, he always feels in control of the room, even when he's not firing guns or brandishing a knife. Sequels followed with replacements of Vincent Pérez (*The Crow: City of Angels*) and Eric Mabius (*The Crow: Salvation*), but nobody could match the role like Lee, an actor who was able to stand out even when makeup surrounded his face and stylish sets encompassed his performance.

CRUEL INTENSIONS

DIRECTOR: Roger Kumble | SCREENWRITER: Roger Kumble | CAST: Sarah Michelle Gellar, Ryan Phillippe, Reese Witherspoon, Selma Blair | GENRE: Thriller | RUNNING TIME: 97 min | MPAA RATING: R

CLASSIFICATION: WEIRD

Cruel Intentions (1999) has the warped appeal of watching a high school performance of an erotic thriller. There's a capable enough cast of young actors that includes the likes of Sarah Michelle Gellar, Ryan Phillippe, Reese Witherspoon and Selma Blair. They're also playing competent and intelligent characters, despite being overly cynical and immoral with their ambitions. The script is written with real bite and sexiness, but it's impossible to shake the hilarious idea that you're watching a group of teens playing *Dangerous Liaisons* dressup. And, yet, it's so earnest about the story it's trying to tell that I admired its audacity, even if I was smirking and giggling the whole way through at its ridiculousness.

Ryan Phillippe plays Sebastian Valmont, a snob at a rich school who gets off on crafty people as much as he does making out with his stepsister Kathryn Merteuil (Sarah Michelle Gellar). But Kathryn won't have sex with her stepbrother so quickly as she fancies a wager. She's pissed off that her boyfriend has dumped her for the sweet Cecile (Selma Blair) and wants her reputation destroyed. The challenge: Sebastian has to deflower Cecile. But, wait, that's too easy for Sebastian. The real challenge lies in sleeping with Annette (Reese Witherspoon), a virgin and the headmaster's daughter. So, new challenge: Sebastian has to deflower Annette who happens to have a boyfriend. If he fails, Kathryn gets his sports car. If he succeeds, Kathryn will have sex with him by blatantly stating. And the games are on!

Sebastian goes about conquering Cecile with blunt and devious strategies. He's not exactly playing it smooth when one of the first questions he asks her is if she's a lesbian. As the plot thickens, he will additionally set his sights on Cecile, who is so naive and dumb he can easily ravish her with oral sex; *"You could be a model...It's too bad you're not sexy."* Lies and deceptions mount so high that Kathryn can't help but get involved in the action as well. In the film's single most erotic scene, Kathryn allows Cecile practice kissing with tongues in an extended close-up sequence of making out on the lawn. But then true love enters the picture, and the sloppy ordeal becomes even more careless.

Whereas other teen sex films find the young protagonists comically stumbling through sex, Cruel Intentions features teenagers that are way too smug and smart about it. Sebastian and Kathryn speak of their sexual affairs and challenges like a married couple that has been battling each other for decades. Watch the mannerisms in the scene where Kathryn taunts Sebastian erotically to seduce Cecile; he refuses, she shoves him back while smugly asking why not and Sebastian straightens out his tie with an aggressive *"Oh, come on, Kathryn - it's too easy."* Is this really how wealthy teenagers speak and act? Not likely, but maybe that's the appeal. Maybe teenagers would like to see themselves to be just as capable as adults in erotic thrillers where the characters are jaded and wicked in their toying with the lives of others with their sexual games. Or maybe they like trashy cinema that can appeal to them.

Cruel Intentions works for its cynical electricity between Phillippe and Gellar who make the perfect villains. Every part of their plan is discussed with snobbish insults and suggestive touching. They place some wit and charm into dialogue that's not exactly the most flattering or subtle for its depraved story. They also help elevate the displeasing ending, strange homophobic plot points and awkward insertion of a black guy into the sordid affairs. It was at least refreshing to see a film where teens are sophisticated about sex, even if it must exist in a trashy fantasy world.

CRUMB

DIRECTOR: Terry Zwigoff | CAST: Robert Crumb, Aline Kominsky-Crumb, Charles Crumb, Jack Harrington | GENRE: Documentary | RUNNING TIME: 120 min | MPAA RATING: R

CLASSIFICATION: BEST

Robert Crumb is by far one of the strangest and most perplexing of underground comic book artists. It's easy enough to see why director Terry Zwigoff wanted to make a documentary about him, even though he had known Crumb for years before deciding to make the picture as Zwigoff had played in his band and traded records. If anyone was capable of understanding Crumb's strange genius of artistry, it was Zwigoff, but I doubt he was prepared for how much material he'd unearth.

Crumb (1994) aims at the artist who was nearly famous and rejected such status at every turn. He became best known for his exaggerated walk pose of the "Keep on Truckin'" illustration, but turned down licensing offers. His band was successful enough to be offered a spot playing on *Saturday Night Live*, but he also turned that down. The only reason his underground comic book character Fritz the Cat had a movie made about him was that his wife signed over the rights. Even making this documentary took much convincing from Zwigoff before Crumb would agree to such a project.

Calling Robert Crumb and his family strange is a vast understatement. One can assume that Robert must have a messed up mind to draw comics of sexual and racial humor with an odd aroma of cynical satire and surrealism. But how could anyone prepare themselves for him admitting that he was sexually attracted to Bugs Bunny as a boy? He'll later divulge that his mother tried to give him and his brother enemas to straighten them out, which mom denies. As for Robert's brother Charles, he presents a strange mirror universe of Crumb's sadness and psychosis where the only frank difference between the two brothers is the level of their success. Charles sadly committed suicide before the film was finished. Crumb's sisters refused to appear.

As much as Crumb will admit to some weird personal info in private, he's not afraid to voice his frustrations at a public lecture, divulging the headaches he received with Keep On Trucking and how he loathed Ralph Bakshi's animated adaptation of *Fritz the Cat*.

In response to his work being poorly portrayed, Crumb killed off Fritz in his comics with an angry ostrich that stabs the character with an icepick.

Crumb is also very standoffish and antisocial for being such an influencing figure. He strolls into a comic book shop and refuses to give autographs to his fans. When asked when and why he was moving to France, he nasally and coldly states that he finds that country less evil than America and refuses to give the exact reason for moving; *"Ask my wife."* He would much rather draw people from afar, preferring to warp and distort them in his caricatures, than talk to them for very long.

There's a lot that *Crumb* reveals which could explain his warped mind. He was obsessed over the character of Sheena as a boy and became very interested in sexualizing big women with large thighs and butts. His offensive material is not immune from scrutiny either, as his comic about a headless woman being raped is placed under a microscope and questioned. Crumb doesn't have a definitive answer for why he draws such vulgarity past the fact that he enjoys drawing figures in general. His best solution seems to be that he's trying to flush out all the sexist and racist thoughts from his mind instead of letting them stew. It makes Crumb all the more odd and creepy, fearing what he would have become if all these images stayed in his head.

I keep a copy of one of The Complete Crumb Comics at my desk and will occasionally flip through a few of the comics, reading his work more like a puzzle of determining whether his illustrations were surreal satire or something deeply disturbing that even Crumb doesn't want to admit. Zwigoff's film is just as perplexing and entertaining to decipher what is going on inside Crumb's twisted mind behind the hat, glasses, and mustache. The film ends with his family moving to France, and I'd like to imagine he found peace there considering his silence since 1991.

THE CRYING GAME

DIRECTOR: Neil Jordan | SCREENWRITER: Neil Jordan | CAST: Stephen Rea, Miranda Richardson, Jaye Davidson, Forest Whitaker | GENRE: Drama | RUNNING TIME: 111 min | MPAA RATING: R

CLASSIFICATION: BEST

The Crying Game (1992) is a movie filled with surprises, one of them being the most shocking reveals in all of movie history. I choose not to spoil it, but the twist becomes such a central focus with how the film shifts and shocks with its unpredictable story that it's almost impossible not to talk about it. It's also an unavoidable reveal, as much as the revelations within *Soylent Green* and *Planet of the Apes*. Even film critic Gene Siskel spoiled the film's iconic scene on *The Larry Sanders Show* for someone who didn't understand the controversial moment and had to have it explained to them in detail.

If you've somehow never heard of or seen *The Crying Game*, see it promptly, but do it in secret. Don't talk to anyone about it until you've seen it for yourself as you'll be able to appreciate better the script that keeps you guessing. You may want to skip this essay until you've seen the film as well. Yes, this is a spoiler warning. I usually don't provide such cautions, but this is a particular case where I'd feel guilty for doing a disservice to anyone who has the movie ruined for them.

Set in Northern Ireland, British soldier Jody (Forest Whitaker) is being held by IRA terrorists in a forest hideout. He's being held hostage for the British government to release IRA prisoners, but is lucky enough that the terrorist guarding him is Fergus (Stephen Rea), a man who still has some humanity left in him. Jody, fearing his execution will be soon, starts talking with Fergus and they soon bond to the point that Jody reveals a snapshot of his girlfriend in London. Things take an unexpected turn and Fergus flees the scene with plenty of big emotions to deal with after a brutal ordeal.

Fergus is next seen in London, where he lies low as a construction worker under a new name. Still carrying the photo of Jody's girlfriend, he seeks her out. Her name is Dil (Jaye Davidson), working in a hair salon by day and singing in a pub by night. The two hit it off well, and a romantic bond soon forms, but there are some guilty feelings that linger in both their minds. Fergus will eventually have to confess how he knew about Dil and who he is in relation to

Jody. As for Dil, well, she has a secret that is revealed in the bedroom with the perfect positioning of the camera.

What makes the film work so well is how it spins its original narrative with twists that come more as surprises than normal developments of the plot. There are no major cues to pick up and no guarantees about how it will all end. We don't know if Fergus and Dil will remain a couple by the end of the movie or if they'll even survive when the IRA comes back into the picture. And I wanted to root for them as they make a surprisingly good couple. Jaye Davidson brings the right amount of vulnerability and dry wit to be an attractive woman and more than just a device for the plot to shift gears in its second act. Stephen Rea also does an exceptional job playing a reasonably complex character with emotions of love, politics, and violence all swirling around in his head. He strives to do the right thing in a world that doesn't give him much of choice in moral paths.

A part of me wants to reveal the film's biggest secrets to discuss the brilliance of deceiving the audience with its themes and tones, shifting between battles of nationalism, individuality, and sex. But another part of me doesn't want to ruin its genuine discovery for first-time viewers. All I'll say is that *The Crying Game* is ripe with genuine originality, earning every left turn it takes with wonderful characters and meaningful arcs. Now see it for yourself and, remember, tell no one!

DARK CITY

DIRECTOR: Alex Proyas | SCREENWRITER: Alex Proyas, Lem Dobbs, David S. Goyer | CAST: Rufus Sewell, Kiefer Sutherland, Jennifer Connelly, Richard O'Brien, Ian Richardson, William Hurt | GENRE: Science Fiction | RUNNING TIME: 100 min | MPAA RATING: R

CLASSIFICATION: BEST

If Alex Proyas' *The Crow* was a successful test of the director's ability to conceive detailed and memorable urban landscapes, then *Dark City* (1998) is his magnum opus. He has imagined a sci-fi world that borrows many elements from other notable movie locations and makes it his own. It is as massive as *Blade Runner*, alive as *Brazil* and decadent as *Metropolis*. And just like those artificial worlds, this city has dark secrets that literally shape the people, buildings, and history. If there were eight million stories in *The Naked City*, then *Dark City* has at least eight billion to tell.

The story takes place in a city with perpetual darkness, the perfect setting for a noir picture. Every night in this city, at the stroke of midnight, every citizen falls asleep and loses their memory. The city and its inhabitants are retooled by a race of pale-faced, bald, teeth-chattering strangers, referred to as the Strangers, that secretly maintain the city underground. Using their powers, they restructure and rebuild the metropolis as they want, with skyscrapers and interiors bending and distorting to their whim. The citizens are implanted with new memories each night, administered with brain injections by the anxious Dr. Schreber (Kiefer Sutherland). Some fulfill the same job while others are moved around. Not a single citizen realizes that their minds and their environments are rewritten every night.

John Murdoch (Rufus Sewell) awakens in a bathtub to discover he has no memories. He has built an immunity to the memory-wiping injections, and his latest dose was incomplete. On this night, he is a serial killer, as he awakens next to a dead body, but can't remember killing anybody. Dr. Schreber does his best to inform Murdoch about what's going on, but can't say much as the Strangers could hear them. It's up to Murdoch to discover the hideous secrets of the city while trying to avoid the cops pursuing him for being a killer and the Strangers seeking him out as a defect of their program.

Detective Bumstead (William Hurt) is trying to capture

Murdoch, but seeks to understand what the killer is going through with questioning that makes too much sense. Murdoch asks Bumstead if he's ever seen the sun in the city and he can't remember; *"I don't think the sun even exists in this place."* There is the torch singer Emma (Jennifer Connelly) that starts to remember Murdoch is her husband. Much like Murdoch, she shares a memory of meeting at Shell Beach, but can't remember much of it. The gaps in memory begin to grow larger with each question Murdoch asks when he discovers that while everyone in this city says they know how to get to Shell Beach, nobody knows precisely where it is.

Dark City is a beautiful blend of film noir and science fiction. The city is a fantastic display of moody lighting and dark streets, while the lair of the Strangers is elaborately metallic and alien. The mystery of the city unfolds with terrifying discoveries as we try to figure out the memories of Murdoch and the intentions of the Strangers. Proyas directs this picture with so much unforgettable scenery and grand ideas that it's a shame the movie wasn't a success at the box office. One year later, *The Matrix* would debut a similar premise that our lives are manufactured. But while *The Matrix* suggested that our lives are one big simulation, *Dark City* implies that there were possibly millions of other simulations we lived through and didn't remember.

DARKMAN

DIRECTOR: Sam Raimi | SCREENWRITER: Sam Raimi, Chuck Pfarrer, Ivan Raimi, Daniel Goldin, Joshua Goldin | CAST: Liam Neeson, Frances McDormand, Colin Friels, Larry Drake | GENRE: Action | RUNNING TIME: 95 min | MPAA RATING: R

CLASSIFICATION: WEIRD

Before Sam Raimi helmed the famed *Spider-Man* trilogy, he had delivered a stunningly original superhero movie with *Darkman* (1990). He wanted to take a whack at developing a film version of *Batman* or *The Shadow*, but couldn't acquire the rights to either and ended up creating his unique hero. Some may argue that Raimi's film is more of a monster movie than superhero affair considering it involves a scientist, horror elements and a costume that looks better suited for *The Phantom of the Opera*. But most monster movies don't feature a thrilling helicopter chase, a giant warehouse explosion and a daring rescue on a towering fight scene.

Liam Neeson plays Peyton Westlake, a scientist on the verge of making a gigantic leap in skin creation research. He has made it as far as the synthetic skin tissue lasting for 99 minutes before melting into goo. A breakthrough happens. When not exposed to light, the skin can last longer. Just before Peyton can shout eureka, mobsters bust into the lab and start wrecking the place. They do so because they're searching for a document of corporate bribes for city developments that Peyton's girlfriend Julie (Frances McDormand) has uncovered. All you need to know is that the mafia forces of Robert Durant (Larry Drake) beat up Peyton, douse him in his chemicals and set his lab on fire.

Burnt to a crisp, Peyton escapes the blaze and survives. He bandages up his hideous face, throws on a dark suit and rebuilds what's left of his lab to get his revenge on the men that tried to kill him. He can still produce synthetic skin for his body, but only for that pesky 99 minutes in the daylight. He's no longer a man; he's Darkman! And, no, he thankfully never says this line.

Darkman's schemes for revenge are quite sharp when armed with a skin replicator. He tracks down a prominent gangster, replicates his appearance and frames him for stealing money and leaving the country. He'll continue to do this for many more mobsters, even brilliantly fooling one of them with a double disguise.

He's still afraid to get his hands bloody though, as with his first victim, played by Sam Raimi's brother Ted, who meets his end when half his body is trapped in a manhole in the middle of busy traffic.

Raimi's style was perfect for a comic book movie in how he stages his shots and angles. Similar to his work on *Evil Dead*, Raimi brings the camera in close and tilts it slightly to create an unease with every scene. Peyton's new persona brings out violent urges for fear of being called a freak, leading to some demonic-style visions where you can see the fire in his eyes as the world around him becomes a living nightmare. The effects of Neeson's full Darkman appearance with charred skin and missing lips make him a grotesque monster worthy of his character's shame about being seen in public. The action is big and exciting with plenty of explosions, a fight scene on multiple levels of steel beams and an extended sequence where Darkman clings to a rope as the villains escape on a helicopter. There's also plenty of Raimi's unique brand of tongue in cheek humor, as in a scene where Peyton's face begins to melt as he runs through a carnival with a stuffed elephant.

Darkman bares a striking resemblance to Tim Burton's *Batman* (1989) in many aspects. The soundtrack was composed by Danny Elfman (*Batman*), echoing a similar tone of operatic themes. Darkman's origins have much in common with The Joker, involving chemicals on the skin that lead to bandages on a face, ripped off to reveal terror. But the most familiar moment comes in the climax where Darkman dangles the villain off a steep drop and lets him fall to his death. Batman seems to kill the Joker more or less by accident. Darkman is more direct and blunt with the villain's fate, where the bad guy tells our hero that he can't kill him as it would be something he couldn't live with. He doesn't realize Darkman is an anti-hero who thinks nothing of dropping his enemy to his doom. While Burton's *Batman* did little to define the hero past being an aloof presence, Raimi knew precisely who the character was and embraced all of his horrific glory.

DAZED AND CONFUSED

DIRECTOR: Richard Linklater | SCREENWRITER: Richard Linklater | CAST: Jason London, Wiley Wiggins, Matthew McConaughey, Ben Affleck, Parker Posey, Renée Zellweger | GENRE: Comedy | RUNNING TIME: 102 min | MPAA RATING: R

CLASSIFICATION: WEIRD

After Linklater displayed he had a keen ear for the dialogue of youth in his plotless movie *Slacker*, he shifted to more of a cohesive narrative with *Dazed and Confused* (1993). Taking place in 1976 Austin, Texas, his easy-going film follows various students on the last day of school and first evening of their summer break. Bullies, potheads, jocks, and nerds are all observed over the course of one wild night. Some will hook up, some will come to terms with their futures, and some will be pounded on by seniors. Linklater lingers on all of them for extended scenes of casual conversations that may not build into a plot, but creates colorful characters that may have a little more on their minds besides beers, buds and babes, even if that seems to be all they want at the moment.

Despite the last day of school being a celebration, there's plenty of lingering issues for many of the partying teens. High football star Randall (Jason Landon) receives a damper notice from his coach in the form of a contract to pledge that he won't do any drugs over the summer as it may jeopardize the championship season. He doesn't want to sign it, but hasn't worked up the courage to throw it back in his face. Perhaps a night of smoking weed will do the trick as he starts thinking a little harder about his future. He may not want to end up like his pal Mr. Wooderson (Matthew McConaughey), a man in his 20s. Wooderson's best years of his life are behind him, still hanging around teenagers to smoke joints and have sex with teenage girls; *"That's what I love about these high school girls, man. I get older, they stay the same age."*

Meanwhile, freshman Mitch (Wiley Wiggins) is on the run from senior Fred (Ben Affleck) and his gang of hazing cohorts. Mitch is one of many freshmen who is being targeted for paddling by the crude and cruel seniors. One by one, his friends are ambushed and beaten for the ritual. Mitch will eventually be caught and paddled mercilessly to the tune of Alice Cooper's "No More Mr. Nice Guy." This may seem like an odd choice in music, but it's entirely in tune with the film's theme of nostalgia. Music can carry memories both painful and fun; Mitch will remember the pain of the paddle while Fred will remember the thrill of the swing. Though Mitch will eventually get revenge on the nasty senior, he'll also find so much more that night after one senior encourages him to come back out for partying, after he has iced his butt.

The film has plenty of themes about the morality and fleeting freedom of the youthful spirit, but never in a preachy or ham-fisted approach. Linklater buries these issues in so much of the 1970s flavor and casual dialogue that any message that can be extracted comes off more organic than required. Linklater lets us in on all the swirling emotions of such a monumental event in being a teenager. We experience all the pride with Mitch finding a girl, the paranoia of the future with Mike (Adam Goldberg) being unsure of his future and the carefree spirit of Wooderson taking life one joint at a time. All of these figures converge at various points, from pool halls to water towers to football fields.

Dazed and Confused can be seen as a snapshot of 1970s teens with aspects of their character that doesn't seem as present in most movies depicting them. Linklater suggests that growing up in this era was fun, but not as fun as you may think. It celebrates the nostalgia as well as embracing its wounds, never shirking the dance-worthy and memorable tunes of the era. It's an aimless film with seemingly meaningless dialogue, but the fly-on-the-wall aspect bodes well with creating a sense of realism of unforgettable characters and situations. It took a believable character from McConaughey to sell a phrase such as *"alright, alright, alright"* and make it as memorable as the 70s themselves. So iconic was this saying that McConaughey would use it for his Oscar acceptance speech years later.

DEAD ALIVE

DIRECTOR: Peter Jackson | SCREENWRITER: Stephen Sinclair, Peter Jackson, Fran Walsh | CAST: Timothy Balme, Diana Peñalver, Elizabeth Moody, Ian Watkin | GENRE: Horror | RUNNING TIME: 104 min | MPAA RATING: R

CLASSIFICATION: WEIRD

Just before Peter Jackson became an Oscar-nominated director for *Heavenly Creatures* (1994) and the *Lord of the Rings* trilogy, he served up a gore bonanza with *Dead Alive* (1992) or Braindead as it's known in Jackson's home country of New Zealand. Jackson had been specializing in horror for years with his homemade alien film *Bad Taste* (1987), and his grotesque *Muppet* satire *Meet the Feebles* (1989), both of which were approached with playful tones for creative kills. *Dead Alive* is a culmination of all the bloody skills he had been mastering into a film that the New York Daily Post fittingly labeled *"the goriest fright film of all time."*

It all begins with a Rat-Monkey, a nasty little creature plucked from a mysterious island and placed in a New Zealand zoo. The disgusting rodent soon sinks its teeth into Vera, an old and controlling mother of her son Lionel. They live in a Victorian mansion where Vera does her best to ruin Lionel's life and make sure he doesn't run away with the lovely Paquita. The Rat-Monkey has infected Vera with a zombie virus, which doesn't take effect until after she dies and then rips off the head of the nurse that discovers her corpse. Let me rephrase that: Vera grabs the nurse THROUGH her cheeks and cuts the head partly off, so it dangles off her neck like an open Pez dispenser.

Despite his mother being undead, Lionel, ever the devoted son, attempts to keep his mother sated. After unsuccessfully trying to give her a funeral, he decides to take care of her at home and keep her from killing others. By this point, she has already bitten a few people, and the mansion is getting a little crowded.

This leads to one of the funniest scenes of any zombie movie; Lionel tries to feed four zombies at a dinner table and finds himself flustered with keeping food in their mouths. One zombie whines as he can't feed himself with a spoon without it going through the back of his skull. Another needs help making sure the food doesn't spill out of the gash in their neck. Lionel also tries to prevent two of the zombies from getting frisky with each other and is unsuccessful, leading to the birth of a zombie baby straight out of *Garbage Pail Kids*. One more undead mouth to feed. The number of zombies in the mansion continues to grow until the film's gruesome climax where Lionel is forced to lay waste to all of them with a lawnmower.

Jackson directs his film with horror both capable and hilarious. He shoots his movie with lots of extreme close-ups and distorted angles to create a sense of anxiety and terror, even when the horror reaches comical levels of slapstick. The characters are also charming enough in trying to make Lionel out to be a likable guy and his uncle Les to be a snobby jerk. Even the secondary characters are fun with the addition of a priest that battles zombies with kung fu (*"I kick ass for the lord!"*).

The horror effects are astounding for a $3 million budget, featuring gory shots that are uniquely original and creatively assembled. Half of a zombie tries to kill Lionel in a bathroom, but ends up trapped in the toilet as his spilled intestines take on a life of their own. A female zombie has its head jammed into a light socket, causing her head to light up like a jack o'lantern. The zombie baby takes hold of an unlucky woman and forces his face through the back of her skull, emerging from the front of her face and taking control of her body somehow.

While other films seem to promise buckets of blood, *Dead Alive* delivers by the metric ton. You need only look to the lawnmower scene where Lionel spills so much zombie blood the floors become slippery. Jackson's film is silly and smart enough to recognize the slipperiness and use it for just the right amount of comedy. He is so unapologetic with his disgusting masterpiece that even the most jaded viewers who find gore yucky will at least chuckle at the sight of a woman punching a zombie baby out of a window. It's the perfect film to throw on at a Halloween party for others to stare in awe while asking what weird movie you put on. Imagine their shock when you tell them it's the same guy who made the *Hobbit* movies.

DEATH BECOMES HER

DIRECTOR: Robert Zemeckis | SCREENWRITER: Martin Donovan, David Koepp | CAST: Goldie Hawn, Bruce Willis, Meryl Streep, Isabella Rossellini | GENRE: Comedy | RUNNING TIME: 104 min | MPAA RATING: PG-13

CLASSIFICATION: WEIRD

Death Becomes Her (1992) plays like a cross between a dark comedy and a slapstick Looney Tunes cartoon. Born from the very visual minds of Robert Zemeckis *(Back to the Future)* and David Koepp *(Jurassic Park)*, it is the story of a love triangle that takes many twisted turns. It all leads up to a scene where Goldie Hawn and Meryl Streep are beating each other with shovels as Bruce Willis contemplates his life choices. There are some astonishing special effects on display, but rather than being in service of creating dinosaurs or flying cars, Zemeckis uses the technology of the time to put a hole in Hawn's chest and twist Streep's neck around.

Such a scene makes the film sound more like a horror, as does the very premise. Doctor Ernest Menville (Bruce Willis) is a plastic surgeon engaged to Helen (Goldie Hawn) but finds himself quickly wooed by the washed-up actress Madeline (Meryl Streep). Helen and Madeline have been rivals for years, leading Helen to be fearful that Ernest will leave her for the blonde celebrity. He assures her that he won't leave her. Comically cut to him marrying Madeline and the crestfallen Helen turning into an overweight slob with an apartment full of cats. Helen soon bounces back and looks better than ever as a younger, thinner redhead that could easily swing Ernest back her way. What's her secret? The age-concerned Madeline wants to know as she'll try anything to maintain her good looks and get rid of the wrinkles.

Madeline is eventually led to a spooky manor where she meets the glamorous socialite Leslie, played by an attractive Isabella Rossellini in costumes that showcase the most skin. Leslie holds the literal potion of youthful immortality, stating how she has taken it and doesn't at all look 71. In exchange for some money and to live a non-public life to keep the potion a secret, Madeline is granted immortality and not a moment too soon as Ernest and Helen are already conspiring to kill her. It's going to take a lot more than a violent tumble down the stairs to get rid of Madeline. And it's going to take more than a shotgun blast to the gut to get rid of Helen, who has also received the potion.

Zemeckis directs his film with a certain eerie allure that echoes shades of Tim Burton. His camera gets in close to the characters and distorts their worlds, pairing well with the film's dark sense of humor; Ernest has to rescue Madeline from the morgue after she is mistaken to be dead for not having a pulse. It was surprisingly fun to watch Streep and Hawn play off each other as bitter competitors that turn violent quickly. But the biggest surprise was Bruce Willis as the hapless doctor who finds himself terrified of these women and the violence they inspire, a significant shift from Willis' usual roles where he is taking charge of situations. Whereas the women in his life don't think twice about consuming the immortality drink, Ernest has to think about it. Life wouldn't be worth living if you had to watch everyone around you die. And when the two ladies only want to make him immortal so that he uses his mortician expertise to keep their bodies looking pristine, eternal life sounds even less appealing.

The film's morbid humor and characters are practically overshadowed by the visual effects, which are mostly the fifth and most gorgeous star of the show. Industrial Light and Magic did an astounding job with compositing and computer graphics that allowed Streep's neck to look twisted and Hawn's gunshot in the stomach a window to the other side. There's some excellent detail at work in these scenes; look at the reflection in the mirror when Streep sits down with her joints twisted in opposite directions. The effects fittingly won many accolades from the Academy Awards, BAFTA and the Saturn Awards. Though Streep was also nominated for a Saturn Award for Best Actress, it may be the only nomination she ever receives; she was soured on the experience of working on such an effects-heavy movie. She liked the results, but said that working on such a demanding project was *"my first, my last, my only."*

DEEP BLUE SEA

DIRECTOR: Renny Harlin | SCREENWRITER: Duncan Kennedy, Donna Powers, Wayne Powers | CAST: Saffron Burrows, Thomas Jane, LL Cool J, Jacqueline McKenzie, Michael Rapaport, Stellan Skarsgård, Aida Turturro, Samuel L. Jackson | GENRE: Horror | RUNNING TIME: 105 min | MPAA RATING: R

CLASSIFICATION: WEIRD

By the time *Jaws: The Revenge* debuted in the late 1980s, killer shark movies were a joke once more. All the shortcomings that Spielberg managed to avoid with Jaws were now more prevalent than ever in a host of bad monster movies. This is why a film like *Deep Blue Sea* (1998) never takes itself too seriously. The age of a shark being a genuinely terrifying monster was over. All you could do now is stage the most ridiculous of films with the most laughable and unexpected of deaths. And for delivering one of the all-time silliest deaths by sharks in cinema history, this movie gets that mindset right.

The plot involves a science experiment where shark brain tissue may aid in the fight against Alzheimer's disease. The operation is carried out in an underwater research station funded by a large corporation, where sharks are held and tested in a special living environment. Security isn't too strong for this facility as one of the sharks breaks out and attacks a boat full of teenagers. A visit to the station is in order for corporate executive Russell Franklin (Samuel L. Jackson). He arrives to meet the station's many colorful members of scientist Susan (Saffron Burrows), shark tamer Carter (Thomas Jane), religious cook Sherman "Preacher" Dudley (LL Cool J), and marine biologist Janice (Jacqueline McKenzie). There are also other crew members that are not worth mentioning considering they're present to be shark food.

Naturally, the sharks begin to go on the hunt once a storm cripples the facility, turning the station into a disaster area of flooding waters and explosions. The sharks that pursue the humans throughout the station are smarter than your average Jaws, made five times more intelligent from the brain experiments. This is the film's silly excuse for how the sharks have memorized the layout of the facility, knowing which corridors to swim down, which doors to bust open and which hatches to pop out of if they want a human snack.

What follows is a violent, exciting and ridiculous escape from the underwater facility. In one of the film's most impressive sequences, the escaping characters have to climb their way across a horizontal ladder with flames above them and a shark in the water below them. Other highlights include Saffron Burrows killing a shark with a power cable while in her underwear and a scene where a shark both kills another human and destroys a control panel in one lunge. And, of course, Samuel L. Jackson receives one of his most exquisite death scenes; his angry monologue is cut off mid-sentence by a shark that pops up out of nowhere.

While *Deep Blue Sea* doesn't offer up any real surprises or smarts in the sub-genre of killer shark movies, it does put forth a quality product for this type of material. The sets look amazing when flooded with water, the characters are likable enough (LL Cool J's character is best friends with a parrot) and nearly every shark attack comes as a shocking and hilarious surprise. The only downside to the sharks is that because they require such quick movements for the right timing of kills, they appear as obvious and dated computer graphics. But who cares; Samuel L. Jackson got eaten by a shark!

DEFENDING YOUR LIFE

DIRECTOR: Albert Brooks | SCREENWRITER: Albert Brooks | CAST: Albert Brooks, Meryl Streep, Rip Torn, Lee Grant, Buck Henry | GENRE: Comedy | RUNNING TIME: 112 min | MPAA RATING: PG

CLASSIFICATION: WEIRD

Albert Brooks' take on the afterlife is the most oddly sensible and satirical in this strangely sweet comedy. According to the logic of *Defending Your Life* (1991), our souls enter a city of purgatory (Judgement City) where we must stand trial before we can move on to the next realm of existence (kids get in free). If you are found guilty of life not fully lived, you're reincarnated on Earth and have to try all over again with your memory wiped.

For the recently deceased advertising executive Dan (Albert Brooks), this will be his 20th time attempting to defend his soul, not realizing that he'd experienced nineteen past lives of cowardice. He thinks of himself as the dunce of the universe, but is informed by his defense attorney Bob (Rip Torn) that he's known souls who have been sent back to Earth a hundred times, though he wouldn't associate with them. Bob informs Dan on all the details of this world, how intelligence becomes a key factor of passing over and how there is no hell; *"Although I hear Los Angeles is getting pretty close."*

Brooks has a bit of fun with the portrayal of purgatory. Everything about this world appears soft, sterile and secure, a cross between a hospital and an airport. Dan arrives in this dimension in a gown while being pushed in a wheelchair, escorted to his hotel by a tram. Every day is sunny and clear in Judgement City that the Weather Channel has this status on a perpetual loop. Food service is instant, and souls can eat as much as they want without gaining a pound.

While waiting for their trial, souls can take in plenty of entertainment. A pavilion allows souls to peer into their past lives, leading to hilarious reactions of old men seeing themselves as little girls and old women seeing themselves as sumo wrestlers. A comedy show features a comedian who asks the audience how they died. Dan has the perfect response: *"On stage, just like you."* His general wit attracts newcomer Julia (Meryl Streep) and a purgatory romance blossoms. Julia has a higher intelligence and as a result, has been issued a better hotel in addition to her more pleasing past lives. They both have a unique and cute relationship with some fantastic dialogue, slightly detached from the more theological talk of their cases.

Most of the movie is spent as a courtroom trial within a windowless conference room. Dan sits in a chair in the middle of the room and has visual records pulled up from his life. Every element of the past is judged as a development of his character from not fighting a bully to negotiating a salary. The prosecution claims that Dan's 11-year-old self wasn't strong enough to face his bully, but the defense argues that he displayed restraint since it was instilled from his toddler days when his parents tried not to fight with each other. The case continues for days as memories are unearthed, and Dan defends his cowardice and bumbling, making such arguments that he wasn't afraid of snowmobiling after an accident, but merely hated the feeling of it on his testicles.

Defending Your Life may appear a little soft in how it takes the surreal setting of purgatory and weaves a light romantic comedy out of its elements, but it's a lovable picture for being just that. Brooks' script doesn't become overly bogged down in the mechanics of the afterlife to focus more on Dan's journey to the next reality by conquering his meekness. Streep is a sweet love interest, Torn is a jovial presence, and Brooks is as amusing as ever with his vocal frustrations and lovable personality. It may sound odd for being a love story in purgatory, but it is one that is filled with humor, humanity, intelligence, and questioning of our existence in the great beyond. It's not exactly the most conventional of romantic comedies and certainly not one to be overlooked either.

DEMOLITION MAN

DIRECTOR: Marco Brambilla | SCREENWRITER: Daniel Waters, Robert Reneau, Peter M. Lenkov | CAST: Sylvester Stallone, Wesley Snipes, Sandra Bullock, Nigel Hawthorne | GENRE: Action | RUNNING TIME: 115 min | MPAA RATING: R

CLASSIFICATION: WEIRD

Demolition Man (1993) proposes the most ridiculous of movie futures, but more for the shifting of culture than impractical technology. In the year 2032, war and violence are practically non-existent in a society that favors the simple and peaceful life. Cops are only instructed to speak sternly with hostile individuals and booths can be found on the streets to boost your self-esteem. It's the perfect world for a criminal like Simon Phoenix (Wesley Snipes) to take advantage of and cause some chaos. The police are so useless that he hardly breaks a sweat beating them to a pulp. All the police can do is stare at him in horror; *"We're police officers! We're not trained to handle this!"*

Phoenix was frozen in the slightly more believable future of 1996 for his many crimes and awakened in 2032 for some unknown sinister purpose. His nemesis of Sergeant John Spartan (Sylvester Stallone) was frozen right along with him and is thawed out of his icebox sentence to catch Phoenix once again. This new world is going to take some getting used to for Spartan, the most immediate being his filthy language which generates an alert and a fine from nearby machines in earshot. His partner on the case is Lieutenant Lenina Huxley (Sandra Bullock), a woman is a big fan of both Spartan and the 20th century. She loves Spartan's action hero attitude with the giddy glee of a fangirl of trying to emulate him, still not quite able to nail one-liners about kicking people's asses.

It's the little details that make the setting of a sterile future so amusing. Stallone is confused that Bullock would take him out for a fancy dinner at Taco Bell, but is informed that Taco Bell was the only food establishment to win the great franchise war (in the UK, this is changed to Pizza Hut). Since procreation is regulated to labs, sex can only be experienced through virtual reality simulators to recreate the act of passion between two people without touching each other. Toilet paper is an outdated concept as bathrooms favor a cleansing technique using three seashells. It's a hilariously strange future that would be terrifying for being so uncomfortably cheerful if it weren't so easy to topple. Snipes can hack into any computer system quickly, and Stallone can use tickets for swearing as makeshift toilet paper. Worth noting is the futuristic cars which were functional concepts built by General Motors.

Not everything in the film works as well as intended. There's an underground collective of dirty homeless people that have rejected this utopian society, led by Dennis Leary who does little more than repeat his typical stand-up comedy routine of angrily ranting. His few scenes feature him going off on long and fast-talking tangents with how frustrated he is with a world where he can't drive fast cars, smoke up a storm or stuff greasy food into his face. It's as if he went off script and nobody had the guts to tell him to stop. Either that or the script called for a Denis Leary rant.

Demolition Man has its brilliant moments, but never fully develops its world, political message, social satire or science fiction elements to elevate past being a solid action picture with a silly sci-fi coating. They do, however, contribute to making the film a lot of fun and charmingly biting in between scenes where Stallone and Snipes battle each other with guns and one-liners. Though there is a conspiracy plot at play, I can't help but feel there's a more frightening aspect missed for such an odd paradise. A world with only Taco Bell eateries and bathrooms with just three seashells for cleaning has to be a nightmare for somebody who can't handle Mexican food.

DICK TRACY

DIRECTOR: Warren Beatty | SCREENWRITER: Jim Cash, Jack Epps, Jr. | CAST: Warren Beatty, Al Pacino, Madonna | GENRE: Action | RUNNING TIME: 105 min | MPAA RATING: PG

CLASSIFICATION: WEIRD

The vast, exaggerated and primary-colored world of *Dick Tracy* (1990) may look garish, but fittingly so for being based on the iconic comic book detective. Whereas other comic book adaptations strove to modernize their style, Warren Beatty's film embraced its limited color palette, weird characters, and flat-looking city. The result is a comic book that looks perhaps too comic-booky, but that just adds to the surreal appeal of what could have been a standard detective picture.

Beatty doesn't try to redefine *Dick Tracy* for a film so much as he redefines film for *Dick Tracy*. He plays the titular detective with the same yellow coat, same simplicity in personality and the same luck of always arresting the bad guys by the end of the story. Beatty plays the role straight with grit and spirit, hot on the trail of the murderous mobsters working for Alphonse "Big Boy" Caprice (Al Pacino). Witnessing Big Boy's goons shooting up a card game, a homeless kid (Charlie Korsmo) tags along for the investigation. Tracy's girlfriend Tess (Glenne Headly) is also along for the ride, but she has competition as the club singer Breathless Mahoney (Madonna) wants to steal him away. Naturally, Madonna has her musical number. Why else would you cast her?

All of the gangsters that Tracy tracks down have appearances and personalities that fit their names. Mumbles (Dustin Hoffman) is a tough suspect to question with his fast babbling of words, but Tracy can apparently understand him while the stenographer scratches her head. Flattop (William Forsythe) appears to have his head flattened on top so that the rest of his face looks oddly stretched. Club owner Lips Manlis (Paul Sorvino), predictably for his name, has some pretty big lips that are large enough to get a hook caught in them. But, of course, Al Pacino steals the show as Big Boy, donning a thin mustache, big chin, and loud suits. Pacino is no stranger to playing a villain, but he's putting everything he has into the role with astounding energy and cruelty. After all, he has to sell himself as a real threat in a movie where he and all his goons look like sideshow attractions.

The production values are unlike anything that was ever seen in a comic book movie with the most deliciously popping of designs. Beatty was committed to the design of Chester Gould's original 1930s comic books by only using seven primary colors of the same shade. He opted for prosthetic makeup to make the characters look almost exactly like the cartoonish concepts of Gould's drawings. The depictions of the flat-looking and multi-colored city make the movie appear massive and grand, even when it looks intentionally fake.

Dick Tracy is a movie that always feels big and otherworldly for being a somewhat straight and overly talky detective story. Is it silly to see a detective run around in a banana-colored trench coat, hauling in criminals who look more like monsters than mobsters? Absolutely. And Beatty makes no excuses for how eye-catching, weird and ugly his world looks. It's impressive that the film turned out as well as it did for how long it took to sort out the rights, nail a script and pick a director. Even more surprising was how this old property was treated as a big summer movie, receiving a marketing campaign as big as last summer's *Batman*. There were McDonald's tie-ins, video games, comic books and toys pushed out to market the film towards kids. In one of the strangest movie marketing moves ever, Madonna used her world concert tour as a promotion by performing her song in the movie ("Now I'm Following You") with someone dressed as Dick Tracy on stage. It was a sight almost as strange as the film itself.

DOGMA

DIRECTOR: Kevin Smith | SCREENWRITER: Kevin Smith | CAST: Ben Affleck, Matt Damon, Linda Fiorentino, Salma Hayek, Jason Lee, Alan Rickman, Chris Rock | GENRE: Comedy | RUNNING TIME: 128 min | MPAA RATING: R

CLASSIFICATION: WEIRD

Religious films tend to brew controversy and protest, be they as satirical as *The Life of Brian* or as challenging as *The Last Temptation of Christ*. Kevin Smith's *Dogma* (1999) indeed generated quite the stir for the inclusion of foul-mouthed stoners, viciously violent angels and stripper muses for this religious-themed comedy. A few big buttons of the religious devout in America must have been pushed when it was revealed in the movie that God is female and Canadian.

Ben Affleck and Matt Damon play the angel duo Bartleby and Loki, banished from heaven and sentenced to an eternity in Wisconsin (genuinely chilling). Bored with their punishment, they're ecstatic to discover that a cathedral in New Jersey is being rededicated with a blessing image of the Buddy Christ, a statue of Jesus giving a smiling and thumbs up. Anyone who enters the cathedral can be remitted of all sin. If Bartleby and Loki can pass through its doors, they can ascend back into heaven. The issue with exploiting this loophole, however, is that it will ultimately bring about the end of existence by proving God as fallible.

All of this is explained to Bethany (Linda Fiorentino) by the angel Metatron (Alan Rickman), and she finds this all a little hard to believe. She works at an abortion clinic in Illinois and finds herself questioning her beliefs for still going to church when she cares very little for Catholicism. She's especially skeptical to hear all this information from an angel that breaks into her room and reveals he has no genitals to rape her. Metatron isn't interested in renewing her faith, however, as he needs her for being the last relative of Jesus that can save the universe. He tells her to follow two prophets that will guide her in stopping Bartleby and Loki. It's weird enough for her to heed such information, but even more bizarre that the prophets happen to be Smith's familiar characters of Jay (Jason Mewes) and Silent Bob (Kevin Smith). She'll additionally meet the stripper/muse Serendipity (Salma Hayek), the black apostle Rufus (Chris Rock) and a white-suited Azrael (Jason Lee).

The script finds all these characters bantering about religious specifics of the intricate plot and silly side conversations to reveal more personality. Rufus explains that he was the 13th apostle, pissed off that he was left out of the New Testament because he was black. Jay has an amusing story about why they're in Illinois, seeking to sell drugs in the town of Shermer where all the John Hughes movies take place, only to realize there is no Shermer, Illinois. There's also some insightfully cynical passages by Loki where he convinces a nun to renounce her faith by explaining religion's oppressiveness with *Through The Looking Glass*.

Unlike Smith's other comedies that are mostly on the nose about geekdom and relationships, he dances the line when it comes to spiritual beliefs in *Dogma*. The film takes the Catholic theology serious enough with following the scriptures, but still has enough creativity to experiment with the material past necessary mockery and adherence to the Bible. There's a sweet moment where Rufus talks about God with such a thoughtful and believable philosophy. He tells Bethany that the creator likes to hear stories, but hates the splintering of beliefs. When she asks if it's bad to have beliefs, he says that ideas are better; *"You can change an idea. Changing a belief is trickier."*

Dogma marked a lot of firsts for director Kevin Smith. It was his most violent film to date, featuring bloody scenes where Damon shoots up a room of executives and Affleck picks up people as an angel to watch them go splat on the concrete. It was his most thoughtful and dense of material, theorizing far more elaborate ideas than the sex lives of superheroes. And, naturally, it was his most controversial of films for being blasphemous enough for Catholics to denounce it; they probably didn't like that Jesus is referenced by Rufus as *"nigga owes me 12 bucks."* It's assuredly not Smith's best work, but certainly his most daring and intelligent with how it aims at religion, armed with insightful knowledge and four-letter words.

DROP DEAD FRED

DIRECTOR: Ate De Jong | SCREENWRITER: Carlos Davis, Anthony Fingleton | CAST: Phoebe Cates, Rik Mayall, Marsha Mason, Tim Matheson, Carrie Fisher | GENRE: Comedy | RUNNING TIME: 101 min | MPAA RATING: PG-13

CLASSIFICATION: WORST

Drop Dead Fred (1991) poses that the worlds of childhood and adulthood are manic, depressing and disgusting. Children are plagued by evil spirits of their creation that encourage them to smear fecal matter on things. Adults have the worst luck as nasty things happen to them in horrific sequences. In the middle of these worlds are imaginary friends that delight in encouraging insanity and vulgarity among their masters. Maybe I'm a bit old-fashioned, but I never had my imaginary friend host a sick party where everyone pukes in a pile.

The movie wants desperately for the audience to sympathize with Elizabeth (Phoebe Cates) and her desire to return to this madness. Her husband has left her for another woman, her purse is swiped, her car is stolen, and she loses her job, all within one day. She returns to her domineering mother's house to recuperate from such an ordeal. During her exploration of her childhood toys, she discovers a jack-in-the-box that explodes open to reveal her imaginary friend Fred (Rik Mayall), dressed in a bright green suit with red hair like a clown without the makeup. With Elizabeth in need of some cheering up, Fred takes it upon himself to cheer her up in the best way he can think of as a childhood creation. This equates to destroying property, throwing food and making Elizabeth appear like a juvenile delinquent in front of the adults.

Rik Mayall manages to deliver the single most annoyingly awful performance of the 1990s, which is saying something for a decade with Jim Carrey and Pauly Shore. It's not enough that the character of Fred has to be destructive and cruel; Mayall makes him loud and obnoxious as well. He screams and shouts at Elizabeth, making her throw dishes, insult others and physically beat up other people. Not only does he turn Elizabeth into a psychological mess, but also breaks the people around her. Her friend (Carrie Fisher) not only believes her story about Fred being an imaginary force of chaos, but is willing to embarrass herself in public when she unsuccessfully tries to beat him up by punching air. She has a date with a man who goes just as crazy as she is for her inappropriate dining behavior. Oh, and

Fred also sinks an expensive boat. That rascal.

I suppose that the message of the film is that you need to be in touch with yourself as a child to build your confidence back up to take control of your life. I'm not sure why she had to learn this lesson from a figure that destroys nearly every aspect of her life. Fred doesn't seem to urge Elizabeth to take control so much as lashing out at everyone and everything around her. This could easily be a psychological horror film if you altered or even removed the comical music.

Strangely enough, the film has developed a small cult following over the years for people who remember the movie fondly from their childhood. I'd implore them to rewatch and reevaluate. Much like the film's imaginary friend, there's a reason we leave things behind in childhood and *Drop Dead Fred* should remain forever locked in the toy chest.

DUMB AND DUMBER

DIRECTOR: Peter Farrelly | SCREENWRITER: Peter Farrelly, Bennett Yellin, Bobby Farrelly | CAST: Jim Carrey, Jeff Daniels, Lauren Holly, Karen Duffy, Mike Starr, Charles Rocket, Teri Garr | GENRE: Comedy | RUNNING TIME: 107 min | MPAA RATING: PG-13

CLASSIFICATION: WEIRD

There's a fearless and almost witty charm to the Farrelly brothers' comedy *Dumb and Dumber* (1994) that portrays Jim Carrey and Jeff Daniels as two foolish men. They are ignorant and childish, but not completely devoid of morality. There is a scene where Carrey's character violently shoots someone to death as he shouts a battle cry. This is naturally a dream sequence as this character has enough sweetness to refuse such an act and not enough smarts to know how to fire a pistol.

Carey plays Lloyd, a limo driver that instantly falls for the beautiful Mary (Lauren Holly) and finds himself stuck with her briefcase after she boards a flight. Having been fired, Lloyd believes this to be the perfect opportunity to seek her out in Aspen for an act of altruism that he hopes will lead to a relationship. His best friend Harry (Daniels) accompanies him, as his dog grooming business isn't going well despite his devotion of transforming his car to look like a dog. With little money and a questionable act of selling a dead bird to a blind child, the two are off on a road trip to return the briefcase and form a love triangle over Mary that she is unaware exists.

The briefcase is pursued by some evil men that desire the monetary contents, but this plot doesn't matter. All you need to know is that Lloyd and Harry are searching for a woman and spend some of the money inside her briefcase. And by some, I mean all of it. What do they spend it on? Still focused on getting into Mary's good graces, Lloyd and Harry decide to ambush her at a charity dinner in the most garish of outfits. Two dolts are smart enough to realize they need formal attire for such an event, but not smart enough to know bright orange and blue are the wrong colors for such an occasion. They additionally don top hats and cane, which they use to stage a sword fight on their grand entrance.

The film is a dare on the audience to see what they'll laugh at in the picture. There is much vulgarity and bodily functions in many of the film's more gross gags. To get revenge on Harry for dating Mary,

Lloyd gives him a massive dose of laxative which results in him having violent diarrhea. Jeff Daniels' expressions are about as amusing as an actor could for a scene where he must violently poop. There are additional scenes involving urination for warmth and a dream sequence where Carrey lights a fart.

But there are still plenty of decent jokes that don't rely on the low brow. When Harry spots a woman walking by with her man, he tells Lloyd to check out the butt on that; *"Yeah. He must work out."* They try to find Mary's last name and believe it to be located on the suitcase; *"Samsonite! I was way off!"* Easily one of my favorite lines is when Carrey addresses a group of guys outside a convenience store, trying to start a conversation, but ending it quickly as he has nothing to say; *"Whoa, Big Gulps, huh? All right! Well, see you later."*

Despite featuring a scene where Jim Carrey states and makes the most annoying sound in the world, *Dumb and Dumber* is one of his more tolerable movies. He plays well off Daniels, and the two have a likable chemistry as idiots that seem more genuinely ignorant than obnoxiously trying for laughs. Most of their attempts at humor come off as funny, and they're even funnier when trying to sound smart and sophisticated with their limited intelligence. The batting average of gags is relatively high, one of the top points being Carrey ripping out someone's heart and placing it in a to-go bag. Again, Carrey does this within a dream sequence as he is not strong or cruel enough for such actions. He and Daniels are just dumb; maybe a little dumber than they appear, but never reaching their dumbest.

ED WOOD

DIRECTOR: Tim Burton | SCREENWRITER: Scott Alexander, Larry Karaszewski | CAST: Johnny Depp, Martin Landau, Sarah Jessica Parker, Patricia Arquette, Jeffrey Jones, Bill Murray | GENRE: Comedy | RUNNING TIME: 127 min | MPAA RATING: R

CLASSIFICATION: BEST

Tim Burton has an eternal infatuation with outsider characters, be they Batman or Pee-Wee Herman. But one of his most influential films on such observations would be *Ed Wood* (1994), a semi-comedic biopic on the real-life director of some of Hollywood's cheapest and worst movies. Burton doesn't just want to mock the director of such travesties as *Plan 9 From Outer Space* or *Glen and Glenda*, but dig deep into the method of his madness. He's not as interested in the man himself as he is in restaging all of his corner-cutting movie-making techniques.

Johnny Depp plays director *Ed Wood*, a mustachioed 1950s filmmaker with dreams so big he can't see the mistakes he is making. Every frame he shoots he believes to be beautiful. Someone on set asks if Wood wants to reshoot a shot where one of his actors accidentally shakes the set. He can't be bothered with such repetition as he's already moved onto the next shot he believes will be just as glorious on film as it is in his head. Depp's enthusiasm perfectly encapsulates Wood's extraordinary nature of a bad movie director. He's a man so sure of his genius that he doesn't believe he's making a bad movie or even a decent movie; only great movies.

If an issue arises with filming, he improvises. When Bela Lugosi dies during filming for *Plan 9 From Outer Space*, Wood replaces him with a double that hides his face behind a cloak. He'll often change the script to fit his needs, altering the Christine Jorgensen sex change story into the transvestite picture of *Glen and Glenda* so Wood could play the role, as he fancied being a transvestite. None of these films did well as they were critical and financial failures. How did his career continue for so long with such dud pictures? He sought to fund from all sorts of odd places, from meat tycoons to local churches. This is a director who would improvise on every aspect of his productions, all with a confident smile on his face for the thrill that he was making his movies.

Wood had a boundless energy to convince other outsiders to

follow him. Wood receives pitch advice from The Amazing Criswell (Jeffrey Jones), a man he can trust for being employed with such little talent, and is later used as an actor in his films. He hires the openly-gay Bunny Breckinridge (Bill Murray) to find transvestites for his movies and is also used as an actor. Wood assembles his odd troupe of the lumbering Tor Johnson (George "The Animal" Steele), the pale Vampira (Lisa Marie) and the washed-up Dracula actor Bela Lugosi (Martin Landau). It's astonishing how long Wood's fiancee Dolores (Sarah Jessica Parker) goes along with him and his weird collective. The only person he receives reliable and sound advice from is Orson Welles, played physically in the film by Vincent D'Onofrio and voiced flawlessly by Maurice LaMarche, who is the master of impersonating Welles.

As much as Wood can't acknowledge or spot his moviemaking flaws, he can't see this group of friends as anything than less than what he wants them to be. Lugosi is a drug addict by the time Wood meets him, but all he can see is the horror movie star and not the frail old man past his age. The actor is depressed, needy, suicidal and hostile towards his fans who think he's as good as Boris Karloff; *"Karloff did not deserve to smell my shit!"* Wood cannot help Lugosi past casting him in movies. It's the only thing he knows how to do and the only way he can look at Lugosi. Casting Lugosi was Wood's special way of lifting the spirits of the actor one more time before leaving this world, granting him one last appearance on the screen, even if it was in one of the worst movies ever made.

Tim Burton's film doesn't just want us to marvel at Wood's blindness to bad, but understand his gleeful spirit and love for a medium he wasn't skilled at doing. Most bad movies are directed by bitter and sleazy men who are more con artists than filmmakers. Ed Wood was a good director in the sense that he loved movies so much he thought he could do no wrong. He aimed to please, even if he only ended up pleasing himself in the end. But considering his pictures are regarded as campy Z-movie classics that are ripe for riffing, I think he succeeded in making people happy with his films, albeit not for the reasons he intended.

EDWARD SCISSORHANDS

DIRECTOR: Tim Burton | SCREENWRITER: Caroline Thompson | CAST: Johnny Depp, Winona Ryder, Dianne Wiest, Anthony Michael Hall, Kathy Baker, Vincent Price, Alan Arkin | GENRE: Science Fiction | RUNNING TIME: 105 min | MPAA RATING: PG-13

CLASSIFICATION: WEIRD

Only Tim Burton could think up a character so strange and sad as *Edward Scissorhands* (1990). He had initially drawn this tragic hero when he was a teenager, spawned from his loneliness, and passed it off to writer Caroline Thompson to see if anything could be done with it. She did not disappoint by turning in a script for an offbeat monster movie with all the surreal and psychological trimmings Burton loved so. It's no wonder he decided to fast-track this film ahead of the sequel to his successful *Batman* movie.

Edward (Johnny Depp) is the artificial creation of an old inventor, excellently played by Vincent Price in his final significant role. They live together in a gothic mansion where the inventor home schools the boy before he puts the final touches on his creation. The hands, obviously, need some work for featuring blades for fingers. But the inventor will not have a chance to install Edward's human hands as the old man suffers a heart attack and passes away. Poor Edward must now face the world alone with his odd scissor hands.

The setting of the gothic mansion may make it sound as though the film takes place in a European country of the late 1800s. It turns out it's just up the hill from an American suburb of the late 1900s. Edward's first visitor after the untimely death of his creator is Peg (Dianne Wiest), a door-to-door Avon salesman. She's a kind soul and decides to take in the odd little creature by housing him at her suburban home. There's a fear that Edward won't fit in with her family, but he does pretty well for a quiet guy with scissors for hands.

That could be because the suburban neighborhood looks and feels almost as odd and artificial as Edward himself. It never feels as though this is a real neighborhood community and more of a strange satire on the storybook depiction of family life. Then again, how believable can you make a suburban neighborhood when there's a gothic castle in walking distance?

Edward soon hits it off with Peg's daughter Kim (Winona Ryder), who loves the man despite him not being able to touch her without leaving a gash. He may not be able to use the waterbed without popping it, but he can still be of great help at cutting hair at the salon, trimming the neighborhood topiaries and carving ice sculptures. Only in Tim Burton's peculiar world could Edward slice up ice at such a rate that the shavings turn to snow to transform a backyard into a winter wonderland. He tries to open his hair salon, but the bank won't give him a loan. There's a romance between Edward and Kim, but not if the tough jock Jim (Anthony Michael Hall) has anything to say about it. And though the neighborhood grows to accept Edward, they can just as quickly turn on him for being dangerous. You probably wouldn't want to go for a jog with him.

 The film has so many original ideas that it's a bit of a letdown the story proceeds down the familiar route of Frankenstein with a grand showdown at the castle. Even with the predictable climax, Burton still delivers on one of his most unforgettable characters being placed in the most dreamlike of settings. It becomes a little lost in the usual Burton surrealness, but never sinking too deep that we can't identify with Edward. Most of the isolation and depression comes through for a character that is slightly distant and silent. It's a fable just weird enough to accept that a man with scissors for hands could make out with a girl or make it snow in summer.

EMPIRE RECORDS

DIRECTOR: Allan Moyle | SCREENWRITER: Carol Heikkinen | CAST: Anthony LaPaglia, Maxwell Caulfield, Debi Mazar, Rory Cochrane, Johnny Whitworth, Robin Tunney, Renée Zellweger, Liv Tyler | GENRE: Comedy | RUNNING TIME: 105 min | MPAA RATING: PG-13

CLASSIFICATION: WEIRD

Empire Records (1995) is a film that takes place over the course of one day in the titular record store. But this isn't any ordinary day for the store. It's Rex Manning day! Every April 8th, the store celebrates the yearly tradition of 1980s rock star Rex Manning (Maxwell Caulfield) making an appearance to sign the autographs of his many old fans. Everyone in the store treats it as a national holiday of sorts, feeling all the giddiness and anxiety that comes with it. It's just one of many weird and cartoonish touches on this snapshot of Generation X.

The small Delaware record store operates with a casual nature to benefit its young employees. But the store owner has decided to sell it to Music City, a competitor that doesn't much care for the staff with their style of dress, hair and body accessories. This could rip apart the family bond of the employees that the adult manager Joe (Anthony LaPaglia) has worked so hard to maintain. It shouldn't come as a surprise that the solution for such a problem is to raise enough money to buy the independence of the store and that it happens to be through music. After all, what type of film would Empire Records be if the original plan of gambling solved the store ownership issue?

Until the film gets to the predictable ending, we follow the many odd teenage employees of Empire. Lucas (Rory Cochrane) is the slyly funny clerk, dressed like a bit of beatnik, that always finds the most peculiar of observations with the most intelligent of jabs; he notices a customer digging rap and metal, recommending that a little jazz would calm any criminal tendencies. Corey (Liv Tyler) is the smart girl well on her way to Harvard. Debra (Robin Tunney) is an employee so troubled she shaves her head to sell her alternativeness. A. J. (Johnny Whitworth) has a crush on Debra he hopes to reveal soon. Other notable characters include Lucas' girlfriend Gina (Renée Zellweger) and the shoplifter Warren (Brendan Sexton III) who isn't as bad as he seems, even when he brandishes a gun in the store. The employees all do their best to run the store in their special way while also ignoring it for their asides, similar to the distractions in *Clerks*.

Despite feeling a little too comfy within its weird walls of quirky characters, there's an undeniably flavorful tone of the era. This is mostly due to the competence of the people behind the picture. Director Allan Moyle had proven with his previous film *Pump Up The Volume* (1990) that he understood the rebelliousness of youth and the type of talk that teens wanted to hear. Screenwriter Carol Heikkinen had previously worked at a Tower Records store and based most of the script on her experiences. The primary cast was young and fresh actors that were mostly unknown, except Liv Tyler being a more significant presence and Johnny Whitworth lying about his age.

The post-production for the film was chaotic. The studio was so nervous about the movie they wanted that roughly 40 minutes worth of cuts were made. This included scenes of the characters smoking weed and using adult language, mostly to ensure that the film could attain a PG-13 rating from the MPAA. These cuts also meant condensing the film down from taking place over the course of two days to one day, making the film feel very off with missing scenes of character development and conversations about music. There was a director's cut released as the Remix: Special Fan Edition, but still only features a fraction of what was initially cut.

Empire Records is almost a quintessential cult movie for trying to encapsulate the music and teen life of the mid-1990s, despite being a box office and critical failure upon release. It has grown into a bit of a phenomenon for the soundtrack featuring noteworthy bands and Rex Manning Day becoming a celebrated holiday among the fans. I never found myself as caught up in the film as the fandom it spawned, considering its standard save-the-old-theater plot and humor that mostly falls flat, but I never felt bored or annoyed with the picture for its charming character chemistry and pleasing musical numbers. Still, it was apparent that the movie was built more for the soundtrack than the other way around.

THE END OF EVANGELION

DIRECTOR: Hideaki Anno, Kazuya Tsurumaki | SCREENWRITER: Hideaki Anno | CAST: Spike Spencer, Amanda Winn-Lee, Tiffany Grant, Allison Keith, Tristan MacAvery | GENRE: Science Fiction (Animated) | RUNNING TIME: 87 min | MPAA RATING: Not Rated

CLASSIFICATION: WEIRD

When the Japanese animated series *Neon Genesis Evangelion* ended in 1996, its last two episodes were too cheap and esoteric for its fans that desired a mix of the conflicting forces of teenage depression and giant robot action. *The End of Evangelion* (1997) was the theatrical answer to the angry fans in one of the strangest TV-to-movie adaptations ever conceived. This film was not intended to be a continuation, remake or spin-off to the series, but a replacement for the last two episodes. And while this movie more or less gave the fans what they wanted, this correction of a film came across more surreally off than philosophically satisfying.

Despite the precursor of an ineffective *Evangelion* recap movie, *Death and Rebirth* (1997), this picture was strictly for fans only. It expects you to be familiar with the current situation of Shinji Ikari, a teenager who hasn't yet recovered from his traumatic giant robot battle of murdering his best friend. It expects you to know the underground organization of NERV, devoted to slaughtering giant biblical monsters with robots made out of said monsters and currently on bad terms with similar military agencies. There is also the matter of the vague Instrumentality Project, intended to advance humanity to the next level of consciousness or transform the movie into one of the most lavish and experimental animated films of the 1990s.

Whereas the TV series managed to find a stable balance of grand themes and action, director Hideaki Anno seems to split them apart into two segments. No, not segments, the term "episodes" is more accurate, as Anno places end credits after the first half of the film, replicating the experience of marathoning the series. For the first episode, the teenage pilot Asuka, freshly awoken from a mind-rape coma, does battle with seven other giant robots with big lips and wings. Meanwhile, the rest of NERV is defending their installation from malevolent forces that lay bloody waste to all the staff. Shinji's guardian Misato does her best to keep Shinji alive in hopes that he'll snap out of his funk and decide to fight in his giant robot again.

The vicious violence fulfilled in the first episode, Anno reserves the last portion for his more artistic and existential ideas for staging Shinji's mental landscape. Some are slightly creative; a live-action shot of an empty theater that forces the audience to look at themselves and contemplate not being there. Others are a little base; a younger Shinji playing alone at a playground in the shape of a woman's body to symbolize the loss of his mother. And some of the symbolism is just lazy, as with a cryptic symbol painted in the skies. There are even meta bits in the imagery, as when flashes of angry death threat emails from *Evangelion* fans briefly grace the screen.

For being so weird and twisted, including an infamous opening scene where Shinji ejaculates over a comatose Asuka, *The End of Evangelion* has become revered among anime fans to sit alongside the works of Hayao Miyazaki and Katsuhiro Otomo. It's probably not a movie to walk into cold, considering how much knowledge of the series is required to grasp its characters and convoluted plot of apocalypse and angels. It's also a bit too experimental, as with the inclusion of a five-minute intermission after the halfway appearance of the end credits, requiring an awful lot of patience for an 87-minute movie. But for being so bizarre, it deserves a watch for touching deeply on the perceptions of depression and the uncomfortable realizations of existence, concepts that are usually foreign for an animation about giant robots.

EVENT HORIZON

DIRECTOR: Paul W.S. Anderson | SCREENWRITER: Philip Eisner | CAST: Laurence Fishburne, Sam Neill, Kathleen Quinlan, Joely Richardson | GENRE: Science Fiction | RUNNING TIME: 95 min | MPAA RATING: R

CLASSIFICATION: WEIRD

Paul W.S. Anderson is best known for such brainless and junky pictures as *Mortal Kombat* and *Resident Evil*, but he came close to making something brilliant with *Event Horizon* (1997). It was mainly a haunted house movie in space, akin to *Alien*, but Anderson aimed for something more original than aliens terrorizing a ship full of human prey. He opted to change the original script from an alien infestation to a supernatural force. He also added in horror so bloody, gory and gruesome that his initial cut was an NC-17 and had to be cut down severely to meet an R rating. The mind reels at what that cut must have looked like, primarily since most of the cut footage was either destroyed or lost. Anderson may have very well made a great film, and we may never see it.

What we do see is a film with lofty goals that falls a tad short, making it just a tad more admirable than Anderson's other works. The film follows the crew of the Lewis and Clark starship, helmed by Captain Miller (Laurence Fishburne) and a team of various engineers and doctors. Their mission is to investigate the Event Horizon starship the disappeared for many years when exploring Proxima Centauri and is now discovered just outside Neptune. Accompanying the crew is Doctor Weir (Sam Neill), who helped develop the Event Horizon's gravity drive that allows it to travel great distances by essentially creating a black hole. He explains how this works by placing holes in a pin-up poster.

When they arrive at the Event Horizon, the crew is all dead and strange recordings have been left behind. Where did the ship go? According to the garbled Latin spoken in the ship's records, it ventured into hell and brought back something with it. Whatever it is has apparently turned the Event Horizon into a spooky vessel that knows your darkest secrets, causes hallucinations and drives you so insane you'll want to tear your eyeballs out. Of course, the crew won't figure this out until it's too late.

The hell ship isn't exactly shocking in its revelations, but it does make for some decent kills, even if most of them come off predictable in design and random in occurrence. One of the crew members has a kid back home, so she'll naturally start seeing her little boy scurrying through the corridors and stupidly fall for him being there. Captain Miller has a terrible secret of leaving someone behind, and that person will return to haunt him as a ghost that shoots flames from his hands. Doctor Weir gets to have some of the best hallucinations about his dead wife urging him to give in to evil with eyes torn from their sockets. All of this and a bathtub of blood fill the ship with plenty of horrors that are more entertaining for their campy construction than true terror. There's always something that seems to make these scenes lose their impact, be it the cartoonish sound effects, lousy CGI or Sam Neil's laughable attempt at screaming in terror.

The production values are comical at times. The opening computer graphics of floating objects in a zero-gravity environment are unbelievably dated; makes you wonder why compositing in a floating book wasn't even considered. If your computer graphics can't make a book look convincing, you either need a bigger budget or your effects team sucks. The haunted house element risks in the third act with a lightning storm raging outside and a flood of blood in the ship's enclosed spaces. The sound effects are so stock a few of them come off as cartoony with the ill-fitting punch, kick and snapping sound effects. I'm surprised Anderson didn't go the extra mile by adding a silly gloop sound for when characters fall into pools of water and are splashed with blood.

Event Horizon was a mess of a production, but has gained a cult following over the years for that very reason. Aside from its spooky factor, the film is a puzzle of trying to put together what went wrong, what was cut and if that NC-17 cut was indeed something unusually remarkable. There are enough stunning visuals of the ship's interiors to be seen as eerily beautiful for sci-fi design nuts, plenty of blood to satisfy gorehounds (including a brief blood orgy) and some laughably blunt dialogue to satiate those seeking a campy sci-fi B-movie (*"Fuck this ship!"*). Sure, there are better haunted house movies in space, but none of them feature Laurence Fishburne punching a shirtless and scarred Sam Neill who babbles about hell.

EXISTENZ

DIRECTOR: David Cronenberg | SCREENWRITER: David Cronenberg | CAST: Jennifer Jason Leigh, Jude Law, Christopher Eccleston, Willem Dafoe | GENRE: Science Fiction | RUNNING TIME: 97 min | MPAA RATING: R

CLASSIFICATION: WEIRD

David Cronenberg's *eXistenZ* (1999) takes place in a future society of video games, but the game consoles are not the standard metallic and slick designs that every movie portrays as the future of technology. Not in Cronenberg's world, where everything is organic, gross, weird and uncomfortably sexual. His vision of a gaming conference doesn't take place in a giant convention center with massive television screens touting the latest tech, but in a small church where the media huddles around a mass of pulsating flesh that connects to their spines to create a virtual reality experience. Organic devices are so in that a terrorist seeking to assassinate someone at the event utilizes a weapon of skin and bone, making it easy enough to sneak through security.

The game developer under attack at the conference is Allegra Geller (Jennifer Jason Leigh), so renowned and controversial enough to be the target of anti-gamer terrorist groups. She is quickly escorted out of the event by security officer Ted Pikul (Jude Law), a man who has chosen not to embrace the virtual reality of video games. It's easy enough to consider his reluctance given that requirements for accessing Allegra's games are through a port in your spine. Ted will eventually have a port installed, but will have the surgery at a gas station run by Willem Dafoe who adores Allegra so much he literally kisses her feet.

The world of *eXistenZ* has us continually asking what the norm is and what is a simulation. We're led to believe that Allegra's virtual reality world exists as a program that only functions if the user can push the plot along by stating the next bit of acceptable dialogue. Both Ted and Allegra have their spinal ports inside the game where all sorts of nasty creatures can crawl up and infect. When Ted examines Allegra's port, he sexually licks the hole. She's shocked, but he explains it was the action of his character and not his desire. Or is it? There's a more in-depth questioning of how we play video games and write off our actions as just being part of the game rather than reflective of our morality that makes us subconsciously sexual and violent.

Cronenberg never harps on this aspect too long, choosing to kick the characters and the viewer further down the fleshy rabbit hole. In their many visions and visits, Ted and Allegra will learn more about the fascinating *eXistenZ* game console. They'll visit a farm where the product is born and assembled like cows. They'll meet a surgeon of the consoles in a scene that dissects the inner workings of its living components. They'll also take in a meal at a restaurant that serves them a disgusting bird dish, but it is not intended to be eaten as its bones form into a gun.

The final scene of the film features a character about to be murdered and asking before the killers shoot if he's still in the game. By the time the film reaches this point, neither the viewer or the characters no for sure. The story leads from rabbit hole to rabbit hole, pulling back endlessly from simulations within simulations. The presentation is very chilling for this ambiguous nature that always keeps you uneasy and questioning everything on screen. The film was released the same year as *The Matrix*, another movie about simulations. But while The Matrix entertained the idea that maybe your reality is false, *eXistenZ* suggests that perhaps fact is a few more simulations away, if it even exists at all.

EYES WIDE SHUT

DIRECTOR: Stanley Kubrick | SCREENWRITER: Stanley Kubrick, Frederic Raphael | CAST: Tom Cruise, Nicole Kidman, Sydney Pollack, Marie Richardson | GENRE: Drama | RUNNING TIME: 159 min | MPAA RATING: R

CLASSIFICATION: BEST

As Stanley Kubrick's final film, *Eyes Wide Shut* (1999) is easily the director's most punishing, puzzling and surreal of pictures. There is a lot of nudity and sex, but it is not meant to be erotic, silly or even grotesque. The sex, despite being prominent and graphic, is merely a foundation for a film that is about the absence of intimacy, the corruption of morality, the emptiness of greed and the draining battle of the sexes. All of this is presented in the mood and atmosphere of an unnerving fever dream where the characters never feel fully in control of their lives, even when they seem to have the advantage of decadence.

Dr. Bill Harford (Tom Cruise) and his wife Alice (Nicole Kidman) seem to have the perfect life as a wealthy married couple. They live in a ritzy part of Manhattan, look beautiful, dress beautiful and attend decorative balls for the wealthy elite. It doesn't take long for the two of them to be quickly seduced by the partygoers. Alice is charmed by a Hungarian with talk of Latin poetry and Bill is pursued by two women who push themselves on him. The party is interrupted for Bill, however, when the millionaire party-thrower Victor (Sydney Pollack) asks for his help with reviving an overdosed hooker in the bathroom. The following evening, Bill and Alice smoke pot and she regales her husband with a fantasy about having sex with a naval officer. They fight, Bill leaves and he then wanders through New York on a dark journey of sex that grows more meaningless and draining with each encounter, slowly losing his own identity.

As Bill proceeds through each strange segment, Kubrick not only tries to make us sympathize with this character, but nearly lose track of him in the haze of his exploration. This is mostly due to Bill never directly becoming involved with the sex presented to him. He entertains foreplay, but never fully engages. Bill never wholly drops off the cliff of morality, merely peering over the edge with fascination and fear. He witnesses the height of this inhumanity when he stumbles onto a secret society that holds rituals of masked orgies. The orgy is more creepy than erotic; when nobody's face can be seen, there is no passion of individuality in the act.

Scene after scene, few perfectly connecting to the more significant story, proves to be intoxicating, each in their manner of acting, lighting, and composition. When Bill and Alice fight, there is a weariness to their argument that feels genuinely uncomfortable and exhausting, due mostly to Kubrick's prolonged production that set a record for the most extended movie shoot, lasting over 15 months. It was worth the time and effort for more than just the stellar acting of Cruise and Kidman. Kubrick perfectly conveys a chilling sense of foreboding terror rumbling beneath every gorgeous shot of the masked ball and every Christmas-lit corner of the evening streets of New York City.

Eyes Wide Shut doesn't offer up to audiences the same iconographic glee of Kubrick's other pictures. In his other films, if you couldn't read the themes, you could at least appreciate the spectacle of a soldier riding an atomic bomb (*Doctor Strangelove*), a detailed space station (*2001: A Space Odyssey*) or a slow-motion fight to classical music (*A Clockwork Orange*). For not being as visually noteworthy in pop culture with its material, it has often been looked down on as the director's lesser work for not being a steamy sex thriller that was never promised; maybe it was by the marketing team, but not by Kubrick. He would never spoil his audience with such simple titillation, nor entertain our expectations of his usual Kubrick-isms. It is his most haunting and challenging picture for trying to decipher all of its themes, visuals, and characters, which may never fully be divulged as Kubrick passed away just six days after submitting the first cut. He fittingly left the world with the gift of a film to be explored, analyzed and theorized to death, a comforting final chapter for the life of a great director.

FACE/OFF

DIRECTOR: John Woo | SCREENWRITER: Mike Werb, Michael Colleary | CAST: John Travolta, Nicolas Cage, Joan Allen, Gina Gershon, Alessandro Nivola | GENRE: Action | RUNNING TIME: 139 min | MPAA RATING: R

CLASSIFICATION: WEIRD

Face/Off (1997) is an acting experiment with some rather intriguing results, where John Travolta tries to act like Nicholas Cage and Nicolas Cage tries to act like John Travolta. This is both a fantastic premise and an irresistible opportunity for Cage and Travolta to flex their acting muscles as they play each other. It provides the perfect foundation for John Woo's stellar action sequences to make the film as much of a delightful romp of car chases and gunfights as it is a fascinating study in actors mimicking each other.

Travolta plays FBI agent Sean Archer and Cage is the terrorist Castor Tony. After recently being captured by Sean, Castor mentions there is a biological bomb under Los Angeles that will explode in a few days. Castor is in a coma and his brother/partner Pollux (Alessandro Nivola) will not talk about the bomb. Desperate times call for extreme measures and it doesn't get more ridiculously drastic than this plan. Sean volunteers for an undercover mission to obtain information about the bomb. He will assume the role of Castor in prison by swapping faces with him. Well, it isn't a swap at first, but once Castor awakens from his coma and forces a doctor to give him Sean's face, it then becomes an even trade.

Cage and Travolta have a lot of fun with these characters as they try to emulate. There's the addition of a microchip inserted on the larynx to make Travolta's character able to sound a little more convincing playing Cage. Where it gets tricky on the actor's part is that both Travolta and Cage have to let just enough mannerisms and speech patterns into the characters to sound like their opposite. In other words, Nicolas Cage is meant to sound like Cage, but with an air of Travolta in his voice. The characters continue to spin webs of deception until they finally meet in the most fascinating of showdowns where they, well, face off against one another; *"It's like looking in a mirror, only not."*

The very concept of the film is entertaining enough with a script by Mike Werb and Michael Colleary, but John Woo does his best to insert some big action with a beefy $80 million budget. An airplane smashes into a hangar with explosive results. Speedboats crash into each other and piers. Even the technology seems just as overblown as Castor is sent to a prison of the future with magnetized boots that keep prisoners grounded to the floor and electronically tracked. Woo must have figured that facial replacement is strange enough that prison gravity boots weren't much of a stretch.

All that stuff is fun, but not nearly as impressive as the personalities at play. Cage is trying to play the role of an imprisoned terrorist to extract information from Pollux, but Pollux is observant enough to be suspicious of his brother. Travolta tries to slip into the part of the husband and father that the FBI agent is seen as at home. Both actors are playing up this material for all its worth, never showing fear of being too crazy with their performances. It's a John Woo film after all; if you're not over-the-top, the action sequences will overpower you.

Face/Off was at one point going to star Arnold Schwarzenegger and Sylvester Stallone, but that casting would probably have turned the film into a comedy as I never thought of Schwarzenegger and Stallone as skilled enough actors to be impressionists. Cage and Travolta, however, have the talent to imitate each other with subtleties and still come off as believably intense and committed to their character's essential personality. They were both already notable stars at this point in their careers, Travolta for his ease in *Pulp Fiction* and Cage for his intensity in *Leaving Las Vegas*. The fact that they can both master trading quirky characters in a John Woo film, where they are always running and gunning, was just them showing off.

FALLING DOWN

DIRECTOR: Joel Schumacher | SCREENWRITER: Ebbe Roe Smith | CAST: Michael Douglas, Robert Duvall, Barbara Hershey, Rachel Ticotin, Frederic Forrest, Tuesday Weld | GENRE: Drama | RUNNING TIME: 113 min | MPAA RATING: R

CLASSIFICATION: BEST

The sun blazes on a hot morning in Los Angeles. Traffic backed up, bumper to bumper. You can practically feel the heat that sticks drivers to their seats in the smoggy gridlock. William Foster (Michael Douglas), with his thick glasses, thin haircut, white shirt, black tie and matching slacks, decides at that moment he has had enough of it all. He exits his car and proceeds to walk towards his destination, eager to explode on anything and everything that has bothered him about this city.

Foster's tirade of a journey home features Douglas in one of his most intense roles of a middle-class man pushed too far. He wanders into a convenience store and finds himself angered at the raised price of soda, causing him to assault everything overpriced with a baseball bat. A stop at the Whammy Burger turns terrifying when Foster brandishes an automatic weapon, threatening to open fire if he can't get something off the breakfast menu. The sight of road crews lounging on the job to run up their budget inspires enough rage for him to take aim with a bazooka and give them something to fix. Douglas is flawless in these scenes that are just as much hilariously over the top as they are shockingly dark.

Not to be outdone by Douglas is Robert Duvall as the pursuing Sgt. Prendergast. It's his last day on the police force with everyone in the office acting as though he's already gone and his wife acting as though he should already be at home. Dreading retirement, he takes an interest in tracking down Foster on his domestic rampage, first recognizing him as a license plate number (D-Fens) and later a bitter man who took the plunge into the dark side. It's easy enough to see why Prendergast is so infatuated with this suspect. They share the same vulnerabilities of being outdated members of society that are cast aside.

Scene after scene of Douglas reveals a little more about both his character's past and mindset. We learn that he had problems at home, is divorced, cannot see his child by court order and was fired from his job as a defense contractor. He has nothing left and doesn't have the energy, personality or smarts to build himself up again. His life is mostly over, and the madness of this thought is what fuels his violent urges for those that get in his way.

In one of the most chilling scenes, he is offered temporary sanctuary by Nick, a gun shop owner and fervent racist that proudly showcases his Nazi memorabilia. *"We're the same, you and me,"* says Nick. Foster disagrees; *"I'm an American and you're a sick asshole."* Foster doesn't think of himself as a Nazi, just a man who wants to get home to his daughter, but he ends up killing Nick when they have a scuffle. Foster may not be racist, but he could be worse for being so blind to the chaos he causes. Nick knew he was a Nazi; Foster still thinks he's a father just trying to get home, even if there is a small part of him that realizes how much of a monster he has become.

There's a bitter sadness to *Falling Down* (1993) layered on top of its shocking and violent nature. It could have quickly taken the route of being a satisfying revenge picture, but Douglas' character doesn't seem to take any major pleasures in his rampage, even if we do. There are a few one-liners he has, as when he comments that a phone booth is busted after he shoots it up, but he never makes them with a sly smile, only casually commenting to alleviate his tension. He is in a constant state of desperation, confusion, and anger as he marches through the city. He is not a hero and does not desire to be one. Duvall's cop character also doesn't want to be the heroic figure that saves the day, and he's not. By the end of the picture, both characters meet and fulfill what they believe they had to do, one struggling not to be irrelevant and one snapping because he is irrelevant. Neither one is a hero; just average men who did their jobs and feared there was nothing left for them when the career was over.

FARGO

DIRECTOR: Joel Coen | SCREENWRITER: Joel Coen, Ethan Coen | CAST: Frances McDormand, William H. Macy, Steve Buscemi, Harve Presnell, Peter Stormare | GENRE: Comedy | RUNNING TIME: 98 min | MPAA RATING: R

CLASSIFICATION: BEST

The Coen Brothers' take on the northern Midwest in *Fargo* (1996) is both savagely satirical and tenderly earnest. Nearly every Minnesotan character speaks in a comically thick accent, with such language as "oh yah" and "you betcha" in their conversations. But there's also a sweet familiarity to their situations. A Minnesotan relays information to a police officer about a funny looking fella that kept spouting that he was *"going crazy up there by the lake."* Cop Marge Gunderson (Frances McDormand) trudges out of her Brainerd home through the snow of a cold morning to get to her car, only to march back inside and inform her husband that the Prowler needs a jump. These moments have a comfy quirkiness for a strangely intoxicating picture of ransom, betrayal, shootings, and bodies in woodchippers.

The pensive car salesman Jerry Lundegaard (William H. Macy) needs some cash to buy up parking lots and decides to attain it by staging a ransom for his wife to be paid by her wealthy father. This is a scheme that is bound to get messy, especially when he hires the short-fused Carl (Steve Buscemi) and the silently violent Gaere (Peter Stormare) to carry out the kidnapping. Messy might be an understatement, however, as everything seems to go wrong. Jerry tries to stiff his conspirator kidnappers by lying to them about the total sum he'll receive from his father-in-law. The father-in-law will stupidly try to go over the heads of everybody and take on the kidnappers himself. Carl will make the big mistake of trying to hide the money in the snow next to a farmland fence. Gaere will momentarily snap out of his passively cold state to place a bullet in the gut or an ax in the chest of anyone who comes between him and his money.

It's a dark picture, but the brightest spot of levity comes in the form of the good-natured Marge, played with a chipper spirit and warm smile by Frances McDormand. Even for being pregnant, she's still able to take a look at a bloody crime scene and start forming theories, only temporarily taking a break when morning sickness might be setting in. She's so sweet that she doesn't grill Jerry too roughly when she suspects he knows something about the recent string of murders. It's not until she has an uncomfortable scene with an old high school flame that lies to her that she decides to visit Jerry a second time, thinking that maybe he wasn't telling the whole truth.

The Coens have conceived a film that delicately balances its gritty crime elements with a sweet glaze of exaggerated Minnesota Nice. There's a delightful contrast between scenes where Carl is violently whipped, and Marge shares a pleasant lunch at work with her hubby Norm. The cold Minnesota landscape is beautifully shot, featuring unforgettable scenes where Marge investigates a car crash in an endless field of snowy white. Even the editing has character, as in a scene where Carl and Gaere take some hookers to bed, quickly cutting from them having sex to watching TV post-coitus.

The film begins with the text of *"based on a true story,"* only to end with the text that the persons and events are fictionalized. While it's funny enough as a jab at movies that claim to be based on real stories, there is an air of truth to its Midwest setting, exaggerated though it may be. It's hard to imagine such an elaborate scheme being real, but it's easy enough to buy the film's closing shot of Marge and Norm snuggled in their small-town home with an upbeat attitude for an uncertain future. No, not all Minnesotans are this innocent and straightforward, but do I know any like Marge and Norm? Yah, you betcha.

FAST, CHEAP AND OUT OF CONTROL

DIRECTOR: Errol Morris | CAST: Dave Hoover, George Mendonça, Ray Mendez, Rodney Brooks | GENRE: Documentary | RUNNING TIME: 80 min | MPAA RATING: PG

CLASSIFICATION: BEST

Errol Morris' documentaries always have some strange fascination with the odd lives of weirdly devoted individuals. *Fast, Cheap and Out of Control* (1997) plays like a smorgasbord of strange in how Morris pointed his camera at four men of perplexing and intriguing careers. Anyone of them could have been the subject of a personal documentary, but having them all presented in the same picture creates almost a window into Morris' mind for what he finds so intoxicating about these people.

David Hoover is a lion tamer for the circus, easily the most dangerous profession present in the film. There is no exact science to this career and always a possibility of injury or death from his predatory co-workers. One minor slip, false move or lacking display of dominance and you could be a lion's dinner. Hoover speaks of how every lion is different and will not always be entirely tamed for every act, requiring him to be quick on his feet and smart with his head, before he loses both. Contrasting with Hoover's words and scenes are segments from old movie clips where lions are presented either as obedient entertainers of their human masters or bloodthirsty beasts eager for some human meat. They make it look so easy in the movies.

George Mendonca is a topiary artist of Portsmouth, Rhode Island. This is a less dangerous profession, but not as simple as it may seem. George specializes in the most elaborate of animal designs that he constructs from greenery, requiring a massive amount of time, energy and detail. Anyone who brushes off this hobby as that of a mere barber is mistaken as he divulges how much work goes into these garden creations. Sure, there are electric tools to make the trimmings more refined, but George is an old guy and prefers the old method of trusty sheers. He's a simple and somewhat sad man for his devotion, realizing that there are lots of major topiary projects he'd like to undertake, but won't live long enough to see them through.

A more chipper career path is that of Ray Mendez, an expert on hairless mole-rats. Determined to study more about this intriguing species that resides underground, he sets up fascinating experiments for deciding how the mole-rats dig, where they live, how they operate within a collective and how dangerous they'd be to hold. They look cute, but are so powerfully adept at digging through material they could put a hole through your hand with their massive teeth. They also don't seem like the most loving of packs considering how they brush off the death of their large families as a matter of numbers and survival.

Rodney Brooks is an M.I.T. scientist that deals with small creatures as well, but ones manufactured and operated by him. His specialty is in the field of miniature, bug-like robots that he spends an incredible amount of time developing and understanding. He has an impressive proposal for studying other planets: send one hundred small robots as opposed to one giant robot, increasing the chance of successful observations if one or two malfunctions. While Brooks' profession doesn't sound as weird and has led to him having a very prestigious career, it still requires much thought and devotion that only people like David, George, and Ray would understand.

There is no vocal commentary from Morris as he leaves all the talking to his four subjects, even positioning the camera perfectly, so it appears they are speaking more towards the audience instead of the interviewer. Morris' sporadic editing style also keeps the film vivid and exciting as he'll often overlap his subjects, bleeding in some of Ray's footage of mole-rats with Rodney's theories on strength in numbers. This brings about connections that Morris hopes to find, but also keep the attention of the audience, refusing to hold on one subject for too long. Intercut between these sequences are various movie clips and cartoons with frenzied and surreal music, relating to how the public might view these areas of focus with simplicity and fantasy.

The film aims to prove there's more to these studies that we may know and even more to the people that devote themselves towards such passions. They are just as obsessed, thoughtful and crazed as Morris and his films, making for his most fitting and personal of documentaries.

FEAR AND LOATHING IN LAS VEGAS

DIRECTOR: Terry Gilliam | SCREENWRITER: Terry Gilliam, Tony Grisoni, Alex Cox, Tod Davies | CAST: Johnny Depp, Benicio del Toro | GENRE: Comedy | RUNNING TIME: 118 min | MPAA RATING: R

CLASSIFICATION: WEIRD

The novels of Hunter S. Thompson do not exactly make for the best movies, as it's hard to put to screen the madness and surreal nature of a writer that is so whacked out on drugs his writings border between poetic genius and rambling gibberish. There was already one failure with the film adaptation of *Where The Buffalo Roam* (1980), where Bill Murray unsuccessfully attempted to play Thompson. But Terry Gilliam was the perfect director to capture Thompson's insanity in *Fear and Loathing in Las Vegas* (1998). Gilliam's whimsical, weird and vibrant style bodes well for Thompson's strategy of gonzo journalism, where he would become ridiculously stoned before launching into his latest writing piece with a blizzard of incoherence.

The film sticks as best as anyone could to Hunter's autobiographical novel of journalist Raoul Duke and his attorney Dr. Gonzo taking a trip to Las Vegas in 1971. Duke is essentially Hunter S. Thompson, the name that has been given to his personification in other fictional works and is played by Johnny Depp. Depp did his best to portray Hunter in the movie by studying the writer in his element, doing his best to embody the inhibited exuberance of the man behind the hat, sunglasses and cigarette holder. Benicio del Toro plays Dr. Gonzo, based on Thompson's friend Oscar Zeta Acosta, with a similar devotion to the restraints of the character. Benicio didn't have the same luxury of studying his character as Acosta mysteriously disappeared in 1974.

As the film begins, they drive towards Vegas with a convertible loaded up with grass, mescaline, acid, cocaine, uppers, booze, and ether. They're not even in the city yet, and already Duke is tripping out and hallucinating bats; *"We can't stop here! This is bat country!"* And from there the story proceeds through aimless and trippy segments of Duke's assignment to cover the Mint 400 motorcycle race, later expanding into covering a district attorney convention. But it's all a hazy fever dream of a trip where Duke and Gonzo inject all of their drugs and experience the oddest of hallucinations. One of the most bizarre moments when the drugs kick in is when Duke attempts to check into the Vegas hotel, freaking out at the carpeted floor patterns seeping onto clothing, the desk clerk transforming into an eel and the bar patrons appearing as lizards. He will later trash his room, snort cocaine during a speech about drugs and try to buy an orangutan.

Hunter S. Thompson reacted to the film as strangely as he does in his writings. According to Gilliam, Hunter was freaking out at the premiere as the film triggered memories of his experience on the Vegas trip with him shouting *"SHIT! LOOK OUT! GODDAMN BATS!"* as he bounced around in his chair. When asked what he thought of the film, Hunter said he liked it and thought Depp did a great job, but would later remark that if he ever saw anyone acting that way, he would probably hit them with a chair. Depp's performance is exceptionally apt, as the actor not only borrowed many of Hunter's clothing and accessories for the role, but voluntarily let the writer shave his head.

While the film is as disjointed and aimless as Gilliam's other films, it is somewhat suited to Hunter's desires of expression. His most prominent hope for the film was that it didn't bore; *"If I'm going to be disappointed, it's because it doesn't make any waves, that people are not outraged."* While it was a commercial failure, it certainly made waves with polarizing critic reviews, calling the film everything from an apt translation to an unwatchable mess. It would also win positive and negative awards, being nominated for the Palme d'Or at the Cannes Film Festival and the Worst On-Screen Couple award from The Stinkers Bad Movies Awards. For being as bold as it was, however, the film has grown a cult status and has become revered enough to be worthy of The Criterion Collection. Over the years, I've come to see it as an oddly amusing picture with sparks of the genius that sometimes rises out of Hunter's ramblings. It's not a masterpiece, but for adapting such material, Gilliam is about as good as it gets.

THE FIFTH ELEMENT

DIRECTOR: Luc Besson | SCREENWRITER: Luc Besson, Robert Mark Kamen | CAST: Bruce Willis, Gary Oldman, Ian Holm, Chris Tucker, Milla Jovovich | GENRE: Science Fiction | RUNNING TIME: 126 min | MPAA RATING: PG-13

CLASSIFICATION: WEIRD

Luc Besson started writing *The Fifth Element* (1997) as a teenager, and it plays very much as a heaping dose of sci-fi pulp that any imaginative teen would love to conceive. It is a world of lasers, robots, snarling aliens, women that know kung fu, elders that babble about legends, big spaceships, and wild hairstyles. Though Besson had slowly been developing the story over the years until he was in his thirties and the script was over 400 pages, he retains a pure wonderment of youthful exuberance in his sci-fi epic.

The story begins not in the far-off future, but in 1914 Egypt, where scientists are investigating an ancient tomb of robotic alien creatures known as the Mondoshawans. They've been safeguarding their secret weapon powered by some magical stones capable of stopping some great evil that seems to show itself every 5,000 years or so.

With most of the MacGuffin nonsense established and out of the way, the film transitions to New York City in the year 2263. As expected from most futuristic science fiction, the city is now a towering metropolis of endless skyscrapers and flying cars. Besson's vision of the future seems fully realized with bustling traffic of flying cars, cramped living environments that allow apartments to reach the skies and comfortable advancements in technology. Getting a bite to eat in the future seems more comfortable than ever when a whole chicken can be cooked in a few seconds and Chinese restaurants can make house calls at your window.

The unlikely hero is taxi driver Korben Dallas, played with the expected scruffiness of Bruce Willis. As with Willis' other action heroes, he's wary enough to have money problems with the government, but wise enough as a former soldier to outsmart a gun-toting burglar without breaking a sweat. He runs across the redhead Leeloo Minaï Lekatariba-Laminaï-Tchaï Ekbat de Sebat (or just Leeloo if you don't have all day), played by Milla Jovovich in an outfit of bandages that is just weird enough to pass as the latest fashion of the future. She has escaped from a lab as she is a clone of that foreboding alien race in Egypt and is the only hope of stopping some great evil that is heading towards Earth. All of this is explained by the Mondoshawans contact of Father Cornelius (Ian Holm), who says they need to collect crystals to save the planet.

Their adventure leads them to space cruise ship, where they must make contact with a blue alien opera singer whose skin glows and voice comes standard with autotuning. Chris Tucker tags along as the loud, eccentric and weirdly dressed celebrity Ruby Rhod, fittingly playing the role of the bumbling sidekick. The crystals are sought by the evil industrialist Jean-Baptiste Emanuel Zorg, played by Gary Oldman with the strangest hair of any role he has played. And working for Zorg is the alien race of Mangalores, appearing as snarling creatures with twitchy facial appendages that could have blended into the background of a *Star Wars* film. They're typically dim and dopey, serving as perfect fodder for Leeloo to beat up with her incredible martial arts skills.

The Fifth Element is very low on originality in its script, relying on the old tale of a reluctant hero helping the great good to stop the great evil, but it's heavy on visual flair. The special effects of the futuristic cities and alien creatures make the film a real treat for the eyes with its detailed and colorful scenes. Some of the standout shots include a mostly nude Jovovich descending into flying car traffic and the opera singer entertaining a crowd with her beautiful voice that switches genres with her ability to remix herself. It's a film that sticks with you more for its delicious eye candy than its plot that drags on with nothing all that unique. The script is not that great when the most memorable line of dialogue is Leeloo's limited speech for identifying herself with *"Leeloo Dallas multipass,"* and that's only because she repeats this phrase.

FIGHT CLUB

DIRECTOR: David Fincher | SCREENWRITER: Jim Uhls | CAST: Brad Pitt, Edward Norton, Helena Bonham Carter, Meat Loaf Aday, Jared Leto | GENRE: Drama | RUNNING TIME: 139 min | MPAA RATING: R

CLASSIFICATION: WEIRD

David Fincher's *Fight Club* (1999) has most likely spawned hundreds, if not thousands, of writings that overly analyze and speculate on the film's many themes of fascism, capitalism, masochism and whatever other isms that can be fathomed. I now better understand the first rule of Fight Club: *"Don't talk about Fight Club."* The film has been talked about and written about to the degree that nearly all of its nuances and hidden meanings have been fully divulged, picking clean every aspect that it's almost pointless to write about the movie. But, hey, what's one more essay?

Edward Norton plays an average office worker that feels the trapping urban lifestyle is draining his soul. He is also the narrator for a big twist later on. The man is an insomniac, desperate for any ray of sunshine in his drab world. He tries an obsession with consumer goods, but it does little to alleviate his depression. He finds a modicum of satisfaction from attending 12-step meetings. He doesn't have a problem, but he feels better about his own life for not being as terrible compared to others less fortunate. It's still not enough. He hungers for more out of a life that is slowly killing him one workday at a time. And the sensation is ruined when non-member Marla (Helena Bonham Carter) attends the meetings, forcing him to find a new session.

And then his life takes an interesting turn when the loudly dressed Tyler Durden enters his life. The Narrator first meets him on a plane as a soap salesman and then a friend when his apartment explodes. Tyler will offer him a place to stay, but only after Narrator entertains him by getting into a fight outside a bar. Later on, another fight. Tyler finally thinks Narrator is ready to be inducted into the secret society of Fight Club, where men come to enlighten through bruises and seek some more significant meaning to their lives one fist at a time.

The film proceeds down a twisty path of surprise reveal about characters and motivations. Many different meanings center around the Narrator's journey to and experiences inside Fight Club. The most obvious is the dangers of consumerism in how Tyler bitterly talks about the subject with Narrator and later makes it play a role in his master plan. Tyler's method of attack, however, seems to favor a theme of fascism that nulls the consumerism angle. The questioning of masculinity comes into play with how the men of Fight Club try to work out their psychological issues with violence, suggesting an aggressive desire to feel something in a society where they're not allowed such sensations. There's also that nasty matter of the id and how it can manifest itself into lashing out at the world. These are just a few of the angles to examine, and you could spend days pulling out any aspect you want for your next school paper or online article.

The film has been described as everything from a coming-of-age drama to a romantic comedy to a psychological thriller to violent exploitation. As such, the film was significantly polarizing for a studio that hated it, critics who were mixed and a disappointing box office gross. In other words, it had all the elements of a destined cult status and became just that. It's a film that begs, no, requires multiple viewings if only to pick apart all its different tones and subtexts. Having watched *Fight Club* at least five times, I continue to debate whether the film is brilliant for never favoring a solidly central theme or a maddeningly mediocre film for the same reason. I'm currently on the positive side to recommend it, but I hesitate to rewatch as I'm sure I'll find something else that makes me rethink it all over again. Few films ever turn into a rollercoaster of admiration after multiple viewings, and there's something about that which makes *Fight Club* a unique film in its own special way.

FORREST GUMP

DIRECTOR: Robert Zemeckis | SCREENWRITER: Eric Roth | CAST: Tom Hanks, Robin Wright, Gary Sinise, Mykelti Williamson, Sally Field | GENRE: Drama | RUNNING TIME: 142 min | MPAA RATING: PG-13

CLASSIFICATION: BEST

"My mama always said life was like a box of chocolates. You never know what you're going to get."

The mentally-challenged Forrest (Tom Hanks) doesn't know what life will present him, but it certainly gives him a lot. He'll be a football star, a war hero, a ping pong champion and a shrimp boat captain, but won't harp too much on his successes. He's a simple man that goes with the flow, even if that current leads him through the violent jungles of Vietnam or the rough waters of the ocean. His life is a remarkable one, filled with innocence and triumph, making *Forrest Gump* (1994) one of the sweetest and unique films of the 1990s.

Forrest has been told since he was a kid that he was dumb, but lived as best as he could through being honest and polite from the supportive nature of his Alabama mama (Sally Field). Though he was picked on by many, he was able to find the best in people. Sometimes it was easy to see; Bubba (Mykelti Williamson) is a man just as simple, but with big dreams of the shrimping business that Forrest admires for the wealth of knowledge he has on shrimp. Sometimes he had to dig deeper; Lieutenant Dan Taylor (Gary Sinise) is so eager to die in the war that he curses Forrest for not giving him a chance. But Forrest manages to bring out the best in them for his persistent attitude towards pleasing others.

The one constant in Forrest's life is Jenny (Robin Wright), his childhood crush that he believes will be his wife one day. Time passes, and they drift apart but will converge at several points in their journeys. While Forrest accepts his draft into the army, Jenny sets off on a hippie lifestyle of drugs, music, and protest. She thinks Forrest will be just a footnote to leave behind, but he's as much a part of her life as he is in the American culture that he inadvertently helps build. They'll end up together, but not without much persistence by Forrest over the course of decades.

Forrest may not be the brightest or most observant of the eras he occupies, but he seems to know just the right things to say about everything he witnesses. When he accompanies Jenny to her old family home where she was once abused, she hurls rocks at the windows tearfully before he comforts her; *"Sometimes there just aren't enough rocks."* He attempts to ask for her hand in marriage, but she refuses, and he is frustrated with her; *"I may not be smart, but I know what love is."* These are lines that could have been melodramatic, but come off surprisingly effective, as in an emotional reveal when Forrest learns he has a son and is both terrified and anxious at this development.

Director Robert Zemeckis delved into a big box of the latest special effects to better conceive the world around Forrest. Not content with restaging critical moments in American history, archival footage was edited with Tom Hanks composited in next to celebrities. He is almost seamlessly transplanted into scenes where he shakes the hand of JFK and sits next to John Lennon on the Dick Cavett talk show. Zemeckis always has a way of directing his films to make them feel real and within our world, even with Forrest's fable adventure through it.

Watching *Forrest Gump* is like witnessing a balancing act of cinema's greatest joys. It is a sweet story that is a fairy tale at times, but never feels artificial and always earned, for as dreamlike as it appears. Tom Hanks' performance is unparalleled for playing a uniquely original character that is unlike any person I may have known with a low IQ, but easily one I'd want to meet. There's an all-encompassing tone where heartbreak can be felt in Vietnam, warmth can be felt at Forrest's home and laughs come from the most genius of Gump commentary on American history. While the film covers a hefty amount of events and emotions, Forrest remains at the epicenter as our guide. He is a simple, charming and honest man with a clean haircut, a nice suit, a box of chocolates and a fantastic story to tell.

FREDDY'S DEAD: THE FINAL NIGHTMARE

DIRECTOR: David Fincher | SCREENWRITER: Jim Uhls | CAST: Brad Pitt, Edward Norton, Helena Bonham Carter, Meat Loaf Aday, Jared Leto | GENRE: Drama | RUNNING TIME: 139 min | MPAA RATING: R

CLASSIFICATION: WORST

Freddy's Dead: The Final Nightmare (1991), the sixth and falsely advertised finale to the *Nightmare on Elm Street* horror series, makes a big case for this to be the final film. It's not that Freddy's death is portrayed here as a convincing demise to keep him away from haunting dreams for good. It's not that this movie brings the villain's reign of terror to a satisfying conclusion. It's that the whole concept of Freddy being a terrifying figure has long past, transforming the man who murdered sleeping teens into a cartoon character. Freddy needed to die before he shared the screen with Bugs Bunny.

This odd shift in tone can be felt in every bloody kill. Freddy constructs a nightmare where a teenager is sucked out of a plane and plummets towards his death. Before the unlucky boy can go splat, however, Freddy pushes a bed of spikes into the landing zone, comically wiping his brow from the exhaustion. Freddy will also try to make someone's ears explode by scraping his claws on a chalkboard and later use the Nintendo Power Glove to kill another teen in a video game. This killer has lost his touch, playing up his kills more for laughs and product placement than horror.

The plot is one of the silliest of the series. It is the year 1999 and Freddy has finally killed all the children of Springwood. Realizing he needs more kids to terrorize, Freddy sends out the last surviving teenager John to find him some fresh meat. John has amnesia and a doctor, along with a collective of her other patients, decide to head back to Springwood to cure his lost memory. If a consistent stream of children to kill was Freddy's plan, it seems like it would make sense for him to plant the seeds of visitors deciding to settle down in the town and raise kids. Nah, Freddy's hungry now and decides to kill these kids the moment they step into his stomping grounds.

If you think the logic of Freddy's dream-killing abilities being bound to the borders of Springwood is ridiculous, there's even more convoluted logic to divulge about the burnt killer's past. It is revealed that Freddy's powers of regeneration come from Dream Demons, appearing as giant sperm with teeth that nestle inside his body. If

Freddy can be drug into the real world, his body can be destroyed, and the Dream Demons won't revive him...for some reason. Freddy also appears to have had a child many years ago, leading to a mystery about who in the group may be his kid with an obvious red herring. It's impressive how underwhelming Freddy is as a character when his entire history and dream logic is spelled out, including flashbacks where the actor Robert Englund appears without the iconic Freddy makeup.

Freddy's Dead plays more like a circus of satire on the franchise than a nightmare of blood and guts. Johnny Depp briefly appears for an anti-drug PSA, only to be comically hit by Freddy with a frying pan. Alice Cooper pops up as Freddy's adoptive father in a flashback, ineffectively playing a drunken abuser. The sorrow of children being slaughtered all but evaporates when two grieving parents are played by Tom Arnold and Roseanne Barr, acting more as though they had crashed the set than had actual roles. And when a movie has to resort to the old gimmick of 3D, during a time when 3D was still cheap and ugly, it was time for Freddy to go to bed.

FROM DUSK TILL DAWN

DIRECTOR: Robert Rodriguez | SCREENWRITER: Quentin Tarantino | CAST: George Clooney, Harvey Keitel, Quentin Tarantino, Juliette Lewis, Cheech Marin, Fred Williamson, Salma Hayek | GENRE: Horror | RUNNING TIME: 108 min | MPAA RATING: R

CLASSIFICATION: WEIRD

From Dusk Till Dawn (1996) comes as a bloody surprise of a picture in how it switches genres halfway through. It begins as a crime film; George Clooney and Quentin Tarantino play bank robbing brothers Seth and Richie Gecko, on the run from Texas law enforcement. Sam tries to keep it together while his hotheaded brother Richie is more prone to rape and kill. To get across the Mexican border, they force the Fuller family of priest Jacob (Harvey Keitel), daughter Kate (Juliette Lewis) and son Scott (Ernest Liu) to hide them in their RV. Holding the family at gunpoint, the Gecko brothers successfully make it across the border and force the Fullers to wait for their contact at a strip club. It's a pretty intense situation for both the Geckos and the Fullers with plenty of character to all of them.

And then the film takes a startling turn. The establishment of the Titty Twister is run by vampires! With a full house of rowdy customers, the strippers and club employees go wild with a massacre of blood and guts on the patrons. Guns are fired, necks are bitten, and the battle is on for humans versus vampires. What's left of the Geckos and Fullers teams up with the cigar-chomping Frost (Fred Williamson) and the pistol-for-a-codpiece Sex Machine (Tom Savini) to survive the night.

The film is a marriage of two minds, blending Tarantino's flair for crossing genres with Robert Rodriguez's skill for well-edited action. It almost feels as though the two of them had conceived two separate films of a crime drama and a vampire action bonanza, having both of them meet in the middle. Tarantino writes his characters to be unique with plenty of exciting things to say, even for the lesser roles of such one-scene characters as Earl McGraw, a Texas Ranger played by Michael Parks that would reappear in Tarantino's *Kill Bill* and Rodriguez's *Planet Terror*. There is room for theological discussions with Harvey Keitel's character of a priest that is grappling with his faith, perfectly paralleling the whole vampire ordeal. You can see Tarantino's name on a script like this with dialogue that is richly keen and in a scene where a stripper played by Salma Hayek makes his character drink booze off her feet, fulfilling the writer's admitted foot fetish.

And then there are Rodriguez's stellar scenes of violence with vampires that look more like bats than humans with really sharp teeth. He loads up the Titty Twister massacre with plenty of gruesome details with severed heads tossed around the room and the house band switching out their guitars for ones made of human body parts. The kills are both gory and hilarious; Fred Williamson impales four vampire strippers on all four legs of a table, and Cheech Marin's head explodes with fluid through his eye sockets when his vampire character swallows a cross. By the time the film reaches its brutal climax, Rodriguez throws everything and the kitchen sink at the screen, as in one scene where a headless vampire transforms into a giant mutant rat. Why? Who cares - it looks cool and gives Clooney something to kill with a jackhammer.

While both Tarantino and Rodriguez were capable of more and would go onto direct better films, *From Dusk Till Dawn* features them having fun with genre material, even if they weren't transcending the material as they usually do. It features a stellar big-screen debut for Clooney, some fantastic production values for a strip club with fire and great effects to please the most demanding of horror fans. Never forget that Tarantino, the director and Oscar-winning writer of *Pulp Fiction*, wrote a film where Cheech Marin has to describe a variety of pussy a strip club has to offer.

FROZEN ASSETS

DIRECTOR: George T. Miller | SCREENWRITER: Don Klein, Tom Kartozian | CAST: Shelley Long, Corbin Bernsen, Larry Miller | GENRE: Comedy | RUNNING TIME: 96 min | MPAA RATING: PG-13

CLASSIFICATION: WORST

Frozen Assets (1992) plays like a failed TV pilot of a one-joke script. Corbin Bernsen plays Zach Shepard, a bank executive whose corporation sends him to run a small bank in Oregon. But it's not your typical small-town bank: it's a sperm bank! Cue the record scratch, double-take look of surprise and the canned laugh track.

Of course, Shepard will not realize it is a sperm bank until he enters the building and the script hopelessly attempts to reap as much comedy from his misunderstandings. He'll enter the lobby and unsuccessfully tries to butter up one of the customers; *"My door is open if you need a hand - two hands. Hey, I'll get down on all fours - that's how eager I am to please."* It isn't until Shepard meets the bank's nurse Grace (Shelley Long) and is led all the way into the freezer of frozen sperm does he finally realize exactly where he is. He finally believes Grace once he is holding a tube of sperm so he can freak out, drop the tube and have Grace catch it with a smile. For this joke to work, however, Shepard had to stupidly miss the words "Sperm Bank" clearly printed on the front door.

Long and Bernsen don't have much of any chemistry as the protective nurse and the smug businessman. They're forced to spit out lines as artificial as the insemination process for their product. He asks where his secretary is and she tells him there are no secretaries in this office. He orders her to retrieve a file, and she starts throwing files in his face. He asks why a hick town needs a sperm bank and she retorts that even hicks can struggle with fertility. The film gets microscopically funnier when Shepard meets Newton (Larry Miller), the local escaped mental patient living with his mother in the small town's local mansion. Miller isn't given anything funny to say, but he at least holds the screen a little more stable with his firm delivery of genuinely terrible content.

A problem arises at the sperm bank! They're faced with a shortage of sperm donations. How do we get the community males to chip in their seed? The solution for the bank is to hold a contest for the largest sperm count, the grand prize being $100,000. To drum up support and give pointers on sperm counts, the teenage cheerleaders of the high school hold a pep rally on how to get those numbers up. One recommendation is not to have sex, sending a panic through the local brothels. This leads to many more lazy and uninspired double-entendres and sex jokes, all of them sounding as though they were plucked from some kid's joke book the writers checked out at the library.

Little is known about this lackluster comedy's production. It was directed by George Miller (no, not the *Mad Max* director) after having finished the much-panned *The NeverEnding Story II: The Next Chapter* (1991). It was written by first-time and only-time screenwriters Don Klein and Tom Kartozian. Not much else is known about the film or why it was made. The most I could dig up was a rumor that Bernsen was so terrible on set that he couldn't remember his lines. I'm willing to bet he just didn't want to say them.

Frozen Assets is a hidden gem of a bad movie. It was a huge box office bomb (grossing $376,008 total) and wasn't reviewed by most critics. It was reviewed by Gene Siskel and Roger Ebert, both giving the film thumbs down on their review program. When they were asked in an interview with Bob Costas about what movie they thought was the worst of 1992, they both promptly responded with *Frozen Assets* in unison. The film was banished to VHS and has become a buried relic of a movie for only the most devoted of bad movie buffs to seek out.

THE FUGITIVE

DIRECTOR: Andrew Davis | SCREENWRITER: David Twohy, Jeb Stuart | CAST: Harrison Ford, Tommy Lee Jones, Sela Ward, Joe Pantoliano, Andreas Katsulas, Jeroen Krabbé | GENRE: Action | RUNNING TIME: 130 min | MPAA RATING: PG-13

CLASSIFICATION: BEST

The 1990s were such a junkyard of movies based on TV shows that most people seem to forget *The Fugitive* (1993) was based on the classic television program of the same name. The film follows the same premise as the television series with the protagonist being wrongfully accused of a crime. He knows who did it, but he cannot prove this. He is imprisoned and sentenced to death, but manages to escape when his bus en route to death row is smashed by a train. Director Andrew Davis is faithful to all of this, but makes the big crash a million dollar spectacle that gets the story off to an explosively impressive start.

But Davis doesn't just punch up the film with big-budget action sequences. He's smart enough not to insult our intelligence by directing characters with just as much firepower in their performances. Harrison Ford plays Richard Kimble, a Chicago surgeon that comes home to discover his wife brutally beaten to death by a one-armed man. Nobody believes Kimble's story about the man who escapes and he is quickly found guilty as all of the evidence points to him. This creates a nightmare for the character which Ford perfectly conveys with his flustered and frantic need to prove his innocence. His blood gets pumping during his escape in the film's fantastic collision sequence. Ford has established in the *Indiana Jones* films that he's a master of fleeing from crushing boulders and once more showcases his amazing skills with avoiding disaster, exiting the crashed bus just before a train slams into it and narrowly avoiding another train car that nearly smashes into him. He does all this while still being shackled at the ankles.

Pursuing Kimble is US Marshal Gerard, played with great wisdom and condescension by Tommy Lee Jones. He throws himself so deep into the case of finding Kimble that he delivers powerful and amusing instructions for his manhunt on searching every warehouse, farmhouse, henhouse, outhouse, and doghouse in the area. His mind is so tactful that he's leagues ahead of his co-workers. While another

Marshal says he is thinking, Gerard tells him to get him a coffee and donut while he's thinking to be of some use. Gerard will slowly come around to understanding the plight of Kimble, but never so merely that it becomes too apparent. You can sense a look in his eyes as the wheels turn in his head that maybe Kimble is innocent if he's willing to go to such lengths to prove it.

Ford never tries to overplay this role with too much melodrama. He knows he's in an action film and brings his usual grit of a growling dog to a movie where he's on the run from the law. A lesser actor would have tried to make the character more fragile for having lost his wife and being betrayed by the justice system. There's no time for melodramatics when you're on the lam in the cold of winter woodlands.

Andrew Davis had proved himself as an action director for such films as *Code of Silence* and *Under Siege*, but he's at his best with this cat and mouse game of Ford and Jones being tactful and intelligent. This leads to fantastic scenes of great exchanges between the two, as well as the astounding chase inside a dam that ends with a daring drop into raging waters. It all makes for a genuine surprise of a thriller, an action picture and a TV-to-movie adaptation in a decade where there were plenty of brainless entries in each category.

GALAXY QUEST

DIRECTOR: Dean Parisot | SCREENWRITER: David Howard, Robert Gordon | CAST: Tim Allen, Sigourney Weaver, Alan Rickman, Tony Shalhoub, Sam Rockwell, Daryl Mitchell | GENRE: Science Fiction | RUNNING TIME: 102 min | MPAA RATING: PG

CLASSIFICATION: WEIRD

Galaxy Quest (1999) is a sci-fi comedy that plucks humor from both the *Star Trek* TV series and its fandom of Trekkies. It's aware not only of the silly cliches of the show, but also the collective of obsessive and scrutinizing fans that surrounded its legacy. William Shatner once performed a skit on *Saturday Night Live* where he addressed the geeky audience of a *Star Trek* convention by telling them to get a life. The sad truth of the old cast of the fictional Galaxy Quest TV show is that this fandom is their life. For every gushing fan that confesses their love of the show, there is another that laughs at the old actors still parading in their dorky costumes.

The cast members, reuniting at everything from conventions to store openings, have grown bitter over time. Alex Dane (Alan Rickman) has become so uncomfortable with wearing the prosthetics of an alien doctor that he's one line repetition away from storming out the door. Gwen DeMarco (Sigourney Weaver) is so tired of being seen as the token female, having once been interviewed by TV Guide on the size of her boobs. The only one who still seems to get a kick out of the attention is the show's lead actor, Jason Nesmith (Tim Allen), but even he will retreat to booze when he discovers how much of a joke he has become as a washed-up actor.

Their lives take a surprising turn when they are approached by actual aliens that have watched the Galaxy Quest program more as a historical documentation than a fictional TV series. Not only have they decided to recruit the original cast to help them fight the evil forces of Mathesar, but they have designed a starship to look and operate exactly as it did on the show. This includes everything from the voice-activated computer systems to the deathtrap of an engine room with clanging, clapping and crushing metal; *"Whoever wrote this episode should DIE."*

Nearly every sci-fi cliche is satirized for a collective of actors that have a tough time adjusting to a world made for their characters. Guy (Sam Rockwell) is exceptionally nervous as the unnamed character of the show that was killed off in one episode he appeared. When assured by his fellow actors that he's not so disposable, he argues that nobody even remembers the name of his character.

Fred (Tony Shalhoub) is such a burnout of an actor that he passively and amusingly accepts whatever convoluted technobabble the aliens tell him about the ship's engineering. Tommy (Daryl Mitchell), who was the child navigator of the starship, finds himself struggling to pilot the massive ship for a role of his childhood that mostly involved him pushing levers forward. And in one of his earliest parts, a young Justin Long plays an obsessed fan that attempts to help the crew over the phone with his sci-fi knowledge, only for his mother to holler at him to take out the garbage.

Galaxy Quest eventually settles into a standard sci-fi plot of starship chases and explosions, but has plenty of fun along the way, thanks to a knowing and committed cast. It's hard not to laugh at Rickman's desire for an onboard pub and hearing Weaver voice her frustrations for repeating whatever the ship computer says; *"That's my one job on the show!"* For its comedic brilliance, it has rightly been deemed as worthy as *Star Trek* for both the acclaim of accolades (winning the same Hugo award *Star Trek* once won) and praise of Trekkies. Whereas the *Trek* movies and TV series continued with their typical cliches, *Quest* had enough smarts to laugh at the cardboard sets while still admiring the genre it's mocking. And much like the *Star Trek* crew, this ensemble is very much a family, albeit one that spends more time bickering about their egos than trying to solve diplomatic issues.

GATTACA

DIRECTOR: Andrew Niccol | SCREENWRITER: Andrew Niccol | CAST: Ethan Hawke, Uma Thurman, Alan Arkin, Jude Law, Loren Dean, Ernest Borgnine | GENRE: Science Fiction | RUNNING TIME: 106 min | MPAA RATING: PG-13

CLASSIFICATION: WEIRD

The future of *Gattaca* (1997) is all about genetic engineering. If you were born from selected genes in a lab, you're labeled as a Valid. If you weren't, you're an In-Valid. The In-Valids are not illegal or exterminated, but it's discouraged as those naturally born are not going to get very far in this brave new society. Valids are more likely to be employed in higher-paying careers while In-Valids are relegated to lesser jobs.

Vincent (Ethan Hawke) is an in-valid and has been diagnosed with disorders that only give him about 30 years to live. His menial job is that of a janitor for a space center, but doesn't accept that he'll die at this job. He dreams of being an astronaut on a mission to one of Saturn's moons. The only way to make it as an astronaut is if you have the right genes. Since this is a future world where genetics is everything, black market DNA brokers exist. And broker German (Tony Shalhoub) knows just the supplier of genes, for a percentage of the profits Vincent will make at his new job, of course.

Vincent strikes up a deal with Jerome (Jude Law), a man who can provide everything an In-Valid would need to pursue the career of their dreams. Every aspect of becoming a valid is covered, from blood to urine to a brand new identity. The identity is Jerome's, as he has the right genes, but still ended up paralyzed and crushed that his career was over too soon. As long as Vincent can pass the daily scans of his work environment, then he, or rather Jerome, will be able to travel the stars. He takes a job as a computer programmer and works his way up, doing his best to conceal his true identity from the nosey Detective Hugo (Alan Arkin) and anyone else who wants to turn him in.

Andrew Niccol, making his feature debut as both writer and director, crafts a remarkable sci-fi world that is cold, calculated and believable. As Vincent narrates the beginning of the picture, we see how his birth went down. Before the baby could even be given to his mother, the doctors have already taken a blood sample and determined his disorders and future time of death. That's quite the excess of next information for new parents to take in. Vincent's office environment features endless rows of computer desks, orderly arranged so that the small workspaces are close to each other in a room that is large enough for echoes. Niccol never overdoes his picture by doing away with typical sci-fi trimmings of flying cars and holograms.

The casting is terrific for such a high-concept picture. Hawke and Law have some great chemistry between the two of them; Hawke is eager to achieve his dream while Law has grown bitter and snarky about losing his shot at space flight. There's a tension between them, but also need to work together for both sticking it to the culture and risking their lives. Uma Thurman does a great job as the love interest of Irene, a co-worker of Vincent who is a Valid, but still not a suitable candidate to go into space. Loren Dean plays Vincent's brother Anton, a Valid that soon closes in on Vincent's scheme and is conflicted about what he discovers.

For the big ideas of *Gattaca* on the subject of genes, it took on considerable interest from the scientific community. Molecular biologist Lee M. Silver of the Nature Genetics journal labeled sci-fi production as a film *"that all geneticists should see if for no other reason than to understand the perception of our trade held by so many of the public-at-large."* Bioethicist James Hughes scrutinized the film for its embellishments on science, arguing that screening of genes is acceptable, real and should be better governed for protecting against genotype discrimination. The film's more significant questions were enough to warrant a viewing in my junior high science class, making me all the more intrigued in biology and a little fearful of the day when every perfect body comes manufactured. It'd be nice to live in a world where our children are given the best genes to live the longest lives, but not preferable if they have to live in a world like *Gattaca*.

GETTING AWAY WITH MURDER

DIRECTOR: Harvey Miller | SCREENWRITER: Harvey Miller | CAST: Dan Aykroyd, Lily Tomlin, Jack Lemmon, Bonnie Hunt, Brian Kerwin | GENRE: Comedy | RUNNING TIME: 92 min | MPAA RATING: R

CLASSIFICATION: WORST

Some screenplays just go so far into messy and amoral content that they are beyond repair. I doubt even the most capable of directors or actors could salvage much from the ill-thought premise of *Getting Away with Murder* (1996). Try as they might, the combined forces of Dan Aykroyd, Lily Tomlin, Jack Lemmon and Bonnie Hunt cannot revive this dead-on-delivery script involving Nazis, murder, and immorality that stretches the definition of a dark comedy.

Jack Lemmon plays Max Mueller, a suburban homeowner suspected of being a Nazi war criminal that was thought to be sentenced to death. The local news covers this story, putting the heat on Mueller and forcing him to make the tough decision of fleeing to South America. But for his neighbor Jack (Aykroyd), this cannot stand. His conscience tells him that he can't let Mueller escape the country without paying for his crimes. What his conscience doesn't tell him is that it might not be a good idea to poison a man you think MIGHT be a Nazi.

True to its title, Jack gets away with murdering his neighbor via poison and the police rule the death as a suicide. The movie is over, right? Not quite. Jack is now angered that he has not been given credit for his work and decides to tip the police off that Max's death was a result of murder by sending them cryptic messages. Going one step further in his insanity, Jack decides to divorce his fiancee (Bonnie Hunt) and marries Max's daughter Inga (Lily Tomlin). All the while Jack feels guilty, but not really, about murdering someone who might not have been a Nazi, but not really.

Outside of being a horrible story, the movie not only isn't funny, but doesn't seem to find much of anything funny for the characters to do. Feeling guilty for murdering Max, Jack seeks therapy and grapples with his guilt with funny lines that fall short of a laugh (*"I'd kill myself, but that would only continue the cycle of violence"*). There's nothing all that funny about the murder itself, nor the confusing and misguided aftermath of Jack's terrible decisions. Squint and you'll see this picture as a dour thriller as if the studio executives decided at the last minute to rewrite this movie to be a different genre. They probably figured hiring funny people could transform this glib tale into a wacky comedy.

It's impressive that such a talented collective could churn out something so despicably awful. Harvey Miller of *Private Benjamin* fame was an accomplished enough screenwriter and director that it's depressing to realize this would be his final picture. Producer Penny Marshall of *A League of Their Own* fame usually backed smart and sweet comedies that it's surreal to see her name attached. The casting is a mess; Dan Aykroyd doesn't quite fit the bill as the nervous killer next door, and the pleasant Jack Lemmon feels miscast in a role where he can't handle a German accent, let alone put on the appearance of a Nazi.

Getting Away With Murder got away with brutalizing its comedy, its potential and our time.

GHOST

DIRECTOR: Jerry Zucker | SCREENWRITER: Bruce Joel Rubin | CAST: Patrick Swayze, Demi Moore, Whoopi Goldberg, Tony Goldwyn | GENRE: Drama | RUNNING TIME: 128 min | MPAA RATING: PG-13

CLASSIFICATION: WEIRD

It's a little strange to think that *Ghost* (1990) is considered a steamy romantic drama among Swayze-Crazy women for a film about the paranormal with a twisty plot of accounting that leads to murders most foul. Of course, most people don't remember much of the story. They do vividly recall the scene where Patrick Swayze and Demi Moore makeout over a pottery wheel to the tune of The Righteous Brothers' "Unchained Melody." You'll never hear that song or look at clay the same way again.

Despite Swayze's character dying about a quarter into the movie, the film does its best to weave some romance and drama out of the recently deceased Sam Wheat. It's no mere coincidence that Sam was murdered by a mugger during his investigation of accounting fraud. Unbelievably, the mugger is connected with the evil Carl (Tony Goldwyn), a co-worker of Sam involved with laundering money. Even worse, Carl is currently dating Sam's girlfriend Molly (Demi Moore) and using her to get to more of Sam's money before killing her. Sam has got to do something and needs to figure out his ghost powers quick before Molly joins him in the next realm. Wait, would that be so bad? Nah, Sam doesn't seem that twisted. Plus, Molly would probably break up with him if he intentionally let her die.

A few ghost rules are established. Sam can speak to cats, pass through matter and move objects if he can concentrate hard enough. Some of these features are discovered early in the hospital scene where Sam accidentally walks through one of the doctors, viewing all of the blood and organs as he passes through in the film's single most shocking and grotesque moment. Other rules are divulged by a scary ghost hobo that dwells in the city subways, played by a booming Vincent Schiavelli. He reveals that the art of moving objects as a ghost requires harnessing all your emotions or something like that. He never quite explains how he's able to ride the subway trains without going through them. That feature must come standard for all ghosts.

Sam can only verbally communicate with the mortal world

through Oda Mae Brown (Whoopi Goldberg), a psychic huckster that is more than a little spooked to discover she can speak with the dead. She cannot see Sam, but hears him perfectly and has some difficulties adjusting to being genuinely saddled as a communicator of ghosts. Goldberg plays this role with the right amount of frustration and perplection. When the paranormal word gets out that she can speak with the dead, all of the New York City ghosts converge on her place of business to try to talk to their living families. I always smile with how frantic she is in this scene, especially when it's discovered ghosts can possess her, and she orders everyone out of both her office and her body. For her performance, Goldberg would win an Academy Award, filed under the "They Won For That!?" category of Oscar wins.

There's one moment that feels like a missed opportunity for playing with the Goldberg character. Swayze wants to feel the touch of Moore one last time and does so by possessing Goldberg's body. This scene plays out in the minds of Moore and Swayze, so we don't see what's happening with Moore and Goldberg as they embrace. Can you imagine how much more provocative and unique it would have been to have a makeout scene between Moore and Goldberg?

Ghost was a rare success of a film for both its box office and accolades. The worldwide gross was a massive $505,000,000, a surprisingly large return on a $22 million budget. In addition to Whoopi winning the Academy Award for Best Supporting Actress, the film also won the award for Best Original Screenplay, in addition to being nominated for Best Picture. It was a big surprise from the new screenwriter Bruce Joel Rubin and comedy director Jerry Zucker (*Airplane!*). While I wouldn't consider the film Best Picture material, it at least has enough playful ideas for bringing humor, romance and darkness to a movie that could have been a bore of a ghost story. The combined talents of Swayze, Moore and Goldberg help elevate a rather silly picture with random demon spirits, an action-packed climax that becomes incredibly violent out of nowhere, a convoluted accounting plot that's not very interesting and a scene where clay is an aphrodisiac. There's enough here to make me a believer (of the story, of course).

GHOST DAD

DIRECTOR: Sidney Poitier | SCREENWRITER: Brent Maddock, S. S. Wilson, Chris Reese | CAST: Bill Cosby, Kimberly Russell, Denise Nicholas, Ian Bannen | GENRE: Comedy | RUNNING TIME: 83 min | MPAA RATING: PG

CLASSIFICATION: WORST

Bill Cosby's days of leading a motion picture didn't just stop with *Ghost Dad* (1990), but came to an apocalyptic crash. His movie career was already going down in flames with the horrendous bomb *Leonard Part 6*, a picture so awful that even Cosby denounced the film while it was being released. *Ghost Dad* wasn't just the final nail in his coffin as a movie star; it was a 16-ton weight dropped from above that crushed his leading man roles instantly.

Cosby slips into the all-too-familiar role of a father. He has three kids, no wife and a busy schedule that prevents him from being home with his children. Bedtime stories are tape recorded and birthdays come with last-minute gifts. If he can finally land that big promotion at work, all of his neglect will have been worth it, but he, unfortunately, dies the day before he acquires his new benefits.

Does that sound tragic? It would be if not for the awkward method of direction where the film leans more towards a sitcom of My Father The Ghost. Cosby meets his end by falling off a bridge, thanks to a Satan-worshipping cab driver that freaks out and leaves him to die. He later discovers he's a ghost when a cop inadvertently urinates on him, and a bus passes through his body where he can see an old woman's underwear.

The logic of Bill Cosby as a ghost is bafflingly confusing. In his spiritual form, he still appears bound by gravity, but can fall through floors and pass through walls. His soul is somehow temporarily transported to London where some crazed paranormal researcher informs that Cosby has until Thursday before he crosses over. Ghosts can apparently be seen in the darkness, but not when the lights are turned on. They cannot form coherent sentences when they first leave their body and have to learn how to speak correctly. All of this does little more than provide a platform for the cheap special effects to do their stuff and Cosby to perform his usual comic antics with much less to work with.

Before Cosby crosses over into the afterlife, he has to complete a corporate merger and pass a physical to ensure he can take advantage of the insurance policy for his children after he passes. In between this rush for securing his family's future, he has plenty of time to become involved with family hijinks. He uses his invisible powers to make his son float for a magic show in his classroom. He disapproves of his teenage daughter's abusive boyfriend and decides to attack him by physically strangling him through the phone, which ghosts can apparently do. Even when an executive committee comes banging on his door demanding to see him, he still makes time to run next door and pester his attractive female neighbor for ghost sex. There's no tone or stakes to any of this idiocy, thanks to the convoluted logic of its story and Cosby's indecipherable actions.

What's most depressing about *Ghost Dad* is how it brought the careers of Bill Cosby and Sidney Poitier, both having worked together on movies for years, to a bitter end. Cosby would no longer star as a leading actor and Poitier would never direct again. It's sad to see them go out on such a horrific misfire of comedy, but perhaps it's better that they stopped before they concocted something far worse. The best that can be said about the movie is that its abysmal failure prevented Cosby from rushing into leading another picture where he must hopelessly flail and blubber his way through ill-thought scripts, hoping some funny voice or face will register a laugh. The most famous TV dad of the 20th century deserved better than *Ghost Dad*.

GHOST IN THE SHELL

DIRECTOR: Mamoru Oshii | SCREENWRITER: Kazunori Itō | CAST: Atsuko Tanaka, Akio Ōtsuka, Iemasa Kayumi | GENRE: Science Fiction (Animated) | RUNNING TIME: 82 min | MPAA RATING: R

CLASSIFICATION: BEST

Japanese animation was perhaps at its grandest height of intelligence with the deeply conceived world of *Ghost in the Shell* (1995). It depicts a future where cybernetics has advanced to a point where every body part can be replaced from arms to eyeballs. Brains are now equipped with implants that allow people to access networks and electronically speak to others with a mere thought. Such reliance on technology naturally leads to hackers becoming a significant threat when they can hack into your mind and alter your vision, actions, and memories. That is where the Japanese security division of Section 9 comes into play as the cyber tactical team that has the smarts to find hackers and the firepower to take them down.

The leader of this unit is Major Motoko Kusanagi, a rarity of a cyborg as her entire body has been artificial since she was a child. She naturally questions her individuality when so much of what made her human is gone. In the opening shots of her mission atop a skyscraper, she removes her clothing to reveal her naked body. Her nipples have no areolas and her genitals no presentation. There's no need for them with a cybernetic organism that cannot have babies, but then why even have breasts at all? Motoko is under a constant quandary if she is a woman or just pretending to be one with what's left of her soul, locked up in a synthetic casing.

Her team has her hands full with a case of the mysterious hacker known as The Puppet Master. They uncover many clues about the whereabouts of this figure, one of which is a sanitation worker that has his mind tampered with to believe he has an ex-wife and daughter. His old memories gone, he is shaken to discover the photo he had of his little girl was a picture of his dog. In the same way that flesh has become easily manufactured, memories also become a lost piece of humanity.

When Section 9 finally captures The Puppet Master, they are surprised to discover it is not a human hacker or a hacker-created virus. It is instead a living being that was born from within cyberspace, composed entirely of data and not an artificial intelligence. The goal for The Puppet Master is to procreate his new species. He does not want to copy himself, but merge himself into a human body and prolong his race. He is the new species that has evolved from this cybernetic future and wants to start the movement towards a shift in human evolution.

The film is a mesmerizing mixture of philosophical ideas and stylish sci-fi action. There are scenes where the characters will indulge in long passages about what it means to be human and how technology has redefined identity. These somewhat static shots are thankfully balanced with some fantastic chases and battles. There are some unforgettable scenes where Motoko tracks a criminal down a watery alley, pummeling him while she conceals herself in thermo-optical camouflage that turns her invisible. Another intense scene features Motoko taking on a spider-like tank that unloads machine guns on her inside a museum.

Director Mamoru Oshii has delivered an intelligent and engaging animated adaptation of the comic book by Masamune Shirow. It is still Shirow's material, but seen through Oshii's unique eyes that can spot more prominent themes to explore. The animation, much like the story's setting, was very far ahead of its time with a combination of computer graphics and cel animation that merged digitally. The music by Kenji Kawai is some of his most notable work for its opening theme of a haunting choir and big drums.

Ghost in the Shell is not straightforward science fiction. It is complicated, intelligent and thoughtful with its strong themes of cybernetics and loss of individuality that Oshii refuses to boil down or skip over. But it's also an excellent atmosphere lofty ideas that always keep the eyes and mind active. So grand is the world of *Ghost in the Shell* that Oshii would return for a 2004 sequel and the franchise would branch off into animated spin-off TV series, TV movies, and direct-to-video movies. It's a technological can of worms that Shirow opened with his comic book and Oshii's film happens to be the most ambitious and intriguing animated interpretation of the lot.

GHOSTS CAN'T DO IT

DIRECTOR: John Derek | SCREENWRITER: John Derek | CAST: Bo Derek, Anthony Quinn, Don Murray | GENRE: Comedy | RUNNING TIME: 90 min | MPAA RATING: R

CLASSIFICATION: WORST

While *Ghost* tried to weave a capable romantic drama around the paranormal, *Ghosts Can't Do It* (1990) took a much creepier route with its themes of love after death. Most films about ghosts feature them coming back for some tasks that must be resolved. In the case of the elderly Scott, he returns for one specific purpose: Sex. How romantic.

Anthony Quinn plays Scott, the old and ill husband of Katie (Bo Derek). Their age gap of thirty years makes their relationship creepy, especially when you consider that Bo Derek is married to the director John Derek, roughly thirty years older than she is. Scott has a heart attack and is informed by the doctors that he can no longer have sex. Well, surely there is more to the age-defying relationship of Scott and Katie than physical acts of love, right? Nope, it's only about sex. Since Scott can't get a heart transplant and can no longer get frisky, he decides to blow his brains out with a shotgun.

Scott then returns to Katie as a ghost, but is apparently only seen in shots where it looks like he's standing in front of a black background with a horrible filter on the camera that makes him look like he's underwater. The only problem is that Scott can't have sex with Katie as a ghost. The solution: Find someone's hunky body that Scott can possess so he can have sex with his younger wife again. I'm sorry, did I write possess? I meant, KILL some hunk so that Scott can take over his body. Oh, and she also has to go to Hong Kong to save Scott's business. This woman puts up with an awful lot for her dead husband. I guess love knows no boundaries of reality, sanity or logic.

The majority of the film wavers between laughably bad decisions and off moments of so-called romance. The erotic tension between Bo Derek and Anthony Quinn is gross at times, as in a makeout scene where she sucks at his bottom lip. There must have been an awkwardness in the air for such a relationship as Bo comes off very stiff and not as committed to the material. Director John Derek tries to get his wife as naked and wet as possible in hopes that you'll forget all about her horrendous acting. It's bad enough that the script has her openly talk to the ghost of her husband and openly admits this to everyone around her, but even worse when coming out of Bo Derek's mouth. Also serving as a distraction from her lousy acting is her array of various hats, most of them appearing as some furry creature from another planet that died on her head.

The film swept the Golden Raspberry Awards, winning Worst Picture (tying with *The Adventures of Ford Fairlane*), Worst Actress (Bo Derek) and Worst Supporting Actor for Donald Trump's cameo as himself, which the closing credits proudly boast "And Yes, That Really Was Donald J. Trump". It was initially released on Australian home video in 1989, but for some reason received a theatrical release in America in 1990. The only good that came of the film was that it brought the directing days of John Derek to an end after a string of terrible pictures featuring his wife. It also stressed the point that not only can ghosts not have sex, but they shouldn't either if it takes this much effort and confusion. And it's unbelievably creepy to imagine that this might've been John Derek's sinister plan after death to continue screwing his wife. Now there is a horror movie.

GLENGARRY GLEN ROSS

DIRECTOR: James Foley | SCREENWRITER: David Mamet | CAST: Al Pacino, Jack Lemmon, Alec Baldwin, Ed Harris, Alan Arkin, Kevin Spacey, Jonathan Pryce | GENRE: Drama | RUNNING TIME: 100 min | MPAA RATING: R

CLASSIFICATION: BEST

David Mamet proves he's a masterful screenwriter by evoking snappy dialogue and gripping drama from the most unlikely of locations: a drab real estate office. Occupying this space are men desperately trying to sell the undesirable property, pulling tactics over the phone of sounding like they have secretaries and busy schedules. In actuality, they are hardly selling a thing and close to being fired.

In walks the hotshot talker Blake (Alec Baldwin), sent from downtown to light a fire under the asses of the men who can't sell. Baldwin delivers his most exceptional performance as a fierce motivator more threatening than inspiring. He makes his insulting intentions quite clear as that of a contest for the sellers. First prize winner receives a Cadillac, the second a set of steak knives and the third is fired.

The salesmen under such pressure include a host of strong talents, from a loudly smug Al Pacino to a quietly scathing Alan Arkin. Pacino's scenes in particular, as the closer salesman Ricky Roma, are a marvel for the actor at his finest, trying to sound like the most intelligent and condescending voice in the room. He's also a masterful negotiator when trying to convince a potential customer (Jonathan Pryce) so well that he can sense and take advantage of his sexuality. He's not messing around here. He wants that Cadillac and will call his competition every nasty word in the big book of expletives as he furiously marches towards his next sale. Alan Arkin and Ed Harris, as salesmen George and Dave, have some great scenes as they secretly conspire to tip the odds in their favor. They know that the office manager John (Kevin Spacey) has hot leads locked away in his office. If they could steal that list of prominent clients, they wouldn't have to worry about coming in third.

But it's Jack Lemmon who steals the show as the sympathetic Shelly. Once a top salesman, he has grown old, and his burdens are high. His sales numbers are too low, his wife is in the hospital, and his techniques are failing. He visits the home of what he believes is a potential client, only to be shot down as he practically begs for a sale with a smile that is fading fast. There was once a fire in his belly, and he's so desperate to get it back that he'll steal leads away from another salesman if he has to. His desperation drives him slowly mad and makes him an easy target for the more cutthroat employees.

Lemmon's exchanges with Spacey, in particular, keeps building with contempt and anxiety. Lemmon tries to buy leads off Spacey, but he refuses. They will later discuss Lemmon cheating that grows more intense until the rawest elements of their characters are laid bare when Spacey decides to destroy Lemmon's career.

Jack Lemmon: Why?
Kevin Spacey: Because I don't like you.
Jack Lemmon: ...My daughter.
Kevin Spacey: Fuck you.

Director James Foley does an exceptional job with making Mamet's dialogue feel real and involving, thanks to weeks of rehearsals to the point where the actors nearly understood every bit of salesman lingo. This created a flawless energy with great actors showcasing their best of abilities with scenes that are written for their strongest of talents. Pacino always feels big, Spacey ever in control, Lemmon always sad and Arkin and Harris ever thinking. It is a tremendously engrossing film where deals are made, dreams are broken, egos explode and rain is always in the forecast.

THE GODFATHER: PART III

DIRECTOR: Francis Ford Coppola | SCREENWRITER: Mario Puzo, Francis Ford Coppola | CAST: Al Pacino, Diane Keaton, Talia Shire, Andy García, Eli Wallach, Joe Mantegna, Bridget Fonda, George Hamilton, Sofia Coppola | GENRE: Drama | RUNNING TIME: 162 min | MPAA RATING: R

CLASSIFICATION: WEIRD

The Godfather is considered one of the best mafia movies ever made and its follow-up *The Godfather: Part II* was a worthy successor. *The Godfather: Part III* (1990), on the other hand, arrives too late for being over a decade after the last picture and with too little to showcase. The previous films had a genuine story to tell of the Corleone family legacy of crime that felt complete, but this final entry of the trilogy comes as such an afterthought it may as well have been called The Godfather: The Next Generation.

The film continues the tale of the Corleone family in 1979, struggling to ease their way out of the world of crime. Michael Corleone (Al Pacino) is now an older man with a slower walk, a diabetic condition and a fervent desire to position his family out of the dirty business. He would like to turn it over to Joey Zasa (Joe Mantegna), but he knows he can't trust him. He wants the best for his children, but knows that he cannot protect them forever. Michael can sense his final days upon him and would rather spend it doing something more besides the tempting leadership position of running the mafia.

What's tougher for Michael than leaving behind the crime business is his struggle to absolve himself of his sins. Can he? Something as massive as ordering the death of his brother Fredo doesn't wash off the soul so quickly. Michael struggles to give his kids a better life by insisting that his son Anthony finish law school and that his innocent daughter Mary. He would instead they not turn out like Sonny's son Vincent (Andy Garcia), a hot-headed man with a violent solution to every problem. Vincent's first meeting results in him biting off someone's ear, much to the chagrin of the weary Michael.

The most apparent black eye on this production was placing an unhealthy focus on the character of Mary. Initially, the role was supposed to go to Winona Ryder, but she fell ill as production was about to begin. In her place, director Francis Ford Coppola recast the role for his daughter, Sofia. This would appear to be fitting casting as Sophia's previous role in *The Godfather* series was playing an infant, but it was the biggest mistake of the movie. Her performance was so terrible that when the film was screened for Oscar voters at the Paramount lot, the usually refined audience cheered as Sofia's character suffers a laughably lousy death, her final word of "dad" sounding more like an afterthought for how casually she speaks after being shot in the chest.

The good news is that the rest of the cast holds up remarkably well. Pacino is in top form as Michael, despite playing a much different version of the character. Joe Mantegna slides perfectly into the role of a mafia man that he became a familiar figure throughout the 1990s as such. Diane Keaton does a brilliant job as Michael's wife Kay, observant and intelligent enough to know that Michael's struggle to resist the crime world is foolish, as she knows who her husband is.

Even for being the weakest of the *Godfather* trilogy and featuring the single worst performance in all three pictures, *Part III* does remain true enough to its roots to not feel entirely out of place. There is still plenty of alliances made, hearts broken, throats slit and shadowy deals behind closed doors. It's a film that struggles to distance itself from the previous entries by asking if a man can change in his twilight years and if the future is indeed doomed to repeat itself. For that, the film is a suitable end for the legacy of the Corleone family. Just skip past the scenes with Sofia Coppola.

GODZILLA

DIRECTOR: Roland Emmerich | SCREENWRITER: Dean Devlin, Roland Emmerich | CAST: Jean Reno, Matthew Broderick, Maria Pitillo, Hank Azaria, Michael Lerner, Harry Shearer | GENRE: Science Fiction | RUNNING TIME: 139 min | MPAA RATING: PG-13

CLASSIFICATION: WORST

The *Godzilla* franchise always had a certain allure for featuring a giant monster portrayed by a man in a rubber suit, stomping around a set of flimsy city miniatures. Aside from the 1954 original, the movies were more of a fun wrestling match to see who Godzilla would fight next, from King Kong to King Ghidorah. With his multitude of sequels and spin-offs, Godzilla is the most iconic monster of Japanese cinema.

But for Godzilla's first American-made adaptation in 1998, all the charm had been drained from what made the monster romp fun. Gone was the rubber suit, replaced by an expensive computer-animated model that seems to borrow more from a T-Rex than the original Godzilla design, looking as though he has back problems. Very few shots of Godzilla are full ones, mostly showcasing his giant feet as he stomps through the city, and for good reason when his mediocre design is finally displayed. One would have to squint and turn their head before even considering this creature to be Godzilla.

As is the tradition of the *Godzilla* series, every human character is entirely uninteresting. All of them are desperately cracking one-liners to stand out, despite the threat of a giant monster ripping New York City to shreds. But is he? Most of Godzilla's destruction appears to be minimal based on his resume. He steps through a few structures, lays some eggs in Madison Square Garden and makes a hole here and there as he bobs and weaves between buildings. He appears more like a rat in a maze than a giant monster taking over a city. Perhaps he should have started small in New England.

In the scenes that don't feature Godzilla, the audience is treated to characters that do little more than talk about the titular monster. Matthew Broderick plays a biologist that studies Godzilla, discovering that it can asexually reproduce and is pregnant. Jean Reno plays a French spy bent on covering up his government's involvement in the creation of the creature. Maria Pitillo plays a journalist that discovers secret information about Godzilla. There are other actors as well, including *The Simpsons* voice actors Hank Azaria and Harry Shearer, but they only serve the purpose of either running around Godzilla's feet or talking about him from afar.

The military fires weapons at the monster, but do little damage. Or at least they shouldn't have done as much damage as they do in this film. The military defeats Godzilla by shooting him off a bridge. He is not killed with a special oxygen bomb or some other giant monster, but good old-fashioned American artillery. Either this Godzilla was too weak, or the Japanese military just wasn't firing the right ammunition.

Director Roland Emmerich, known at the time for the blockbuster of *Independence Day*, paints this picture with his brand of embarrassing comedy. As revenge against the critics that badmouthed his movies, the inept New York City mayor and his assistant are modeled as parodies of critics Roger Ebert and Gene Siskel. When Siskel and Ebert reviewed the film, they found the insertion petty and also a wasted opportunity in that Godzilla never ate or squashed them. Even Emmerich's satirical edge is laughably awful.

Despite an astounding budget, it's incredible how much the movie doesn't show us. We cannot watch a panicking crowd loot the stores of New York City, as Harry Shearer has to tell us about this over the radio. We don't see Godzilla smash a hole through a skyscraper, only witnessing the aftermath of his path of destruction. For a director who loves to make things blow up, Emmerich sure doesn't showcase any memorable moments, almost as if he's ashamed to be making a *Godzilla* movie. It indeed becomes evident in how Godzilla's trademark move of atomic breath was substituted for "power breath" in which he can blow a harsh wind.

In an attempt to move past this misfire, Toho Studios quickly produced *Godzilla 2000* (1999) to remind everyone of what an actual *Godzilla* movie looks like. And just to make sure this horrid American version of Godzilla would never return, Toho killed him off in *Godzilla: Final Wars* (2004), in which the American CGI Godzilla appears for only a few seconds before the original rubber-suit Japanese Godzilla obliterates him with atomic breath. Long live the rubber-suited Godzilla!

GODZILLA VS. DESTOROYAH

DIRECTOR: Takao Okawara | SCREENWRITER: Kazuki Omori | CAST: Takuro Tatsumi, Yōko Ishino, Yasufumi Hayashi, Sayaka Osawa, Megumi Odaka, Masahiro Takashima | GENRE: Science Fiction | RUNNING TIME: 95 min | MPAA RATING: Not Rated

CLASSIFICATION: WEIRD

Godzilla is not himself in *Godzilla vs. Destoroyah* (1995). He has destroyed the island on which he resides, broken out in rashes of lava all over his body and his nuclear reactor of a heart is experiencing a meltdown. He is dying and decides to go on one last city-destroying rampage before heading off to that big monster island in the sky.

Godzilla's opponent for his twilight days is the creature Destoroyah, born from the Oxygen Destroyer that once killed the king of the monsters, that awakens in its first stage as an army of crab people. This finally gives the human characters a small enough opponent to fight in these movies where they're usually being squashed under the feet of giant monsters. Now they were being savaged by goofy-looking crab people. I suppose that's progress. The crabs eventually combine to form the giant monster of Destoroyah, and it's a sight to behold. He's a massive horned beast that towers over Godzilla, appearing as a demon straight out of hell to escort the monster king to the underworld.

This is easily the most somber of *Godzilla* pictures for effectively making the audience feel something for a monster that consistently demolished Japan. His son, Junior, has now grown from the ugly little beast of Son of Godzilla to the fully developed creature that looks like a chip off the old block. But when the father can't revive his son after he is brutalized by Destoroyah, Godzilla is filled with great grief and rage. I never thought I'd see a Godzilla capable of such emotion, but here it is, and it's surprisingly moving.

The human forces are little more useful and exciting for this *Godzilla* movie. The Japanese military has sound weaponry and strategy to quell Godzilla's meltdown to at least protect the planet if they can't entirely save Tokyo. Masahiro Takashima returns from the previous Godzilla film as Lt. Sho Kuroki, bring both consistency and character to scenes where people stand around talking about the monster or reacting to his destruction. There is also a great cameo with Momoko Kôchi reprising her role of Emiko from the 1954 original film.

There were a lot of ideas for Godzilla's proposed final film in both the conception and marketing. An initial plan featured the current 90s iteration of Godzilla battling the ghost of the 1954 original version, a premise that was pitched as *Godzilla vs. Godzilla*. Godzilla had become such an icon that the Toho studio came up with a brilliant promotion of postcards with the large text "Godzilla dies." A bronze statue of Godzilla was erected a few days before the film's release and would be showered with coins and tobacco by fans to commemorate the monster's death.

There was no doubt that this wasn't going to be the final *Godzilla* film, but *Godzilla vs. Destoroyah* does a fantastic job making us believe it was the last stand of Japan's most celebrated monster. His death caused such a reaction in Japan that fans angrily demanded he be resurrected. And considering the hack job Roland Emmerich would do on the first American-made *Godzilla* movie from 1998, Toho was quick to produce their next *Godzilla* film ahead of schedule.

GOOD BURGER

DIRECTOR: Brian Robbins | SCREENWRITER: Dan Schneider, Kevin Kopelow, Heath Seifert | CAST: Kel Mitchell, Kenan Thompson, Abe Vigoda | GENRE: Comedy | RUNNING TIME: 95 min | MPAA RATING: PG

CLASSIFICATION: WEIRD

As movies based on *Saturday Night Live* skits were becoming prominent in the 1990s, the Nickelodeon studio decided to follow the trend. Based on a skit from the network's comedy series *All That*, *Good Burger* (1997) follows the innocently idiotic burger shop employee of Ed, played with wide-eyed enthusiasm from Kel Mitchell. His head is so far in the clouds that his aspirations have been cheerfully met as a full-time employee at the Good Burger restaurant. Unable to take even the most simplistic of orders, he's somehow managed to maintain his job that he holds so dear. I doubt he could survive at any other position with both his idiocy and sincerity.

Ed finds kinship in Dexter (Kenan Thompson), an unlucky high school student who takes a summer job at Good Burger to pay off a car accident. But he may not have this post for long as some competition has moved in across the street. The new Mondo Burger establishment aims to make burgers that are more massive, bent on directly crushing Good Burger. The only hope for the lowly Good Burger is Ed's secret sauce mixture that Dexter profits from promoting, and Mondo Burger aims to procure. In between flipping burgers, Dexter and Ed still find time to have dates and discover Mondo's hideous experiment of creating bigger burgers.

Most of the movie's humor derives from how Ed is unable to communicate or understand the world around him. The evil Mondo Burger manager Kurt issues a threat towards Ed for him to watch his butt, causing Ed to spin in a circle to observe his behind. He's unable to read basic emotions, turning tender moments into silly ones *("I don't remember what my dad looks like either, but at least I get to see him every day")*. Even something as simple as waking to an alarm clock brings about enthused bemusement *("Whoa! A clock!")*. It's juvenile humor, bordering on questioning if Ed has autism, but Dexter's straight-man reactions even out most of his stupidity.

Physical gags also play a substantial role in the comedy. The opening sequence features Ed rushing to work on the street in which he is nearly hit by a car, accidentally abducts a baby and disrupts a basketball game by switching the ball out for the baby. Dexter and Ed later go in lousy drag to infiltrate Mondo Burger, leading to much overacting with Kenan and Kel's best (or worst) female voices. And since Mondo Burger is experimenting with making meat bigger, you can bet there will be plenty of messy explosions. It just wouldn't be a 1990s Nickelodeon production if someone wasn't covered in something slimy.

Among the many odd choices the movie makes is how it uses its guest stars. Sinbad plays Dexter's teacher as a man stuck in the 1970s with his big hair, dated clothing, and an attention span easily distracted by being compared to Shaft. Abe Vigoda acts like the oldest employee of Good Burger, hobbling around the kitchen with an always weary expression, occasionally helping the protagonists when he's not dozing off or using an oxygen tank. George Clinton pops up as a mental patient who starts up a dance number in a mental institution, fittingly singing the song "Do Fries Come With That Shake?". Carmen Electra acts as a henchman hired by Mondo Burger to seduce a sexually dubious Ed into revealing his secret formula. Does Ed even know about sex? The only celebrity that appears as himself is Shaquille O'Neal; he orders Good Burger after a game so Kenan Thompson and Kel Mitchell can rush to his side and fawn over the basketball legend.

Good Burger could have easily just been another forgettable kids movie of the 1990s, but it's too iconic and quotable for youth comedy of the era to ignore. There's a wealth of silly performances, some great music, a genuinely good heart and a plot so ludicrous that it's surprisingly funny for its audacity. If it were a fast-food item, *Good Burger* would be a half-pound of cheese on a sesame bun. And sometimes you're just in the mood for a half-pound of cheese; it's not good for you, but damned if it isn't delicious.

THE GOOD SON

DIRECTOR: Joseph Ruben | SCREENWRITER: Ian McEwan | CAST: Macaulay Culkin, Elijah Wood, Wendy Crewson, David Morse, Jacqueline Brookes | GENRE: Drama | RUNNING TIME: 87 min | MPAA RATING: R

CLASSIFICATION: WORST

Macaulay Culkin was such a sweet little boy in the *Home Alone* movies that it's bizarre to think he'd follow up such films with *The Good Son* (1993). The little boy had gone from a cute kid turned home defender to an evil child turned murderer. Culkin's father fought for this role, reasoning that it would be a chance to display that Macaulay could play more than just a cute kid. To be fair, he didn't play many cute kids after this role or any role for that matter.

To enjoy such a picture requires one to divorce themselves from the fact that young children are the key players in a rather dark thriller. Mark (Elijah Wood) has just experienced the death of his mother, and his life is about to get worse when he meets his evil cousin Henry (Culkin). Henry is not evil in the sense that he beats up kids for lunch money or leaves flaming bags of dog poop on people's doorsteps. He'd much rather watch his sister drown in icy water or throw a dummy into oncoming traffic to cause a giant accident. Mark observes the crashing cars with his mouth agape while Henry smiles devilishly, relishing in the chaos of destruction.

I suppose the appeal of *The Good Son* is the shocking nature of how one kid can be the most inhuman of monsters. It's later revealed that Henry was responsible for the death of his baby brother Richard by drowning him in the bathtub. His motivation: Richard was playing with Henry's favorite rubber duck. When the mother later questions if Henry murdered his brother, he coldly responds, *"What if I did?"*. The movie goes to such extreme lengths to make Henry such a vile killer I'm surprised there was no third act reveal of him being the spawn of Satan.

He'd have to be possessed. What child under twelve would possibly have the guts to kill a dog for pleasure, frame his cousin for potentially fatal accidents or speak to his cousin with such threats as *"Don't fuck with me"*? This kid is not a serial killer in the making - he's a serial killer in his prime with several kills already under his belt and ready to slaughter more.

Considering nobody believes Mark as he desperately tries to

prove Henry is a bad seed, I have to wonder how many other murders he's committed, perhaps in preschool or kindergarten, burying his classmates' corpses in the school floorboards. That's a morbid thought, but, then again, the movie is nothing but a series of morbid scenes. There's no deep moral questioning of Henry's condition, no shred of humanity to his murders or even consequences for his actions (the car pileup is never investigated by local authorities). All that's present is a showcase for how creepy and despicable Culkin can play a serial killer - a role he perhaps should have waited another ten years to perform - where he continues to kill until someone kills him.

This was a Hollywood production run amok with celebrity attachment and commercial revisioning. It was intended by screenwriter Ian McEwan to be a movie low on budget, but high in class. After much shifting of writers and directors, along with the messy casting of Culkin with conditions for his appearance, it turned into the exact opposite. The movie exists more as an oddity for how Elijah Wood, the hobbit from *Lord of the Rings*, was terrorized by Macaulay Culkin, the kid from *Home Alone*. Considering what happens to them in the dreadful finale of the picture, it's a little too telling of their career paths as well, making the movie far more depressing and ugly than it already is.

GOODFELLAS

DIRECTOR: Martin Scorsese | SCREENWRITER: Nicholas Pileggi, Martin Scorsese | CAST: Robert De Niro, Ray Liotta, Joe Pesci, Lorraine Bracco, Paul Sorvino | GENRE: Drama | RUNNING TIME: 145 min | MPAA RATING: R

CLASSIFICATION: BEST

Goodfellas (1990) begins with Henry Hill talking about how he always wanted to be a gangster. They always seemed to be his heroes the way they controlled everything from business to respect. Everybody seems to know them, and nobody seems to beat them. This is the life Henry wants. By the end of the picture, however, it won't be as appealing.

Henry (Ray Liotta) narrates this picture to give us his perspective on his love affair with crime. It seemed like such a sweet deal to be in that much control of so much money that he wouldn't know what to do with it all. One thing he does with it is lavish it on his new wife Karen (Lorraine Bracco), who also narrates portions of this story. She's initially terrified of this lifestyle, but Henry soon intoxicates her on the drug of power and glamour. She reasons that this is all these blue-collar boys can do and accepts their illegal activities to favor her luxurious lifestyle. A mistress makes the relationship worse, and the kids only add to the burden.

Working with Henry are his mobster pals Jimmy (Robert De Niro) and Tommy (Joe Pesci). They're in this together for life when they end up killing a made man of the Gambino family and cover up his murder. They chop up the body, bury it and then rebury it when they realize the burial site is slated for development. There isn't much tension about the murder between them because killing is just part of the business to an uncomfortable degree. This is especially true with Tommy as the hot-headed talkative one of the trio. He doesn't like being called funny, and when Henry says he's funny after telling an amusing story, Tommy will become so agitated he starts threatening him with a gun. Tommy won't shoot him because he's friends with Henry, but he's crazy enough to shoot Spider in the foot for not getting him a drink fast enough. Tommy considers it an accident and Spider has his foot fixed, only for Tommy to get pissed off again the next night and shoot him until he is dead.

Henry's life of crime continues to mount with more tension and dirty tactics. He becomes part of a massive heist at JFK airport, only for the police to find the car, leading to most of his heist partners ending up whacked. He starts smuggling cocaine by having others carry it in diaper bags; Karen fawns over the baby that was brought over while Henry unloads the merchandise and tests it in the same room. The fights between Henry and Karen heat up further to the point that they're pointing guns in each other's faces, their children watching in sadness.

By the time the story gets to 1980, Henry is a paranoid wreck. He looks overworked and is continually sweating. Every moment in the car has him looking up at the sky for a police helicopter. The title cards have now stopped tracking years and now displays the exact time of day as that is all Henry can think about. His legacy is coming to an end, and he realizes he better switch gears quickly if he doesn't want to end up like all the others.

Unlike a lot of gangster pictures, Scorsese doesn't try to humanize the mobsters too much. He makes them real with little details of their celebratory moments of family and conversations over drinks, but never makes them charismatic enough to be likable. They're sick people and end up suffering the consequences of their evils. They're so drowned in their aspirations they can't recognize when it may be their turn to go down. Most of the time when the authorities bust them happen out of one mistake of a phone call made or someone pissed off. If you're going to kill someone, you better hope they don't have family in the FBI. One of the gangsters believes he is being invited to be a made man, only to enter into an empty room and realize it's a trap. Before he can curse, he's shot in the back of the head. This is how this world works and why Henry is relieved when a cop points a gun at his face and tells him to surrender. The mafia wouldn't ever give him such notice.

For being such an all-encompassing and well-made picture, *Goodfellas* is often cited as Scorsese's best film ever made. It's a masterpiece of unforgettable performances, well-written scenes (some of them ad-libbed by the actors) and phenomenal cinematography for the iconic unbroken shot through a restaurant. In the pantheon of mob movies, it is without question one of the best for letting us understand how the minds of such violent and terrible people functioned. You might not want to be a gangster when your best friend is one misplaced word or facial expression away from whacking you.

GRAND CANYON

DIRECTOR: Lawrence Kasdan | SCREENWRITER: Lawrence Kasdan, Meg Kasdan | CAST: Danny Glover, Kevin Kline, Steve Martin, Mary McDonnell, Mary-Louise Parker, Alfre Woodard | GENRE: Drama | RUNNING TIME: 137 min | MPAA RATING: R

CLASSIFICATION: BEST

Lawrence Kasdan's *Grand Canyon* (1991) could have quickly turned into sentimental drivel with its overly ambitious themes of an ensemble picture, but it is held together firmly by his sharp and intriguing dialogue. His film follows various characters around Los Angeles in different stages of their lives, but all of them are thinking about more than the current situation. Take the opening scene where the lawyer Mack (Kevin Kline) has his car break down in a bad neighborhood. He's about to be mugged by some black punks until the black mechanic Simon (Danny Glover) comes along to confront them. Simon makes the kids retreat with his words, but words not of the immediate and rather the essence of each other's character. Their exchange is one of considerable intimidation and respect on a higher plain than most street arguments. Mack gets a ride from Simon to the auto shop, and their conversation leads from vacations into finding our place in the world.

Kasdan crafts characters that always seem to be openly seen as frightened people in one way or another. They seek more and find more out of the world they occupy. Mike doesn't just want his encounter with Simon to be a random one, desiring to develop a more significant relationship. Meanwhile, his wife Claire (Mary McDonnell) finds an abandoned baby that perfectly clashes with her fear of an empty nest with her son going off to college. Mack's best friend is Davis (Steve Martin), a producer of violent movies who is all about the gory money shot. When Davis is shot in the leg and has his watch stolen, he has an epiphany about grotesquely violent movies and vows never to make one again. And there are even more personal stories connected with all these figures.

The film spends so much time building these players up that we not only grow to like them, but understand them on a more profound and perhaps even spiritual level. We're allowed to peer into the dreams of Mack and Claire, finding themselves both freed and troubled by the world. They both want to believe that their run-ins with strangers weren't a coincidence, as though it were their destinies to become involved. It sure beats the alternative that the world is just random chaos and violence that can erupt unexpectedly at the worst times. And there is violence in this movie that always creates an undercurrent of unease, making the more pleasant moments of human connection all the more earned and warm.

The Grand Canyon is referenced and becomes a focal point for the characters and their comprehension of humanity. The geographical landmark had been forming for millions of years before they were born and will still be developing long after they've passed away. There's an all-encompassing sensation that Kasdan taps into about adults who have lived a life they thought they understood, only to realize there is more to their existence. The film is mostly about their desire to find that extra sensation of life's grander pleasures and meanings, hopefully before it's too late. *Grand Canyon* has strong enough writing, directing and acting to triumph over the many cliches of such a premise and breathe with the humanity of real people with real problems in a real world.

GREMLINS 2: THE NEW BATCH

DIRECTOR: Joe Dante, Chuck Jones | SCREENWRITER: Charles S. Haas, Chuck Jones | CAST: Zach Galligan, Phoebe Cates, John Glover, Robert J. Prosky, Robert Picardo, Christopher Lee | GENRE: Comedy | RUNNING TIME: 106 min | MPAA RATING: PG-13

CLASSIFICATION: WEIRD

Director Joe Dante must have realized that he could never top the tongue-in-cheek charm of the horror comedy *Gremlins*, which explains why he doesn't attempt to duplicate such a tone in the sequel. *Gremlins 2: The New Batch* (1990) goes straight for the comedy jugular, reaping any goofy gag and satirizing any figure it can. It's very fitting that Dante hired *Looney Tunes* director Chuck Jones to feature Bugs Bunny and Daffy Duck fighting over the opening title card for the movie. This sets the tone perfectly for a comedy extravaganza of a monster movie where anything can happen and usually does, no matter how ridiculous or cartoonish it may be.

The mystical rules of the adorably furry Mogwai still apply: Don't expose them to light, don't feed them after midnight and don't get them wet. Doing so will cause the Gremlins to spawn forth and wreak havoc on the human race. The cute little Mogwai by the name of Gizmo returns to have the unfortunate luck of birthing more of the green devils, now within the confines of a giant city skyscraper where the returning heroes of Billy and Kate (Zach Galligan and Phoebe Cates) now work.

This time, however, the Gremlins have more variety. There's a smart Gremlin that has grown intelligent enough to speak words clearly with the droll tone of an English professor. There's a silly Gremlin with big eyes and little smarts. There's a Gremlin with wings that can fly. There's an electric Gremlin made entirely of electricity. There's even a shameless product placement Gremlin with the Warner Bros. logo tattooed on its chest.

There's a thin plot of Billy and Kate trying to stop the Gremlins, but the story is mostly abandoned to make way for more Gremlin antics. The tower the Gremlins terrorize, owned by the Trump-like billionaire Daniel Clamp (John Glover), is also packed with colorfully absurd characters and departments. Grandpa Fred (Robert Prosky) is an Al Lewis parody that introduces B-movies in a Dracula costume on a cheap television stage. Microwave Marge (Kathleen Freeman) host a cooking show on a set ripe for some dangerous antics of boiling water and exploding cookery. Gizmo's cute dancing number does little to sway the evil Doctor Catheter (Christopher Lee) from his desires to dissect the creature. Paul Bartel plays a snooty theater manager who becomes slightly peeved when Gremlins disrupt the movie. And there is a host of hilarious cameos from the likes of Hulk Hogan and Leonard Maltin.

The Gremlins are voiced by the familiar talents of Howie Mandel as the adorable Gizmo and Frank Welker as the evil Gremlins, but the variety of Gremlins leads to an extended cast of voices. Tony Randall is most notable as the voice of the intelligent Brain Gremlin, bringing a bizarre sophistication to the usually blithering puppets. Director Joe Dante himself voices two Gremlin variations, cartoon voice actor Mark Dodson provides the voice of the Daffy Gremlin and *Muppet* director Kirk Thatcher voices the rest.

This film is an insane stroke of satirical madness that is, as Joe Dante himself describes it, *"one of the more unconventional studio pictures, ever."* Dante was awarded total creative control, triple the budget of the original movie and access to more cameos than any of his other pictures. The result is a film that is so unbelievably cheesy, inventive, silly, commercial and shameless that it essentially sealed the tomb for the *Gremlins* franchise as no sequel could ever hope to be so bombastic.

GROUNDHOG DAY

DIRECTOR: Harold Ramis | SCREENWRITER: Danny Rubin, Harold Ramis | CAST: Bill Murray, Andie MacDowell, Chris Elliott | GENRE: Comedy | RUNNING TIME: 101 min | MPAA RATING: PG

CLASSIFICATION: BEST

The premise of *Groundhog Day* (1993) is so simple and so genius that it was one of the most inventive comedies of the decade. TV weather reporter Phil (Bill Murray) is assigned to Punxsutawney, Pennsylvania to cover the annual Groundhog Day celebration. He can't stand being in a town of hicks and despises his job with an ironic and cynical tone towards everyone. It's the same deal every year; the groundhog Punxsutawney Phil awakens from his sleep and ventures outside. If it sees it's own shadow, it will mean six more weeks of winter. It's a silly and superstitious event that everyone seems to enjoy except Phil, soured by wasting his time on such a news story. Phil can't wait to leave Punxsutawney and for this day to be over.

But he cannot escape this town or this day as he is condemned to repeat Groundhog Day over and over again. He tries everything to figure out why this day is on a perpetual loop, but still can't escape the repetition, even when committing suicide. A lesson must be learned, and there are no clear means of escaping this maze. Phil has to figure this out on his own and learn from his mistakes. He's got all the time in the world to solve this dilemma.

Every morning begins the same. He awakens in a bed and breakfast to Sonny & Cher's "I Got You Babe" over the clock radio, a song that will probably drive him bonkers long after this experience is over. He is greeted by an old friend of an insurance salesman on the street that he considers an energetic jerk, followed by an unfortunate step into a puddle. His lovely producer Rita (Andie MacDowell) wants to stay in Punxsutawney longer to cover more news, and the cameraman Larry (Chris Elliott) puts up with Phil's lousy attitude with a smile and a can-do attitude. Phil is rude to all of these people and every single person in Punxsutawney. Maybe a change in attitude will break this eternal day.

This structure of *Groundhog Day* could have become tiring, but Bill Murray makes it work with one of his best performances. Murray had been known at the time for playing an intelligent guy that could deliver laughs with both booming loudness and subtle delivery. He applies that same technique to a man who seems distant and grumpy, appearing as the smartest guy in the room with nobody to talk with. He plays Phil with a quiet desperation of a man who hides behind a wall of jokes and jabs, fearing he'll run out of bricks when reality pushes him down. This performance could be seen as the prototype for his more notable deadpan roles in *Rushmore* (1998), *Lost in Translation* (2003) and *The Life Aquatic with Steve Zissou* (2004). It's a far more exceptional performance of a curmudgeon than his more manic character in the Christmas Carol comedy *Scrooged* (1988).

Despite not being very religious, *Groundhog Day* has been hailed as a spiritual comedy for its cross-religious themes of selfishness, reflection, purgatory, and reincarnation. It's rather remarkable to read such praise for a comedy with a rude protagonist who questions if he's god; *"I'm a god. I'm not *the* God... I don't think."* Director Harold Ramis partially based the script on the Buddhist lore of taking 10,000 days for someone's soul to evolve, with the original draft featuring 10,000 repetitions for Phil; Ramis thankfully shortened the repeating days to 40. No matter how you interpret it, the film stands strong as one of the most original comedy ideas with one of Murray's best performances as a man who changes enough of himself to be more of a better person than a saint. As Rita points out to Phil, *"You're not a god. You can take my word for it; this is twelve years of Catholic school talking."*

GUMMO

DIRECTOR: Harmony Korine | SCREENWRITER: Harmony Korine | CAST: Linda Manz, Max Perlich, Jacob Reynolds, Chloë Sevigny, Jacob Sewell, Nick Sutton | GENRE: Drama | RUNNING TIME: 89 min | MPAA RATING: R

CLASSIFICATION: WORST

Don't be fooled by Harmony Korine's arthouse ramblings on Middle-American squalor. *Gummo* (1997) has all the trimmings of an avant-garde piece, but no point to its weird and glib world other than to point out how strange and ugly it all is. This is a mean, vile and smug picture that can't decide if it wants to be a morbid comedy or a sad portrait of American life. There's a scene where a boy sits in a bathtub, eating spaghetti on a tray, with bacon hung on the bathroom walls. Don't read too much into the significance of the bacon.

The film is set in Xenia, Ohio, a town that was hit by a tornado 20 years ago and still hasn't recovered. Any rising from the ashes seems unlikely given the citizens of this dirty and depressing area. Solomon is a rat-faced little boy who spends his days talking with a pimp that tries to sell him on sleeping with his Down syndrome sister. Tummler is a teenager who is first introduced drowning a cat and then finding out his girlfriend has breast cancer while making out in a wrecked car. Bunny Boy, an unknown child that wanders Xenia dressed in bunny ears, is attacked by little boys in cowboy costumes until they grow bored with him playing dead. And, in one of the oddest insertion of a director, Harmony Korine plays a drunk that comes onto a gay dwarf.

Each scene presents more disgusting elements of the Ohio community, showcasing the worst and most depressing examples of humanity. Two skinheads beat each other to a pulp in a dirty kitchen. Solomon and Tummler get revenge on a cat poacher by breaking into his house and taking his catatonic mother off life support. Two sisters meet an elderly child molester. There is not an ounce of love or human decency anywhere in this picture, as even a more casual moment of an ADD tennis player speaking to some ogling girls comes off more mean than sweet.

Gummo was intended as a personal project for Korine, inspired by his hometown of Nashville, Tennessee. He identified with the trailer trash of the area and desired to make a film around such strange individuals that did them justice, taking a more in-depth look at the poor, destroyed and bad parts of southern towns. He wants us to peer into the corners to find what creatures feast on the rotting innards of the country. Perhaps it was intended to identify and understand America's ugliness, but all *Gummo* convinced me of is to accelerate faster when driving through these areas.

HACKERS

DIRECTOR: Iain Softley | SCREENWRITER: Rafael Moreu | CAST: Jonny Lee Miller, Angelina Jolie, Fisher Stevens, Lorraine Bracco, Matthew Lillard, Penn Jillette | GENRE: Science Fiction | RUNNING TIME: 107 min | MPAA RATING: PG-13

CLASSIFICATION: WEIRD

Hacking computer systems doesn't have the same visual and intense allure of a bank heist, but they certainly do in Iain Softley's *Hackers* (1995). Rather than showcase the usual dull display of code, this film doesn't even bother with trying to be accurate with computer hacking of the era, opting to turn computer data into a virtual reality experience. Nothing is boring about hacking into a database when it looks like you're infiltrating the world of The Lawnmower Man. Is it laughably inaccurate for being a techno-thriller? Absolutely. That's also part of its charm that favors a cyberpunk style over nerdy smarts.

The hacker punks are known by their handles. Dabe (Jonny Lee Miller) was once known by the hacker alias "Zero Cool" when he was 11-years-old, but was caught and sentenced to a childhood without computers or phones. Now attending a new high school at the age of eighteen, he plans to get back into the hacking game with his new handle of "Crash Override." Armed with a silly name that sounds high-tech for the era, Crash makes his way into the underground collective of hackers, committed to taking advantage of the system with their battle cry of *"hack the planet!"*

But there are no dorks of pocket protectors and glasses allowed in this hacker group, as these are not the traditional nerds you'd expect to be obsessed with breaking into databases. There's the female hacker "Acid Burn," played by a short-haired Angelina Jolie, so obsessed with technology she'll stop a session of making out to boast to her friends about her new computer. The snappy-talking Puerto Rican hacker "The Phantom Phreak" (Renoly Santiago) is knowledgeable enough to be the reliable one for exposition and hacking strategies. "Cereal Killer" (Matthew Lillard) is the wild one of the bunch with his constant crackle and odd dreads. "Lord Nikon" (Laurence Mason) is so named for his photographic memory, and Joey (Jesse Bradford) hopes to have his memorable handle someday as well. Maybe he needs some dreads to impress his fellow hackers.

The villain of the picture is known as "The Plague" (Fisher Stevens), a bearded manager of computer securities for a giant corporation. Much like the more underground hackers, he commits cyber-crimes, but on a much larger scale of hacking into military systems to sink a tanker. And he wants Crash Overrides collective to take the fall for hacking they didn't do. And so the petty thieves that broke into television signals and corporate systems for fun must prove their innocence, staying one step ahead of the bumbling authorities.

The hacking plot is silly, but presented with such a rebellious attitude for its dubious material I couldn't help but love its audacity. Very little of the hacking involves actual code, opting instead to fill computer screens with wild typography, floating numbers, and trippy computer graphics. Most of the hacking scenes look less like the users are breaking into systems and more as though they've cracked the universal code of all life. The technobabble for creating tension in describing the penetration of computer systems is laughable, but also earnestly committed to this world's idea of technology. Penn Jillette is a master of magic, and in this film, he sells us on the trick that he appears to know what he's talking about. Pay no attention to what the characters are typing; look at the crazy colors, stylish costumes, and slick editing!

Hackers became part of a new genre of films known as hacksploitation, dubbed as such for distorting computer hacking to seem more grand, wondrous and dangerous in the movies than it is in reality. Where the film falls apart in its lingo, it makes up for a weirdly sweet romance between Crash and Acid, a high-speed thriller plot with a tanker on the line and a rebellious nature for portraying hackers as the new punk gangs of the future. It's enough to make you want to hack the planet, for as silly and lame as that phrase sounds today.

HALF BAKED

DIRECTOR: Tamra Davis | SCREENWRITER: Dave Chappelle, Neal Brennan | CAST: Dave Chappelle, Jim Breuer, Harland Williams, Guillermo Díaz, Clarence Williams III | GENRE: Comedy | RUNNING TIME: 82 min | MPAA RATING: R

CLASSIFICATION: WEIRD

Dave Chappelle's stoner comedy *Half Baked* (1998) was more than just another giggle and cough on weed culture. His script, co-written by his writing sidekick Neal Brennan, combs every aspect of dope dealing for any comedy nugget that can be mined for the silliest of scenes. They don't exactly find gold, but indeed enough insightful material to be worthy of all its snickering.

A stoner foursome lives under the same roof, using their collective salaries from their little jobs to indulge their evening habit of getting high. Thurgood (Chappelle) is both the narrator and a master of the custodial arts (*"or a janitor if you want to be a dick about it"*). Scarface (Guillermo Díaz) is a hot-headed Cuban working as the cook of a fast-food chain, easily angered by the cashier speaking loudly over him. Brian (Jim Breuer) is a giggling mess, working at a record shop which Thurgood describes as the perfect job for a stoner. Kenny (Harland Williams) seems to be the most successful of the lot as a kindergarten teacher. Life is simple and smokey until Kenny stupidly kills a police horse by feeding it junk food and is sent to prison. To free their friend, Thurgood and company decide to make bail for their friend by selling weed they swipe from a pharmaceutical laboratory at Thurgood's workplace.

The trio dubs their business Mr. Nice Guy, attracting all sorts of odd customers. One of which happens to be the rapper Sir Smoka Lot (also Chappelle), a stoner so insecure he lets all his feelings out over a bong. But when Smoka Lot's regular supplier Samson Simpson (Clarence Williams III) hears there is competition, he intimidates the charitable entrepreneurs with threats of violence and crossbows. Also balanced on top of this plot is Thurgood's romantic difficulties in wooing Mary Jane Potman (Rachel True), Scarface bonding with his new dog friend, Kenny befriending his prisoner bodyguard (Tommy Chong) and Brian trying to call upon the powers of Jerry Garcia's ashes. It all sounds crazy and wild, but it, unfortunately, plateaus towards the end, even for a climax of the heroes fighting a room full of Simpson's sexy female warriors where a boob pops out.

There is a host of celebrity cameos who are given their own scenes to fill out Thurgood's catalog of pot smokers. Willie Nelson plays the Historian Smoker, regaling Thurgood with tails of dime bags costing a dime and condoms being lame. Snoop Doggy Dogg pops out of the shadows as the Scavenger Smoker, bumming puffs off other potheads for free. Jon Stewart is the Enhancement Smoker, bestowing his wisdom of how pot can improve everything from the illustrations on dollar bills to *Scarface* (*"You ever seen* Scarface...*on weeeeeed?"*). I have no clue if these smokers are of true titles, but Chappelle's writing and narration sell them so well.

Not all of the jokes hit as well as they should. Trying not to spend all of what little cash he has on a first date, Thurgood steers Mary Jane to cheaper alternatives. The money counter in the corner of the screen goes down with each purchase, but goes up after he sneakily snatches a handful of cash from a homeless man without remorse. Remember, Thurgood is the hero of this picture.

Half Baked has its moments of insightful and cartoonish skits, featuring a brand of humor that Chappelle would later perfect with the more biting *The Chappelle Show*. There was enough strangeness and satire in this wild script to be worthy of a few laughs, even if I felt I had to be high to appreciate all of its silliness truly.

HAMLET

DIRECTOR: Kenneth Branagh | SCREENWRITER: Kenneth Branagh | CAST: Kenneth Branagh, Julie Christie, Billy Crystal, Gérard Depardieu, Charlton Heston, Derek Jacobi, Jack Lemmon, Rufus Sewell, Robin Williams, Kate Winslet | GENRE: Drama | RUNNING TIME: 242 min | MPAA RATING: PG-13

CLASSIFICATION: BEST

Kenneth Branagh's *Hamlet* (1996) is the most definitive of film interpretations for Shakespeare's play. It features the largest ensemble of A-list actors, the most gorgeous of settings and with the most extensive script that covers nearly every inch of the original material. Branagh became inspired to create such a product after hearing a full version of *Hamlet* performed on BBC Radio in 1992 and then another for the stage that same year. He wanted to be the one that brought such an all-encompassing version to the big screen. He greatly succeeded.

Branagh plays the title role of the Prince of Denmark with great enthusiasm and love for the text, making the avenging madman so much fun to watch. In the crucial scene of the first act, when he is visited by the ghost of his father, Hamlet's wide eyes and whispers of astonishment make him just as terrifying as the ghost. During the Danish wedding of Claudius and Gertrude, he remains alone and dressed in a black that contrasts beautifully with the castle of gold and white. Branagh doesn't just want us to pay attention to his soliloquy with such a decadent setting, but make us appreciate his loneliness of such a large environment that breeds his madness.

The story remains the same as it ever was, but with strong talents and high production values. The ghost of Hamlet's father appears with smoke and dread to deliver the news that he was murdered by Claudius, but with just the right amount of atmosphere so that his performance isn't overshadowed by theatrics. Branagh also has enough faith to keep the Elizabethan English intact to respect the text and deliver on the drama.

It helps that he's working with a cast strong enough to commit to this material. Derek Jacobi can bring more dimension to the deceptive usurper Claudius than the simplistic villain he's usually portrayed as in shorter versions. Julie Christie plays Gertrude with a lust for Claudius that makes their marriage seem more believable for the era. The play that Hamlet stages to insinuate Claudius' dirty tactics takes on a whole new level of engagement when veteran actor Charlton Heston takes on the role of the Player King, receiving his scene to flex his legendary acting muscles. And the list of talent goes on, from Kate Winslet's Ophelia to Timothy Spall's Rosencrantz. Even the lesser roles of bit players are filled out by such notable actors as Robin Williams, Jack Lemmon, Judi Dench and Billy Crystal.

The film is a visual masterpiece for being a rarity of being shot on 70mm film, a format that would not be used again until 2012 with *The Master*. It was the last excellent Shakespeare film adaptation of the century, as the more modern adaptations of another *Hamlet* (1991), *Romeo + Juliet* (1997) and yet another *Hamlet* (2000) were underwhelming. While it wasn't a box office success, it did receive massive critical praise, was nominated for several awards and has been hailed as one of the best adaptations of *Hamlet* ever made, if not of all of Shakespeare's works. It also happens to be the longest, clocking in at over four hours, that a shorter version was edited down for its theatrical release of three-and-a-half hours. Trust me; the four-hour version is worth it for delivering on great perspective, beauty, and intrigue like no other interpretation of the old play.

HEAT

DIRECTOR: Michael Mann | SCREENWRITER: Michael Mann | CAST: Al Pacino, Robert De Niro, Tom Sizemore, Diane Venora, Amy Brenneman, Ashley Judd, Mykelti Williamson, Wes Studi, Ted Levine, Jon Voight, Val Kilmer | GENRE: Action | RUNNING TIME: 170 min | MPAA RATING: R

CLASSIFICATION: BEST

A major selling point of *Heat* (1995) was the pairing of Al Pacino and Robert De Niro together on screen. They only share one scene together where they talk, but it's one hell of a scene at that. Pacino is detective Hanna, and De Niro is top-tier thief McCauley. Pacino has been tracking De Niro for days and pulled him over. A shootout could occur here, but they get a cup of coffee instead. They quietly and carefully choose their words about their choices in lifestyle and how they won't hold anything back if they run into each other again on opposite sides of the law. It is one of the best scenes for the calm before the storm. And that's saying something for a movie with one of the most incredible shootouts in movie history.

This pivotal moment strengthens the inner world of cops and robbers. They exist in a bubble outside of the rest of society. McCauley hangs out at a bar and strikes up a conversation with the beautiful Eady (Amy Brenneman), lying to her about being a salesman. As their discussion grows more intimate and personal, she asks if he travels for his work and if he feels lonely. He responds, *"I'm alone, I am not lonely."* It's a brilliant and sad line about his path, punctuated by the soundtrack that mixes synth and guitars to create a tone that is equally somber and sexy. McCauley can't fall in love with his line of work, but can't help himself.

Meanwhile, Hanna is on his third marriage to Justice (Diane Venora), and it's not going well. She is always frustrated with him and his obsession with work. He would rather keep tales of murders and dead babies in the office where it belongs. In truth, work is the only place he resides, surrounded by sick people and cold corpses. He spends so much time involved with police work that he knows little else. This is the bond that he and McCauley share and the only thing they still have in common before they must commit to the duel they signed themselves up for when they picked up their guns.

There is no reason for McCauley to go on as he has enough money and a place to go. Hanna should be at home working on his marriage and relationship with his teenage daughter. But they need this in their lives. There's a thrill that comes with every aspect of their jobs from the staking out to the big heist. And once the heist is on, after much precision in planning from the thieves that will pull it off and the cops that will foil it, it's one of the most intense shootouts between the police and the criminals in city streets. The thieves were smart enough to know how to deal with hostages and make it out with the money, but their bout with the authorities is all about wits. Automatic weapons are fired in a bloody chase, the gunshots echoing so loudly you can hardly hear anyone speak. As with the rest of the film's banter and planning, there's realism to this scene where the true scale and power of a downtown gunfight are felt.

It's as though Michael Mann had such a fantastically grand action scene in mind, but wanted to do everything in his power for his film to earn this cinematic achievement. He dramatically succeeds with a script that contains intelligence, passion, and humanity. Pacino and De Niro are no strangers to roles of flawed men with guns in tow, but *Heat* features them at their best in roles of articulate individuals careening towards an explosive end they know they can't avoid.

HEAVYWEIGHTS

DIRECTOR: Steven Brill | SCREENWRITER: Steven Brill, Judd Apatow | CAST: Tom McGowan, Aaron Schwartz, Shaun Weiss, Tom Hodges, Leah Lail, Paul Feig, Kenan Thompson, Jeffrey Tambor, Jerry Stiller, Anne Meara, Ben Stiller | GENRE: Comedy | RUNNING TIME: 100 min | MPAA RATING: PG

CLASSIFICATION: WEIRD

Fat kids usually fulfill a simple role in most movies, acting mostly as pudgy mascots continually eating and typically disgusting. But *Heavyweights* (1995) features a primary cast of tubby kids heading to fat camp. It doesn't sound like a pleasant summer activity for Gerry (Aaron Schwartz), but, as his fellow camper Roy (Kenan Thompson) points out, every kid there will be fat, and so nobody can make fun of your weight. It's a place where the fat kids get to mock the skinny people as the minority.

Camp Hope doesn't sound at all bad by the time Gerry arrives. The counselors are enthusiastically encouraging, there are go-karts to race, and the cabins come stocked with candy contraband from the campers that have mastered the art of smuggling sweets. The other campers find it cute that Gerry was able to sneak in a sleeve of Oreos when they unveil their massive stash of junk food that could put any prison smuggler to shame.

A problem arises when the camp enters bankruptcy and is sold. The new owner is Tony Perkis (Ben Stiller), a cross between a pompous seminar speaker and a ruthlessly condescending fitness instructor. He plans to restructure camp to better focus on fitness, aiming to take off the pounds as quickly as possible. With the aid of his commanding German assistant Lars (Tom Hodges), he wipes out all elements of fun from camp by destroying the go-karts, refusing meals and keeping the fat kids exhausted continuously to the point that death from hiking seems possible. When the other counselors prove useless in resolving the situation, it's up to Gerry and his gang of campers to best the maniacal Tony with their quick methods of capturing him to run the camp how they see fit. They must have been to the Home Alone school of crafts given their ability to trap Tony in a cage of chicken wire electrically charged by bug zappers.

The film goes through the typical tropes of underdogs. Since Tony doesn't seem to be enough of a significant story component, the camp setting adds in extra plot segments to give the kids more to do. There's a neighboring camp of girls that visit the boys at a dance where they're too shy to speak to one another before eventually deciding to dance together. To end on a more triumphant note after exposing Tony, the boys must also compete in a physical camp competition where they will triumph over the more athletic and winning-obsessed kids. Naturally, the winning trophy and kiss from a girl come standard for Gerry's perseverance.

What's remarkable about this picture is how many early careers blossomed from such a strange film. Ben Stiller blew up as a comedic talent and would become a better known evil fitness guru in *Dodgeball* (2004). Paul Feig would continue acting for a few more years before becoming the director of such comedies as *Bridesmaids* (2011) and *The Heat* (2013). It was the first feature writing credit for Judd Apatow, who would become the legendary comedy director/producer of *The 40-Year-Old Virgin* (2005) and *Knocked Up* (2007). Kenan Thompson would continue to be a comedic talent on TV's *All That* skit show until later appearing in the kid comedy *Good Burger* (1997) and then becoming a regular on *Saturday Night Live*.

Heavyweights is an odd little film, more noteworthy for its early talent that would improve past this simple bit of weight-challenged wish-fulfillment. The tone and comedy are all-too-familiar, yet the premise itself feels oddly original. There isn't a lot of competition for movies that take place at a fat camp, featuring slow-motion footage of boys devouring junk food to the tune of classical music. There's nothing quite like it, and there probably won't be another movie like it. Whether that's a good or bad thing is up for debate.

HIGHLANDER II: THE QUICKENING

DIRECTOR: Russell Mulcahy | SCREENWRITER: Peter Bellwood | CAST: Christopher Lambert, Virginia Madsen, Michael Ironside, Sean Connery, John C. McGinley, Allan Rich | GENRE: Science Fiction | RUNNING TIME: 100 min | MPAA RATING: R

CLASSIFICATION: WORST

The Highlander was a cult film for its campy story of immortal warriors, an engaging atmosphere with fun action and a stellar soundtrack by Queen. But the laughable sequel, *The Highlander II: The Quickening* (1991), tarnishes the Highlander series and its mystical elements. The most insulting of developments was the retooling of the Immortals, a collective of Scottish warriors that cannot die unless they are beheaded. Their origins were shrouded in mystery, but *The Quickening* finally reveals who they indeed were: aliens from the planet Zeist.

It takes the movie only a few moments to confuse the viewer. The story starts in 1999, but then flashes the title card of taking place 25 years later. The movie later cuts to the planet Zeist with the title card of 500 years prior. The Immortals tried to wage war on Zeist, but were soon banished to Earth for an eternal life sentence, hence their names. But the Immortals can die, sort of. One character states that Immortals can live forever on Earth until they return to Zeist, but you can die on Earth under certain circumstances. The Immortals left on Earth for over 500 years are Connor MacLeod (Christopher Lambert) and Juan Sánchez Villa-Lobos Ramírez (Sean Connery).

Earth's problem in 1994 is the fading ozone layer. MacLeod has a solution to this problem and by 1999 has developed an electromagnetic shield with scientists to protect the Earth from radiation. He is successful, but there's a big catch: it's perpetually night and always a balmy 99 degrees. It sounds like a fair compromise, but things only get worse by 2024 from a social perspective. Hope is lost in humanity; a greedy corporation now runs the shield, crime runs rampant in the streets and terrorists seek to take down the shield.

The terrorists have a good reason to blow up the shield as it turns out the ozone layer has been repaired and no longer needs such a power-sucking device to keep Earth habitable. But, of course, the greedy David Blake (John C. McGinley) can't let people know about that. To take down the shield, Louise Marcus (Virginia Madsen) seeks the aid of the legendary McLoud. Back on Zeist, the evil General Katana (Michael Ironside), the man who stopped the rebellion of the Immortals, has been monitoring MacLeod and doesn't want him coming back to Zeist. MacLeod was already banished never to return, but I guess Katana would feel better if he knew this rebel was dead.

This is an idiotic script on multiple levels. Past the ridiculous retconning of the backstory of the Immortals, the whole idea of shielding Earth doesn't make the least bit of sense. For a planet where there is no day, it sure doesn't look as though much has changed over the course of 23 years. Sure, it's dirtier, and there's more crime, but wouldn't there be a massive change in the production of food, culture, and buildings? I guess all movie futures look the same. The whole Zeist plot is shamelessly inserted so MacLeod has someone equal to fight and revive Juan so that Sean Connery can cash a paycheck. Considering Connery received $3.5 million for only shooting nine days, he made out like a bandit.

In an attempt to salvage the film, a few different cuts were made for home video release. The director's cut, also known as the Renegade Cut, featured new prologue text to fix the story to the specific date of 2024 rather than jumping around timelines and planets. Another cut for DVD in 2004 featured modern computer graphics and voice-over by Christopher Lambert. But these are all band-aids on a film that is fundamentally flawed and incomprehensible at its core.

The Quickening of the title refers to the lifeforce of a beheaded Immortal being absorbed into another Immortal. It has also been described for the *Highlander* TV series as "receiving of a sacrament or a massive orgasm." I suppose *The Quickening* sounds better than MacLeod's Orgasmic Decapitation Adventure, though they both make the same amount of nonsense.

HOME ALONE

DIRECTOR: Chris Columbus | SCREENWRITER: John Hughes | CAST: Macaulay Culkin, Joe Pesci, Daniel Stern, John Heard, Catherine O'Hara | GENRE: Comedy | RUNNING TIME: 102 min | MPAA RATING: PG

CLASSIFICATION: WEIRD

John Hughes' script for *Home Alone* (1990) touches on a relatable aspect of childhood, albeit from a fantastical angle. There's an air of excitement and anxiety when you're a kid, and you occupy the house without parent or babysitter. There's great freedom in deciding what you'll eat out of the fridge and great fear in the noisy furnace in the basement. But Hughes treats this picture's cute little kid with the same outlandish nature he gave to *Ferris Bueller's Day Off*. A kid terrified of being alone in his house probably wouldn't be able to devise elaborate traps to foil burglars, but it's still fun to imagine being that handy at such a young age.

8-year-old Kevin McCallister (Macaulay Culkin) is someone you want to root for being plucky. He's the youngest of his massive family that includes several siblings and cousins, all occupying the same enormous house for the holidays. He seems only to be noticed whenever his cousins want someone to mock, or his parents want someone to blame. Despising his family, he makes a wish that he could be all alone. The next morning, the family scrambles for the airport and accidentally leave Kevin behind, not realizing what they've done until they're en route on the plane.

This is an astonishing development for Kevin to finally have his wish granted, believing his whole family indeed has vanished into thin air. Free to roam about the house, he learns to come to grips with his fears of being alone in addition to taking care of the house. He conquers many milestones including the act of applying aftershave (*"AHHHHH!"*), buying groceries and confronting the mysterious old neighbor who isn't at all scary once you get to know him.

Kevin will have to grow up quick, however, as his quiet home becomes the target of house robbers Harry (Joe Pesci) and Marv (Daniel Stern). One might figure this would be the moment when Kevin confesses to the cops or a neighbor that he's alone and needs help. But Kevin seems so determined to keep this level of independence that he's willing to fight for it. Harry and Marv shouldn't be too hard to fend off with their bumbling nature; Harry being the hot-headed mastermind and Marv being the cackling idiot. But Kevin takes no chances. He sets his home up as an elaborate trap for the burglars. They slide down slippery stairs, take irons to the face, burn their hands, burn their heads and step on Christmas bulbs their bare feet. This all staged as slapstick antics, but the film pushes the definition of slapstick when Marv's bare foot is pierced by an exposed nail. That seems a little more horrific than the lighter traps of Harry being feathered and knocked in the face with a paint can.

Home Alone was directed by Chris Columbus, the director behind *Adventures in Babysitting* (1987), and he brings that same level of a daring adventure to a familiar aspect of childhood. It is such an odd Christmas film with its multiple levels of sentimentality, holiday spirit, and cartoonish violence. In the same way that Hughes wrote his movies to be appealing for teens, his script appealed to me as a kid for how much the child protagonist can do on his own. It's a pleasantly warped bit of wish fulfillment. A cute kid such as Kevin can make a run to the store, make amends with their neighbor at church, set the record straight with Santa Claus and be home in time to cook themselves a macaroni dinner before waging war on criminals with B.B. gun in hand. It's just that weird and just that fun.

HOME ALONE 2: LOST IN NEW YORK

DIRECTOR: Chris Columbus | SCREENWRITER: John Hughes | CAST: Macaulay Culkin, Joe Pesci, Daniel Stern, John Heard, Tim Curry, Brenda Fricker, Catherine O'Hara | GENRE: Comedy | RUNNING TIME: 120 min | MPAA RATING: PG

CLASSIFICATION: WEIRD

"We did it again!"

Home Alone 2: Lost in New York (1992) finds the McCallister family on another frantic family Christmas trip where they once again lose their son Kevin, reprised once more by Macaulay Culkin. This time, however, they make sure that Kevin is on the shuttle to the airport before they depart, even when they're just as late and scrambling as they were in the last picture. Now they make a new mistake. In the hustle of the airport, Kevin boards the wrong flight and finds himself alone and bound for New York City.

Unlike the last film that somewhat touched on the fears of being all alone in the house, Lost in New York doesn't carry as much concern. It's already been established that Kevin is more than capable of handling the bumbling bandits of Harry (Joe Pesci) and Marv (Daniel Stern), making their eventual run-in not nearly as terrifying as it should be. Kevin isn't in a tight spot either as he has his dad's wallet, allowing him to use a credit card and fool the Plaza Hotel into approving its use for checking in. There's another lonely old person to befriend, but somehow a homeless lady who feeds pigeons (Brenda Fricker) doesn't hold the same eeriness as the mysterious elderly neighbor.

That being said, the film still presents plenty of near-miss opportunities for Kevin to continually be on his toes and prevent him from kicking his feet up too high in luxury. He may have fooled most of the Plaza Hotel staff, but the concierge Mr. Hector (Tim Curry) is a little more wise to Kevin's ways. It's not every day that a kid comes into your hotel and starts speaking with the same tone as an adult with his parents nowhere to be found. To keep the staff fooled, Kevin makes excellent use of his environment. He uses an inflatable pool toy to stage his father being in the bathroom, using recordings of his Uncle Frank to create the illusion complete. In one of the film's funniest moments, Kevin uses the audio of an old mobster movie to intimidate Hector and accuse him of making out with his staff. Curry's commitment to such a ridiculous role of Hector makes him stand out for his unforgettable reactions and is the sole reason to watch this movie.

The climax eventually leads to a vacant townhouse where Kevin will once again stage traps for the pursuing Harry and Marv. As with everything in this sequel, the traps are overblown to an absurd degree. Far more elaborate and twice as violent, the bandits experience an excruciating wrath from Kevin. Bricks are smashed into skulls, nails pierce groins and shelves crush ribs. The bandits should by all accounts be dead after such an ordeal, but the film firmly establishes the cartoony aspect of all this when Marv briefly turns into a skeleton when being electrocuted.

Though the sequel lacks a certain warmth of the previous picture, *Lost in New York* is absurdly aware enough of its nature to have fun with its exaggerated material. The comedic cast of villains at play is strong with Curry, Pesci, and Stern carrying most of the film's slapstick and reactions, while Rob Schneider and Dana Ivey provide comedic backup as additional hotel staff. The New York City setting has a grand presence for taking place during Christmas, featuring a brief moment of wonder when Kevin sneaks into Carnegie Hall to watch a performance of "O Come, All Ye Faithful."

No, it's not an essential Christmas movie; it's overly commercial for featuring the advertising tie-in of a tape recorder, the indulgence of a toy store, the fattening of a hotel minibar and a cameo by Donald Trump. But it's also aware of its strengths and knows that it's not about a more profound message for the true meaning of Christmas; it's about watching Tim Curry sneer about ordering a pizza and Daniel Stern being shot in the ass with a nail gun.

HOOK

DIRECTOR: Steven Spielberg | SCREENWRITER: Jim V. Hart, Malia Scotch Marmo | CAST: Dustin Hoffman, Robin Williams, Julia Roberts, Bob Hoskins, Maggie Smith, Charlie Korsmo | GENRE: Adventure | RUNNING TIME: 144 min | MPAA RATING: PG

CLASSIFICATION: WEIRD

Spielberg's take on the classic tale of *Peter Pan* is easily the most surreal of interpretations, coming in somewhere between a silly adventure, cumbersome adult drama, and corporate product. In this picture, intended as a sequel to the traditional tale, Pan has become an executive that has lost his youthful ways. Neverland is a glorified theme park of treehouses and painted trees, where lost boys can skateboard and play basketball in their forest community. Captain Hook is built up as a terrifying presence that runs his pirate hook across walls when kidnapping children, only to be seen as the familiar nut of a deranged pirate. All of this makes *Hook* (1991) such a bizarre concoction of fantasy that I find so fascinating for being so off.

Peter (Robin Williams) has grown up and become a short-tempered and smart-mouthed yuppie. He has children of his own, but is so caught up in work that he misses his son's ball game, sending someone from the office to tape the game for him. His kids are sweet and act as eccentric as most imaginative children, but he can't stand these kids and will often explode on them. And then Captain Hook (Dustin Hoffman) comes to take them away, and Peter is too late to save them. He returns home to discover the kids gone and the walls scraped with a hook. It's a terrifying sight that makes the evil pirate of Neverland seem like a frightening monster of horrific intent. It's a bit of a letdown when he turns out to be more of a slurring pirate captain that is secretly depressed and suicidal for Peter's return. Hook is just as disappointed to discover that Peter isn't his same old self for appearing fatter, plainer and unable to fly.

To save his kids, Peter must learn to be Pan all over again by being trained by the Lost Boys. They've been busy since he's been gone and their new leader is Rufio (Dante Basco), a sword-wielding teenager with apparently three mohawks. He doesn't believe this out-of-shape lawyer could be the legendary Peter Pan, but with some exercise, happy thoughts and a pretend feast, he'll soon be crowing in no time.

Williams and Hoffman make the best of what they can for roles with characters that are a little too dark and sad for such an uproarious adventure of ship battles and sword fights. Williams has a quick wit for a nervous man who thinks Neverland is a drunken haze while Hoffman's delivery is an odd mixture of silly and sinister. There are some surprising supporting roles here as well. Julia Roberts plays the chipper little fairy Tinkerbell if you can see her past the bright aura and obvious compositing. Maggie Smith provides the gentle voice of the old Wendy to remind her grandchildren that magic is real. Bob Hoskins blends well as the bumbling villain sidekick of Smee, doing his best to talk the captain out of killing himself. Peer close on Hook's ship and you'll see an array of stars hidden behind dirty pirate makeup, including David Crosby, Jimmy Buffett and Glenn Close in a beard.

The film is a treasure trove of funny lines I often find myself regularly quoting. One of the smaller Lost Boys feels around Williams' face to rediscover the Peter Pan he once knew; *"Oh, there you are, Peter."* Captain Hook's mockery on the irritation of children is relatable enough for a parent; *"I want a cookie. I want to stay up. I want, I want, I want, me, me, me, me, mine, mine, mine, mine, now, now, now."* And the reaction of Pan's daughter Maggie when she finally discovers the truth about her father always makes me laugh; *"Peter Pan is my...dad?"*

Hook is a movie I can only recommend for the nostalgic joy of looking back on a film so surreal and weird. For a movie that was intended as an adventure picture for children, a demographic that Spielberg is usually a master with appealing towards, it's a surprisingly adult. The script features depression and yuppie jokes that will soar over the heads of kids, as well as a convoluted origin about how Peter wanted to run away as a baby. That being said, there's a certain childlike appeal for a swashbuckling adventure of kids boarding ships and besting pirates in combat. And what kid didn't love cheering for Rufio with a battle crow?

HOOP DREAMS

DIRECTOR: Steve James | SCREENWRITER: Steve James, Frederick Marx | CAST: William Gates, Arthur Agee | GENRE: Documentary | RUNNING TIME: 170 min | MPAA RATING: PG-13

CLASSIFICATION: BEST

Hoop Dreams (1994) began as a 30-minute TV movie for PBS that snowballed into a three-hour documentary. The initial three weeks of footage focused on kids playing on a basketball court. The cameras followed two of them back to their homes. As the filmmakers continued to film, they realized the story could not end with them as kids. And for the next five years, the cameras would follow them all the way from playing in the streets to playing professionally for high school teams to their tragic exits.

The two subjects are William Gates and Arthur Agee, black teenagers of the slums of Chicago with aspirations of playing professional basketball. They come from low-income families, but are still hopeful these dreams can be achieved. They are targeted by a scout for St. Joseph's High School and accepted into the school. And though they'll have financial assistance, they'll still have to make the long 90-minute commute to the school's location in Westchester. Both William and Arthur, along with their families, are convinced that this will be the best of opportunities. After all, NBA star Isiah Thomas started here and, as the school continues to suggest, they could be just as lucky.

Despite all their effort, things don't go as planned. Arthur is dropped from St. Joseph's and they won't release his transcripts without a payment of $1,300 for tuition. He cannot graduate high school without them and St. Joseph's doesn't consider this their problem. They're only interested in Arthur as a basketball player. If he can't play, that scholarship is dropped. No matter. Arthur still makes the best of his abilities at Marshall and leads their team to be third in the state. He works at Pizza Hut for minimum wage, later using his success at Marshall to attend Mineral Area Junior College, a Missouri campus of few black students that are mostly basketball players.

William fairs better to be kept on at St. Joseph's, but then the unthinkable happens. He has a torn ligament and has to have it repaired. William does his best to make a speedy recovery, but another injury occurs when he returns to the basketball court. His confidence dwindles, despite the best help he receives from the Nike All-American Summer Camp. He'll eventually find a better deal at Marquette that offers him a four-year-scholarship, whether he plays basketball or not.

The way I write about this movie probably makes it sound as though it's a sports drama. It's not. At least not at its core anyway. The real meat of the documentary comes in the pressures that surround the lives of Arthur and William. Arthur's mother Shelia sacrifices the most to do what's best for her and her son. She is living on aid that dwindles further once Arthur turns 18. They cannot afford gas or electricity, relying on a lantern to find their way around their dark home. Despite her husband leaving, her back in pain and her options for a job limited, we watch her overcome to graduate from nursing school in the film's single most triumphant moment after a series of sad ones.

Hoops Dreams is three hours long, but it's so engrossing that I didn't want it to end. We learn enough about Arthur and William, as well as their families and worlds that we want to know what happens next. Ultimately, Arthur and William did not make it into the NBA and never became the next Isiah Thomas or Michael Jordan. They'll never be basketball legends, but are just as inspiring for how much better their lives turned out in the end.

HOT SHOTS!

DIRECTOR: Jim Abrahams | SCREENWRITER: Jim Abrahams, Pat Proft | CAST: Charlie Sheen, Cary Elwes, Valeria Golino, Jon Cryer, Kevin Dunn, Bill Irwin, Lloyd Bridges | GENRE: Comedy | RUNNING TIME: 84 min | MPAA RATING: PG-13

CLASSIFICATION: WEIRD

In an age where cliche action pictures were abundant, *Hot Shots!* (1991) came about to give the genre an excellent overblown satire to shake some sense into filmmakers. Similar in style to the likes of *Airplane!* and *The Naked Gun*, this parody picture aims precisely at the silliest of campy action pictures, *Top Gun*. And it'll take down a few other movies along the way.

Charlie Sheen plays the role of Topper Harley, satirizing the Tom Cruise role from *Top Gun* as a maverick pilot called back into the US Navy for a secret project. He meets with his therapist Ramada (Valeria Golino), who recommends that he doesn't go back to duty for his psychological issues. He refuses her warning, including a warning about the hallway being too dangerous with exposed wiring. He will, however, pursue a romance with her. Back on duty, Topper grows to despise fighter pilot Kent Gregory (Cary Elwes), who finds Topper unfit for combat. He'll also meet Jim "Wash-Out" Pfaffenbach (Jon Cryer), a pilot with distorted walleye vision.

There's a whole plot about Topper being called in for a specific reason with Operation Sleepy Weasel to prove pilots over planes, but that doesn't matter with a movie like this. The script is packed with wall-to-wall jokes that are launched at the screen with machine-gun speed. Sometimes the dialogue goes for the simplest of bits, as when Sheen and Elwes fight over Golino. She says they're acting like children, to which they respond with a childish battle of *"am not"* and *"are too,"* made all the more hilarious with their stern deliveries. The film also goes for many brilliant sight gags that come faster and funnier than the characters at times. Take the scene where a slew of jet pilots land on an aircraft carrier. One takes a handicap parking spot, angering a passing soldier in a wheelchair. Another starts unloading groceries out of the cockpit. And another removes their oxygen mask to reveal how hideously it has reshaped their mouth during flight.

The film has an uncanny ability to take all the typical tropes of action movies and reap as much comedy from them as possible. There's a moment when we know one of the pilots is not going to make it back from his next mission because his life seems too perfect. Just before he goes up in the air, the pilot's wife surprises him with a visit, tells him they finally acquired their dream home, gives him a new life insurance policy that he forgets to sign and mentions that he has found a solution for global warming that he'll divulge when he returns. The pilot's name is revealed: Dead Meat.

In case *Top Gun* wasn't a funny enough target, the movie goes about parodying other films with the same amount of inspiration. Sheen tries to be erotic with Golino in a scene reminiscent of *9½ Weeks* where they sexually feed each other food. But rather than indulge in fruits, Sheen feeds her a cold pizza. That premise alone is funny, but made extra hilarious how Sheen rolls up the pizza and licks the end as though he were rolling a cigarette. He will later place food on her body that is somehow hot enough for him to grill an egg and some bacon. Nothing says romance like midnight breakfast.

Hot Shots! was directed by satire master Jim Abrahams, previously helming such comedy classics as *Airplane!*, *Top Secret!* and *The Naked Gun*. It has the same wit and timing as those films, complete with the most elaborate of slapstick, as with an ambulance that takes the worst care of patients en route. The cast includes a young Charlie Sheen delivering a refreshingly deadpan performance and Abrahams regular Lloyd Bridges bringing innocence to such a stupid character. Not all of the jokes hit with huge laughs, but there are enough speed and force in each of them rapidly shot on the screen that I rarely noticed the lesser ones, making *Hot Shots!* more notable than just being a *Top Gun* parody.

HOT SHOTS! PART DEUX

DIRECTOR: Jim Abrahams | SCREENWRITER: Jim Abrahams, Pat Proft | CAST: Charlie Sheen, Lloyd Bridges, Valeria Golino, Brenda Bakke, Richard Crenna | GENRE: Comedy | RUNNING TIME: 86 min | MPAA RATING: PG-13

CLASSIFICATION: WEIRD

Hot Shots! Part Deux (1993), most likely using the French word of two for the one joke of the poster's slogan "Just Deux It," proceeds as a victory lap of its highly satirical predecessor. Whereas the previous picture mostly satirized *Top Gun*, this sequel takes palpable aim at the *Rambo* franchise. Adding to that, however, is a timely nature for mocking Saddam Hussein, current movie conventions and a handful of other movies in its cavalcade of parody.

Topper Harley (Charlie Sheen) has ditched the pilot life to retreat to a village in Tibet, where he can engage in fighting competitions and fix up the village huts with some recommendations by Bob Villa. But when Hussein presents a new threat to the world, Topper is reactivated as a soldier and is sent into the war zone of Iraq with his Rambo cosplay. Even the colonel briefing Topper on his assignment is played by Richard Crenna, the very same actor who briefed John Rambo in the *Rambo* trilogy of action pictures. As with all the actors, he is devoted to the script with deadpan grace, explaining Topper's importance as a soldier using Goldilocks and the Three Bears as an analogy. That's hilarious enough, but watch the very subtle delivery of Sheen reacting to this story as though he were a bewildered and innocent child.

Topper's mission is to plunge into Iraqi territory and rescue the captured soldier played by Rowan Atkinson. He is aided by a crew of ridiculous mercenaries that includes Miguel Ferrer, Michael Colyar, and Ryan Stiles. Valeria Golino is also present on the mission, reprising her role as Ramada from the previous movie, acting like an old flame for Topper. And Lloyd Bridges also returns, this time as the President of the United States, conceiving all sorts of wild and crazy ideas for solving the war, such as relocating the entire Middle East to Minnesota; *"Why go over there to fight? We can do it right here at home, and get in some good fishing while we're at it."* There is also a brief cameo by Martin Sheen, passing by Charlie Sheen's boat as though they're in different movies, both of them shouting encouragingly, *"I love you in Wall Street!"*

Director Jim Abrahams manages to find humor not just in easy parody, but also the smallest of additions for comedy. Take the opening scene with a humorous depiction of Hussein's bedtime routine. He packs a lunch in his lunchbox, has crackers in bed and sucks up the crumbs with a portable vacuum cleaner. In an early scene of a Tibetan village barn that holds fights for money, look in the background for a Subway sandwich shop with the specialty of a pig snout sandwich. A shootout inside the interior of a small fishing boat features Topper saving a vase that falls off the shelf. These are the smaller bits that prove *Part Deux* is capable of any gag in any setting and always keeps the eyes on the lookout for more amusing stuff in the background.

Part Deux not only finds funny things to exploit from other movies, but also trends in film. In a brilliant send-up of movie violence, an onscreen counter is displayed for how for how many soldiers Sheen kills in one scene. As the bodies add up, the digital credits signal when the movie has beaten the high scores of *Robocop* and *Total Recall*, eventually reaching the rank of *"BLOODIEST MOVIE EVER!"*.

There's nothing more insightful I can say about *Hot Shots! Part Deux* without just listing every single joke. So I'll close with this hilarious image: Saddam Hussein and his little dog are frozen solid by Lloyd Bridges and smashed into a thousand pieces. The pieces melt from a fire, and he reforms like the T-1000 in *Terminator 2*. But because he rebuilds himself with parts of his dog, Hussein spends the rest of the movie with a dog face. Dog-faced Saddam always makes me laugh.

THE HUNCHBACK OF NOTRE DAME

DIRECTOR: Gary Trousdale, Kirk Wise | SCREENWRITER: Tab Murphy, Irene Mecchi, Bob Tzudiker, Noni White, Jonathan Roberts | CAST: Tom Hulce, Demi Moore, Tony Jay, Kevin Kline, Paul Kandel, Jason Alexander, Charles Kimbrough, Mary Wickes, David Ogden Stiers | GENRE: Drama (Animated) | RUNNING TIME: 91 min | MPAA RATING: G

CLASSIFICATION: BEST

Disney's animated heroes and heroines tended to be beautiful and enchanting figures. *The Hunchback of Notre Dame* (1996) stands distinctly apart in how the lead is not a handsome fellow. He has a massive hump, a drooping eye, and an odd smile, appearing more as an Igor-like supporting character than a true hero. Sure, he's a character not as repulsive in Disney animation with his big eyes and cheerful smile, but he still doesn't fit as neatly next to Prince Charming.

Notre Dame is a much darker premise for a Disney animated film that the inclusion of comic relief gargoyle statues does little to offset the grander tale of social themes. The film opens on perhaps one of Disney's darkest opening songs, as a gypsy mother suffers a bitter end at the hands of the corrupt Judge Claude Frollo (Tony Jay). Before Frollo can kill her ugly baby as well, the cathedral's archdeacon witnesses this atrocity and condemns him to atone for his sins by raising the child. The boy grows up in the cathedral belltower to become Quasimoto (Tom Hulce), a man with a disfigured face that is spoken more of as a monster by Frollo. Locked away from society, his only friends are three gargoyles (Charles Kimbrough, Jason Alexander, and Mary Wickes) that only he can see. They provide the comic relief because, hey, this story gets pretty dark.

He decides to go against Frollo's rules and leave the Cathedral for the annual Festival of Fools, where he is declared King of the Fools for what the citizens believe to be a mask. When they discover that's no mask on his face, Quasimoto is tied down and tortured in public for being a freak, with Frollo looking down on him in the background. Rushing to the foreground, however, is the gypsy Esmeralda (Demi Moore) coming to his rescue. She pities him, but when Esmerelda becomes a new target of Frollo, Quasimoto takes pity on her and grants her sanctuary in the cathedral. It isn't long before Quasimoto finds himself caught up in a war between gypsies and Frollo's forces, but captain Phoebus (Kevin Kline) is hesitant about his duties as he has fallen in love with Esmerelda.

The movie weaves a story far more intricate than most Disney features, complete with a love triangle, tolerance, loneliness, guilt, and spirituality. It deals with harsher themes and delivers strong results. It will not end happily with the hero getting the girl because there is more than one hero. Someone is going to get hurt.

The Disney animation studio gave the story their usual treatment of breathtaking hand-drawn animation and catchy songs, but they carry a heftier punch for dealing with such material. In one of the film's best musical sequences, "Hellfire," Frollo secretly confesses his infatuation for Esmerelda that he views as a sin for craving a gypsy. His motivations are a swirling mess of guilt, helplessness, lust, and rage. Take a moment to appreciate how extraordinary this musical number is for its operatic depiction of judging saints, Tony Jay's powerful vocals and being a Disney song about killing a woman the villain desires.

The Hunchback of Notre Dame is remarkable for many reasons. It takes grim material and, despite some comic relief additions and animal mascots, delivers on most of the grander themes present in the original story. It takes an ugly character and turns him into the hero, even for as cuddly as the Disney designers make him for this movie. Above all, it's another masterpiece from the Disney Renaissance age with a more unconventional story.

I COME IN PEACE

DIRECTOR: Craig R. Baxley | SCREENWRITER: Jonathan Tydor, David Koepp | CAST: Dolph Lundgren, Brian Benben, Betsy Brantley | GENRE: Science Fiction | RUNNING TIME: 91 min | MPAA RATING: R

CLASSIFICATION: WEIRD

Among Dolph Lundgren's strangest roles, *I Come In Peace* (1990) is one of his silliest misfires. This was a film that had so many problems it couldn't even decide on a title. The script was initially titled Lethal Contact. The title during production was Dark Angel. That title was too familiar, so it was changed to *I Come In Peace*, but future releases labeled it once again as Dark Angel. This indecisiveness sets the tone for a sloppy production of a bizarre script of cops, aliens and vibrating disks that kill people. And because it's such a silly title, I'm calling it *I Come In Peace*.

Lundgren plays Houston detective Jack Caine, a cop who doesn't go by the book to get the job done. He shirks regulations to pursue the white collar drug dealers, known uncreatively as the White Boys, those same criminals that killed his partner. He has a new partner of FBI agent Larry (Brian Benson). The two of them not only have to foil the White Boys, but stumble onto an extraterrestrial threat of the alien drug dealer Talec (Matthias Hues), appearing as a white-haired warrior from Highlander with the tech and mannerisms of the Terminator. This alien is not here to deal, but to harvest his latest crop. On his planet, human endorphins are considered a top drug. And if there are alien drug dealers, an alien DEA agent (Jay Bilas) isn't far behind.

Caine has to stop Talec's plan of filling people up with drugs, extracting their endorphins and killing them in the process. If Talec is successful in his extraction, Earth could become a prime target for other alien drug dealers to drain our brains. The cops will need to stop him, but they'll have to match his strength and dodge his spinning disc that can slice throats.

That's a very wild story and maybe too ambitious for such a cheap production. The alien gun is mostly a modified Calico M950, and Talec's deadly disc is mostly a CD with sharp edges. Lundgren feels very awkward trying to play the no-nonsense detective next to the more frantic Benson, but it's surprising how much of this chemistry works. It's no *Red Heat*, but the relationship has its small moments of charisma or at least as much as Lundgren can muster with his accent. He does sound more at ease than he did in *Rocky IV*.

But the film falters significantly with a cluttered plot for a story that doesn't need this much baggage. Caine has a girlfriend of a coroner, played by Betsy Brantley, stressing that her beefy boyfriend should be focusing on their relationship. What's this unneeded and uninteresting romance arc doing in my sci-fi action picture? It doesn't exactly pair well with the bloody and gory scenes of aliens harvesting brains.

Director Craig R. Baxley was a former stuntman, and he knows how to shoot some fantastic scenes where the hulking actors do their stunts. There's a tremendous fight in a convenience store robbery, where Lundgren can roundhouse kick a criminal with a fluidity I didn't expect for a guy with legs like tree trunks. Matthias Hues does all his stunts as the villain, which is pretty impressive for scenes where there is fire and explosions all around him. Sure, it's a little too goofy for its presentation that appears as the last gasp of 1980s action pictures, but there's an admirable and inventive spirit at play for the special effects and out-there story. And you can't take a movie like this too seriously; not with such lines as *"Fuck you, space man!"* and *"But you go in pieces, asshole!"* in response to the villain's titular catchphrase.

IN THE MOUTH OF MADNESS

DIRECTOR: John Carpenter | SCREENWRITER: Michael De Luca | CAST: Sam Neill, Julie Carmen, Jürgen Prochnow, Charlton Heston | GENRE: Horror | RUNNING TIME: 95 min | MPAA RATING: R

CLASSIFICATION: WEIRD

In the same way that Stephen King's *Misery* played on the reality of an author being targeted by fans, John Carpenter's *In the Mouth of Madness* (1994) focuses on what happens when the author's work targets the fans. It's a film that takes significant influences from the maddening works of H.P. Lovecraft, the title itself being a jab at the author's novella *At the Mountains of Madness*. Between drawing references to both King and Lovecraft, Carpenter almost goes as nutty with the material as the characters.

Horror writer Sutter Cane has gone missing. The last book he wrote before his disappearance was a best-seller that caused his readers to go mad. Insurance investigator John Trent (Sam Neill) is called in to investigate Cane's publisher of Arcane Publishing. While hearing about this case, he is attacked by Cane's former agent, who has gone insane and murdered his whole family after reading Cane's books. The agent's last words before being shot dead by police are asking if Trent has read Sutter Cane. Having never read his work, Trent figures he should probably start for this assignment.

Trent meets with the publishing director (Charlton Heston) and Cane's editor, Linda Styles (Julie Carmen). He also reads Cane's books and discovers a clue in all his book covers; a series of red lines that when combined form a map to a New Hampshire town present in the novels. Both Trent and Linda venture off to the area and discover the village of Hobb's End, a fictional town from Cane's stories. That's creepy. Even creepier, the residents seem to resemble characters from the books as well.

And it only gets crazier from here, as Trent's initial skepticism about this all being a publicity stunt are proven wrong. Cane's total disappearance was planned by Linda, but none of the frightening elements of Hobb's End were the work of the scam. Typical spooky town frights are abounding, but what's scarier is how Trent slowly loses his grip on reality. He keeps seeing suicidal people, grotesque monsters and ghoulish apparitions that are straight out of the books. Trent cannot leave town, continually being transported back if he tries to go. And by the time Trent finally meets Sutter Cane (Jürgen Prochnow), a terrible truth is revealed about his existence, that Trent was meant to fulfill a specific purpose of Cane's next novel.

It wouldn't be a John Carpenter horror film without some surreal and twisted imagery, and this film offers plenty. The monsters that pursue Trent are uniquely designed as a mess of claws, teeth, eyes, tentacles and contorted limbs. The settings are genuinely strange and nightmarish, featuring a church that transforms into a watery tunnel that bridges fiction and reality. There's an ambitiously odd moment where Cane tears apart his face as though he were ripping a hole in a book, shifting the sense of dimension. Carpenter always keeps our eyes peeled for how distorted Trent's reality becomes. Notice how each time he is transported back to Hobb's End how much more blue his world becomes. Sam Neill throws everything he has into this role of a man slowly losing his sanity, making it one of his best performances. Considering he's working with acting legends David Warner and Charlton Heston, Neill holds his own pretty well.

It's impossible to talk about the film without revealing its most prominent and most shocking twist. All I'll say is that it is very Lovecraftian for featuring creatures from another dimension and the apocalypse. For these elements, the film is considered the final film in Carpenter's Apocalypse Trilogy, the other movies being *The Thing* (1982) and *Prince of Darkness* (1987). While *In the Mouth of Madness* is not quite Carpenter at his best for its jump scares and seemingly random monsters at times, it remains one of his more underrated works as a psychological horror and a love letter to Lovecraft.

INDEPENDENCE DAY

DIRECTOR: Roland Emmerich | SCREENWRITER: Dean Devlin, Roland Emmerich | CAST: Will Smith, Bill Pullman, Jeff Goldblum, Mary McDonnell, Judd Hirsch, Margaret Colin, Randy Quaid | GENRE: Science Fiction | RUNNING TIME: 145 min | MPAA RATING: PG-13

CLASSIFICATION: WEIRD

Roland Emmerich deserves a modicum of credit for taking a standard flying saucer script as *Independence Day* (1996) and filling it with unforgettable imagery. A giant saucer hovers over the White House, shoots down a laser and causes a massive explosion that catches a helicopter in its fiery path of destruction. It's a great shot, and there are several more where the saucers obliterate other landmarks and send out smaller ships to do battle with jet fighters. All that stuff is fine; it's the garbage script between all these visual marvels that make the movie more odd than entertaining.

The movie follows a host of characters during this alien invasion and none of them all that unique. David (Jeff Goldblum) is the scientist that has the honor of nervously stating the exposition of the aliens using our satellites to coordinate an attack, thus allowing him to construct a big countdown timer before all the ships blow up monuments; *"Times up."* Steven (Will Smith) is the cocky military pilot that has the most one-liners and celebrates with cigars, committed to winning this war before committing to his fiance. Thomas (Bill Pullman) is the President of the United States that must race to the helicopter while holding his young daughter before the aliens obliterate Washington. And so on and so on, as the movie introduces a host of colorful characters of various races and professions, from crop dusters to exotic dancers, all coming together to combat the aliens. Some do more than others.

Though the script is old with its story, the visuals were the latest in special effects. The destruction of major cities is grand and epic, complete with skyscrapers exploding and hordes of terrified citizens fleeing from explosions. But these effects come off more grand than spectacular. The hovering saucers that obliterate cities are only impressive for their size and not their design. Zoom too far out, and it'll appear as though giant frisbees are attacking Earth. Zoom in too far, and you'll probably see a random assortment of junk painted and glued to the ships' exteriors.

This is the type of big-budget B-movie that has to run high with preposterousness to make any of it work. The aliens are apparently not only stupid enough to use our satellites to coordinate their global attack, but have possibly already been here as one of their starships is being held at area 51. The motivations of the aliens are revealed in one brief scene where the aliens make contact with the silliest of dialogue; the President of the United States asks what they want, and the alien's answer is that they want all humans to die, for no particular reason. Goldblum's breakthrough idea to stop the aliens comes to him in a drunken stupor, and his father mentions he'll catch a cold lying on the floor. Cold? Like a virus? Computer virus? Eureka! And, of course, the computer virus will work inside the alien's central computer systems, despite not having any knowledge of their operations.

Independence Day was THE blockbuster of the decade, debuting on July 3, 1996, and ranking in $817 million globally. Its success launched a new sub-genre of disaster pictures, which were more about large-scale catastrophes than the characters within them. And for carrying a patriotic theme with a harrowing monologue Bill Pullman delivers before a battle, it was considered a quintessentially American film, occupying nearly every American VHS home library. The film doesn't hold up as well over time for still being very cheesy with its characters and plotting, but it's worth checking out for the silly script, a benchmark of special effects and the first film of Will Smith's career to be a significant box office success. And to think his movie career finally took off with him punching aliens while hollering at them; *"Welcome to Earth!"*

THE IRON GIANT

DIRECTOR: Brad Bird | SCREENWRITER: Tim McCanlies | CAST: Jennifer Aniston, Harry Connick, Jr., Vin Diesel, James Gammon, Cloris Leachman, Christopher McDonald, John Mahoney, Eli Marienthal, M. Emmet Walsh | GENRE: Science Fiction (Animated) | RUNNING TIME: 87 min | MPAA RATING: PG

CLASSIFICATION: BEST

Brad Bird's *The Iron Giant* (1999) stands out substantially from a decade where American animated movies were either Disney musicals or wannabe Disney musicals. There's no need for musical sequences, comic relief sidekicks or plush-worthy mascots in an animated film with a precise, creative and profound story to tell of a boy and his robot. That may explain why Warner Bros. wasn't sure how to promote this film and how it went criminally unnoticed during its theatrical release.

The film follows Hogarth Hughes, a typical little boy of the 1950s with the interests of science fiction, comic books and owning a pet. His waitress of a mother (Jennifer Aniston) doesn't approve of him having a dog or a squirrel, so you could imagine how peeved she'd be if she discovered Hogarth bringing home an iron giant from the stars, voiced by Vin Diesel. The robot doesn't know where he came from and isn't familiar with Earth. Hogarth, excited to have a robot pet, teaches him about everything from speaking words to reading comic books to hiding in the barn from mom. They have fun together, especially when Hogarth is taken for rides in the palm of the giant's hand.

Realizing he can't keep the giant at his home, Hogarth needs to find him food and shelter. The junkyard owned by the local beatnik Dean (Harry Connick Jr.) can provide both. Dean IS a cool guy and likes Hogarth enough to help him, but doesn't like the giant. But when the giant's ability to rip and bend metal can help with his artwork, Dean starts to come around and teach the robot a little something about creativity. While the giant remains hidden from the public, his damage to public property has not gone unnoticed. Government Agent Chet Mansley (Christopher McDonald) arrives in town to investigate and is quickly convinced there's something big in this town when half his car is found eaten. He targets Hogarth as a potential lead, making the boy's concealment of the robot all the more stressful.

The film's animation style comes off as a cross between a Norman Rockwell painting and a golden era *Superman*. While the mechanical giant is rounded and clunky enough to come straight off the pages of a sci-fi comic book, the human characters all appear in bright colors with a consistent blush on their faces. These may seem like clashing forces for the humans being animated in traditional 2D while the giant was rendered with cel-shaded 3D animation, but it syncs up surprisingly well for two mediums colliding.

There's a very touching scene where Hogarth confronts the giant on his side during the night, walking along his arm as the giant's illuminating eyes cast shadows on the boy. The combination is so seamless that the audience won't be distracted and can better focus on the scenes strong concept of Hogarth teaching the giant about death: *"It's bad to kill, but it's not bad to die."* Hogarth's words will come in handy for the giant when the military forces threaten him led towards the town that activates his defense systems, making him look more convincing as an invader from Mars. It will then be up to the giant to decide if he wants to be nothing more than the gun he was programmed to be or the hero of Superman he aspires towards.

The Iron Giant, for being such an original animated film, was a commercial failure with the strangest of marketing. It would later become recognized as a classic from Brad Bird when his work on *The Incredibles* (2004) made him better known as a top-tier animation director. The film holds up considerably over time for its astonishing animation style, fun characters and deep tone that has been known to provoke a few tears when the rusty bot saves the day alone; *"I go. You stay. No follow."* For being a charming tale about a boy and an alien robot, it has often been compared to Spielberg's *E.T.* for the similar characters and story. Brad Bird's response to such comparisons: *"E.T. doesn't go kicking ass."*

THE ISLAND OF DR. MOREAU

DIRECTOR: John Frankenheimer | SCREENWRITER: Richard Stanley, Ron Hutchinson | CAST: Marlon Brando, Val Kilmer, David Thewlis, Fairuza Balk | GENRE: Science Fiction | RUNNING TIME: 96 min | MPAA RATING: PG-13

CLASSIFICATION: WEIRD

The Island of Dr. Moreau (1996) is such a trainwreck of a film that it has to be seen to be believed. It was tough during the 1990s to get veteran actor Marlon Brando to agree to a role, but he was somehow convinced to play a figure that spends most of the movies in robes while babbling about being a god, or possibly the Pope based on the way he dresses. It features creatures designed by the famed special effects artist Stan Winston, but the results are more goofy than intimidating. You haven't seen weird until you've watched an overweight and bespeckled Brando play piano for a werewolf-like creature that wails and grunts, hilariously asking with a whimper *"What am I?"* I'd like to think the movie itself is asking the same question.

Based on the H.G. Wells novel, the story follows Edward Douglas (David Thewlis) after he crashes his plane into the sea. He is picked up on a boat by Montgomery (Val Kilmer) who takes him to the mysterious Moreau's Island. The island seems nice enough with beautiful scenery, roomy accommodations and the lovely Aissa (Fairuza Balk) providing some dance. Montgomery keeps assuring he'll radio for help, but keeps putting it off. Something doesn't smell right on this island when Montgomery locks Douglas in his housing for his own good.

Curious, Douglas ventures out at nightfall and happens upon a lab where he witnesses the birth of a mutant baby being birthed by mutants. The island has a whole village of them, created from the mad experiments of Dr. Moreau. And, wow, once Brando appears as Moreau, it's one of the silliest character introductions of his entire acting career. He is escorted in his makeshift jungle Popemobile, wearing massive amounts of white makeup, large sunglasses, a Sunday hat that seems made for beekeeping and red lipstick because I guess it contrasts well with the white powder.

Moreau tries to explain to Douglas his secret experiments of trying to breed a higher form of life. All Douglas can see are freaks that have had their DNA tampered with. Of particular creepiness is

Moreau's little assistant, whom Moreau will later play music with as the little guy plays a smaller piano on top of a big piano. It's a scene so absurd that it was then satirized in *Austin Powers: The Spy Who Shagged Me*. The mutant beasts are given drugs to prevent regression and embedded with pain implants so that Moreau can control them if they get out of line. Naturally, they'll find these implants, remove them and revolt.

One of the silliest moments is the death of Brando's character. When the mutants remove their implants, they state the laws of being human that Moreau had established and proceed to eat his flesh in a hammock. This should be an emotional and dark moment, but the ridiculous line delivery of the mutants makes the scene about as comical as the moment they tear off Brando's arm with the wristwatch still attached.

The story behind the production of *The Island of Dr. Moreau* is far more intriguing than the movie itself, so much so it became a documentary film, *Lost Soul: The Doomed Journey of Richard Stanley's Island of Dr. Moreau* (2014). The original director, Richard Stanley, was fired after only three days of shooting, becoming an emotional wreck as he began tearing up documents and disappearing in the shooting location of Australia, later visiting the sets in disguise. The second director, John Frankenheimer, got into heated arguments with Val Kilmer and Marlon Brando, as well as being overly critical of the Australian crew. Kilmer and Brando started making more extensive demands out of personal problems; Kilmer's wife had filed for divorce before filming began and Brando's daughter had recently committed suicide, both events stalling production.

With all these issues, it's amazing the film was even finished and stands as one of Brando's worst movies, which is reason enough to give this weird film a watch.

JACK

DIRECTOR: Francis Ford Coppola | SCREENWRITER: James DeMonaco, Gary Nadeau | CAST: Robin Williams, Diane Lane, Jennifer Lopez, Brian Kerwin, Fran Drescher, Bill Cosby | GENRE: Comedy | RUNNING TIME: 117 min | MPAA RATING: PG-13

CLASSIFICATION: WORST

Robin Williams can do well in a role where he is given a strong enough character, but he's working with very little in *Jack* (1996). As the titular character, Williams plays a boy with Werner syndrome; he'll grow much faster than average humans. By the time he's twelve, he appears as a fully grown adult, body hair and all. By the time he's twenty, he will most likely die. It sounds sad, and it could've made for high drama if the screenplay wasn't so poorly written to be more about the obvious jokes. It is easily the biggest waste of Williams' talent in a film that never finds enough comedy or drama for him to take advantage of.

To be fair, Williams does what he can with such a character as Jack. He does his best to nail the mannerisms and manic nature of a ten-year-old boy, excited to finally go to a real school after being homeschooled for so long by a tutor (Bill Cosby). The kids mock, giggle and cower at the new kid in class for his large stature, receding hairline and increasing arm hair. The expected jokes occur. He tries to sit in a desk built for fifth-graders, only to have it break under the pressure of his weight. How could the sweet teacher (Jennifer Lopez) not notice this before he had to embarrass himself? She makes up for this oversight later on by gently talking to Jack over gummy bears and trying to let him down kindly when he asks her to the dance. These scenes are mere glimpses of a better movie buried in bad decisions.

The boys of Jack's class begin to accept him, but more for his physical advantages of looking like a 40-year-old man. They pick him for their basketball game since he can tower over every kid on the playground. They will later take advantage of his ability to pass himself off as a substitute principal, buy nude magazines and make the most significant farts. This is not Robin Williams at his finest for a film where he hangs out in a treehouse with ten-year-old boys, farting into a coffee can and then lighting it on fire. And, of course, the treehouse will succumb to Jack's weight, telegraphed when it first shakes upon his entry.

It's remarkable how an accomplished director as Francis Ford Coppola could deliver such a dull movie. It's as though he wanted to make a film where Robin Williams pretends to be a kid, but didn't care to flesh the story out past its dubious checkpoints of heartwarming moments and juvenile jabs. Nothing takes off here in a movie that jumps all over the place. Jack's parents (Diane Lane and Brian Kerwin) have a somber talk about Jack growing up when they're alone on the night of his first sleepover. But before any meaningful dialogue can occur, the film quickly cuts to Jack and his friends making a gross dish of ketchup, worms and other nasty foods to be eaten on a dare.

Films such as *Big* and *Vice Versa*, where adults pretend to be kids, are amusing because there is a temporary role reversal. We know in the end the child inside these adult bodies will return to the average life of a kid once more. *Jack* doesn't have that luxury with no resolution for extending his life as death looms over his shoulder early. A writing assignment in class about what the students will be when they grow up depresses him. Heart problems force Jack to stay out of school, and he's further depressed. This leads to Jack getting drunk in a bar, starting a fight and being arrested. The only possible way this film could get any darker was if Jack sleeps with a prostitute and begins taking drugs off the streets. Given Coppola's direction, I'm not sure which he'd play up for laughs.

Similar to *Kindergarten Cop*, this is a film that never finds a specific audience. The poster features Jack's name written with crayons, and there are childish jokes in this script, but the movie is rated PG-13 and contains many adult elements too dour for kids to relate. Coppola had a great premise to work with here, but his retreat into uninspired and sitcom territory is about as depressing as Jack's descent into sadness for realizing his fate. You can only have Williams play up the role of a kid who is awkward around adults, gross around boys and pensive around parents for so long before the bit runs out of gas. And Coppola was running on fumes with this movie, hopefully not literally.

JACK FROST

DIRECTOR: Troy Miller | SCREENWRITER: Mark Steven Johnson, Steve Bloom Jonathan Roberts, Jeff Cesario | CAST: Michael Keaton, Kelly Preston, Mark Addy, Joseph Cross | GENRE: Comedy | RUNNING TIME: 101 min | MPAA RATING: PG

CLASSIFICATION: WORST

Not every creature born from the Jim Henson Creature Shop can be a winner, nor can each one enhance a lame idea for a character. The studio was tasked with trying to create a convincing snowman that was able to talk, emote, move its arms and roll across the snow. In hitting all these technical aspects, they succeeded. But to what end? Interestingly enough, there was a horror movie of the same title with a snowman that killed people, which was far less terrifying than the highly-technical snowman of *Jack Frost* (1998).

Before we get to the snowman, however, the movie spends an awful lot of time whipping up a depressing and off tone. Michael Keaton plays the musician Jack Frost (yes, this is his actual name), leader of the band uncreatively titled The Jack Frost Band. He has an 11-year-old son at home, Charlie (Joseph Cross), and a lonely wife, Gabby (Kelly Preston), both of which desperately miss him when he's on the road. When Jack finally decides to stop all the gigs and go home to his family, fate sends him hurtling off the road and dying in a car crash. Charlie and Gabby are heartbroken, still crying months after his death. What a fun Christmas film for the whole family!

I can only fathom that they tried to make the first act so depressing in hopes that the second would be more forgivable for all its incoherence, creepiness and wasted potential. Before Jack's death, he bestowed on Charlie a harmonica that would call him home if played. Through some unexplained magic, Jack returns in the form of a snowman. And here is where the film hits its biggest flaw: living snowman look creepy in live-action. They always seem playful and charming in the animated specials of *Frosty the Snowman* and *The Snowman*, but the creation of the snowman for this film, a combination of practical and computer effects, is frightening. His beady eyes, large mouth cavity, and thin twig arms are something straight out of a kid's nightmares. Charlie's initial fear of the snowman is more than understandable, and I'm surprised he accepts his dad's new form so readily.

Nothing intelligent is done with Jack as a snowman. Being made of snow, he's somehow able to throw snowballs at rapid-fire speed with his twig arms. He helps Charlie ward off some bullies in a snowball fight that turns into a cartoonish chase on sleds. Later, Jack will coach Charlie with his hockey and encourage him to join the hockey team. I understand that Jack is trying to be the kind dad he never had the time to be, but wouldn't there be more to talk about with someone who died and came back as a snowman. Is Charlie not even slightly curious what the afterlife is like? Hockey tryouts don't seem as important in comparison.

Jack Frost is so ignorant of its potential it becomes more cynical, surreal and frightening than the warm family entertainment it was most likely intended to be. Charlie seems so sad after dad's death, but can only think about how to best his bully once Jack returns in snowman form. And I dare anyone to explain to me what exactly goes down in the ending, which finds Michael Keaton's soul glowing in a twister of snow. But above all the sentimental drivel and magic without rules, the talking snowman is still the biggest sin. Worth noting is that the killer snowman from the horror movie *Jack Frost* (1997) was more approachable and funny by comparison. And that snowman was intended to be a frightening monster that killed people.

JACOB'S LADDER

DIRECTOR: Adrian Lyne | SCREENWRITER: Bruce Joel Rubin | CAST: Tim Robbins, Elizabeth Peña, Danny Aiello | GENRE: Horror | RUNNING TIME: 113 min | MPAA RATING: R

CLASSIFICATION: BEST

We are not meant to understand how the titular character of *Jacob's Ladder* (1990) sees strange and frightening images of terror in his daily life. That's not the point. The film doesn't venture out of Jacob's mind, favoring to keep us locked inside his psychological cage of paranoia and dread. We experience every ounce of his nightmare that exists in an uncomfortable void between heaven and hell. We share his unsure and fearful nature of reality he has been reshaped into one that makes the eyes widen and the stomach turn. There's no light at the end of the tunnel for Jacob, and it's a fantastic film to watch for how everything starts to go black.

Tim Robbins plays the strung-out veteran of Jacob, a man who has seen plenty of death in Vietnam. He lives in 1975 Brooklyn with a Ph.D. he doesn't use, an ex-wife he misses and a job at the post office. Something is wrong in his life. He is nearly run over by cars and subway trains. He starts seeing visions of blood and faceless monsters. In one of the film's weirdest moments at a party, he watches on the dance floor as a woman is raped and gored by a tentacle monster, barely visible behind strobe lights. He is the only one who can see this.

With his friends dying around him, Jacob believes the Army may have performed experiments on him and his fellow soldiers. He tries to recall a time on the battlefield where their memories were lost when they grew dizzy. Jacob remembers being airlifted to a hospital, but not much else. Seeking other Vietnam veterans for help, he tries to piece together what exactly happened at the hospital. The veterans back out and the visions continue to grow more strange, surreal and frightening with each transition and awakening.

Even with such blunt imagery, there is a constant questioning of Jacob's reality and timeline. Is he experiencing hallucinations from some science experiments or is it all psychological from the war? Are the visions of his past what happened or how he wants to remember them? The answer becomes more evident towards the end of the movie, but the skillful editing and multidimensional performance of

Robbins keep the mystery all the more intriguing to follow.

One scene that is crucial to understanding Jacob's mind takes place in a hospital that may or may not be a hallucination. He is placed on a gurney and wheeled across a slippery and bloody floor of organs and body parts. Jacob watches the rooms he passes by and starts seeing more scary figures and symbols of his regret. When the doctors begin to operate on him, Jacob tries to make a case for his sanity. But what if these doctors are not a hallucination? What if they're something far more frightening that Jacob refuses to face?

Without giving too much away, the ladder of the title refers to life and death, up towards heaven and down towards hell. Jacob finds himself caught in the middle, fearful of pursuing either direction. There are happy moments of love in his life, as well as darker ones of guilt. And when it gets dark, the film turns pitch black to an unsettling degree. It's a fun film to pick apart for its themes and imagery, but deeply disturbing for its presentation.

There's a moment where Jacob hallucinates a doctor jamming a syringe into his temple. In that same instance, Jacob realizes a horrible truth and the needle is suddenly less painful than the chilling realization of what is going on. It's a scene that never fails to frighten me for its implication about one's mental state being so warped you can't differentiate between dreams and reality, hallucinations and real violence, heaven and hell. *Jacob's Ladder* is the type of scary film that crawls inside your head and refuses to leave. Fair warning.

JASON GOES TO HELL: THE FINAL FRIDAY

DIRECTOR: Adam Marcus | SCREENWRITER: Jay Huguely, Dean Lorey | CAST: John D. LeMay, Kari Keegan, Erin Gray, Allison Smith, Steven Culp, Steven Williams | GENRE: Horror | RUNNING TIME: 88 min | MPAA RATING: R

CLASSIFICATION: WORST

Not to be outdone by *Freddy's Dead* (1991), New Line Cinema decided to put the other horror franchise icon of Jason Vorhees to rest, for good this time (sort of, but not really). But for the final film of Jason's classic run as the killer of Camp Crystal Lake, *Jason Goes To Hell* (1993) whips up such ludicrous writing that proves the series has jumped the shark with its ninth entry. Hell can't come fast enough for Jason.

Now more mangled than before, Jason Vorhees pulls another trick out of his magical bag of convenient powers. After being blown to bits by the FBI, his still-beating heart mesmerizes the coroner into eating it up, causing Jason to possess his body. And for the rest of the movie, Jason will continue possessing bodies until he can find another member of his bloodline that he can infest and be reborn as the killer once more. This makes *Jason Goes To Hell* the biggest tease of the series as you won't see the killer don his new hockey mask until the very end of the movie. Most of the running time features Jason in the form of either a glowing spirit, a tentacle monster that protrudes out of mouths or a nasty little demon that claws its way out of bodies. All of this convoluted logic for Jason's game of host body hot potato makes me pine for the more straightforward entries of a masked killer slashing up camp counselors.

The new rules for killing Jason is that he can only be killed by someone from his bloodline and only with a mystical knife. This information is relayed by the film's most eccentric and wild character of Creighton Duke, played by a gleeful Steven Williams trying to ham up the role as far as possible. He bestows this knowledge onto Steven Freeman (John D. LeMay), portrayed as the nerd who would usually learn the most about Jason and then be killed off. But in this picture, Steven is the hero more or less who will be the one to connect the dots with the aid of his female companion Jessica (Kari Keegan).

There was never much logic to the *Friday the 13th* movies, but this one is easily the most farfetched. None of Jason's rules are fully explained, leaving plenty of loopholes and random actions to his demonic powers. The special effects of his soul are cheesy, protruding into bodies as small beams of light. And the inevitable ending of Jason being drug down into the underworld is both underwhelming and confusing; hands drag him down into the dirt while a heavenly spotlight targets his body that is attacked by more beams of light. Are the lights supposed to be the souls he has claimed over the years? Possibly, but who knows or cares by the end of the picture?

The film does at least feature a few solid kills. When Jason jumps to another body, his previous host of an officer begins to melt to the floor with his skin turning gooey and his jaw falling off. Jason grabs the head of a diner employee and forces him into the deep-fryer. But for every gruesome and creative kill, some less stellar ones are either lame in conception (elbowing someone in the face, smashing heads together) or merely occur off-screen. In a horror franchise that prides itself on blood and gore, even the kills become a tease for not featuring the gruesome money shots audiences have come to expect from the series. It's a little late for subtlety if that was indeed what this young director was going for.

The film's only moment of genuine excitement came in the ending stinger. Jason's mask, left behind in the dirt, is drug into hell by the claws of Freddy Krueger. The potential of a fight between the horror figures of Freddy and Jason instantly lit a spark of anticipation for their future bout. It's too bad that movie would not come for another decade, further adding to the film's long and tedious list of teases.

JAWBREAKER

DIRECTOR: Darren Stein | SCREENWRITER: Darren Stein | CAST: Rose McGowan, Rebecca Gayheart, Julie Benz, Judy Greer, Chad Christ, Ethan Erickson, Carol Kane, Pam Grier | GENRE: Comedy | RUNNING TIME: 87 min | MPAA RATING: R

CLASSIFICATION: WORST

Jawbreaker (1999) takes all those snobby, superficial girls you knew from high school and tries to make them even more inhuman. It begins with the teen girl collective known as the Fearsome Four playing a joke on their member Liz (Charlotte Ayana) for her 17th birthday. The other three members of Courtney (Rose McGowan), Marcie (Julie Benz), and Julie (Rebecca Gayheart) want to treat her to a birthday breakfast, but plan to do so by kidnapping her as masked criminals and driving her to the diner in a trunk. Unfortunately, they use a jawbreaker candy as a gagging device, and she chokes to death on the ride over. Why a jawbreaker of all things? Perhaps they were too prudish to buy a proper rubber ball gag from a sex shop.

The rest of the film is a black comedy of trying to cover up Liz's death for all the hilarity the movie thinks it can muster. But do we care if these girls are caught? I didn't, but the film presses on anyway. To cover up the murder, Courtney pretends to be Liz's mother over the phone to say she'll be absent from school. That buys some time, but they still have to make it look like they didn't kill Liz. Their solution: stage her corpse in bed, so it seems like she was raped to death.

Overhearing this inhuman scheme is the school outcast, Fern Mayo (Judy Greer). The murdering trio can't have her blab and decide to buy her silence by making Fern (what else?) a popular member of their clique. This, of course, involves giving Fern a makeover and instructing her on the finer aspects of being a popular girl, such as never eating lunch. But, surprise, Fern turns out to be even more despicable and nasty than the three girls that murdered their friends. Are THEY surprised by this development? A girl who favors being popular over informing the police about a murder would have to be pretty evil. Meanwhile, a detective played by Pam Grier investigates the disappearance of Liz, but is just as clueless as the girls. She believes almost every ridiculous lie that is told and seems to ignore every bit of evidence that points to the murderous trio in bright neon letters.

Jawbreaker is the type of movie that requires the most idiotic of characters to justify stretching its material. The only moment of tension comes when Jennie is suddenly overcome with a brand new emotion she hasn't felt within her clique: guilt. As punishment for considering turning herself in, the other girls shun Jennie, and her popularity drops like a rock. And the battle for being popular in high school continues as the cover-up gets messier, to the point where Courtney has sex with a stranger (Marilyn Manson) in Liz' bed so she can frame him as the rapist. All of this leads up to the senior prom to blame the evilest girl of the pack by playing her recorded admission of murder over the speakers. But if high school students were to hear this news about their prom queen, would their initial response be to pelt her with food? Those tomatoes seem better suited for fixing the prom queen results or cheating on a test.

It's not that a movie about the bad girls of high school can't be funny. Mark Waters proved it in 2004 by directing *Mean Girls*, a savage teen clique comedy with real smarts, and so did 1988's *Heathers* with an accidental death that plays out with more cleverness and wit. By comparison, *Jawbreaker* is about as pointless and junky as the candy itself.

JINGLE ALL THE WAY

DIRECTOR: Brian Levant | SCREENWRITER: Randy Kornfield, Chris Columbus | CAST: Arnold Schwarzenegger, Sinbad, Phil Hartman, Rita Wilson, Robert Conrad, Jim Belushi | GENRE: Comedy | RUNNING TIME: 89 min | MPAA RATING: PG

CLASSIFICATION: WEIRD

When Arnold Schwarzenegger wasn't mowing down bad guys with big guns and big muscles, he found himself wrapped up in ill-written comedies as an average guy. Perhaps the most bizarre of these projects was *Jingle All The Way* (1996), a commercial Christmas movie in which Arnold finds himself sliding into a ball pit and being accused of touching little children by angry moms who whack him with purses. He's a long ways away from *Total Recall* and *Terminator 2*.

It's a scenario that many parents are familiar with during the surge of the highly-sought Tickle-Me Elmo dolls and Buzz Lightyear action figures during the holiday season. Turbo Man is the hot toy for Christmas and Harold (Schwarzenegger) has completely forgotten about it on the day before Christmas Eve. Believing he can merely swing out on the morning of Christmas Eve to pick it up, he quickly discovers how rare this toy is and how chaotic the fight is for it. In his race around the Twin Cities area of Minnesota, he encounters several obstacles, including mentally unstable mailmen, conning Santa Clauses and maniacally laughing salesclerks.

You'd think after Schwarzenegger had to fight his way out of a counterfeit toy operation and is nearly arrested by the raiding cops that he'd call it quits. No toy on Earth could be worth so much hell, but Arnold's character is apparently a glutton for punishment. He returns home only to fail in stealing the toy from his neighbor, ruining his Christmas decorations and punching a reindeer in the face. Don't worry, the reindeer survives, and they share a beer afterward.

All of this ultimately leads to the sappy ending of family being more important than gifts, but it comes seemingly out of nowhere after eighty minutes of commercialism mayhem. I couldn't help but laugh at such a revelation after so much lunacy, including a fight for Turbo Man with ridiculous costumes, kidnapped kids, grappling hooks and jetpacks.

There are a few supporting roles that greatly stand out in this picture. Phil Hartman is undeniably watchable as the overly chipper and profoundly manipulative neighbor that can't wait to swoop in and steal Howard's wife. Sinbad provides some great improv as a mailman pushed over the edge to acquire Turbo-Man for his kid. Many of his unscripted scenes featured him bouncing his ranting off of Schwarzenegger, who responded quite well with his unscripted responses. And it's hard not to fall a little bit for Jake Lloyd as Howard's honest child who sounds like a genuinely commercial-fed kid, even if he must choke out the forced moral message in the climax. It's still funny seeing him as a homeless drunk in one dream sequence.

The movie takes place in the Twin Cities of Minnesota, but takes a substantial amount of liberties with the area. Minneapolis and St. Paul are treated as though they're the same city, explaining why the police are labeled as Twin Cities Police. The film seems to be handling the entire Twin Cities area as one city given how Howard can race from Minneapolis to Bloomington to St. Paul to Edina before the sun has even set.

Even more evidence of the movie's fable quality is the grand Wintertainment Parade of large displays on par with the Macy's Parade. The actual parade in Minnesota was the Holidazzle, a far quainter event down a smaller Minneapolis street at night, but I guess that setting wouldn't work as well for Schwarzenegger zooming around the city in a jetpack.

Jingle All The Way is a Christmas oddity in how it addresses the issue of Christmas commercialization, but also revels in its madness. One could quickly bust out an essay on the destructive nature of holiday commercialism in this picture, but it's too overtly silly and unbelievably baffling to take that seriously. There's just something that always makes me smile about how ridiculous it is that Schwarzenegger screams at Phil Hartman over the phone to drop a cookie. Like Christmas with out-of-touch in-laws, it's best to sit back and appreciate the bizarre spectacle.

JOHNNY MNEMONIC

DIRECTOR: Robert Longo | SCREENWRITER: William Gibson | CAST: Keanu Reeves, Dolph Lundgren, Takeshi, Ice-T, Dina Meyer | GENRE: Science Fiction | RUNNING TIME: 96 min | MPAA RATING: R

CLASSIFICATION: WEIRD

The futuristic world of *Johnny Mnemonic* (1995) features the most hilarious and preposterous means of data transfer. In the year 2021, there are data couriers, people who use their brains as data storage devices. Valuable information can be uploaded into their minds and then downloaded at another location. This is apparently a benefit as the courier can travel incognito and nobody will be aware that such an individual is carrying valuable information.

Today, we can laugh at such an idea as data encryption is more secure and sound, but the concept is still flawed within the 1990s era when the internet wasn't as secure or understood. Plane tickets alone would cost too much money to justify the transfer, and there's a high chance your courier could be ambushed or inexplicably die and your data could be stolen or lost forever.

Another major drawback to such a service is the sacrifice of the courier. Johnny (Keanu Reeves) has been making good money doing this for a job, but has lost his childhood memories as a result. He may be able to get them back with an operation after completing one last task. Ah, but it's never "one last job" with these movie heroes. Johnny's mind apparently holds 160 gigabytes of data, and his latest job has him transporting 320 gigabytes. To fit the information, Johnny must upload the content directly into his brain, profoundly affecting his psychological settings and possibly remove more memories. What a vicious cycle!

For the rest of the movie, Johnny is running from gun-toting bad guys that want what's inside his brain. Two groups are pursuing: one a pharmacological company and the other the Yakuza. There's a betrayal from one of Johnny's trusted partners, a rebellious, anti-establishment gang (led by Ice-T), a sexy love interest (Dina Meyer), an evil businessman (Takeshi Kitano) and a showdown at an old factory that specializes in belching fire. Oh, and there's a lost password and ticking clock for getting the information out of Johnny's brain. If he can't figure out the encrypted password and dump the data in time, his mind will melt.

The very concept of *Johnny Mnemonic* is silly, but the film reaches peak silliness when Johnny starts accessing the internet in virtual reality. Reeves slaps on a metallic visor and electronic gloves to enter a computer-generated world, making the corny graphics of Hackers seem subtle. This scene is an absolute riot for cutting between the Lawnmower Man style visions of surfing the internet and shots of Keanu Reeves swatting at air as he pretends to be an expert hacker. The scene is supposed to make him appear intelligent and calculative for the way he infiltrates records, but it'd be impossible for even the best of actors to look sophisticated in such dorky equipment.

Director Robert Longo and screenwriter William Gibson wanted this film to be a smaller and more artistic effort, but they couldn't get the financing. Only after Sony showed great interest in cyberpunk stories with the growing culture of technology did the film finally receive a $30 million budget. For going from no money to heaps of money, the project was drastically altered to the point that Gibson was disgusted with the script, despite writing it himself. The final result was another hacksploitation picture with ridiculous technobabble and computer graphics that did not age well. Sony's marketing campaign of staging an internet scavenger hunt was more creative than this weird tale of storing data in brains. Considering that our minds apparently hold less than a terabyte of info in this movie's version of the future, I think we're better off with email encryption and external drives.

JUDGE DREDD

DIRECTOR: Danny Cannon | SCREENWRITER: William Wisher, Jr., Steven E. de Souza | CAST: Sylvester Stallone, Armand Assante, Diane Lane, Rob Schneider, Max von Sydow | GENRE: Action | RUNNING TIME: 96 min | MPAA RATING: R

CLASSIFICATION: WORST

The most glaring of deviations that *Judge Dredd* (1995) makes from its comic book source is that of the titular anti-hero's helmet. As the most aggressive of dirty cops in a futuristic dystopia, he never once removed his large helmet in the comics, revealing only his stubbly chin and constant frown. But because Sylvester Stallone is attached to star, his whole face must be seen on screen, as apparently nobody would recognize Stallone by his stature and voice. That's just surface level, however, as many more problems were plaguing this big screen adaptation of the *2000 AD* comics in which Dredd appeared.

The setting is that of a dystopian future where crime runs rampant with gangs that shoot at each other within the towering city blocks of Mega-City One. Law enforcement has been entirely replaced by Judges, bulky-armored soldiers that act as literal judge, jury, and executioner. When confronting criminals big and small, Judges state the nature of the crime, pass judgment and carry out the sentence. The crime of stealing results in a sentence of serving time in the Isolation Cubes. The killing of a Judge naturally results in death, carried out on site with a really big gun.

As the most professional of the Judges, Dredd (Stallone) gets to see the most action and spout the most one-liners. As Dredd lists the offenses for a criminal murdering a Judge, the offender guesses his sentence will be life. Dredd shoots him and coldly corrects; *"Death. Court's adjourned."* It's a corny line, read with a caveman slur by Stallone, and it only gets worse from there as when he must shout, *"I never broke the law, I AM THE LAW!"* The only actor that comes close to firing back with a more indecipherable slurring is Armand Assante, barking at Stallone with a sneer and growl so ridiculous his character may as well be half dog.

To make Dredd likable, since he's apparently not intelligent or cool, the plot presents a story where he is framed for a crime he didn't commit. Off comes the helmet and in comes the off-putting comic relief of Rob Schneider as Stallone's shrimpy and annoying sidekick on the road to proving his innocence. Their prison transport is downed from the sky en route, and they're off on a buddy adventure through the dangerous wastelands of the future, filled with mutants and murderous robots, not nearly as intimidating as they should be for a gritty future. How scary can wasteland cannibals be when they cook their victims over a spit-roast and have dials on their foreheads to channel their moods?

Judge Dredd is a futuristic action picture so fast and chaotic that it never slows down for a moment to explore its dystopian world. There's no deeper examination or satire of the police state, no exciting angle to Dredd being framed by a clone and no family drama between Dredd and his spiteful brother. Perhaps the movie is so anxious to speed through its story in hopes that we won't question its stupidity, as when a flying motorcycle somehow crashes into a hologram.

This is a comic book movie that has all the visuals of sci-fi pulp with none of the intelligence, placing bullets before brains. You don't even have to take my word for it. The original character creator John Wagner stated that this wasn't a *Judge Dredd* story and Stallone would admit that the production was such a mess he couldn't tell if the movie was going for comedy or drama. *Dredd* fans would have to wait 17 years later for a more proper film adaptation with *Dredd* (2012), a film that better understood the world, the tone and that Dredd shouldn't take off his helmet.

JUNGLE 2 JUNGLE

DIRECTOR: John Pasquin | SCREENWRITER: Bruce A. Evans, Raynold Gideon | CAST: Tim Allen, Martin Short, Lolita Davidovich, David Ogden Stiers, JoBeth Williams | GENRE: Comedy | RUNNING TIME: 105 min | MPAA RATING: PG

CLASSIFICATION: WORST

Jungle 2 Jungle (1997) could be considered an apt remake of a foreign movie for being just as tedious as the French hit film *Little Indian, Big City*. What Disney forgot was that while *Little Indian, Big City* was a box office success, it was savaged by critics as one of the worst movies of 1996. The only reason that film escaped this book was that *Jungle 2 Jungle* exists.

Tim Allen plays New York commodities broker Michael, racing through the hustle and bustle of city life as he jumps from selling futures on the stock floor to divorcing his wife through paperwork. His life hits a snag as he must journey to the Amazon to have his ex-wife sign the divorce papers so that he can be newly married according to his busy schedule. But when he arrives in the Amazon, making faces and verbal jabs at the yucky jungles ill-suited for his business suit, Michael discovers he has a son he never knew about.

Dubbed by the local tribe as Mimi-Siku (Sam Huntington), the son seeks to follow his father back to New York as he has promised a tribal chief he will bring back the flame from the Statue of Liberty torch. And if you think he's going to shirk that loincloth and blowgun before he gets on the plane, you'd be wrong.

Most of the movie requires checking your brain at the door to buy into the logic of this premise. You must be able to accept that kids would even be the slightest bit interested in a plot about the stock market and Russian mobsters. You must be able to accept that Mimi-Siku can walk through a New York City airport in loincloth without being accosted by security. And you must accept the disappointment when Mimi-Siku discovers that the torch on the Statue of Liberty is not a real fire because nobody had the heart to tell him it was a statue. On second thought, leave your brain in the car.

The comedy present is strictly fish-out-of-water gags in which a boy from the Amazon cannot adjust to life in the city. He disgusts Michael's fiancee with his fancy for lizard guts. He shocks Michael's broker pal (Martin Short) by cooking his prized fish over a fire in the backyard. Mimi-Siku's pet tarantula will often escape and cause others to shriek and scurry, turning the pet into a weapon that literally keeps Russian mobsters at bay. His blowgun is left out so Tim Allen can shoot a dart into a cat and put it to sleep so Allen can have some simple slapstick with its body.

This is not exactly Tim Allen at the height of his career. When he isn't toying with a cat's unconscious body, he's doing his best to crack his classic dad jokes to an out-of-towner. He bestows the wisdom to his son on the importance of keeping the toilet seat down after use, less a war of the sexes be prompted. He enlightens his son on the idea of monogamy, a foreign concept to Mimi-Siku. As much as Tim Allen tries to inject some smart snark into this script, he can do little to deter the abundance of lame jokes that all rely on the same gimmick.

Jungle 2 Jungle doesn't work as the sly comedy of a father trying to bond with his son, the kiddie slapstick of an Amazon in the city or whatever the whole stock market subplot was supposed to be. The only mystery of the picture is why the title itself was spelled with a 2. Perhaps such awkward naming was put in place to ensure a sequel will never happen.

JURASSIC PARK

DIRECTOR: Steven Spielberg | SCREENWRITER: Michael Crichton, David Koepp | CAST: Sam Neill, Laura Dern, Jeff Goldblum, Richard Attenborough, Bob Peck, Martin Ferrero, B. D. Wong, Samuel L. Jackson, Wayne Knight | GENRE: Adventure | RUNNING TIME: 127 min | MPAA RATING: PG-13

CLASSIFICATION: BEST

Spielberg's dinosaur picture *Jurassic Park* (1993) marked a unique development in the use of computer graphics for adventure pictures. The initial plan was to use practical effects to conceive the prehistoric creatures, but the cost was far too high for results that were not up to Spielberg's standards. Computer graphics were the only way to go in this situation that had advanced to a level of being a marvelous spectacle. The first full shot of a dinosaur reveals the entire body of living, moving, lumbering Brachiosaurus is as surprising to witness as it is for Sam Neill and Laura Dern who stare with their mouths agape.

The jovial industrialist John Hammond (Richard Attenborough) has made two significant investments in reviving the extinct species on a Costa Rican island. The first is the bioengineering company InGen, responsible for extracting dino DNA from preserved mosquitos and recreating everything from Velociraptors to T-Rexes. The second is the Jurassic Park theme park that will house the dinosaurs and merchandise. But a theme park of dinosaurs carries many dangers for featuring such towering and dangerous creatures. As the uneasy Doctor Ian Malcolm (Jeff Goldblum) points out in this operation, *"If the Pirates of the Caribbean breaks down, the pirates don't eat the tourists."*

To alleviate the concerns of investors and scientists, Hammond invites Dr. Malcolm, paleontologist Alan Grant (Sam Neill) and paleobotanist Ellie Sattler (Laura Dern) to the island for a demonstration. They, unfortunately, arrive the same day when computer programmer Dennis Nedry (Wayne Knight) sabotages the park systems and steals company information for a rival. With the park security measures turned off, dinosaurs run rampant and start chowing down on unlucky humans, beginning with the park's lawyer. While Ellie tries to restore power to the park, Grant is stuck in the park's expansive nature environment with Hammond's grandchildren of Lex and Tim.

The film is a mix of wonder and terror, featuring scenes where dinosaurs seem majestically gentle and others where they bite off limbs. But it's mostly a monster flick for fleeing from everything from a towering T-Rex and agile Raptors. The special effects by the ILM studio were stunning for the time, mixing practical dinosaur animatronics and cutting-edge computer graphics, which still holds up today as a marvel of filmmaking.

The cast is practically shoved into the background with all these fantastic dinosaur shots, but there are still a few memorable character moments. Goldblum plays up his role with some of the best lines (*"Your scientists were so preoccupied with whether or not they could that they didn't stop to think if they should."*). I love how he finds just the right snarky comment for every situation. Neill and Dern are not as compelling with their subplot about settling down, but they're likable enough for this adventure. Other notable actors present include Bob Peck as a no-nonsense games warden (*"Clever girl."*) and Samuel L. Jackson as a cigarette-chomping engineer (*"Hold onto your butts."*).

Jurassic Park was promoted towards kids with plenty of merchandise, but some adults feared the picture might have been too violent for the little ones. Having been in that concerning demographic, it didn't bother me in the least as I viewed the picture with as much excitement as I imagine kids felt seeing the original *King Kong*. 22 years later, I'd be sitting in a theater watching the revival of *Jurassic World* next to two little girls. They stared up at the screen with the same amusement as the adults. I would later share an elevator with a little boy gushing about seeing *Jurassic World* for the second time, excitedly telling me about the good dinosaurs teaming up to fight the bad dinosaurs with the same glee I once had.

Most kids should be fine. They can handle some prehistoric terror, which is why I was drawn to *Jurassic Park* in the first place and still enjoy it as a genuinely thrilling adventure picture.

JURY DUTY

DIRECTOR: John Fortenberry | SCREENWRITER: Neil Tolkin, Barbara Williams, Samantha Adams | CAST: Pauly Shore, Tia Carrere, Brian Doyle-Murray, Stanley Tucci, Abe Vigoda, Charles Napier, Shelley Winters | GENRE: Comedy | RUNNING TIME: 88 min | MPAA RATING: PG-13

CLASSIFICATION: WORST

Not only was Pauly Shore an insufferable comedy actor, but he seemed to gravitate towards unbearable projects. *Jury Duty* (1995) is perhaps his most agonizing of pictures for its annoyingly dumb premise. Shore plays Tommy, an aimless slacker whose mother (Shelley Winters) coddles him and father (Charles Napier) despises him. Facing a dad who wants to kick him out, he is overjoyed to be chosen for jury duty as it means free food, board and $5 a day for being sequestered. The rest of the movie involves him trying to keep the trial going so he can continue to mooch. I feel for the unfortunate jurors trapped with this jerk for days upon days.

The case he is assigned to is a murder trial for the Drive-Thru Killer, a fast-food employee who was fired and then murdered everyone in the establishment that let him go. Not only does Tommy try way too hard to keep this trial going, but the movie goes out of its way to make him so unbelievably annoying that there is no reason he would still be on the jury. Why would he not be thrown out after continually harassing jurors, talking back to the judge and making sexual advances on fellow juror Tia Carrere?

Strangely enough, *The Simpsons* had an episode with a similar premise a year before this film. The episode featured an assault trial where Homer Simpson was on a jury and was enraptured of being sequestered in a hotel. Within the confines of that episode, Homer found more funny stuff to do in the trial and in the hotel than anything Shore could muster in 88 minutes. I'm not saying the three writers required for this script were ripping off *The Simpsons*, but they needed to take better notes if they were.

Many of the film's "jokes" are either too half-thought or straightforward. Tommy owns a small dog that is addicted to watching *Jeopardy*. Why? It's apparently been the dog's dream, but Shore doesn't explain how he knows this and the script doesn't reveal why this is funny. Also not disclosed is why every fast-food employee that testifies is required to wear their uniform when put on the stand.

Bodily functions naturally play a significant role in Shore's comedy, and there's an extended sequence where he has to take a long and audible urination while the rest of the jury listens outside the bathroom. Every scene plays out with lame joke after lame joke, from cutting a single noodle with a plastic knife to his little dog having little dog accessories.

It's bad enough that Shore is awful in this movie, but even worse that several veteran actors are dragged down with him. Abe Vigoda plays the judge and at one point is manipulated into shouting *"penis, penis, penis"* as he bangs his gavel. Shelley Winters performs in her last US role as the mom who fears for her son becoming a milkman. Billie Bird also delivers her final performance in a nothing role. Tia Carrere feels wasted in a position where she's initially furious with Shore when she discovers he was intentionally prolonging the trial, but then falls for him again when he admits he's changed (uh huh). And while Richard Riehle has never been a great actor, even he deserves better than to be seen in his underwear while surfing.

Shore had a microscopic appeal of a young recluse in such throwaway pictures as *Encino Man* (1992) and *Son In Law* (1993), but those films were appealing for him playing a high school and college student. The party was over now, and Shore needed to graduate to something higher as he couldn't continue to play the dopey kid. Rather than move on to different projects, he stayed with terrible scripts and his same bland brand of "hip" youth comedy stylings. Much like the character he plays in *Jury Duty*, he's coasting on his expected behavior that would eventually lead to the downfall of his acting career.

KAZAAM

DIRECTOR: Paul Michael Glaser | SCREENWRITER: Christian Ford, Roger Soffer | CAST: Shaquille O'Neal, Francis Capra, Ally Walker | GENRE: Comedy | RUNNING TIME: 94 min | MPAA RATING: PG

CLASSIFICATION: WORST

Shaquille O'Neal must have had a fervent desire to move on from being an NBA star to a movie star to accept such a role as a genie in *Kazaam* (1996). It's not that he is a terrible actor, having proved his ease as a basketball player in *Blue Chips* (1994), and it's not that he's unsuited for a family film. There's a certain charm to his presence that can make him a lovable enough giant for kids to look up to (literally). It's just too bad he had to come packaged in a silly costume for this worthless piece of childhood wish-fulfillment.

Shaq plays the genie Kazaam that somehow transfers his home from a magical lamp to a 1990s boombox, thus making the mystical genie concept more modern and urban. I'm not sure if this shift in housing also brings about his ability to rap unless he indeed has been a mediocre singer for 5,000 years. Max (Francis Capra) discovers the genie and could use some wishes for his life that is filled with bullies and a missing father. But, wow, is this genie annoying. Remember how fun it was to hear Robin Williams' genie from *Aladdin* exit the lamp and beam with excitement? Kazaam's entrance comes complete with threats to kids, spoken in the form of rhymes. He seems very intimidating for his size and attitude, but for some reason ends the scene begging for the skeptical Max to make a wish.

Max can't be bothered with such fantasy elements as he's more concerned about his absent father, whom he recently learned is living in the city. Now Max has something to wish for, and Kazaam aids the kid in his quest. They find his father in a nightclub and discover he is involved with an illegal music pirating operation. Dad isn't ready to be the father Max needs, but maybe he'll come around by the end of the picture. The nightclub owner, Malik (Marshall Manesh), wants Kazaam's power for himself. Also, Kazaam finds his rapping abilities can get him a record deal, and he starts ignoring Max.

Does this sound like a kids movie? All this talk of music pirating, record deals, lost fathers, nightclubs and violent goons feel strangely out of place for what should have been a story about a boy and his genie. There's even a point where Max is kidnapped by the villain and tossed down an elevator shaft. This kills the kid, meaning we'll have to endure a magical sequence where Kazaam learns to appreciate life and revive the dead, thanks to magic, I guess. Oh, and Kazaam also turns human. Whatever.

The wishes are nothing impressive. One of Max's first wishes is for the sky to rain with candy. But, wait, I thought the genie didn't know that much about the people of this era. How would he know that M&Ms are Max's preferred candy? Maybe he heard an ad for them on the boombox? Seriously, what went down inside that boombox?

I don't see why Shaq had to play such a wonderful character considering the ease of the rest of the cast. Francis Capra didn't know much about his father and John Costelloe used to be a firefighter. Why couldn't Shaq be the basketball playing genie? It's far more fitting than the film's attempt to make him a rapper. The most he'll get to do is contort the villain into a basketball and slam-dunk him into a garbage chute.

Even though the film was blasted by critics and wasn't a financial success, Shaq didn't regret the movie. He told GQ magazine in an interview that movies were his dream and that he was happy to be a part of one; *"I was a medium-level juvenile delinquent from Newark who always dreamed about doing a movie. Someone said, 'Hey, here's $7 million, come in and do this genie movie.' What am I going to say, no?"* Well, yes, he could have refused and held out for a better movie that made better use of his talents. His future acting gigs found him playing himself, a role that is better suited for Shaq than that of a rapping genie.

KINDERGARTEN COP

DIRECTOR: Ivan Reitman | SCREENWRITER: Murray Salem, Herschel Weingrod, Timothy Harris | CAST: Arnold Schwarzenegger, Penelope Ann Miller, Pamela Reed, Linda Hunt, Richard Tyson, Carroll Baker | GENRE: Comedy | RUNNING TIME: 111 min | MPAA RATING: PG-13

CLASSIFICATION: WEIRD

Kindergarten Cop (1990) is such an odd concoction of genre blending that it's surprising how much of it holds together. It starts off as a typical Arnold Schwarzenegger action picture with the big hero playing John Kimble, a gung-ho detective hot on the trail of convicting a drug lord (Richard Tyson). The story then shifts to a kindergarten classroom in the suburb of Astoria, Oregon. Between the dangerous drug lord plot and sweetly pleasant school setting, the film becomes a balancing act of a violent detective story with cute kindergarten antics.

Here is how the two stories connect. The drug lord is conspiring with his bad mom (Carroll Baker) to track down his ex-wife and son that have gone into the witness protection program. Schwarzenegger chases after him in his dirty coat, grizzled complexion, intimidating sunglasses and trademark cocky attitude. But he cleans up his look when he has to go undercover as a kindergarten teacher to seek out the drug dealer's son and protect him. Kimble's food-loving and currently ill partner Detective Phoebe O'Hara (Pamela Reed) informs him to leave the gun behind for the school day. When Schwarzenegger states teaching the class will be an easy job, she reconsiders him bringing the gun.

Most of the action acts as bookended segments, the majority of the film focusing on the cute antics of the kindergarten students and Schwarzenegger's hilarious attempts to both run the classroom and uncover the drug dealer's son. He wastes no time by immediately questioning the kids with a game called *"Who Is Your Daddy and What Does He Do."* The rules are self-explanatory, and it leads into many short clips where the kids say the darndest things. Sometimes it's cute when they describe their dad's facial features and other times hilarious for not fully realizing what they're saying; *"Our mom says our dad is a real sex machine."* While still amusing, it doesn't slow down the movie, as Kimble does gain a few possible suspects from this questioning.

A few subplots develop around this case. Kimble befriends fellow teacher Joyce (Penelope Ann-Miller), taking pity on him being unprepared for handling kindergarteners and soon forming a tender romance. A case of child abuse with one of his students is discovered, and Kimble takes it upon himself to violently punish the abusive father. Kimble's unconventional teaching methods become of interest to the strict Principal Miss Schlowski (Linda Hunt). She slowly comes around to his skills and admires his abilities to punch child abusers.

What makes the film work is that Schwarzenegger makes a genuine commitment to both tones of his character. He slips into the gruff action hero with ease, but has a certain charm as the big and lovable teacher. There's a moment on his first day when he loses all control of the classroom and shouts for them to shut up, leading to an outbreak of crying. He runs out of the school in frustration to grab something from his car. I expected the gun, but he grabs his pet ferret instead to calm the class. As the story progresses, there's a gentleness to his approach with children that makes him a rather effective teacher.

Kindergarten Cop seems as though it would be a fun family movie from the premise and poster, complete with kids crawling over Schwarzenegger and the title being written in crayon. But the film is rated PG-13 and for a good reason. The violence is never understated, leading to moments when people are hit by cars, beaten with baseball bats and shot in different parts of the body. All of these violent moments also occur inside the school, featuring scary moments where the library is set on fire, and Richard Tyson abducts his son with a gun in hand. While these scenes make the film seem strangely dark when contrasted with the more innocent laughs, all of it works and make sense within its bizarre writing that defies genres. It may not be suitable for the intended audience if there even is one, but it's an oddly hilarious picture for being as audacious to feature everything from dark alleys of gun-toting gangs to sunny classrooms of efficient fire drills.

L.A. STORY

DIRECTOR: Mick Jackson | SCREENWRITER: Steve Martin | CAST: Steve Martin, Victoria Tennant, Richard E. Grant, Marilu Henner | GENRE: Comedy | RUNNING TIME: 98 min | MPAA RATING: PG-13

CLASSIFICATION: BEST

Steve Martin's *L.A. Story* (1991) is a romance both sweet and scathing for its depiction of the weird culture of Los Angeles. The atmosphere is that of a paradise for its residents, but a paradise with parks of stationary bikes, restaurants of the small dishes better suited for artwork and street muggers that are polite enough to introduce themselves like waiters at a table. It is the perfect playground for Steve Martin to flex his comedic muscles, as well as serve up a loving valentine to both the city and his then-wife Victoria Tennant.

Martin plays local weatherman Harris K. Telemacher, a man who fits neatly into this strange society of first-world problems; *"I've had seven heart attacks, all imaginary."* Life has become so routine that he finds himself stuck in a rut. As he describes in his opening narration, he is depressed, but doesn't know it because he's so happy all the time. He's bored with his job for being so easy, as every day is a sunny day in this town. Even his drive to work that goes off-road through alleyways and neighborhoods has become part of the daily grind, residents waving him by as he accelerates through their yards.

And then a shift occurs. Harris loses his job, his girlfriend (Marilu Henner) is having an affair and starts receiving helpful advice from an electronic highway sign. There's a new sense of freedom in his life to find something new; it's not every day that a sign on the highway gives you romantic tips. He pursues a new relationship with the sexy model SanDeE(STAR) (Sarah Jessica Parker). If you think her name is hard to spell, try pronouncing it the way she does. At first, she offers a liberating experience for him, but there's still something missing in his life. Finally, he meets the British journalist Sara (Victoria Tennant) and knows who his true love is. She's doing a piece on L.A. lifestyles and Harris figures he's just the weatherman for the job. But with Sara trying to reconcile with her ex-husband, he fears he may have to settle for SanDeE(STAR) and get used to writing that weird name on all her birthday gifts.

Steve Martin's screenplay, which he had apparently been working on for about seven years, is smart with its satire of L.A.

There's an ample opportunity for him to go overboard in a scene on the freeway where his character has to shoot at other drivers, mocking the consistent violence in traffic. And while it is hilarious watching Steve Martin shoot a pistol wildly at other drivers firing back at him, there's an easy-going soundtrack on top of the scene and a casual conversation that follows, making the scene much funnier for being just another day in L.A.

The script is also written to give enough range for Martin to be at his highest levels of comedy. One of the best segments of the film features him rollerskating into an art museum and offering up an in-depth artistic interpretation of a painting that is only the color red. He has a remarkable grace to how he unstably skates across the room and then hilariously speaks of how an art makes him *"emotionally erect."*

What I love most about *L.A. Story* is how it has the pacing of a Zucker comedy, but the casual atmosphere of a light romance. It's a fantasy world where the characters feel so comfortable in their warm existence that their obliviousness to life's grander means of purpose and emotional satisfaction makes them cute for being so superficial and weird. There's a moment when a collective of the wealthy elite sit at a table ordering drinks; their requests are a decaf coffee, decaf espresso, double decaf cappuccino, decaffeinated coffee ice cream and half double decaffeinated half-caf, with a twist of lemon. Harris orders the lemon and everyone else soon requests a twist of lemon as well. It becomes clear in this scene that the funniest character is Los Angeles itself.

LAKE PLACID

DIRECTOR: Steve Miner | SCREENWRITER: David E. Kelley | CAST: Bill Pullman, Bridget Fonda, Oliver Platt, Brendan Gleeson | GENRE: Horror | RUNNING TIME: 82 min | MPAA RATING: R

CLASSIFICATION: WEIRD

"I'm rooting for the crocodile. I hope he swallows your friends whole."

There's no pussyfooting around the campy nature of a creature feature like *Lake Placid* (1999). There'd already been a resurgence in this genre with snakes in *Anaconda* (1997) and sharks in *Deep Blue Sea* (1998). A crocodile was the next logical evolutionary step. It's a production that realizes it will be seen more like a goofy monster picture, attributing to the movie's biggest strength and weakness as a self-aware genre picture.

Set in the rustic sticks of Maine, the local lake (not named Lake Placid for some reason) has become a danger zone after a game warden is bitten in half. Could an alligator have done such a thing? Sheriff Hank (Brendan Gleeson), Fish and Game officer Jack (Bill Pullman), paleontologist Kelly (Bridget Fonda) and mythology professor Hector (Oliver Platt) aim to find out. They're perplexed in their investigation of the lake to discover flipped canoes, a severed toe, and a decapitated moose head. It turns out there's an enormous crocodile in the lake, made evident from a scene where it comes out of the water to eat a bear. Since the bear was attacking two of our human characters, maybe he's a kind enough crocodile that just wants to be left alone to eat in peace.

Local elder Mrs. Bickerman (Betty White) seems to be on good terms with the oversized croc, feeding him cows on a regular basis. Sure, the croc ate her husband, but they seemed to know the risks of owning such a pet. I can even understand her lying to the authorities about his death considering the overreaction such info would cause. She was right. Rather than restrict the area to anybody looking for some fishing, the only solution for the crocodile is too kill it or capture it, depending on whoever argues their plan the loudest. As a result, it's easier to root for her as she's rooting for the monster to get rid of these stupid people. She also has quite the mouth on her; *"If I had a dick, this is where I'd tell you to suck it!"*

But, again, why attack it? The giant croc is on a secluded lake and not a public beach or mainstream river. There's no danger of it hurting anyone as long as you just stay away. Wouldn't you want to stay away from Giant Croc Lake? Wouldn't it be safer to study it in a lake than to go to all the trouble of removing him from his environment? These plans all involve the characters making foolish decisions that include going scuba diving in the lake and airlifting a cow as bait. But weren't the visitors initially appalled by Mrs. Bickerman feeding the croc a cow in the first place? Whatever.

The whole movie is just an excuse for giant croc action, and some of it is deliciously cornball. The scene where the massive creature drags a bear down into the water is pretty amusing the way the bear claws to the ground, and there's a spectacularly bizarre moment when the croc latches its jaw onto a helicopter. I was surprised that the special effects were by the famed Stan Winston Studios were somewhat competent. They constructed a 30-foot extended crocodile model to be used in the picture, and it looks believable. It almost makes up for the goofy computer graphics of the croc's more physically-demanding kills.

Lake Placid would continue as a franchise years later when cheap creature features became a bigger deal. These included *Lake Placid 2* (2007), *Lake Placid 3* (2010), *Lake Placid: The Final Chapter* (2012) and, the fight everyone had been waiting for, *Lake Placid vs. Anaconda* (2015). Most movie franchises that take this route of sequels and crossovers that go straight to TV or video often carry some amount of disappointment that the franchise had to take a dip in quality. This is not the case with *Lake Placid*, a monster movie so blatantly campy it seemed to know it was destined for such a legacy.

LAST ACTION HERO

DIRECTOR: John McTiernan | SCREENWRITER: Shane Black, David Arnott | CAST: Arnold Schwarzenegger, F. Murray Abraham, Art Carney, Charles Dance, Frank McRae, Tom Noonan, Robert Prosky, Anthony Quinn | GENRE: Action | RUNNING TIME: 131 min | MPAA RATING: PG-13

CLASSIFICATION: WEIRD

Arnold Schwarzenegger's career as an action hero had reached such a height in the early 1990s that it had to be satirized at some point. *Last Action Hero* (1993) wasn't exactly the most thoughtful of satires, but it does have its charming moments of playing with action movie cliches. It overblows most of what we expect out of a typical Schwarzenegger film with the big lug kicking men several feet into the air, revealing an absurd arsenal he keeps on him at all times and being so strong he can crush a walkie-talkie effortlessly with his grip. There could have been more comedy here, but the movie seems to rest easy on Schwarzenegger carrying more of a straightforward action picture than a knowingly satirical one. That being said, it's still an uproarious action picture for a script that has a few bits of commentary and meta humor struggling to be heard in an action-packed film of explosions and car chases.

The young teenager Danny (Austin O'Brien) frequents a New York movie theater to escape from his crime-infested neighborhood and the thoughts of his recently deceased father. He enjoys action movies so much that he finds himself zapped into one by a magical ticket. Danny is trapped within the world of Jack Slater, played by Arnold Schwarzenegger with his usual amount of grit and goofs. Danny has seen all of Slater's movies and knows that Slater has to stop the evil villain Tony Vivaldi and fight his henchman, Mr. Benedict. Because it's a Schwarzenegger action picture, Danny knows the villains can't win. But when Mr. Benedict escapes the movie world to Danny's reality, there's a higher chance he could win. Benedict's new plan involves killing the real Arnold Schwarzenegger to get rid of Jack Slater. And if you think that makes the movie strange, just wait until the grim reaper appears to state some exposition for the finale.

The movie is at its best when Danny starts questioning all the unbelievable aspects of the movie world. To prove to Jack that he's a character played by an actor, he takes him to Blockbuster Video to show him a copy of *Terminator 2*. It's not Schwarzenegger, but Sylvester Stallone on the cover. I wonder who would be on the cover of Twins. Danny acts as a spoiler for using his library knowledge of action movie cliches to predict what will happen next. He points out where the bad guy would be located in town, and Slater is offended that some kid trumped all his police training to figure out his case. The more Slater talks to Danny, the more he becomes self-aware of being trapped in a movie, struggling to question the very formula he's doomed to repeat. He argues that his shouting police chief is only good for comic relief and tries to surprise Danny with unexpected one-liners; *"Rubber baby buggy bumpers!"*

The script was initially written by writers Zak Penn and Adam Leff as a satire of typical action pictures that mocks a formula similar to Shane Black's work. But, in an ironic twist, Shane Black himself was called in for rewrites. And this relates to the biggest problem with *Last Action Hero*; it's an action comedy that isn't sentient enough to realize it's trapped in a predictable plot. The final result is a film that never takes full advantage of being an action parody and transforms into another campy Schwarzenegger movie of big action and dorky one-liners. I laughed at the movie, but only about as much as I would any other ridiculous Schwarzenegger romp. It's worth it for Danny's imagination of Schwarzenegger playing *Hamlet*, chomping a cigar as he throws Claudius through a stained-glass window to his death; *"You killed my father! Big mistake!"*

THE LAWNMOWER MAN

DIRECTOR: Brett Leonard | SCREENWRITER: Brett Leonard, Gimel Everett | CAST: Jeff Fahey, Pierce Brosnan, Jenny Wright, Geoffrey Lewis | GENRE: Science Fiction | RUNNING TIME: 103 min | MPAA RATING: R

CLASSIFICATION: WEIRD

The Lawnmower Man (1992) plays as the strangest of Stephen King adaptations for warping his short story into a silly tale of the dangers of virtual reality. As far as movies using virtual reality as a component of the story, this is one of the most ridiculous uses by far. A company by the name of Virtual Space Industries is conducting tests on chimpanzee subjects to see if their intelligence can be improved with virtual reality and drugs. Okay, admit it, scientists; you just wanted to dope up some monkeys and watch them play video games. They couldn't have been serious to think that chimps playing a shooter video game was going to somehow make them smarter. Because watching the footage of a CGI video game with chimp sounds over the footage is just too weird to be taken that seriously.

But Dr. Lawrence Angelo (Pierce Brosnan) is taking this research seriously. He has neglected his wife and devoted all his time into placing chimps inside gyroscopic spheres, putting ridiculous electronic equipment on them and watching them play games. But now his research requires a human subject. He decides to use Jobe (Jeff Fahey), a greenskeeper with mental problems. Jobe lives in a shed owned by the local priest who beats him and quotes scripture. The rest of the town looks down on him. But Angelo believes Jobe to be the perfect subject to use an intelligence boost. He surely won't use this power to get revenge on everyone that beat and mocked him.

At first, things are looking up for Jobe after his sessions. He masters Latin and finds himself a girlfriend. But then the crazy drugs and virtual reality grant him telepathic powers and the loose rules of this sci-fi story go straight out the window. Jobe has virtual reality sex with his girlfriend and ends up melting her brain. Outside of virtual reality, he sets people on fire with his mind and digitizes their molecules with some of the strangest uses of death by special effects. Not only are the kills silly, but so is Jobe's appearance of wearing a virtual reality suit straight out of *TRON* as he walks the streets on a quest for revenge.

By the third act, Jobe decides to abandon his body for the form of pure energy inside virtual reality or cyberspace (or whatever). His virtual form, appearing as a semi-realistic face with a golden version of those *TRON* suits, desires to enter the mainframe of every computer system on Earth. What will he do once he gets there? We don't know, but he does tell Angelo that he'll let everyone know he has arrived by making all the phones on the planet ring at once. We don't know what he'll say if people answer. My best guess is that everyone will hear that ugly sound when the local line is currently on the dial-up internet.

The best the film had to offer was the use of computer graphics for rendering the virtual reality environment. Though blobby and without textures, these scenes felt smooth and otherworldly, better reflecting how a virtual reality video game would look in the early 1990s. The animations were created by Angel Studios, a company that would fittingly move into developing video games and became better known as Rockstar San Diego for developing the notable games of Midnight Club and Red Dead Redemption. So incredible were the film's computer-generated sequences that a few of them would be separately featured in the animated video anthology *Beyond the Mind's Eye*.

The movie had little to do with Stephen King's original short story. In fact, the script once had been entitled Cyber God, reformatted to take advantage of the Stephen King attachment. The movie was going to be called Stephen King's *The Lawnmower Man*, but King hated the divergence from his original story so much that he sued to have his name removed from the film's title. It's easy enough to see why King disassociated himself with this movie for its mess of ideas that were more impressive on a technical level than any of its laughable story. It's still worth a look just to see Jeff Fahey's nightmarish computer-generated character crucify a metallic Pierce Brosnan. Most movies with computer graphics at the time didn't feature imagery that twisted.

THE LAWNMOWER MAN 2: BEYOND CYBERSPACE

DIRECTOR: Farhad Mann | SCREENWRITER: Farhad Mann | CAST: Patrick Bergin, Matt Frewer, Austin O'Brien, Ely Pouget, Camille Cooper, Kevin Conway | GENRE: Science Fiction | RUNNING TIME: 92 min | MPAA RATING: PG-13

CLASSIFICATION: WORST

The Lawnmower Man 2: Beyond Cyberspace (1996), sometimes called Jobe's War, does its best to both separate itself from the first film and be even more silly with its technobabble plot. For starters, it ignores the fact that Jobe left behind his body to become pure energy so he could escape into computer systems and control the world. It was implied by the ending of the first film that Jobe was successful when all the telephones in the world rang at once, as Jobe mentioned that would be the signal of dominance. He must not have made it as scientists discover Jobe's body in the wreckage of the exploded research facility and can revive him. All of the phones ringing must have been a coincidence.

Jobe (now played by Matt Frewer) is given reconstructive surgery, but has lost his memory. An evil company headed by tycoon Jonathan Walker (Kevin Conway) wants to use Jobe for their research with a computer chip that could dominate the world. They hook Jobe back into the virtual reality world so he can regain his memory and that strange gold suit he was wearing. A key difference that is noticeable right away with the virtual reality scenes is that the computer-generated characters have been done away with, favoring live-action actors in front of computer-generated backgrounds. Or, as we see later, live-action characters in live-action environments. Either virtual reality in this world has improved immensely in graphic detail, or the filmmakers were just too cheap to be bothered with CGI footage.

Skipping ahead to the *Blade Runner* style future (with the title card "The Future"), Jobe's old kid friend Peter (reprised by Austin O'Brien) is now a hacker hanging out with other tech-talking teens living in the subway systems. While flying through a game in cyberspace, Peter reconnects with Jobe, though it takes him creating a lawnmower to remind Peter who he's talking to. Jobe tells him to find virtual reality developer Dr. Benjamin Trace (Patrick Bergin) as he has important information about his MacGuffin of the Chiron

Chip. It isn't until Trace finally speaks with Jobe that he realizes he wants to control the world (again) and stages a hacking battle for the fate of the planet. It couldn't have been a coincidence that director Farhad Mann of *Max Headroom* fame had cast Matt Frewer who played *Max Headroom*. Frewer doesn't even try to embody the character of Jobe; he's Headroom 2.0 as he is constantly cracking jokes and appearing aggressively reactive. I can't blame him as you'd have to ham up a role with such ridiculous lines as, *"I don't need the Chiron Chip anymore. I've *become* the chip!"*

Everything about *The Lawnmower Man 2* was destined for disaster. The budget was so low that old computers from the 1980s were donated for this 1990s film about the future of technology. The central plot involves an overly intricate explanation for the merging reality and virtual reality that essentially translates to creating the internet. The technobabble is some of the worst of any hacksploitation picture of the 1990s, throwing as many high-tech words into the script without understanding a single word. All of this doesn't make it a surprise that producers locked the director out of the editing room as they attempted to save the film in editing. Based on the horrendously low box office of $2 million total, they didn't salvage much.

LEAVING LAS VEGAS

DIRECTOR: Mike Figgis | SCREENWRITER: Mike Figgis | CAST: Nicolas Cage, Elisabeth Shue, Julian Sands | GENRE: Drama | RUNNING TIME: 112 min | MPAA RATING: R

CLASSIFICATION: BEST

Nicolas Cage's acting career is ripe with roles where he goes over the top, but his manic nature was best suited for Mike Figgis' *Leaving Las Vegas* (1995). He plays Ben; a man crippled with alcoholism that is eating away at him fast. He loses everything to his drinking - his family, his friends and now his job as a screenwriter. With his massive severance check, he takes off to Las Vegas where he is determined to drink himself to death. While in Vegas, Ben meets the hooker Sera (Elisabeth Shue) and they soon form a bond that goes beyond sex. But the drinking continues, even when they move in together. Nothing will stop him from killing himself.

Cage's performance in this film is one of the best of his career. He plays a man that is so addicted to booze that he cannot survive without a drink. While at the bar, he quickly goes from being a loud charmer to a simpering mess; one moment he's coming on strong to the lovely Valeria Golino, the next he's desperately pleading that he wants her to go home with him. He is so sad and lonely that he seems to have drunk himself to the point of no return. So dense is his drinking that he forgot about the wife he once had. Did she leave him? Did she die? All Ben knows is that she's gone.

What's truly sad about this story is that Ben is thoroughly committed to ending it all at the bottom of a bottle. When he moves in with Sera, he strictly forbids her from asking him to stop drinking. She agrees, but with quiet pity. Ben will not judge Sera's profession too harshly. They love each other, but not for anything so simple as sex or companionship. There's something there that makes them gravitate towards each other, making them feel needed and loved as they are trapped in their vices they will not let go. Ben's drinking will eventually kill him. Sera's line of work is dangerous. One of Sera's worst decisions comes at a motel where she services four drunken high school athletes, and things turn ugly. She is killing herself just as much as Ben, and there's an unspoken kinship in such devotions.

The film was directed by Mike Figgis, quickly, cheaply and without permits. He keeps his movie focused on the suffering of Ben and Sera, refusing to muddy up his picture with unnecessary explanations or exposition. This plot is never once played for melodrama. Every scene carries a beautiful darkness that is never overplayed and always cuts deep. In a gentle scene, Ben opens a present from Sera. It's a flask. He goes quiet and puts his fist to his mouth, overcome with emotion for a woman who understands his drinking; *"Looks like I'm with the right girl."* He says this tragically with a smile for realizing how unconditional their love is, that Sera would buy the gun he is killing himself with.

Nicolas Cage went on to become a bit of a joke of an actor, which is why I'm compelled to always look back to this film as Cage at his best. His performance would garner multiple awards, including the Academy Award for Best Actor. If you ever doubted his abilities as an actor, I highly recommend checking out this film where he played a drunk capable of great pain, depression, frustration, edgy humor and tender passion, sometimes all within the same scene. This is not a great movie with Cage starring; this is Cage making a good film even better.

LEON: THE PROFESSIONAL

DIRECTOR: Luc Besson | SCREENWRITER: Luc Besson | CAST: Jean Reno, Gary Oldman, Natalie Portman, Danny Aiello | GENRE: Action | RUNNING TIME: 133 min | MPAA RATING: R

CLASSIFICATION: WEIRD

Luc Besson's *Leon: The Professional* (1994) plays like an American rendition of his previously acclaimed picture *La Femme Nikita* (1990). This means that it was nowhere as compelling for watering down most of the bitter sadness of an assassin lifestyle, but Besson still does his best to give the film its edge of action better suited for American audiences. It's bigger with more violence and explosions, but also has the uneasy tones of pedophilia for the film's heroine being a 12-year-old girl. The result is a film that grabs your attention when something explodes and makes you recoil when she tries to act sexy.

The girl is Matilda (Natalie Portman), who considers herself tough and wise enough to make it on the streets. She comes home to her apartment one day to discover that her entire family has been murdered by the crooked DEA enforcer Stansfield (Gary Oldman). She spots the hitmen right outside the door and quickly walks to her neighbor's apartment, quietly pleading for him to let her inside before the killers figure out she was the last target. The neighbor is Leon (Jean Reno), a hitman with more experience killing people than anything else. They soon form a bond and a trade of services. Leon will teach her all the skills he knows as a professional hitman to exact her revenge on the man that murdered her family. In exchange, Matilda will clean up his place and teach him how to read.

As you may have guessed, Matilda is a lot stronger than Leon, but in more ways than one. A 12-year-old would probably be adept at reading, but would she be able to make references to Bonnie and Clyde or Thelma and Louise? Considering what she's been through, most of Leon's lessons come a little natural with holding guns, aiming them and firing them. She is so consumed with revenge that she doesn't seem to be too afraid of the mission that lies ahead. A little fear could do her wonders though. For example, it might be a good idea to be a bit fearful of your relationship with a man thirty years older than you. The movie quickly shifts into several shades of uncomfortable when Portman starts to come on to Leon on more than one occasion, leaving him aghast with each of her advances.

It's important to note how this film, even with all its grit, is a fantasy. It'd have to be if you think about it for a few minutes. Matilda is only twelve, but able to teach Leon how to read within a few days. Leon takes Matilda out for target practice on a New York City rooftop, where she shoots a target in the park with fake bullets. The city doesn't seem overly alarmed that there's a sniper in the park or observant enough that there's a girl in green shorts and a man in black aiming a gun on a roof in broad daylight with no cover. And I'll spare you the analysis of the climactic shootout where Leon is apparently smart enough to know where his targets are coming from and have time to hang from the ceiling while shooting at them.

The film overcomes its fantastical and off-putting romance with a strong cast. Portman, despite her age, never feels as though she's trying to sound harsh, throwing herself believably into the role of a confused and brave young woman. Reno is distant and hesitant, but also capable of genuine heart and charisma, even for a cornball scene where he tries to cheer up Portman with a puppet. Gary Oldman is always fun to watch as the hot-headed villain, delivering his lines with remarkable snark and fury. One of his best scenes features him frustratingly forming a plan for taking down Leon, urging an associate to send everyone after him. The associate nervously asks what he means by everyone, and Oldman clarifies: "EVVVERRYYYYONNNNE!"

Besson has style to spare, and he uses everything from his bag of tricks to make this film shine. He shot the film in New York with remarkable cinematography as though he were trying to shoot it like Paris. His action scenes are big and loud with a lot of excitement and violence. The only problem is that Besson's film feels so fantastical that it doesn't take much advantage of Portman's youth or loss of innocence. And when those creepy moments come when she starts kissing Reno, you feel about as eager as Reno to quickly move on to the next action sequence.

LIAR LIAR

DIRECTOR: Tom Shadyac | SCREENWRITER: Paul Guay, Stephen Mazur | CAST: Jim Carrey, Maura Tierney, Jennifer Tilly, Swoosie Kurtz, Amanda Donohoe, Anne Haney, Justin Cooper | GENRE: Comedy | RUNNING TIME: 88 min | MPAA RATING: PG-13

CLASSIFICATION: WEIRD

Jim Carrey can be hilarious if he is given a funny premise with some direction and character. *Liar Liar* (1997) provides him both, allowing Carrey to appear both likable enough to sell the role of a dad and manic enough to showcase his uncanny ability for slapstick. Unlike his previous films, Carrey doesn't have to fulfill the added baggage of a character intended to be stupid (*Dumb and Dumber*) or insane (*The Cable Guy*). He proves with this film that he can be just as energetic as he was in his previous films, but still be more human than cartoonish, despite his rubbery face.

Carrey plays Fletcher, a yuppie lawyer that has risen in his profession by spinning tales inside courtrooms. The court buys his lies, but his five-year-old son Max (Justin Cooper) doesn't buy his excuses for breaking promises. His ex-wife Audrey (Maura Tierney) is getting tired of his lies as well, but she knows there's still a fun father buried under his career. Max decides to take some action on this issue and uses his birthday wish to force his father to tell the truth finally. It takes hold quickly. Soon after Fletcher has sex with his boss Miranda, she asks how it was for him. He smiles for a lie, but the wrong words come out: *"I've had better."* She is appalled, and so is he.

And there you have a genius premise for a comedy with a lawyer that cannot tell a lie. This leads to many brilliant scenes where Fletcher's secrets come spilling out like a flood of embarrassing honesty. One of the best moments finds him being pulled over by a cop who asks if he knows what traffic violation he committed. Fletcher, bound by honesty, quickly states every law he broke, from speeding to failing to yield at a crosswalk. He also can't help himself from admitting that he has unpaid parking tickets, throwing open his glove compartments with tickets spilling out. It's usually pretty awkward to watch protagonists in films embarrass themselves for the sake of a laugh because you don't want to see them fail. This movie is somewhat unique in that the mistakes are out of his control and will make him a better person, even if he has to fight it every step of the way.

It's especially hilarious watching Carrey test out the logistics of how this spell works. He picks up a blue pen and tries to say that it's red, but his words strain, and his voice prevents him from telling a simple lie. He later tries to restage a birthday wish with Max to take back the wish, but Max isn't sure he wants his father to go back to lying, especially when he can ask him any question. Max's questioning of his dad is cute, and Carrey delivers funny responses, one of them poking fun at his career.

Max: If I keep making this face [makes a silly face] will it get stuck that way?

Fletcher: Uh-uh. As a matter of fact, some people make a very good living that way.

The honesty is given a countdown, but Fletcher still has to make it through the most significant trial of his career without lying. More funny scenes occur as well as Carrey's desperation to find a loophole. He finds one: If he is physically unable to continue, the trial can be rescheduled. He flees to the bathroom where Carrey proceeds to beat himself up in his most physically demanding bit of comedy he's ever accomplished. The judge asks him who did this and he responds *"a desperate fool at the end of his pitiful rope."* Unfortunately, the judge also asks if Fletcher can continue and he tearfully answers yes. And there's also the plot about Fletcher potentially losing custody of his son, leading to a fantastical landing of a plane before it entirely takes off.

Liar Liar fits into that odd little category of PG-13 family films with humor and concepts aimed at the older kids. It works well with Carrey performing slapstick bits for the younger crowd and spouting dirtier jokes for the adults. If you want to like Carrey, this is one of his few films of the 1990s that portray him as a likable enough guy to appreciate his unique brand of comedy. And if you hate Carrey, you can still indulge in watching him beat himself up.

LIFE IS BEAUTIFUL

DIRECTOR: Roberto Benigni | SCREENWRITER: Roberto Benigni, Vincenzo Cerami | CAST: Roberto Benigni, Nicoletta Braschi, Giorgio Cantarini | GENRE: Drama | RUNNING TIME: 116 min | MPAA RATING: PG-13

CLASSIFICATION: BEST

Life is Beautiful (1997) manages to find the sweet spot between sincerity and tragedy, both of which can be difficult to weave in a story that takes place in a concentration camp during the Holocaust. There had been some movies about the Holocaust in the years prior, from the unblinking *Schindler's List* (1993) to the draining documentary *Shoah* (1985). But here is a story so innocent and heartfelt for trying to maintain a sense of childhood wonderment in the most inhuman of historical events.

Guido Orefice (Roberto Benigni) seems to have been born with the gift to make others smile. His energy alone is enough to perk up anyone with a sense of humor, and his personality is charming enough to attract the lovely Dora (Nicoletta Braschi) from marrying a more affluent and arrogant man. They wed, run a bookstore and have an equally charming son, Giosuè (Giorgio Cantarini).

Life seems sweet in Italy until World War II breaks out and Guido's family is sent to a concentration camp, on Giosuè's birthday no less. Dora is separated from Guido and Giosuè, leaving Guido to protect his son from the horrors of the camp. To shield Giosuè from learning the truth, he explains that this whole ordeal is a game of points. You earn these points by hiding from the camp guards and lose points by crying, asking for your mother or complaining about being hungry. The winner will receive a tank. Guido sells this concept authentically enough so that Giosuè buys into it and listens to his father. It's the only way he knows how to protect him.

We see both sides of Gudio that represent the fearful father and the playful parent. When he speaks to his son about the game, it feels like a dark comedy at times the way Giosuè remains chipper about winning and how Guido makes funny commentary on the camp guards. But when his son goes into hiding or keeps quiet, the darkness sets in that he may never see his wife or make it out alive. There is considerable danger in the camp as his Uncle Eliseo is executed in a gas chamber. Giosuè only narrowly avoids being gassed because he didn't want to take a shower and decided to hide while all the other children were executed.

Benigni both wrote and directed the film, carefully trying to balance the film's fable nature with real war. He makes the situation feel real, but never makes it overly dark. He based much of the character on his father, a man who had spent time in a concentration camp and used humor as a coping mechanism. For being such a tricky film that his friends advised against producing, Benigni made sure to keep certain aspects historically inaccurate not to cheapen the Holocaust, making the setting better fit the story of a father and son trying to survive in a horrific environment.

Predictably, the film drew much controversy when it premiered at the Cannes Film Festival for trying to place charming humor into a sensitive subject. But Benigni's film was not aiming to be specifically a comedy or historically accurate drama. He favors a story that plays on the swirling of emotions for such an event, not all of these feelings the expected ones. As he explained in his philosophy for the story, *"I'm a storyteller: the crux of the matter is to reach beauty, poetry, it doesn't matter if that is comedy or tragedy. They're the same if you reach the beauty."* And there was plenty of beauty in this film.

LONE STAR

DIRECTOR: John Sayles | SCREENWRITER: John Sayles | CAST: Ron Canada, Chris Cooper, Clifton James, Kris Kristofferson, Matthew McConaughey, Frances McDormand, Joe Morton, Elizabeth Peña | GENRE: Drama | RUNNING TIME: 135 min | MPAA RATING: R

CLASSIFICATION: BEST

Lone Star (1996) is John Sayles' best work as a film about the old wounds, dark discoveries and subtle sweetness of a Texas border town. The central story concerns the corpse of a former sheriff that is discovered in the desert by current Sheriff Sam Deeds (Chris Cooper). The skeletal remains determine that this was a murder and there's speculation that the killer is Sam's late father, former Sheriff Buddy Deeds (Matthew McConaughey). Sam is prepared to open up the case to find out what happened, but may not like the other skeletons he unearths.

This is not an easy case for Sam. Buddy is remembered as a local hero of the community that business leaders and government figures would rather Sam not drag a hero's name through the mud with such a scandal. Sam has good reason to prove his father's guilt as the two clashed on many occasions. But even Sam is not ready for the cathartic tale of how his dad came to kill the corrupt Sheriff Charlie Wade.

His case brings up more than just memories of his father. After releasing a kid who was accused of stealing car radios, he meets the child's mother, Pilar (Elizabeth Pena). They were high-school sweethearts and hadn't seen each other since their parents forbid them to date for racial reasons. They continue to meet over the course of the case and slowly begin to gravitate towards each other, culminating in a sweet moment where they dance in an empty restaurant.

Sam questions many individuals throughout the town to uncover the real story of his father's secret crime of killing a Sheriff. They reveal, in their perspectives, how Wade was a psychotic jerk, always one insult away from drawing his gun or punching someone to the floor. His cocky and violent nature towards others give everyone in town enough reason to want him dead, but Buddy seems most likely as he didn't stand for Sam's evil. They traded enough threats in their conversations to make anyone in earshot believe that a showdown was in their future.

As with John Sayles' other ensemble pictures, the story splinter off to follow the bigger picture of these characters and their town. Big Otis (Ron Canada) ran the only black bar back in Wade's time. We not only hear his recollection of Wade, but follow his son, Colonel Delmore Payne (Joe Morton), working at the local army base. He's estranged from Otis and has his own family with the story additionally following Delmore's son with a conflicted view of his future. We also follow a young Army Private speaking about her career with her commanding officer, and there's another story about some illegal immigrants trying to lay low.

Sayles sets up this border town to feel lived in with a rich history, most of it waiting to be unlocked from the many elders that have stored away from the darker spots of history. This is thanks to the astounding cast that meld beautifully into these roles. Chris Cooper has a tall and gruff exterior for a Sheriff, but has a thoughtful tone to his voice as he questions the older fellas with plenty to tell. Elizabeth Pena always lights up the screen when she's present, bringing some rays of sunshine to Cooper's somber journey. Kris Kristofferson is chilling for playing a guy with an itchy trigger finger and a nasty personality. And Matthew McConaughey has that familiar ease he hides behind, making himself more aloof with his intentions than Kristofferson.

Lone Star is part western, part tragedy and part romance. It paints a picture of a Texas town with the ghosts of segregation, murder and love haunting all its residents. There are no obvious moments of drama that Sayles takes advantage of, even with the climactic reveal of the story behind Wade's true killer. Every conversation feels natural and exciting, never racing towards the solutions as it moseys between characters and takes in the colorful atmosphere. There is enough personality and culture here to make it John Sayle's masterpiece of an original American movie.

LOST HIGHWAY

DIRECTOR: David Lynch | SCREENWRITER: David Lynch, Barry Gifford | CAST: Bill Pullman, Patricia Arquette, Balthazar Getty, Robert Blake, Natasha Gregson Wagner, Gary Busey, Robert Loggia | GENRE: Horror | RUNNING TIME: 134 min | MPAA RATING: R

CLASSIFICATION: WEIRD

David Lynch has an uncanny ability to make the simplest of spaces seem creepy and otherworldly. He turns a rather large home with plenty of space into a dreamlike reality just from the lighting and camera angles. He also makes his story a slow burn of terror, so we feel just as trapped as the characters, being only as in the dark as they are, figuratively and literally. It's the perfect atmosphere for another one of Lynch's twisted films that are easier to explain in their moods than their plotting.

The story begins with Fred (Bill Pullman), a successful enough saxophone player to afford a beautiful house, hearing a mysterious voice over his house's intercom system: *"Dick Laurent is dead."* Who is Dick and how did he die? That question isn't important at the moment. More significant is the recent arrival of videotape that his wife Renee (Patricia Arquette) finds at the door. They play the tape and find it to be footage of someone videotaping their house. They'll later receive another tape, this one with the camera going into their bedroom while they sleep. That's scary enough for Fred and Renee, but Fred is more shaken by once seeing a strange man on Renee's shadowed face and later having a dream where he murders her.

And then the film reaches its creepiest moment at a party for a friend. Fred runs into a wide-eyed, pale-faced man referred to only as The Mystery Man (Robert Blake). He states that he's met Fred before as he's been in his house. Fred doesn't remember him. The Mystery Man goes on to state that he's currently inside his home, handing Fred a cell phone to call and confirm he is there. The Mystery Man speaks the truth, and it only gets more terrifying.

Lynch makes the perspective of this picture evident early on when the police visit his house to question him about the tapes Fred received. The cops ask if he owns a video camera the intruders could have filmed with and he states he doesn't own one because he prefers to remember events his way and not the way they happened. It is then that we realize not everything we're seeing is the truth and that

Fred's reality is scattered in bits and pieces. The tapes represent the truth, as do his dreams which foreshadow his dark future. Or do they? Lynch's refusal to pin down Fred's perceptions keeps the film as a puzzle and always makes it appealing to analyze endlessly.

Some scenes throw us completely for a loop, just when we think we have the mystery solved. When Pullman's character is imprisoned for murder, the guards look in his cell one day to discover he has been replaced with the teenager Pete (Balthazar Getty). He is released from prison for not having any charges against him and works with a gangster played by Robert Loggia and meets his mistress played by a much different Patricia Arquette. Is this the same woman as Dick's wife or just a coincidence? Is she real or just a cobbling of memories? And who is Pete supposed to be? I have theories, but I've probably spoiled too much already.

Lost Highway (1997) isn't so much about piecing together lost memories as it is comprehending the perspectives that shape our truths and determining whether or not they are valid. Similar to how Lynch conceived *Twin Peaks*, it deals with the splitting of character and timelines that splinter and contort towards some darker truth. And he does it all with extreme violence, somber sex, moody music by Lynch staple Angelo Badalamenti and haunting imagery that is sure to spawn nightmares. It's another darkly engaging example of how Lynch can crack open our skulls and mess with our minds, daring to delve into areas most filmmakers would fear to tread.

MAD DOG TIME

DIRECTOR: Larry Bishop | SCREENWRITER: Larry Bishop | CAST: Richard Dreyfuss, Gabriel Byrne, Jeff Goldblum, Ellen Barkin, Diane Lane, Gregory Hines, Burt Reynolds, Richard Pryor, Billy Idol, Paul Anka, Rob Reiner, Michael J. Pollard, Henry Silva, Larry Bishop, Kyle MacLachlan | GENRE: Comedy | RUNNING TIME: 93 min | MPAA RATING: R

CLASSIFICATION: WORST

Mad Dog Time (1996) is a crime comedy that literally takes place in another galaxy. It'd have to. How else would one explain such a picture devoid of laughs, thrills or personality? It could also have been put in place to improve the appeal of this dull parade of an A-list ensemble that spends the entire movie milling about. This was yet another film born from the wave of Tarantino-ism, with every director aiming to let dialogue play out longer than it should while gangsters flood the screen. But while Tarantino made his long passages crackle with charisma, writer/director Larry Bishop makes his film of gangsters and nightclubs about as appealing as a third-rate soap opera where more care was put into the sets than the script.

Jeff Goldblum plays Mickey Holiday, a hitman with a long list of enemies. He works for the crime boss Vic (Richard Dreyfuss), but is having an affair with his girlfriend (Diane Lane) and her sister (Ellen Barkin). Vic has been in a mental hospital for quite some time and is finally being released. There are plenty of gangsters in line to kill Vic and overtake his organization, including the likes of Gabriel Byrne, Kyle MacLachlan, Gregory Hines, Burt Reynolds, Billy Idol, etc. And the battle is on for Vic's business.

The fights for the crime throne all start and end the same way. A handful of characters enter a room, speak in hard-boiled cliches and then somebody is shot, usually while sitting. Their dialogue is unbelievably dull, talking about the plot or detailing how they're going to shoot someone. Did this director learn anything from Tarantino? His films were brilliant because his characters spoke beautifully about everything besides the plot, finding insight in talk of burgers and television shows. Are the lives of these gangsters so dull that this is all they ever talk about? Every encounter plays out like the least exciting part of any crime movie where we wait for the inevitable moment of someone to get shot so that something more interesting can happen. The most entertaining thing that happens between scenes are some Rat Pack songs.

Larry Bishop, the son of Joey Bishop, seems to have made this film in an attempt to replicate the classic Rat Pack pictures for the 1990s. He loads his picture up with lots of styles, where his massively talented cast are dressed up in fancy tuxedos, sexy dresses and occupy swanky clubs. But then there are stranger sets that seem to take place in warehouses with mafia office furniture placed for characters to sit and shoot from, resembling the set decoration of a play trying to make the most use of the stage. I think the script is intended to be comedic, but the few attempts at humor are uninspired and lame. One scene features Byrne's character of Ben being shot as he collapses on one key of a piano, leading to Goldblum's throwaway joke, *"I judge a man's life by the way he dies, Ben. Your life was, uh, one note."*

The most significant appeal of a movie like *Mad Dog Time* is that so many great actors were gathered together in the same room to look good and shoot guns, but the film offers up nothing else. Most of the actors seem so bored with this dialogue that they deliver their lines so dryly I'm surprised they didn't start falling asleep in the chairs they occupy for shootouts. And how much fun can a shooting be when nearly everyone is sitting down? This is a film so boring it feels like a waiting room for these actors, passively playing their nothing roles while hoping for a better movie to come their way.

MALCOLM X

DIRECTOR: Spike Lee | SCREENWRITER: Spike Lee, Arnold Perl | CAST: Denzel Washington, Angela Bassett, Albert Hall, Al Freeman Jr., Delroy Lindo, Spike Lee | GENRE: Drama | RUNNING TIME: 202 min | MPAA RATING: R

CLASSIFICATION: BEST

There must have been enormous pressure on director Spike Lee for *Malcolm X* (1992). Having made a name for himself with *Do The Right Thing* (1989), a film which dealt with racism sharply and smartly, all eyes were on this black filmmaker to deliver some compelling commentary on the life of the black rights activist. What's surprising is that this film feels more rounded and whole than the reactionary piece most were expecting. But this is still very much a Spike Lee movie, albeit one that pays more homage to *Malcolm X* as a human being than a figure with an excellent biography.

With such a massive running time, Lee leaves plenty of room to learn as much as we can about Malcolm Little. We learn that his dad was a preacher who subscribed to the belief that there is no hope for the blacks in America and that the only salvation lies in Africa. His father was murdered, and his mother was institutionalized, leading to him being raised with a foster family. He had a bright mind in school, but was driven into the jobs of a Pullman porter and later a gangster. Before he was Malcolm X, he was Detroit Red, indulging in sex and robberies. He would be arrested for burglary. While in prison, Malcolm learns of the Black Muslims that take him under their wing and teach him to be more proud and angry to be black.

And then Malcolm picks up where his father left off, now with more fire in his belly to stir up the black community. The film follows him through this rough life that leads him from preaching on street corners to rallying his brotherhood in the streets to making a pilgrimage to Mecca. And then, after a long journey of transformation, his assassination.

Denzel Washington stars as Malcolm, and he gives this figure a wealth of dimension. We watch him shift significantly from being an obscure loser to an adept criminal to an awakened rebel. This is not a comfortable role for playing a man that changes back and forth between being the loudest voice in the room and then the most distant. At one point in his life, he's wearing a zoot suit in Harlem and then later donning a robe in Mecca. Denzel eases into all these critical moments of Malcolm's life with such grace that he disappears into the role, where we feel more like we're watching Malcolm X than just Denzel playing him.

A film so significant about a life so iconic was not an easy feat for Spike Lee, having taken on an immense project that had been in development hell for decades. He wanted to include Louis Farrakhan in the script, but was prevented from doing so when Farrakhan sent him death threats. He wanted a large budget for the picture, but was refused for not being a director with a big enough box office draw. The decision to go with Lee as the director drew heavy criticism from the likes of black nationalists and the United Front to Preserve the Legacy of Malcolm X. Lee would joke on the DVD commentary that he and Denzel had their passports at the ready if the film were so bad they'd be rushed out of the country.

They remained, and so does the film. Lee's portrayal of Malcolm felt honest, engaging, entertaining and educational. His movie is a fantastic effort that is always gorgeous to look at from the colorful streets of Harlem to the dark corners of prison. Every scene feels well-shot when even Malcolm examining the dictionary in the prison library holds our attention. Most importantly, and surprising for Lee, the film takes such an in-depth look into Malcolm's life that it's much more than a movie about race. It is also about dignity and personal change in a man who is soldiering on to make himself complete. And up to his demise, we feel there were maybe one or two more steps left in his evolution that was tragically cut short.

MAN BITES DOG

DIRECTOR: Rémy Belvaux, André Bonzel, Benoît Poelvoorde | SCREENWRITER: Rémy Belvaux, André Bonzel, Benoît Poelvoorde, Vincent Tavier | CAST: Benoît Poelvoorde, Rémy Belvaux, Jenny Drye, Jacqueline Poelvoorde-Pappaert, Malou Madou, André Bonzel | GENRE: Drama | RUNNING TIME: 95 min | MPAA RATING: NC-17

CLASSIFICATION: BEST

In the first shot of *Man Bites Dog* (1992), we see a man strangle a woman to death on a train. In the next scene, he's finished preparations to dump the body in a river and is explaining this process to someone behind the camera. The offscreen characters documenting this murderer probes further into the process as the killer describes the specifics of disposing of dead bodies, including children and midgets. It's a vile moment which left me questioning why the documentarians in this dark tale of fiction were okay with filming such a psychopath take lives. But the following scene has the killer dropping the body off a bridge, only for the corpse to splat anticlimactically in a very shallow river. It's amusing, and I laughed, leading to a questioning of my morality.

The man committing the murder is Ben (Benoît Poelvoorde), and he is being filmed by a documentary crew. He is a witty and charming guy when he's not killing, able to hold conversations about everything from architecture to poetry. He has friends and family that he regularly visits, always with a big smile on his face. Of course, he doesn't shy away from talking about his profession. During one conversation, Ben talks about how he chooses his targets; *"What I avoid are young couples. They stink of poverty. It's unpleasant. But old folks are loaded for sure!"* He will later make racist remarks about his victims, at one point urging the film crew to pull down the pants of the black man he just killed to see if the myth is true about all black guys having big dicks.

The crew obliges him out of charm, fear, and money. Ben is financing the documentary, and so the filmmakers feel they must help him out when he asks for their assistance in handling dead bodies. There is always the tension that the killer could turn on them at any moment, making them all the more likely to take orders from him. Ben looks at them as both his friends and foot soldiers, able to speak freely with them about anything and explode on them when he needs something done. They go along with his rationalization that he's just a regular guy trying to make an honest living, even though he takes out a competing serial killer to protect his fame.

There's a strange fascination with such a mockumentary that shifts between being a darkly comedic satire and exploitation that is even darker. It is remarkably edited to showcase a man who is a charm around his old stomping grounds and an inhuman monster when on the job. He enjoys his career too much to the point where he starts staging his kills for the camera. He breaks into a home and smashes someone's face into a bathroom mirror, commenting how it reminds him of a movie. He then makes the mic operator bring the mic in close so they can pick up the sound of the victim's neck snapping.

The film is a dare on our morality. It attempts to humanize Ben in casual conversations and dehumanize him in the act of slaughtering his victims without a shred of humanity. It's vile, sadistic and perverse for showcasing such a violent psychopath. It's especially horrific when he murders a little boy's parents and then suffocates the kid to death, thinking more of his skills than his actions. But it's up to us to decide how far we're willing to accept Ben as a human being before we see nothing but evil, questioning the media's love affair with violence. Some people like these types of characters to a point and *Man Bites Dog* tests the limits of acceptance before we're entirely disgusted.

MARS ATTACKS!

DIRECTOR: Tim Burton | SCREENWRITER: Jonathan Gems | CAST: Jack Nicholson, Glenn Close, Annette Bening, Pierce Brosnan, Danny DeVito, Martin Short, Sarah Jessica Parker, Michael J. Fox, Rod Steiger, Tom Jones, Lukas Haas, Natalie Portman, Jim Brown, Lisa Marie, Sylvia Sidney | GENRE: Science Fiction | RUNNING TIME: 106 min | MPAA RATING: PG-13

CLASSIFICATION: WEIRD

Whereas *Independence Day* attempted to replicate the flying saucer pictures of the 1950s for the modern age, *Mars Attacks!* (1996) seeks to satirize and pay homage to the very subgenre of campy science fiction. Though technically based on a line of trading cards, the movie derives most of its comedy from the sci-fi B-movie classics of *Invaders from Mars* and *Earth vs. the Flying Saucers*. It was the perfect follow-up film for Tim Burton after completing his bio-pic on *Ed Wood*, the infamous director of the terrible sci-fi picture *Plan 9 From Outer Space*, as Burton must have still had aliens on the brain.

Burton treats the invasion of aliens as a disaster farce with a fantastic roster of actors to experience Earth's destruction from giant saucers. Jack Nicholson plays the President of the United States as a smugly smiling politician more concerned with his political career than the fate of Earth. Less manipulative and more frantic is his wife played by Glenn Close, a woman who is more worried about the aliens damaging the chandelier than the planet. Pierce Brosnan plays the insightful professor, always seen with a long pipe in his mouth, believing the Martians are misunderstood individuals that can be reasoned with in proper conversation. Rod Steiger is the military general, convinced that the only safe route is to launch nukes at the aliens. Both are proven wrong. Also along for the ride is Annette Bening as a new age nut, Danny DeVito as a rude gambler, Jim Brown as a former boxer, Jack Black as a dopey soldier and Tom Jones as himself.

Despite the incredible cast trying their best for a laugh, the aliens steal the show. Their designs are uniquely creepy for having no eyelids, no lips and brains they wear over their skulls. They speak in their amusing language of one word repeated: *"Ack!"* Their intentions for Earth are not to make peace, increase their galactic military influence or harvest humans as food. They seem to be invading Earth more for the pleasure of toying with Earth's population for laughs.

When the humans make contact, they send back the message of *"We Come In Peace,"* only to whip out their ray guns and zap everyone into skeletons. They apologize and appear before Congress, but fool us all and zap more humans. Sarah Jessica Parker is abducted by them, and they remove her head to be placed on a dog's body, with the dog's head put on her body. I doubt this experiment has any scientific purpose outside of looking funny. Their assault on Earth is darkly amusing with them angling the Washington monument to fall on some people and using the statues of Easter Island as bowling pins. Their antics on the ship amused me the most where they walk around in their underwear and mock nearly every Earth transmission they receive.

The movie's only major misstep is that it's perhaps too on the nose with its many satires. Burton commits himself so true to the spirit of these alien invasion cliches that I started to wonder if he doesn't question if he was making more of an earnest homage than a dark satire. Most of the characters nearly outstay their welcome for their preoccupations that I began to wish the film was more about the aliens than the humans. Can you imagine how surreal and amusing it would be for Burton to make an alien invasion movie entirely from the alien perspective with *"Ack ack ack!"* being the only dialogue?

Mars Attacks runs a bit out of steam towards the end, but there's enough zaniness present to make it one of Burton's biggest, weirdest and darkly amusing pictures. It was far more enjoyable than the likes of the other alien invasion picture, *Independence Day*, released the same year. Unlike that film, Burton implores us to laugh at the silly aliens, the cliche characters and the ridiculousness of what simple solution defeats the aliens. In this case, it's Slim Whitman's "Indian Love Call."

THE MASK

DIRECTOR: Charles Russell | SCREENWRITER: Mike Werb | CAST: Jim Carrey, Peter Riegert, Peter Greene, Amy Yasbeck, Richard Jeni, Cameron Diaz | GENRE: Comedy | RUNNING TIME: 101 min | MPAA RATING: PG-13

CLASSIFICATION: WEIRD

Some comedic actors have such a way with their actions that they appear as to be limited by reality. In the same way that Robin Williams was in his element for voicing an animated character in *Aladdin*, so too is Jim Carrey in step with his mostly cartoony role in *The Mask* (1994). Through some breakthrough computer graphics, Carrey can perform as a green-faced, zoot-suit wearing maniac that has escaped from a Bob Clampett cartoon, running amok in our dimension. His antics are not only zany, but amazingly accurate to cartoon visuals.

Before Carrey breaks into the zaniness, he puts in the grunt work of rooting for his hapless character of Stanley Ipkiss. He works a thankless job at a bank, isn't cool enough to get into local clubs, has an unreliable car and his landlady is continuously complaining about the volume level in his apartment. Life sucks when your only best friend is a dog. But his personality is about to get an upgrade when he discovers a mysterious mask. When placed on his face, he transforms into a green-faced force that breaks all the rules, be they of decency or physics.

Acting like a hyperactive joker was Jim Carrey's usual mode for this era, but he shines more brightly here due to both the fantastic special effects of his Mask persona and the contrasting personality of Stanley. He's a meek enough character that his comical outbursts of robbing the bank, crashing the club and hooting at the lovely Tina (Cameron Diaz) feel more vindicating than placing Carrey at his maximum level of annoyance from the start. His eyes can bug out, his jaw can drop to the floor in awe, and he can flatten himself without feeling a thing; *"Look, ma, I'm roadkill!"*

Stanley's whirlwind of energy is noted by both the police and the local mafia. The cops want to bring the masked maniac to justice while the gangster club owner Dorian Tyrel (Peter Greene) would prefer to have the powers of that mask for himself. This leads to many silly scenes where Stanley bests criminals and law enforcement with his cartoon antics. How does he escape a swarm of police that corners him? With a song and dance number, of course, donning a Mexican dance outfit and using his hypnotic powers to convince every officer to bounce along to "Cuban Pete." It is such a catchy and fun sequence that I never found myself questioning how the mask also gave Stanley the godlike powers to make anyone join him in a conga line.

The Mask, for being based on a comic book, is very much a superhero film, but not the traditional kind. Stanley's mask persona doesn't exactly save people or uphold justice, playing more like a cross between the Hulk and the Joker. The character was more violent in the comics, but there were enough gritty superheroes in the 1990s that the more lovable chaos was a welcoming presence. Not every joke hits, however, especially a prison scene where Stanley coaches his dog into grabbing the keys from a sleeping guard. But most of the bits are intelligent enough to hold a relatively standard plot of cops and robbers.

The film was a genuine discovery of how well special effects can enhance Carrey's frantic acting and how impressive Cameron Diaz could be in her first feature role. Still, there were so many computer graphics used to make Carrey appear like a cartoon character that it begged the question of why not just make *The Mask* an animated cartoon, considering the mask falls on Stanley's dog that is almost entirely CGI. *The Mask* would later be adapted into an animated series, but would not be nearly as inventive or brilliantly animated as Carrey was in this film. It's rather strange how live-action computer animation looked more cartoony than hand-drawn television animation at the time. The times were indeed changing.

MATINEE

DIRECTOR: Joe Dante | SCREENWRITER: Charles S. Haas | CAST: John Goodman, Cathy Moriarty, Simon Fenton, Omri Katz, Robert Picardo, Dick Miller, John Sayles, Naomi Watts | GENRE: Comedy | RUNNING TIME: 99 min | MPAA RATING: PG

CLASSIFICATION: WEIRD

Matinee (1993) is Joe Dante's love letter to an era that was gripped with great fear and escapism. Taking place during October 1962, he crafts a charming tale that effortlessly weaves together the Cuban Missile crisis, young love, campy monster movies and the fear of nuclear annihilation. It all blends with ease given how Dante lived through this time as a kid, citing the film as semi-biographical of his childhood. This makes *Matinee* his most personal film, as well as his most underrated.

John Goodman plays the shameless huckster of movie producer Lawrence Woosley, traveling the country with his band of followers willing to play any role. If he needs some religious leaders to stir up controversy about his new movie to spark interest, his pals Herb (Dick Miller) and Bob (John Sayles) will get the job done. If he needs a nurse to pretend to make statements that the movie is so scary waiver forms need to be signed, his lovely assistant Ruth (Cathy Moriarty) will fill the role. If he needs a man in a suit to run up and down the aisles to enhance the experience, Herb and Dick can force a local punk kid into playing the part.

Woosley doesn't just sell theaters on a movie; he sells an experience. Similar to the theater tricks of William Castle, Woosley employs many theatrical displays to enhance the picture. When the monster grabs a woman's bottom in the movie, the theater seats will deliver an electric jolt to the audience. A costumed monster will attack the audience during the scary moments. His "Rumble Rama" machines make the theater quake with every explosion and attack by a giant monster. He later divulges his ideas for making a ghost come out of the screen and drip blood all over the audience. Blood-o-Rama is one of the working titles of this technique. And though these elements appear as goofy gimmicks of their time, it's not too dated considering the modern implementation of D-BOX, which adds simulated motion to theater seats.

Woosley's latest stop is in Key West, Florida during the height of the Cuban Missile Crisis. The monster movie he brings with him to premiere is Mant, the campy horror story of a creature that is half man and half ant. During his trip down, Woosley is already forming the next movie in his head: Man-o-Gator. Or was it Alli-Man? It's a working title.

While setting up a sneak preview of his picture with all his experience-enhancing tricks, the movie mostly sticks to the perspective of the kids in Key West. The new kid in class Gene has a father in the military and is worried about his safety during the Bay of Pigs, as is his little brother Dennis. To distract himself, he'll often take Dennis out to the movies. He also has the bonus of a girl at school that fancies him, the intelligent and honest Sandra. His new friend Gene also happens to find a girl, but has the added trouble of a jealous prison poet telling him to back off. These kids are incredibly cute and surprisingly smart, as in one scene where the savvy Sandra questions the uselessness of air raid drills. Calling out how covering your head does nothing to protect you from a blast of radiation was grounds for detention in those days.

Goodman does a fantastic job playing Woosley as the most charming of hustlers. At his core, however, Woosley is a figure that cares deeply about the movies. When talking to Gene about his process for making movies fun, he delves into a philosophy about what makes monster movies so exciting and personal. He then delivers one of the sweetest descriptions of going to a movie theater:

"You see, the people come into your cave with the 200-year-old carpet. The guy tears your ticket in half - it's too late to turn back now. Water fountain's all booby-trapped and ready; all the stuff laid out on the candy counter. Then, you come over here, to where it's dark - there could be anything in there. And you say 'Here I am. What have you got for me?'"

And *Matinee* has plenty for everyone. A young romance with relatable kids. A paranoia of communism and nuclear holocaust in an age of uncertainty. A corny monster movie with deliciously campy and nostalgic scenes. A satirical dance on the movie-going experience of a different era. A daring rescue amid a crumbling theater. A charming score by Jerry Goldsmith. What more could one ask for from a movie? Maybe a coming attraction of Man-o-Gator. No, wait, Gal-o-Gator!

THE MATRIX

DIRECTOR: The Wachowskis | SCREENWRITER: The Wachowskis | CAST: Keanu Reeves, Laurence Fishburne, Carrie-Anne Moss, Hugo Weaving, Joe Pantoliano | GENRE: Science Fiction | RUNNING TIME: 136 min | MPAA RATING: R

CLASSIFICATION: WEIRD

The Matrix (1999) was a mishmash of genres that fused into a style all its own. The Wachowskis took inspiration from the likes of Hong Kong action films, cyberpunk anime and the sci-fi writings of Philip K. Dick. The combination of all these led to a phenomenal action picture with a thought-provoking notion that our reality is a simulation. There were plenty of movies that used such a theme, including *Dark City* (1998) and *eXistenZ* (1999). Those films had more significant ideas with such a concept, but *The Matrix* ended up being the most notable for having the flashiest special effects of people dodging bullets and performing kung fu.

Keanu Reeves plays a strung-out guy who is the computer programmer Thomas Anderson by day and the hacker Neo by night. He begins to see something strange with a repeated cryptic phrase and suited men pursuing him. He soon meets the sunglasses-wearing hacker Morpheus (Laurence Fishburne), informing him that his world is not real. Offering him the truth, Neo is awakened in an apocalyptic world to realize that machines have programmed his whole life. Escaping the program, he meets other hackers rebelling against the machines that are using humans as batteries of bioelectricity as the sun has blocked out their unlimited means of power. Wouldn't humans make the worst means of generating energy? Couldn't they use wind, gas or coal as an alternative to solar energy? I can't imagine the robots would care all that much about the pollution.

Neo can reenter the human simulation of the Matrix with newly-learned superhuman abilities, now ready to perform martial arts and leap across rooftops in a single bound. He'll need all of these skills if he wants to best the many programmed agents inside the simulation devoted to killing the hackers that wish to free all humans from the game. The agents are fully armed with big guns and just as capable against the rebels in hand-to-hand combat. They have a mission in trying to crack the secret information about the hackers and their base of operations in the real world. The Matrix can't be exited easily, requiring a ringing telephone to be used as a means of escape, and creates a quandary of what to do when the agents capture one rebel. Do the hackers kill the captured rebel by forcefully removing his plug from the simulation to prevent him spilling information or do they try to rescue him?

The unique ideas begin to dissolve towards the end of the picture, as it's foretold that Neo may be *"The One,"* a messiah that can save all of humanity within the simulation. This essentially equates to making the hero incredibly strong when it seems that all hope is lost. He finds all the cheat codes for this video game of a world.

Outside of its standard storytelling aspect of the all-powerful savior that saves the day, the film's action sequences are remarkable and set a new tone for the action movies that would follow in the early 2000s. The film's most iconic scene features Neo dodging the bullets fired by an agent, bending himself backward and angling himself out of the paths of the bullets. The scene is shot in slow-motion while the camera rotates around Neo. The camera will also revolve around the female rebel Trinity (Carrie-Anne Moss) as she gracefully jumps into the air and kicks an opponent in the face. These are the film's most iconic scenes and would be parodied to death in the years that followed.

The Matrix became such a hit that it opened up a whole new can of worms for movies. The film's wire work created a new template for staging action sequences in *X-Men* (2000), but also generated a new interest in Hong Kong films that used it more prominently, leading to the popularity of the martial arts picture *Crouching Tiger, Hidden Dragon* the following year. The themes of a simulated world spawned a plethora of theory books on the subject, using the movie as a basis. *The Matrix* franchise exploded with two sequels (*The Matrix Reloaded*, *The Matrix Revolutions*), a tie-in video game (Enter the Matrix) and an animated anthology film (*The Animatrix*). The footprint it left on cinema is astonishing for two filmmakers who previously made a little lesbian noir (*Bound*). Neo said it best: *"Whoa!"*

MEET THE DEEDLES

DIRECTOR: Steve Boyum | SCREENWRITER: Jim Herzfeld | CAST: Steve Van Wormer, Paul Walker, A. J. Langer, John Ashton, Robert Englund, Dennis Hopper | GENRE: Comedy | RUNNING TIME: 93 min; MPAA RATING: PG

CLASSIFICATION: WORST

Meet the Deedles (1998) could be considered the death of the goofball duo formula for the 1990s. It could also be considered the end of surfer culture at the theater, considering how painfully bland and overused the slang of "dude, " and "bud" becomes in this picture. Disney wanted to capitalize on this culture, but they didn't understand what to do with it in this grand mess of a family comedy.

The Deedles are two surfer teenagers who lounge about in Hawaii on their father's dime, despite both "teens" appearing in their early twenties. But dear old dad is tired of their aimless lives that revolve around surfing and cutting class, leading him to send them off to Wyoming to gain some character. The boys decide the best way to prove themselves to pop is to assume the role of prairie dog control experts for Yellowstone National Park.

Now that's a ridiculous enough premise right there, but, wait, it gets more ludicrous. Yellowstone requires prairie dog experts as they are being overrun with these pests that are secretly controlled by the mad ex-park ranger, Slater (Dennis Hopper). His evil scheme is to use the prairie dogs to divert the water flow of the Old Faithful geyser onto his land. He aims to name this new attraction (what else?) New Faithful. To enact his plan, he sets up an underground base beneath a trailer where he monitors Yellowstone from multiple cameras. Hopper was the quintessential villain choice of the 1990s, but this is by far one of his worst characters just for how bizarre and surreal of a silly antagonist he portrays. His role in *Super Mario Bros.* is far more coherent by comparison.

The Deedles themselves are a dim pair, but also baffling in how they bounce between capable humans and braindead weirdos. One moment they're pulling each other's fingers to make themselves fart, the next they're hacking into the CIA website. They're smart enough to form an elaborate plan to get rid of the prairie dogs, but are dumb enough to toy with a helicopter that they nearly crash. In between their idiotic "whoa, bud" jokes and blandly expositional smarts, they spend their time making Hawaiian drinks, hosting luaus and finding means of surfing in Wyoming. There is no consistency to any of their antics, making Beavis & Butt-head appear as geniuses.

What's most surprising about this picture was the casting. This was one of the first roles for Paul Walker, who ended up having a fruitful career in the Fast and the Furious movie series. Robert England, better known as Freddy Krueger from *A Nightmare on Elm Street*, plays a hick of a henchman. Members of Oingo Boingo make a guest appearance as a band playing at a party, Steve Bartek being the most prominent as the film's composer. Even the bear hired for the movie, Bart the Bear, was a celebrity with his appearances in *White Fang* and *The Edge*. This was, unfortunately, his last role as he was euthanized from complications with cancer two years later.

This isn't so much a movie as it is a quilt of stupidity, stitched together from tired and ill-thought ideas. The Deedles concoct a special gas known as Gastro Castro, which makes people poop themselves in an extended sequence of fart jokes and one gross-out gag where a flock of birds crap all over one of the rangers. The Deedles become sidetracked at the airport in a pointless scene where they make drinks via a remotely controlled mini-bar. One Deedle falls in love with one of the female rangers, which causes him to see cartoon hearts and be hounded by the ranger's furious dad (also a park ranger). So many of these uncreative and laughless scenes are stacked on top of one another with little story that the movie quickly turns into a relentlessly annoying headache.

Meet the Deedles is an agonizing experience, spouting such ridiculous slang as *"preemo party-pooper"* and making such lame jokes as *"this cave's about to cave."* There was one memorable quote: *"Lynch the Deedles!"*

MIGHTY MORPHIN POWER RANGERS: THE MOVIE

DIRECTOR: Bryan Spicer | SCREENWRITER: Arne Olsen | CAST: Karan Ashley, Johnny Yong Bosch, Steve Cardenas, Jason David Frank, Amy Jo Johnson, David Yost, Jason Narvy, Paul Schrier, Paul Freeman | GENRE: Action | RUNNING TIME: 95 min | MPAA RATING: PG

CLASSIFICATION: WORST

Japanese television programs of heroes in tight spandex that battle monsters with giant robots, known as sentai, quickly became a phenomenon in the 1990s with the American adaptation of *Mighty Morphin Power Rangers*. The show lifted footage from Japanese sentai shows and filled in the non-action segments with American teenagers. The Japanese footage of spandex and robots were the best part of the show by far. Proving this point is *Mighty Morphin Power Rangers: The Movie* (1995), the American franchise's first stab at not using any Japanese footage, replacing the practical effects of the giant robots with the limited means of budgeted computer graphics. It's a movie that makes one pine for the corniness of the Japanese rubber suit monsters and flimsy cardboard sets.

The six leading heroes are nothing all that impressive as teenagers that maintain a secret identity during high school hours, but discreetly don the tight costumes when monsters attack their city of Angel Grove. They will also call on their giant robots of Zords when the monsters turn big, per the formula of the show. They speak the language of buzzwords and catchphrases in a manner that makes the dialogue of the *Teenage Mutant Ninja Turtles* sound Shakespearean. So bland are the Rangers that color coordinates their superhero names, labeled as Red Ranger, Black Ranger, etc. This arrangement makes them easy to spot in fight scenes, easy to remember when buying the right toy for your kids and easy to forget any personality these Rangers might have beneath the suits that cover any hint of them being human.

The villain is Ivan Ooze (Paul Freeman), a cackling monster who looks like Al Lewis if he fell into a vat of purple dye. Despite his sinister nature, there isn't much to this villain past his looks, his only memorable line being a bit about comparing the Black Plague to the *Brady Bunch Reunion*. His evil plan is to use an infectious ooze to turn the adults of Earth into slaves that will help him build an army. When the army is finished, he will then convince the adults to commit suicide. This sounds like a job for the Power Rangers, but they won't be on Earth for a while. Ivan's first assault was on the Power Rangers' command center, where their jar-dwelling master Zordon is dying, forcing the Rangers to venture off the planet and seek a cure. This, of course, leads to the Rangers receiving new costumes and new giant robots. You can't have a Power Rangers movie without a new product to push.

There's such a vapid nature to how everything in *Power Rangers* was assembled with little character and lazy writing. This script is so dull with handling a great power known only as the Great Power, also referred to by an even more lame title of the power of Ninjetti. Ivan's giant monsters are referred to as Ecto-Morphicon Titans, a name that rolls off the tongue and out of mind. The climactic battle of the Rangers new Zords versus Ivan's forces is some of the most indecipherable computer graphics ever put to film, appearing too off in compositing to be believable and too poorly staged to enjoy its action. Give me those old rubber suits and cardboard sets any day! Sure, they were cheap, but they age a little better than this poorly-rendered trash.

The film is devoid of any story, character or visual splendor that it comes across as another shameless cash-in of a theatrical commercial, its accompanying merchandise being video games, comics, and toys. Some might argue that the film is harmless for featuring wholesome teens, light violence, and science fiction elements that are targeted for kids. The people who believe this probably think that Cocoa Puffs are a healthy breakfast.

MISERY

DIRECTOR: Rob Reiner | SCREENWRITER: William Goldman | CAST: James Caan, Kathy Bates, Frances Sternhagen, Richard Farnsworth, Lauren Bacall | GENRE: Horror | RUNNING TIME: 107 min | MPAA RATING: R

CLASSIFICATION: WEIRD

The mere mention of *Misery* (1990) conjures up wincing for the most painful of tortures that is enough to make anyone turn their head in horror. It's a scene you wish you could forget, where Kathy Bates has tied James Caan to the bed and placed a block of wood between his feet. She then picks up a sledgehammer and, with one mighty swing, smashes his foot inward, breaking his ankles with a bone-chilling sound effect. And to think this was all over a novel.

Caan plays famous author Paul Sheldon, best known for his romance novels featuring the character of Misery Chastain. He's ready to leave behind this series, however, having just completed his manuscript for the final story of Misery where she dies in the end. A blizzard prevents him from getting home and ends up in a car crash in the middle of the Colorado wilderness. Thankfully, he is rescued by nurse Annie Wilkes (Bates), a big fan of his work that is more than willing to attend to his injuries. Unfortunately, she is allowed to read Paul's latest manuscript and is not too happy that Misery's demise. She becomes so infuriated with his writing that she holds him, hostage, to destroy his manuscript and write a new Misery novel. Nobody knows where Paul is and Annie is too resourceful and dangerous to escape from. This is fandom to the darkest extreme.

Outside the home, the hunt is on for the missing author. Local sheriff Buster (Richard Farnsworth) is on the case and intelligently tracks down clues to the whereabouts of Paul, the most significant lead coming for a shopkeeper that sold an awful lot of typing paper to Annie. Don't expect much from his arc outside of being the one person who could save Paul, but ultimately doesn't.

The acting talents of Caan and Bates are in top form for this picture. Caan plays the author with a certain sense of control and subtlety, acting carefully around his obsessed fan as though he's dealt with this kind of behavior before. Bates, who won an Academy Award for this performance, is the perfect antagonist of a woman who goes from sweet to sinister in a snap. There's madness to her character that always felt bubbling and present, but never overblown.

She is a terrifying monster and not just because she could break our ankles.

The story is based on the Stephen King novel of the same name and comes off as a very personal premise for King's career. The inspiration came from a number of sources including King's drug addiction and dreams he has had, but the biggest would arguably be the response to his novel *The Eyes of the Dragon*, as it was more fantasy than horror. King is known for far more than fear, but his fans didn't seem as interested in him pursuing different stories. As with most of King's books, he took this truth in the rejection of fandom and spun it into a terrifying story that is just as frightening for the audience as it is for a successful author.

Misery is considered one of the better movie adaptations of Stephen King's novels, but mostly from the perspective of respecting the text. Director Rob Reiner does a sufficient job of reaping King's words and faithfully displaying them on screen, but does little more than that. The script was such a straight adaptation that William Goldman's screenplay was easy enough to translate over into a Broadway play. But it's the performances of Caan and Bates that stand out and make this film engaging enough to follow. Well, that and, you know, the whole smashing of ankles bit.

MORTAL KOMBAT

DIRECTOR: Paul W.S. Anderson | SCREENWRITER: Kevin Droney | CAST: Linden Ashby, Cary-Hiroyuki Tagawa, Robin Shou, Bridgette Wilson, Talisa Soto, Christopher Lambert | GENRE: Action | RUNNING TIME: 101 min | MPAA RATING: PG-13

CLASSIFICATION: WEIRD

When producer Lawrence Kasanoff told Midway Games that he could develop the violent video game *Mortal Kombat* into a movie, they said he was full of crap. When he presented New Line Cinema with the script, executives told him they hated it, only reluctantly agreeing to greenlight the picture. Kasanoff showed them all by not just making the first video game movie with a coherent production, but also the first blockbuster of the sub-genre. Where *Super Mario Bros.* and *Street Fighter* went down in flames, *Mortal Kombat* (1995) featured better character, camp, and creativity to bring in a big audience.

Unlike most video game movies of the era, this film had a straightforward story (somewhat). There is a secret fighting tournament between Earth and Outworld, another dimension of great evil, magic, and monsters. If Outworld can win the championship, Earth will be invaded. Earth needs some heroes for the tournament, and thunder god Raiden (Christopher Lambert) has a few in mind. He assembles the team of Shaolin monk Liu Kang (Robin Shou), Special Forces officer Sonya Blade (Bridgette Wilson) and action movie star Johnny Cage (Linden Ashby) to be Earth's defenders. They don't easily believe Raiden's story, but once they arrive at the island for the tournament to meet with soul-stealing warlords, ice-shooting ninjas, and four-armed giants, they come around quickly.

With such a simple plot, director Paul W.S. Anderson was better able to focus on the meat of this action picture. Robin Shou was cast not because of his marquee value, being virtually unknown in America, but because of his impressive martial arts training. Anderson wanted the fight scenes to feel like real fights, and Shou gave him not only stellar scenes of great action, but also a surprising amount of charisma. He bodes well for his many scenes, whether he's throwing a kick or bantering with his comrades.

Cary-Hiroyuki Tagawa always makes me laugh for sternly

committing to scenes that are cornball for a villain, but he throws himself so well into the role that he makes the villain both memorable and fun. Christopher Lambert seems to be having just as much fun as a smirking wizard, evident from him being such a good sport with volunteering to shoot on location in Thailand as opposed to shooting all his scenes in Los Angeles. The only character that seemed to have the most problems on set was Goro, the four-armed warrior that required many puppeteers and two voice actors; Kevin Michael Richardson voicing the dialogue and Frank Welker the growls. The puppet continuously broke down, preventing filming his scenes in Thailand and creating a joking catchphrase on set: *"Goro won't come out of his trailer!"*

Despite the malfunctioning puppet, this film has a surprisingly high-spirited production. The fights have some great choreography in some fantastic locations, from a well-lit beach to a dark hell-like dimension of flames and rickety bridges. Of course, it helps that the film has an amazingly catchy and blood-pumping techno theme song by Praga Khan and Oliver Adams, perfect for a dance at the nightclub or a workout at the gym.

Mortal Kombat is worthy of being the first financially successful video game movie for grossing $122 million worldwide. It's probably not the most faithful adaptation for not including the blood and gore that made the games controversially famous. It's not even the best action film for its slightly goofy story and corny moments of overacting (right from the first shot when Cary-Hiroyuki tries to look menacing). But it's still a fun movie for its technical charm and committed actors. And at a time when films based on video games were mostly incoherent messes, this was a step in the right direction for the sub-genre for not being a Flawless Victory.

MORTAL KOMBAT: ANNIHILATION

DIRECTOR: John R. Leonetti | SCREENWRITER: Brent V. Friedman, Bryce Zabel | CAST: Robin Shou, Talisa Soto, Brian Thompson, Sandra Hess, Lynn Red Williams, Irina Pantaeva, James Remar | GENRE: Action | RUNNING TIME: 95 min | MPAA RATING: PG-13

CLASSIFICATION: WORST

When *Mortal Kombat* (1995) became the first video game based movie to be a blockbuster hit, New Line Cinema wasted no time in commissioning a sequel. So quick, in fact, that they didn't bother to regroup the previous cast and crew. Most of them were busy with other projects, but part of me wants to believe they just weren't interested in coming back for a script that was slapped together fast to push into production as soon as possible. The result was *Mortal Kombat: Annihilation* (1997), a film that was so cheap and flimsy it's a wonder that New Line Cinema didn't decide to just release this movie on, home video instead of embarrassing themselves at the theater.

The story picks up directly where the first film left off with a portal to the Outworld opening in the skies. Out of the portal comes some of the most laughable costumes that seem better suited for *Power Rangers* villains. Emperor Shao Kahn, looking dorky in his skull mask, has invaded our realm with his minions of Sindel (Katana's mother) and Sheeva (a four-armed female and distant cousin of the previous film's Goro character). Since most of the original cast did not return for this film, Kahn does the filmmakers a favor and kills Johnny Cage quickly upon his arrival, removing the chance of any scenes that remind you how much better the original actor was.

The warriors of the Earthrealm have six days to defeat Kahn before he can overtake their world. The familiar fighters of Liu Kang (reprised by Robin Shou), Katana (reprised by Talisa Soto), Sonya (not Bridgette Wilson-Sampras) and Raiden (certainly not Christopher Lambert) have to find some more warriors and new fighting abilities. They travel via a ridiculous contraption of a rolling ball built for two that I swear is intended as sex furniture based on the thrusting the two passengers have to do to propel the contraption.

Liu Kang learns a new ability in his travels, the act of Animality where a fighter can transform themselves into their spirit animal or something like that. True, Animality is a finishing move from the video games, but it won't be used to finish a fight in this picture. Instead, in some of the most astonishingly awful computer graphics of the late-90s, Liu Kang will transform into a dragon to do battle with another giant creature to pad out a fight scene. It's bad enough that the computer graphics look ugly, but it's even worse on a conceptual level for favoring this scene over more creative martial arts.

This film is a confusing mess on every level. The martial arts rely on wirework so many times for pushing and pulling characters during fight scenes that the blatant use of it in *Crouching Tiger, Hidden Dragon* seems subtle by comparison. Several new characters appear in ridiculous costumes, most notably the android of Cyrax that looks remarkably like a melted generic action figure. Sub-Zero returns, but didn't he die in the last movie? Oh, nevermind; it's his twin brother. But wait, Scorpion is back, and he also died in the previous film. Is he a twin as well?

While *Mortal Kombat* did not promptly return to the theaters for a third film, a series entitled *Mortal Kombat: Conquest* was developed for television with even sillier plots and costumes. By the time this show was canceled, I had found myself questioning just who *Mortal Kombat* was for. The video games were a significant allure for me as a kid for being so bloody violent to a level that made it taboo. While the *Mortal Kombat* video games continued for their inventiveness in developing violent fights, *Annihilation* was so bereft of competent ideas that killed any chance of the franchise receiving a movie trilogy.

MRS. DOUBTFIRE

DIRECTOR: Chris Columbus | SCREENWRITER: Randi Mayem Singer, Leslie Dixon | CAST: Robin Williams, Sally Field, Pierce Brosnan, Harvey Fierstein, Robert Prosky | GENRE: Comedy | RUNNING TIME: 125 min | MPAA RATING: PG-13

CLASSIFICATION: WEIRD

We know that Robin Williams is a capable enough comedian to pull off all sorts of impersonations, but *Mrs. Doubtfire* (1993) puts him to the ultimate test of looking the part as well as acting it. He must not only work as a kindly old British nanny, but must look like one. It sounds like a script that's a recipe for disaster, but is a somewhat intoxicating comedy just for how well Williams throws himself into a role that requires him to flex his impersonation muscles while at the same time displaying emotional heartache. A lesser actor would not have sold such a ridiculous character.

Williams is perfectly cast for the role of voice actor Daniel Hillard, a father that embraces the wild nature of his three kids. This angers his wife Miranda (Sally Field) enough to divorce him. And since Daniel was recently fired over a morality dispute with his director, he has limited custody. What's a dad to do? Sure, he finds a new job and tries to be a more responsible person, but that's not enough for a father; he needs to see kids. Enter his character of Mrs. Euphegenia Doubtfire; an old British persona Daniel sells with his gentle voice and a state-of-the-art costume created by his makeup artist brother Frank (Harvey Fierstein). This is no mere simple drag outfit, as Williams slips on everything from a chubby bodysuit to dentures. We still know it's Williams, but a squint of the eyes and cock of the head would make me think otherwise.

The role is sold well enough that Miranda hires on Mrs. Doubtfire. Daniels uses this as a rare opportunity to start over with his kids. He becomes sterner and caring past his manic pushover nature, acting as the parent Miranda always wanted. But he'll also have to contain his rage for Miranda's new boyfriend Stu, played by the charmingly British hunk Pierce Brosnan. Daniel maintains his Doubtfire character around Stu, but has enough wit to fight him off both figuratively with the graphic mention of Miranda's vibrator and physically with a piece of fruit. And he'll also have to balance his true identity by holding down a steady job and proving as a man that he's still a capable father. All in a day's work for Daniel/Doubtfire.

The story of *Doubtfire* isn't a uniquely original one, especially for the climax where Daniel has two dinners reserved at the same restaurant on the same night, one as Daniel and the other as Doubtfire. He can't afford to miss either and finds himself running back and forth between tables and changing in the bathroom. It's a predictable enough scene, but succeeds from Williams' committed performance that never goes too far off the rails. He is surprisingly collected and witty for a scene where any other actor would be frantic and awkward. When Williams forgets to change out of the Doubtfire attire when he goes back to the table of his boss that is expecting Daniel, he plays it cool as though he had intended to return as a woman.

Admittedly, *Mrs. Doubtfire* is not up to snuff with other drag comedies, from the uproarious *Some Like It Hot* to the intelligent *Tootsie*, but it does satisfy with Williams' performance alone. He spent four hours in makeup every day. It's a wonder he was not only able to deliver laughs in such an elaborate costume, but also evoke a bit of heart from his character's plight. Not a lot, but just enough to fall a little for the film's sentimentality. His role was so essential to making the movie work that when Williams, unfortunately, committed suicide in 2014, development plans for a sequel were immediately canceled. Nobody else could fill those pantyhose.

THE MUPPET CHRISTMAS CAROL

DIRECTOR: Brian Henson | SCREENWRITER: Jerry Juhl | CAST: Kermit the Frog, Miss Piggy, The Great Gonzo, Rizzo the Rat, Fozzie Bear, Michael Caine | GENRE: Comedy | RUNNING TIME: 86 min | MPAA RATING: G

CLASSIFICATION: WEIRD

One of my favorite actors in the role of Ebenezer Scrooge from Dickens' *A Christmas Carol* is without question Michael Caine. He just happens to be performing as Scrooge in *The Muppet Christmas Carol* (1992), where he must share the screen with puppets that are mostly acting for laughs. That just makes me appreciate Caine all the more as an actor that never tries to be as silly as his co-stars. He plays Scrooge straight to the point where he looms over the entire Muppet ensemble, sometimes literally. There's real emotion in his performance that feels genuine and true to the character and not just a family-friendly Scrooge for a Muppet movie.

Familiar Muppets fill out the bulk of the roles, their personalities fitting firmly into the story. The meek and lovable frog Kermit plays Bob Cratchet, a forgiving man (frog?) that is thankful for what little he has. Fozzy Bear fits snuggly into the jovial shoes of Scrooge's former employer Fuzzywig or, in this case, Fozzywig. Regular hecklers Waldorf and Statler are both cast in the role of the haunting spirit Marley, rewritten from one character into two brothers. Other Muppets are cast in background shots or secondary roles. One of my favorites is the patriotic eagle Sam being cast as Scrooge's old headmaster, referring to the field of business as *"the American way."* Another Muppet quickly enters the frame and stresses to Sam that this story takes place in England.

The hook-nosed Gonzo is interestingly cast as Charles Dickens, both as the narrator and participant observer in this story. He provides some essential descriptions and amusing banter with his co-star Rizzo the Rat, the only Muppet cast as himself in this picture. With Rizzo continually questioning the story, Gonzo always seems to have the smart and amusing answer on the telling of this tale.

Rizzo: How do you know what Scrooge is doin'? We're down here and he's up there!
Gonzo: I told you, storytellers are omniscient; I know everything!
Rizzo: Hoity-toity, Mr. Godlike Smarty-Pants.

For the roles of the three spirits of Christmas, the Jim Henson Creature Workshop developed some unique designs that embody more of the spirit of *A Christmas Carol* than the zaniness of Muppets. Christmas Past appears as a doll-like child that floats with a warm glow. Christmas Present is a bearded giant, looking soft in felt for such a beefy figure. Christmas Future is a predictable design of a grim reaper figure, but still rendered spooky enough with elongated limbs and a draping cloak that Gonzo abandons this segment of the film out of fear.

The musical numbers are some of the finest produced in any Muppet movie. From Scrooge's cold introduction of the townspeople singing about how terrible he is to the chipper and warm melody of Caine singing "The Love We Found," every melody is a joy for the ears, expertly written by the legendary Paul Williams. One song that has been lost over time was "When Love Is Gone," a sad goodbye from when a younger Scrooge leaves his first love, Belle. This song was only included on the VHS release, but is not missed as most every kid remembers fast-forwarding through this somber scene that slows down the picture.

The Muppet Christmas Carol is a little heavy on dialogue and light on Muppet wackiness, especially for Michael Caine committing seriously to his starring role. But it's for that reason it stands out as a charming and emotional picture brimming with catchy songs, captivating performances, dazzling visual effects and a warm Christmas spirit. It has enough respect for both Dickens and Muppets to be an engaging family film that doesn't dumb down the source material too much for the younger crowd. Rizzo asks Gonzo if all this talk of death and ghosts is too spooky for kids; *"Nah, it's all right. This is culture!"*

NAKED GUN 33⅓: THE FINAL INSULT

DIRECTOR: Peter Segal | SCREENWRITER: Pat Proft, David Zucker, Robert LoCash | CAST: Leslie Nielsen, Priscilla Presley, George Kennedy, O.J. Simpson, Fred Ward | GENRE: Comedy | RUNNING TIME: 82 min | MPAA RATING: PG-13

CLASSIFICATION: WEIRD

There were plenty of notable comedic talents from movies of the 1990s, but Leslie Nielsen deserves the most credit as one of the funniest men of the decade for his unflappable performances. His comedic antics were first introduced as the doctor in the classic spoof *Airplane!*, but he indeed came into his own as the lead cop Frank Drebin from *The Naked Gun* movies, based off the TV series which he also led. The key to his comedy is how straight he speaks his amusing lines without cracking a smile. It was a requirement for nearly every actor in these spoof pictures of the time, but nobody could nail this formula quite like Nielsen.

Naked Gun 33⅓: The Final Insult (1994) finds Frank happily married to his wife Jane (Priscilla Presley) and retired from the police force. His new problem is Jane's desire to have a baby. She goes to work as a lawyer and her biological clock rattles when it turns out every woman in the court has a kid they brought with them to work, including the stenographer that burps her baby between reading back statements. When the prospect of trying to have a child becomes a stricter ordeal, Frank decides to secretly go back to work in stopping the new threat of terrorist Rocco (Fred Ward). For this mission, he'll have to go undercover in prison to work his way into Rocco's gang and discover his sinister plans to set off a bomb at the Academy Awards.

Writing about the plot is pointless for a film such as this that is wall-to-wall gags with the highest batting average of any comedy of the decade. Nielsen gets in plenty of hilarious lines he delivers so seriously that they're twice as funny for his devotion. He incites a prison riot by complaining that the food is like gruel and the prison's Chateau le Blanc 68 should not be served at room temperature. His narration offers up great parody on classic detective lines, rewriting familiar phrases and passages to sound more bizarre and silly; *"Like a blind man at an orgy, I was going to have to feel things out."*

Priscilla Presley is just as funny, but more for her commitment to physically demanding gags. She dons electric lingerie for a romantic evening and has her hair shook into all sorts of weird styles by another frantic woman. Anna Nicole Smith plays the sinister love interest with legs that go on for so long she appears to have extra knees in an extended reveal. And I couldn't get enough of the antics of the straight cop Ed (George Kennedy) and his absent-minded co-worker Nordberg (O.J. Simpson), who is easy to distract with a puzzle or a phone that doesn't ring.

The film has a lot of fun with satire when the third act takes place entirely at the Academy Awards ceremony, run by a frantic director (Joe Grifasi) with a fistful of medication. The nominations are hilarious (*"Shannen Doherty, "Basic Analysis" - One woman's triumph over a yeast infection, set against the background of the tragic Buffalo Bills' season of 1991."*) as are the nomination categories (*"Best Actor in a Columbus Film"*). There's a running gag of Nielsen being mistaken for Phil Donahue, but also passing as Weird Al after swiping his passes to get inside the show.

Though the numerical label of 33⅓ was a joke, *The Final Insult* was no lie. It was intended to end the trilogy, writing off Leslie Nielsen's character for good. It was the final role of O.J. Simpson as he would enter his murder trial soon after. The film received mixed reviews and was nominated for two Golden Raspberry Awards for Worst Supporting Actor (O.J. Simpson) and Worst New Star (Anna Nicole Smith). That being said, the trilogy still went out on a high note by maintaining its speed of comedy, committed actors and unparalleled ability to evoke a laugh. David Zucker and Pat Proft would not make another *Naked Gun* movie, though they did write a script with a great title: *The Naked Gun 444.4*.

NATURAL BORN KILLERS

DIRECTOR: Oliver Stone | SCREENWRITER: Richard Rutowski, Oliver Stone, David Veloz | CAST: Woody Harrelson, Juliette Lewis, Robert Downey, Jr., Tommy Lee Jones, Tom Sizemore | GENRE: Drama | RUNNING TIME: 119 min | MPAA RATING: R

CLASSIFICATION: BEST

The world of *Natural Born Killers* (1994) was one of overblown satire, or at least one hopes it was. When released in 1994, during the OJ Simpson murder trial that gripped America, Oliver Stone's violent and chaotic vision of media and murder running amok together was disturbingly prophetic. It is a film that became the subject of considerable controversy for its viciously ultra-violent content and copycat murders. The murderers and those that wanted the film banned missed the point entirely, further solidifying Stone's theories of the media's disgusting glorification of violence and how we interpret it.

Woody Harrelson and Juliette Lewis play serial killers Mickey and Mallory that start to become household names with the public's obsession in their media coverage. They playfully slaughter anyone they meet, usually leaving one survivor or a rolling camera to spread the word of their rampage. And even if it's only one guy inside a store, they still need to take him out; *"If I don't kill you, what is there to talk about?"* Their aggressively violent antics create a sensationalism within the media where teenagers look up to them as counter-culture idols. One young man interviewed for the cameras states that Mickey and Mallory are the best things to happen to mass murder since Manson. The boy next to him agrees; *"But they're way cooler!"*

The film follows the chaos seen not only through the eyes of the killers, but through the neon and cheap lens of television. The most surreal of these interpretations come in the form of showcasing Mallory's origins of a troubled home life. Rodney Dangerfield plays her piggish and putrid father, and the scene at home features a sitcom laugh track. But the laughs are mounted on top of Dangerfield saying the nastiest and hurtful things to his family. He proceeds to sexually harass his daughter by fondling her body and talking explicitly about raping her, set against an audience that laughs and cheers at his foulness. The "live studio audience" finds this scene humorous either out of Dangerfield's timing or for being programmed by a network to laugh on command. Anything can be sold as funny to a TV audience if you sell it with such a formula, even when the visuals break into harsh black-and-white to show there's no parody in Mallory's father squeezing her ass.

The people that surround the killers are just as flawed and odd. Keeping the closest tabs on Mickey and Mallory is Wayne Gayle (Robert Downey Jr.), a ruthless tabloid TV journalist so eager to get the exclusive interview with these icons that he practically wants to become their intern. Tommy Lee Jones plays prison Warden McClusky, overjoyed to have Mickey and Mallory imprisoned in his building for the chance to be on television. These two characters have become so high on the media buzz, as they believe they're just doing their jobs until the dark turning point of a prison riot turns them into weaklings that cause them to ask where they went wrong.

Stone's picture comes loaded with as much style as it has substance. The film shifts between all sorts of cinematic techniques. Color leaves the screen for instances of black-and-white that changes tones dramatically. The camera whips around rooms, tilts the perspective and becomes drenched in different filters. The film itself will shift from 35mm to Super 8. Animated cartoons appear, and newsreels flood the screen as Gayle salivates over editing his segments. These visual choices enhance the picture in more ways than one; the green lighting signals the sickness of Mickey's mind and the quick editing perfectly portrays the nonstop madness of the killers that everyone is caught within.

Natural Born Killers isn't so much a violent film as it is a film about violence, more appalling for how people react to Mickey and Mallory's murders than the murders themselves. It doesn't overload the screen with blood and guts, choosing just the right moments to showcase the carnage and not desensitize the viewer as much as the media circus. It's easy to get caught up in the three-ring act of serial killers, but Stone wants to take us outside the big top and make us look at the filthy ropes holding it in place. This is a movie ripe with parody and shock, with Stone throwing all the violence and media eroticism at the screen in hopes that we'll see more than just entertainment in its chaos.

THE NIGHTMARE BEFORE CHRISTMAS

DIRECTOR: Henry Selick | SCREENWRITER: Caroline Thompson | CAST: Danny Elfman, Chris Sarandon, Catherine O'Hara, William Hickey, Glenn Shadix, Paul Reubens, Ken Page | GENRE: Comedy (Animated) | RUNNING TIME: 76 min | MPAA RATING: PG

CLASSIFICATION: WEIRD

There is a debate about whether *The Nightmare Before Christmas* (1993) is a Christmas or Halloween film for featuring elements of both. It could be argued it's more for Halloween based on the abundance of horror characters and for being released theatrically on Halloween weekend of '93. But for Tim Burton, who conceived the original story, it was a celebration of two holidays that kids adore. And while Burton stepped down from directing this movie to work on *Batman Returns* (1992), his mark of weird and wonderful is all over this stop-motion animated picture, as well as featuring some original touches by the film's director Henry Selick.

The story concerns the boney Jack Skellington (Chris Sarandon), the skeletal Pumpkin King of Halloween Town who seeks something more out of life. Halloween town is certainly a unique marvel with all sorts of grotesque monsters and warped buildings, but it would probably lose its charm if you saw it every day. Jack goes strolling through the woods and stumbles into Christmas Town, a village of snow, presents, joy and Santa Claus. He's amazed by this discovery and impressed by a holiday that's all about peace and goodwill. There's a need in his soul to make Christmas a part of his life.

Unfortunately, Jack goes about promoting Christmas in the worst ways for both Christmas Town and Halloween Town. He decides to kidnap Santa Claus and assume the role of Santa himself, employing the citizens of Halloween Town to assemble the gifts that will be distributed to the children of Earth. This naturally frightens Santa and worries Halloween Town about Jack. He's a nice guy that wants to do the right thing, but is too ambitious and weird for his own good. He wants his fellow helpers to make Santa feel comfortable in Halloween Town, but they hand over the jolly fat man to Oogie Boogie, a sinister sack of bugs that wants to torture the icon of Christmas.

Jack's attempt at being Santa Claus does not go well. He rides to Earth with a sled pulled by skeletal reindeer. He leaves children frightening presents of snakes and voodoo heads. Jack believes he is doing justice to the holiday, but starts to get the message once the military tries to shoot him down. Maybe delivering Christmas presents isn't the best job for living skeletons.

The stop-motion animation on display is a technical marvel that redefined how the medium would evolve. Teams of animators not only constructed otherworldly sets, but dozens of different bodies and faces for the vivid characters. Rather than push and nudge facial movement with clay, plastic head models of specific facial changes were created to make the animation smoother and the seams less distracting. The musical numbers by Danny Elfman are some of his most catchy tracks ever composed. The opening number of "This is Halloween" is such a memorable melody it's practically become the theme song for the entire holiday, melding perfectly with classic Halloween songs. I'd like to point out this is a Disney movie as well, making it Disney's most unconventional of animated musicals of the 1990s.

The film became a launching point for both Burton and Selick that continued with animated projects. Burton would later direct the stop-motion animated musical *Corpse Bride* (2005), despite criticisms that he was rehashing *Nightmare* with a similar art style and story. Selick would continue working in stop-motion, eventually working with the Laika studio to direct *Coraline* (2009), an even darker animated fantasy. And the movie itself has become one of Disney's most cult classic of animated films for its macabre style, grand music and a uniquely twisted tale of merging holidays. Not all of it holds up over time, but it's still a great movie for older kids who want something a little more twisted out of their animated film.

NORTH

DIRECTOR: Rob Reiner | SCREENWRITER: Alan Zweibel, Andrew Scheinman | CAST: Elijah Wood, Jon Lovitz, Jason Alexander, Alan Arkin, Dan Aykroyd, Kathy Bates, Faith Ford, Graham Greene, Julia Louis-Dreyfus, Reba McEntire, John Ritter, Abe Vigoda, Bruce Willis | GENRE: Comedy | RUNNING TIME: 87 min | MPAA RATING: PG

CLASSIFICATION: WORST

The premise of *North* (1994) is not only too contrived and stupid for a kid's movie, but also insultingly cruel. The titular character of a little boy, played by a young Elijah Wood, decides that he is going to divorce his parents. North makes this decision not only because his parents ignore him, but because he feels he's too good for them as a child prodigy. Thanks to a scummy lawyer, he manages to convince a judge that his parents don't deserve him and to let him experience a summer of trotting around the globe to select his new parents. This picture is staged as a fable of sorts, but comes off more like a bad reality show where families plead with the talented North to be their son.

The potential families that North interviews are all cartoonish stereotypes. He goes to Texas to interview a family, played by Dan Ackroyd and Reba McEntire dressed up as cowboys who lost their son in a stampede. If you think their odd explanation for their son's death isn't funny, just wait until you hear their song and dance number about it. Next. He visits a Hawaiian couple (Keone Young and Lauren Tom) that wants to use North's butt-crack to appear in ads and increase tourism. Next! He visits an Alaskan Inuit family (Graham Greene and Kathy Bates) that live in an igloo, serves him (what else?) Eskimo pie and send their old off to die on ice slabs in the ocean, even though the Inuit haven't done this in ages. NEXT! He visits the Amish, but they don't have electricity and North thankfully cuts this trip short.

All the while Bruce Willis keeps popping up as the costume donning mentor, existing as someone outside the crazy adults for North to vent towards. Willis has the honor of stating some of the film's worst lines. He first meets North and cracks a bad joke about his name; *"That's my favorite direction."* He makes garbled metaphors that make no sense and are probably intended to be funny for being so stupid; *"Remember, kid, if you can't stand the heat, stay out of Miami."*

North asks him to clarify the metaphor, and he doesn't; *"What metaphor? You ever been down there in August? Your balls stick to your leg like crazy glue."* Oh, and you have to love the film's copout of an ending that proves the screenwriters wrote himself into a corner with this story.

Director Rob Reiner has said that some of his best jokes are in this picture, but I'm not sure where they were located. Did he think kids would get a kick out of a husband joking about his wife being barren? Was it amusing to make light of an Inuit tribe sending their elderly off to die on floating ice? Or is the mere sight of Bruce Willis in an Easter Bunny costume hilarious? If this is the best Reiner has to offer, he sucks at comedy for relying on stereotypes, puns and outdated humor that wouldn't be funny in the 1960s.

Film critic Roger Ebert despised *North* so much that he admitted a sinister force came over him while writing his review, causing him to write *"I hated this movie. Hated, hated, hated, hated, hated this movie. Hated it."* This was a film so unfathomably awful that it reduced a Pulitzer Prize-winning writer down to the most simplistically savage of criticisms. There's not much more to say other than that I share his emotional reaction for hating, hating, hating, hating, hating this movie.

NOTHING BUT TROUBLE

DIRECTOR: Dan Aykroyd | SCREENWRITER: Dan Aykroyd | CAST: Chevy Chase, Dan Aykroyd, John Candy, Demi Moore | GENRE: Comedy | RUNNING TIME: 94 min | MPAA RATING: PG-13

CLASSIFICATION: WORST

Nothing But Trouble (1991) is such an inhuman comedy in that it relies more on its makeup and production values than anything vaguely human. It is a bitterly ugly film which plays as a wicked cross between a backwoods kidnapping and a haunted house of terror. This is a picture that tries so hard to be a cruel and dark comedy that it seems to forget to give us a reason to care about any character on screen that is either a putrid pile of makeup effects or a potential victim to be ground up into bones. I can only fathom that Dan Aykroyd assembled such a picture to see if his audience could both puke and laugh at the same time. If there were any laughs to be had, they're buried in barf.

Chevy Chase plays New York City financial publicist Chris, casually agreeing to drive lawyer Diane (Demi Moore) to Atlantic City with his annoying Brazilian clients in tow. They get a little crazy with their driving in the backwoods of New Jersey and are taken into custody in the village of Valkenvania. For their sentencing, the wealthy collective is brought to the mansion of local judge Alvin Valkenheiser, played by Dan Aykroyd under what must have been pounds of makeup. Valkenheiser is easily the most disgusting character Aykroyd has ever played, featuring clammy skin, balding hair, colored teeth, a large gut and a protruding nose that looks like a penis in some shots. Not gross enough? What if I told you the nose is detachable, allowing the viewer to see the exposed nasal cavity and muscle tissue beneath the prosthetics? How this film got away with a PG-13 rating for featuring such a scene is beyond me.

Valkenheiser runs a strict, deadly and elaborate operation of maintaining law and order. He will execute major offenders on his grounds, but by placing them on a roller coaster that launches them into a grinder that launches their bones into a pile. If the unlucky guests don't want to lose their skin, they're forced to endure Valkenheiser's elaborate house of horrors. He invites them to a dinner of gross hot dogs, making his entrance by descending from the ceiling on a platform and passing condiments across the table via a motorized toy train. I don't know how many takes it took for Aykroyd to make his character consume a hot dog in the most disgusting way possible, but he nailed it.

In the most surreal of scenes, Tupac Shakur drops by with Digital Underground to provide the soundtrack for a shotgun wedding between Chevy Chase in shock and John Candy in drag. I can't imagine how Tupac felt about his theatrical debut, composing music with an accompanying penis-nosed Aykroyd on piano. Even more putrid than this character was the addition of Valkenheiser's diaper-wearing mutant grandchildren of Bobo and Little Devil, one of which is played by Aykroyd in another heaping portion of makeup. Their banter is unbelievably tedious, especially when they are easily wooed by Diane. All of these scenes are only vaguely intended as humorous by the light and silly soundtrack. One could easily replace this with an intense Hans Zimmer score and have an unpleasantly vile and mean horror film.

Nothing But Trouble was the first and only film to be written by, directed by and starring Dan Aykroyd and it's easy to see why he never put on the directing hat again. The film swept the Razzie nominations for all the major awards, from Worst Picture to Worst Actor to Worst Actress. The only positive nomination was for the Saturn Award of Best Make-up. On this designation I'll agree; I had to look twice to be sure that was John Candy in drag and Dan Aykroyd in a diaper. Maybe part of me just wanted to believe they wouldn't stoop so low.

OFFICE SPACE

DIRECTOR: Mike Judge | SCREENWRITER: Mike Judge | CAST: Ron Livingston, Jennifer Aniston, Stephen Root, Gary Cole | GENRE: Comedy | RUNNING TIME: 89 min | MPAA RATING: R

CLASSIFICATION: BEST

Mike Judge had proven in the realm of animation that he had an eye for satire, be it centered on brain-dead teenagers (*Beavis and Butt-head*) or Texas suburban life (*King of the Hill*). For his first live-action movie, he aimed at the world of office cubicles in *Office Space* (1999). He already created the template for this humor with his animated short Milton, depicting a meek employee that silently vowed to set the building on fire after his passively demanding boss gently talks his way into forcing others to do his bidding. So hilarious were these characters that they were included in the movie, played by Stephen Root and Gary Cole as their most memorable of comedic roles.

The focus of the story, however, is the more relatable character of software updater Peter (Ron Livingston). The daily grind of working at Initech has taken its toll on him. The agonizingly slow speed of morning traffic, the constant chattering of his nearby co-workers and the neverending requests from his manager Lumbergh (Cole) have forced him into a corner of questioning the direction in his life. His charismatic co-workers Michael (David Herman) and Samir (Ajay Naidu) offer him no help. When Peter asks what they think about working at Initech when they're fifty, Samir scoffs and jokes that it'd be nice to have that level of job security.

But then Ron has an epiphany while seeing a hypnotherapist at the request of his girlfriend. All his worries about work vanish, and there's an honest, carefree nature of his rejection of his burdens. He no longer cares if his boss gets mad at him or if his girlfriend breaks up with him. More at peace with his happiness, he finally works up the courage to ask out the waitress Joanna (Jennifer Aniston) and divulge his philosophy about not going into work.

> *Joanna: Won't you get fired?*
> *Peter: I don't know, but I don't really like it, and, uh, I'm not gonna go.*

Peter eventually will return to the office and turn it upside down by removing cubicle walls, refusing to finish his TPS reports and being as brutally honest to company consultants trying to determine if he should keep his job. The plot eventually spins out of control into a scheme of getting revenge on Initech after Peter's Zen-like state of mind wears off and his co-workers are fired. While the story takes a strange shift in its third act, it is still a fun ride of office place satire throughout, right up to the ridiculously explosive finale.

Part of what keeps the comedy consistent is Mike Judge's ability to conceive hilarious characters that are just as much relatable as they are cartoonish. There's dimension to such simple figures as Tom (Richard Riehle), a paranoid office veteran that fears he'll lose his job, but also has the ridiculous idea of marketing a Jump To Conclusions game akin to Twister. It's hilarious how Michael isn't just a bitter office nerd, but also a closeted rap lover and overflowing with disgust for his last name being Bolton for the obvious celebrity joke. The quietly pensive Milton (Root) has the familiar aroma of the timebomb beta employee who is one desk change away from setting the cubicles aflame.

Office Space has its quotable lines, raunchy talk, memorable characters and a triumphantly hilarious sequence where Peter and company destroy a printer with a baseball bat. But at its core is a definite intelligence and philosophy on the existentialism of the nine-to-five world and the human desire to reject it. Peter has had plenty of time to think about this and forms the perfect answer for the old career question of what you'd do if you had a million dollars. He responds that he'd do nothing if he had the money to do so. But as his mustachioed neighbor Lawrence (Diedrich Bader) points out to him, money is not always the path to such enlightenment; *"Take a look at my cousin: he's broke, don't do shit."*

ON DEADLY GROUND

DIRECTOR: Steven Seagal | SCREENWRITER: Ed Horowitz, Robin U. Russin | CAST: Steven Seagal, Michael Caine, Joan Chen, John C. McGinley | GENRE: Action | RUNNING TIME: 105 min | MPAA RATING: R

CLASSIFICATION: WORST

Steven Seagal makes the big mistake of turning his action picture *On Deadly Ground* (1994) into a movie about environmentalism. It's not that Seagal's concern for the Alaskan wilderness feels false, but it isn't suited for his usual genre of explosive action. It's hard to take any grand message about saving the Earth seriously when his picture spends so much time filling it up with gunfights, car chases, and explosions.

He should have thought about this concept a little longer to realize how counterintuitive it appears. Seagal plays Forrest Taft, a man who puts out oil fires and discovers that the soon-to-open Aegis oil rig off the coast of Alaska is cutting corners with faulty equipment to meet the operational deadline. If the rig continues to operate in this manner, it will cause many oil leaks and pollute the environment. Taft's solution: Blow it all up! It doesn't sound like a very heroic resolve for a hero that is supposed to have a substantial opinion about saving the planet.

But this is the world that Seagal always occupies and the only way he can make a point. In his movie and his mind, Seagal can do no wrong. He is referred to by the Inuit people as everything from the Chosen One to the Spirit Warrior. He gets to defend the natives by getting into ridiculous bar brawls, grabbing someone by the testicles at one point for them to shout, *"MY NUTS!"* He speaks with native elders about his spirituality and oneness with nature and goes on a vision quest. You know, before blowing up an oil rig.

The villain he fights is the evil Aegis Oil boss Jennings, played by a black-haired Michael Caine. Jennings and Taft were once friends, working side by side for the almighty dollar. But Taft soon discovers that money can't buy happiness or spirit animals. What good will all that money do you if there's no environment left to spend it in? Taft needs to do something. Something drastic. Something explosive! It's a good thing there are plenty of racist oil workers to punch. Soon, Taft teams up with the beautiful activist Masu (Joan Chen), a woman who captured his heart when she first threw oil at him in protest. It's love at first splash. She spends most of the movie blending into the background, never getting very involved in the action.

Jennings sends waves of hitmen to take out Seagal, played by the likes of John C. McGinley, Sven-Ole Thorsen, and R. Lee Ermey. They go through all the expected motions. They search through Alaskan villages for Taft, and if they can't find him, they start killing the innocent natives along the way. They're given silly kills where they fall into helicopter blades and are caught in explosions. You'll begin to notice a pattern to this film's method of direction, where balls of fire act as filler.

The entire film is an embarrassment of Seagal trying to make an action film with an environmental message, but it reaches its highest levels of absurdity with Taft's ending speech to the Alaska State Capitol. He speaks of the dangers of pollution and how greedy corporations are destroying the planet. This statement initially went on for eleven minutes, but was cut down to seven minutes after a test audience complained about overly preachy it was. The total amount of footage he shot for this was forty minutes worth. How full of yourself do you have to be to rant for such an extended period on the environment? *Captain Planet* only needed half an hour with commercials, and his lessons stuck better than this so-called savior Seagal has portrayed himself.

There are a lot of dopey and silly Seagal pictures, but *On Deadly Ground* is among his most hilarious of misfires for believing that the world's environmental problems can be solved with punching, bar brawls, and refinery explosions. I'd love to see how he handles the issue of healthcare.

ONE FALSE MOVE

DIRECTOR: Carl Franklin | SCREENWRITER: Billy Bob Thornton, Tom Epperson | CAST: Bill Paxton, Cynda Williams, Billy Bob Thornton, Michael Beach | GENRE: Drama | RUNNING TIME: 105 min | MPAA RATING: R

CLASSIFICATION: BEST

There is tension in almost every scene of *One False Move* (1992). Three criminals burst into a house of people, shouting as they wave guns and demand money. A police chief shares an awkward dinner with two officers, one of them black, when he slips out the N-word while describing the criminals. An affair that led to a child breeds a heated conversation of old wounds. Every scene left me wondering who was going to get a lashing, be it tongue or gun.

But to capture that sense of being on pins and needles, director Carl Franklin spends plenty of time letting us understand these characters that are misguided and flawed in one way or another. The criminal trio of Ray (Billy Bob Thornton), Fantasia (Cynda Williams) and Pluto (Michael Beach) go on a murderous rampage for money and drugs. Ray is the muscle as an intense killer who isn't afraid to shove guns into faces, but twitchy enough to pull the trigger too soon. Pluto is his contrast as a killer that is more calm and collected, rarely speaking unless it's about the job at hand. Fantasia falls somewhere in the middle as Ray's girlfriend who is confident enough to kill someone, but fragile enough to be shaken by a child at a crime scene.

Chasing after them is a pair of LAPD detectives that enlist the aid of Star City Police Chief Dixon (Bill Paxton). He seems to be a happy husband, a friendly man about town and is ecstatic to be working with other detectives that he nearly crashes his car to relay his excitement towards them. He's a little ignorant and a bit gung-ho about his chances of working in L.A., to the point that the detectives joke about him behind his back. But as the story continues, he seems to have a bigger role in this case and isn't as innocently naive as he appears.

While the plot has its fair share of surprises, the most prominent draw is the characters that bring an unease to any scene. When the criminal trio stops at a gas station, they catch the glance of a cop in the store. There's a scent of suspicion and death in the air, but violence will not occur here. It will happen further down the road when they are pulled over. But who will shoot first? It could be Ray with his temper, Fantasia with her fear or Pluto with his cold-hearted nature. These characters are built up brilliantly over their squabbles that we know them well enough, but have no clue about how this will all play out for them. And when the violence erupts, it's never subtle or telegraphed. Anyone could die at any moment, and that prospect becomes possible as each situation for the criminals and the cops goes south in one way or another.

One False Move always keeps the tension high by never ramping down towards its finale, as storylines intersect and violence mounts. There is no typical chase or an easy shootout to cap off the picture. There is enough drama within these characters that cheapening it with action cliches would be a disservice to the smart script and strong cast. The real grit of this movie comes from the fascinating characters that seem to be one moment away from exploding with anger or shooting someone. The unpredictability of the picture makes it easily one of the most gripping crime stories I've ever seen, right up to its revealing, bloody and poignant final scene.

THE PEOPLE VS. LARRY FLYNT

DIRECTOR: Miloš Forman | SCREENWRITER: Scott Alexander, Larry Karaszewski | CAST: Woody Harrelson, Courtney Love, Edward Norton | GENRE: Comedy | RUNNING TIME: 129 min | MPAA RATING: R

CLASSIFICATION: BEST

If Hugh Hefner was a classy figure of peddling pornography, Larry Flynt was the filthy entrepreneur that desired the dirty. He didn't care if his Hustler magazine was lacking in articles and text. Flynt knew his audience was only flocking to the publication of the pictures of nude women and a lacking raunchiness. He thrived on untapped offensiveness that launched him into being a millionaire with his smutty photos and dirty cartoons. His parodies were so outrageous that he would soon find himself in court being sued by Reverend Jerry Falwell.

And so we have a clashing of free speech versus bad taste. In one sense, we want to hate Larry and see him go down in flames. He's a lewd hillbilly and a shrewd businessman that dabbled in moonshine and loves to sleep with the women he photographs. And, yet, he makes a strong case for us to accept with his filthy mind and magazine; *"If they'll protect a scumbag like me, then they'll protect all of you. Because I'm the worst."* Larry is the type of guy you want to hate for finding the loopholes to his pleasures, but can't deny his intelligent reasoning. After all, if Falwell was successful in taking down Larry's publication for a slanderous parody, what's to stop him from taking down any other form of media that criticizes him or hurts his feeling? For that matter, what's to prevent anyone else from shutting down Falwell and his sermons?

Larry (Woody Harrelson) is portrayed as a smut peddler with an eye for what sells. He thumbs through the popular Playboy publication and has several gripes: the breasts don't look real, the pictures are too fuzzy and articles too sophisticated. He asks a room full of guys if they read Playboy and questions them on the articles. It boggles his mind that seven million people buy the magazine and nobody reads it, believing that Playboy is so out of touch with the common man that it mocks its readers. He thinks he has found an untapped market of the smut scene, favoring the more raw and real approach to showing nude photos that Playboy would shy away from printing. Once he was lucky enough to acquire and print nude photos of Jacqueline Onassis, all eyes were on Hustler, oglers, and opposers.

The film follows Larry's rise in popularity and his associates that are along for the ride. Althea Leasure (Courtney Love) is a bisexual stripper that quickly becomes the love of his life, even if she was underage when she submitted her first photos. Their marriage faces many troubling mountains that they somehow overcome. Larry becomes close with his lawyer, Alan Isaacman (Edward Norton), a man who Flynt believes will look upon him as the best client for being fun, rich and always in trouble. He eventually flocks to Ruth Carter Stapleton (Donna Hanover), who converts him to a born-again Christian.

Summoned to court multiple times for the vulgar content of Hustler, Larry quickly turns into the crazed and dazed freedom fighter of pornographers, wearing shirts that say "Fuck This Court" and an American flag diaper as he testifies. He's been touting the truth of free speech is absolute for so long that he now views the trials for his magazine to be a circus where he is the clown running the show.

While Harrelson gives one of the most exceptional performances of his career for a man that grows paralyzed while maintaining his vulgarity, the startling revelation of the film is Courtney Love. She arrived at her first meeting with the director as a mess, still high on drugs. Forman didn't want to hire her, but then realized would be perfect for the part, based more or less on her unintentional method acting. He would hire her so long as she stayed sober for filming. She agreed and attributed her sobriety to Forman, leading to a surprising upturn in her career.

The film's most memorable scene features Flynt up on a stage with a slideshow behind him, flipping between photos of the graphic nudity of his magazine and the graphic violence of war. He asks which is worse and we're reluctant to point our disgust towards war atrocities. He's making a scene with his argument, but he's not wrong. Morally, we'd much rather look at images of breasts and vaginas than gore and guts. The media and the MPAA would disagree, and that's just twisted enough for a man like Flynt to make his case and be an essential aspect of American freedom, despite his disgusting and crude nature.

PHILADELPHIA

DIRECTOR: Jonathan Demme | SCREENWRITER: Ron Nyswaner | CAST: Tom Hanks, Denzel Washington, Jason Robards, Mary Steenburgen, Antonio Banderas | GENRE: Drama | RUNNING TIME: 126 min | MPAA RATING: PG-13

CLASSIFICATION: BEST

Director Jonathan Demme begins *Philadelphia* (1993) with the warmest and inviting of movie openings. We see multiple shots of the city, from massive sky shots of the towers to the close-ups of local businesses to the distant shots of homeless and destitute on the streets, all set to the gentle tune of Bruce Springsteen's original song "Streets of Philadelphia." It establishes the personal tone for a timely story about AIDS and homosexuality, two controversial subjects that caused the more ignorant to view such conditions and orientations with discrimination.

Andrew Beckett (Tom Hanks) finds himself going from being a top lawyer at his firm to being fired for having AIDS. He had the disease long before they even knew, making regular hospital visits with his partner Miguel (Antonio Banderas), but the firm didn't know about this either. It's easy to understand his concealment, as when the company first notices a skin lesion on his forehead, quickly yank him off their most significant case and fire him. In the heat of AIDS paranoia, Andrew believes he was fired for his illness and needs to prove it in court.

He enlists the help of lawyer Joe Miller (Denzel Washington), a man known by everyone in Philadelphia as the guy from TV for his many commercials, always carrying a business card to chase any case. He's thrown the trial of his life when Andrew asks him to take on his case of discrimination. Miller is reluctant to represent Andrew as he despises homosexuals and is mocked by his peers for pursuing such a case. He figures it will be good exposure for his career, but he isn't prepared for the pressures of both homophobes and homosexuals that surround him. He is prone to emotional outbursts about sexuality, but tries to stick with the case as it's his job. When a colleague jokes if Miller is gay, he asserts his stance and assures him that he's only doing his job; *"Some of these people make me sick. But a law's been broken here. You do remember the law, don't you?"*

The film is mostly about the courtroom battle. Washington's character begins with opening statements about how this won't be the fantasy court case you see on TV and in movies, but there will be a few familiar scenes. Washington will be granted a moment to make a grand statement about homosexuality as the music swells. The attorney for the defense of the firm (Mary Steenburgen) will eventually lose her appetite for such dirty accusations of Andrew. It's still powerful and relevant stuff with some strong acting by Washington and Hanks, as well as the no-nonsense judge played by Charles Napier, but predictably strong as the finest of Oscar bait.

The good news is that the screenplay by Ron Nyswaner avoids a few of the more significant traps of making a movie such as this. A perfect example is featured in the scene where Andrew returns to his old home, greeting mom and dad with his lover Miguel. A lesser film would have played this up for the drama of insultingly fearful and ignorant parents, but mom and dad are not ashamed of their boy. It's the most touching scene in the film, past the inevitable trial results and Andrew's ultimate fate.

Philadelphia should feel as though it should be more contrived for such a standard plot on topical issues, but Jonathan Demme's direction evokes a bigger heart out of this material. He has the patience and steadiness to let us meditate and focus on the more profound moments of humanity as Hanks' character begins to wither away. Demme doesn't turn the camera away and knows how long to hold on the facts, the emotions and the controversy. He doesn't just want to showcase a trial on AIDS discrimination, but wants us to recognize its true impact past the immediate, the simplistic and the cliche.

PI

DIRECTOR: Darren Aronofsky | SCREENWRITER: Darren Aronofsky | CAST: Sean Gullette, Mark Margolis, Ben Shenkman, Samia Shoaib | GENRE: Drama | RUNNING TIME: 84 min | MPAA RATING: R

CLASSIFICATION: WEIRD

Recommending a movie like *Pi* (1998) is not easy, even with the allure of being the first film of director Darren Aronofsky. It is an independent film about numbers and a man who obsesses over them. Where others only see the numeric alphabet, one man sees more. He combs through every combination, pattern, correlation, and equation. What's he looking for? Nothing short of the meaning of all existence. It sounds boring, almost as though it's a documentary on numeracy, but Aronofsky's bold direction and inquisitive screenplay help make a movie about one man's obsession a stroke of both genius and madness.

The man attempting such an experiment is Maximillian Cohen (Sean Gullette), a mathematician, number theorist, computer programmer and social hermit. He has isolated himself from the world of numbers, shunning the outside world as he surrounds his apartment with computers. The few times he leaves his apartment features him speaking briefly with a few figures, including a kid in the complex that likes to test Max's ability to calculate any equation quickly.

He instructs his latest computer program to make stock predictions, but has encountered an error when it spits out a 216-digit number. He thinks nothing of the computer bug until he realizes that the stock price listed after the number had accurately predicted a crash. Maybe there is something special about these numbers. He learns from his old mathematician teacher Sol that this particular figure has been seen before. There must be something to these numbers. Later, in a coffee shop, he learns from a Hasidic Jew that some Jewish scholars believe the name of God has 216 letters. Now, this is getting creepy.

The film is intriguing not because Max's hypothesis is correct, but that he thinks it's accurate. He spends so much time drowning in his theories about numbers that he can't recognize his symptoms of a man losing his mind. There is so much torment in his mind that he begins to experience headaches and nosebleeds, as the stress of cracking numerical secrets increases his paranoia and restlessness. Others try to tell him to relax and take a break to clear his mind, but he can't be bothered with them. He believes he is on the path to a significant breakthrough and shuts down almost every aspect of his life to work towards this goal.

A film such as this could easily have run the risk of being a laughably inaccurate and preposterous thriller, but Aronofsky takes great care to make the struggle of Max seem real and not just a MacGuffin plot for him to go crazy. There is no MacGuffin, and it's Aronofsky's job to convince us that Max believes there is one. Max's approach to math and physics feels real and detailed enough that we almost agree his crazy theories. There are others who want what Max is searching for: a Wall Street firm wants the ability to predict stocks, and a synagogue wants to learn that elusive name of God finally. This makes Max even crazier. If he eventually uncovers the secret equation to all existence, what will he do with it?

For being shot on a small budget in grainy black-and-white, *Pi* is an intelligently involving thriller for its high concepts and simple settings. It touches on many interesting theories of the golden spiral and chaos theory, but presents them in a manner that is chilling for what happens when we dwell on them for too long. Most thrillers find the heroes risking their lives to solve some mystery; *Pi* finds its hero risking his sanity.

THE PLAYER

DIRECTOR: Robert Altman | SCREENWRITER: Michael Tolkin | CAST: Tim Robbins, Greta Scacchi, Fred Ward, Whoopi Goldberg, Peter Gallagher, Brion James, Cynthia Stevenson | GENRE: Comedy | RUNNING TIME: 124 min | MPAA RATING: R

CLASSIFICATION: BEST

The Player (1992) is the type of movie that is hard to imagine being greenlit for such a savage satire of the movie business. It was based on a novel by Michael Tolkin, conceived from his bitter frustrations of working as a screenwriter in Hollywood. Robert Altman was the perfect director for such an adaptation, given how much trouble he'd had with Hollywood and his previous films not being very successful. It's somewhat poetic that this scathing attack on the Hollywood machine was what led to Altman's return to Hollywood-produced movies once more.

Tim Robbins plays studio executive Griffin Mills, a man who is patient enough to sit through a pitch for *The Graduate 2*, but smart enough to realize it's a horrible idea. His life moves fast and slick with listening to many screenwriter pitches, turning away dozens, dealing with his dopey new story executive Larry (Peter Gallagher), attending Hollywood parties of various celebrities and reading over scripts while in a hot tub with his editor/girlfriend Bonnie (Cynthia Stevenson). His life may appear sweet, but he's quickly set on edge when he starts receiving death threats in the form of postcards and faxes from a screenwriter. Having turned down several screenwriters over the course of his career, it could be anybody who wants him dead.

Doing some detective work, Mills believes he has found the vindictive screenwriter and attempts to negotiate a movie deal to end the harassment. Mills has not only picked the wrong culprit and agitated him over the edge with his stalking, but also ends up murdering the writer in an alley. Now Mills is not only still being harassed by some unknown screenwriter, assaulting him with more letters and placing a rattlesnake in his car, but he becomes a prime suspect in the murder case. Oh, and he's also dating the dead screenwriter's wife, thus raising more suspicions of his actions.

Keeping in step with Altman's traditions, several scenes were improvised with new dialogue being written on the set and many of those scenes with overlapping dialogue. Take for instance the scene when Robbins is questioned by Detective Avery (Whoopi Goldberg) in a police station. In between their conversation, the detective will ask a nearby co-worker about the last movie they saw and then another if they have seen her brand of tampons around the office. This direction ensures there is always something interesting happening in the frame, even when it's a scene meant to keep the murder plot moving as fast as Mills' busy schedule.

What's most admirable about the satire in *The Player* is how well Altman sells the cynical world he portrays. About sixty-five celebrities appear as themselves in this picture, many of them A-listers. When an Oscar-bait film within the movie is tapped for Julia Roberts and Bruce Willis to play the leads, Roberts and Willis appear on the screen in roles indicative of their careers with an earnest portrayal. There are even some brilliant commentary moments as in the opening scene of an unbreaking shot around the studio following different conversations, one of them about the unbroken opening shot from Orson Welles' *Touch of Evil*.

Altman has suggested that his treatment of *The Player* was a very mild satire. It's a bit of a humble statement considering how well his direction picks several targets and sends them up with an unrelenting parody that is humorous, twisted and meta. It does make one wonder, however, that if this is what he considers mild satire of Hollywood, what would the movie have been at its most vicious? We may never see that movie with such talent, but *The Player* is still a bit of a miracle that it went as far as it did with such ribbing of the city where movies are made, stars are born, and screenwriters are a dime a thousand.

PLEASANTVILLE

DIRECTOR: Gary Ross | SCREENWRITER: Gary Ross | CAST: Tobey Maguire, Jeff Daniels, Joan Allen, William H. Macy, J. T. Walsh, Don Knotts, Reese Witherspoon | GENRE: Comedy | RUNNING TIME: 124 min | MPAA RATING: PG-13

CLASSIFICATION: BEST

Pleasantville (1998) starts with the amusing concept of 1990s teenagers being trapped in a 1950s sitcom and ends with an insightful and uplifting commentary on how society shifts. The film directly attacks the notion that the 1950s were an ideal time when compared to the more dour outlook of the future, breaking away from the nostalgia we harbor for yesterday. And it does so with some of the most remarkable and beautiful of special effects that blend black-and-white film with vivid color.

For the high school student David (Tobey Maguire), he finds great joy in escaping to the reruns for Pleasantville, a classic sitcom in the style of *Leave It To Beaver* and *Father Knows Best*. His encyclopedic knowledge and obsession with the program don't seem as strange when everything in the present appears awful. His sister Jennifer (Reese Witherspoon) is rude, his mother fights with her ex-husband and his teachers stress how a multitude of developments have inherently doomed his future. Retreating into television doesn't sound so bad when everything in Pleasantville seems so simple and happy.

David's obsession attracts the attention of a TV repairman, uniquely played by Don Knotts of *The Andy Griffith Show*, who bestows on him a magical remote that traps David and Jennifer inside the world of Pleasantville. For David, it's a dream come true to occupy a town where he knows everyone in the neighborhood and everything that will happen. For Jennifer, it's a nightmare world where bras are too pointy, and boys consider holding hands to be second base.

Placed in the roles of a brother and sister to the prim family of Betty (Joan Allen) and George (William H. Macy), they discover this world is a little too simple and planned. Geography classes never venture past Main Street; the basketball team never misses a shot and the diner manned by the kindly timid Mr. Johnson (Jeff Daniels) has a routine for serving up little more than cheeseburgers. The slightest tweak to this world causes it to shake, as when David is late for his job of opening the diner, leaving Mr. Johnson a little terrified about who would set up the tables while he cleans the counter.

A Pandora's box is opened when David and Jennifer start changing this world, both intentionally and unintentionally. Some changes are as simple as David suggesting that Mr. Johnson could change up his routine, while others are as major as Jennifer coaxing a meek high school student into sex. These disturbances to the natural order cause people to appear in color. Why does this happen? The initial theory is that people turn this color when they have sex, but this is quickly dismissed when Jennifer sleeps with one of the residents has yet to become.

The color is change itself, and it's spreading like a virus. Betty, after pleasuring herself in the tub, refuses to make George dinner, sending shockwaves through his bowling buddies. Mr. Johnson becomes inspired by a book of fine art and starts painting masterpieces on the windows of his diner. The chairman of the Chamber of Commerce (J.T. Walsh in his final performance) approaches this colorful revolution with fear, leading to book burnings and violence against colored individuals. Sound familiar?

Sure, the parable of *Pleasantville* becomes very blunt with its uplifting themes of embracing change, but it's a message worth shouting from the rooftops. For as grim as the future may seem for all its uncertainty, don't forget there was a time when art, books, and sex were a taboo. This film suggests that the 1950s appeared so comfy because there was no challenge past which cheeseburger to order or which girl to ask to the prom. For that reason, *Pleasantville* is as essential in its biting social commentary as it is hilarious with its savage satire towards sitcom convention.

POINT BREAK

DIRECTOR: Kathryn Bigelow | SCREENWRITER: W. Peter Iliff | CAST: Patrick Swayze, Keanu Reeves, Gary Busey, Lori Petty | GENRE: Action | RUNNING TIME: 122 min | MPAA RATING: R

CLASSIFICATION: WEIRD

Point Break (1991) is the finest of action movie cheese. It features a preposterous script, overblown action and is oozing with machismo, with a dash of homoerotic tension added in for good measure. Oh, and it was directed by Kathryn Bigelow, the Academy Award-winning director of *The Hurt Locker* (2009). Who says women can't lead testosterone-pumping action films?

Keanu Reeves plays rookie FBI agent Johnny Utah, insultingly referred to by his hard-ass boss as *"young, dumb and full of come."* He is tasked with infiltrating a gang of bank robbers known as the Ex-Presidents, pilfering only the registers of banks in their rubber masks of US Presidents. Johnny's partner of FBI Agent Angelo Pappas (Gary Busey) identifies that one of the robbers has a tan and that a DNA sample leads to the beach. They're surfers! Johnny grabs a board and carefully makes his way into the group by meeting the leader Bodhi (Patrick Swayze), a surfer so charming that he may just convince Johnny to switch sides. And after much surfing, Johnny starts to fall for both Bodhi's philosophies on life and his ex-girlfriend (Lori Petty). But when it comes to the robberies when lives are on the line, Johnny is conflicted. Banks are robbed, people die on both sides, and it all ends with a transcendent suicide by surfing.

This is a film that walks a weird line between being a crime thriller, a philosophical meditation and an action picture of surfing and skydiving. It is unbelievably silly, but somehow works as effectively as Bodhi's ability to charm Johnny with talk of surfing legendary waves and crushing capitalism. The movie takes itself seriously, so we don't have to. There isn't any questioning in the script why Johnny would go skydiving with Bodhi when he realizes his cover has been blown. Johnny shouldn't have done such a dangerous stunt after such a revelation, but then we wouldn't get the fantastic stunt of fighting in free-fall with guns for a parachute.

The cast runs the table of overacting and underacting. In the underacting category, Keanu Reeves, fresh off his *Bill & Ted* fame, feels so wooden as if he's afraid his righteous dude personality will slip out. He is so devoid of emotion that by the time he displays some in a moment when he fires wildly into the sky to refuse shooting Bodhi, it's hilariously off, despite being a fitting enough personality for an action star. On the other end of the spectrum, Gary Busey brings his usual insanity (*"I was in this bureau when you were still popping zits on your funny face and jerking off with the lingerie section of the Sears catalog"*) and McGinley brings a snarky crudeness (*"Guess we must just have ourselves an asshole shortage, huh?"*). Patrick Swayze hits the sweet spot for a story such as this, embodying an intoxicating level of wisdom and stupidity. He's a villain with a brain or at least as big a mind as a movie of surfing bank robbers will allow.

 Bigelow's direction helps elevate a ridiculous script into an action picture worthy of campy cult status. She directs some fantastic action sequences that always feel thrilling and inventive, from chases through Santa Monica to skydiving fights through the air. Every scene looks remarkably well shot, and the music by Mark Isham keeps the film focused on its moody atmosphere. And for as contrasting as the actors are with their various ranges of quality, they work well together with their conflicting emotions and loyalties. All of this makes *Point Break* more than just an odd film about surfing bank robbers; it is THE film about surfing bank robbers.

POKEMON: THE FIRST MOVIE

DIRECTOR: Kunihiko Yuyama | SCREENWRITER: Takeshi Shudō | CAST: Veronica Taylor, Ikue Ōtani, Rachael Lillis, Eric Stuart, Ken Gates, Philip Bartlett | GENRE: Adventure (Animated) | RUNNING TIME: 75 min | MPAA RATING: G

CLASSIFICATION: WORST

It was nearly impossible to avoid the *Pokemon* craze of the late-1990s. As much as my classmates and I loved to talk smack about the franchise amongst each other in the school hallways, we all played the video games, watched the TV show and attended *Pokemon: The First Movie* (1999) on opening night. Looking back, I still have no shame in being sucked into the commercialism of the video games and the show. The movie, on the other hand, had me question my loyalty to the *Pokemon* mantra of catching them all.

Based on the TV series, the movie picks up with the familiar characters, assuming that the small audience is up to date on the show and the Pokemon. The crowd I saw it with were very astute. They knew all about Ash Ketchum, a young trainer venturing across the world to become a master trainer of Pokemon. They recognized his traveling companions of Misty and Brock, as well as his rivals of Team Rocket, a trio of bumbling criminals bent on capturing Ash's beloved Pikachu. The kids were also aware of all 150 Pokemon, made easy to remember with a rap song that played on the television series. Those children got the most out of the movie. The unwitting parents dragged into the theater were up a creek without a water-type Pokemon.

Mewtwo is the first Pokemon to be created by man as a clone of a legendary Pokemon known as Mew. Angered by his origins, he takes out his revenge on humanity by capturing Pokemon and breeding his super clones to reform the world he despises. He lures unknowing Pokemon trainers to his secret island and springs the trap on them. It's up to the plucky trainers to free the Pokemon and show Mewtwo the error of his ways.

Tension mounts over whether or not we'll ever be able to see that cute Pikachu coo again. And I guess the fate of humanity hangs in the balance or something. There could be something to be said about the loss of individuality with Mewtwo applying his anger over being a clone to the order of the world. But don't dig too deep into that area, as the screenwriters apparently didn't bother to explore it much either. The majority of the picture is fighting. Lots and lots of fighting with more effort invested into the animation and soundtrack than emotional stakes in any of this violence.

The movie does have a moral message wedged into its script, but it's about as forced as a Public Service Announcement. When the cloned Pokemon battle the original Pokemon, it's implied to be a sorrowful battle the way Nurse Joy observes the carnage and declares that Pokemon should not have to fight like this. How are Pokemon supposed to fight? I never saw much of a difference between this battle and the other official Pokemon matches. I guess it takes an encounter with clones to realize the futility in capturing creatures and forcing them to fight for your honor (or gym badges).

It's been said that the original intent of the first *Pokemon* movie was to act as a finale to the series and it's easy to see how this could have been brought about. The ultimate conclusion that the characters reach the climax is the realization that fighting is wrong. If this were indeed the end of the *Pokemon* series, Ash and the other Pokemon trainers would reform their ways. They'd release their Pokemon from their Pokeballs and not raise them for combat. Such an ending is not in the cards for this runaway franchise as the movie ends with Mewtwo returning everybody to land and wiping their memories of all the events.

In the end, nobody learns anything and Pokemon will fight once more in another movie just as dour and contrasting to the usually chipper TV series. It's an unfortunate example of a picture that wants to feature a powerful message and then immediately toss it out the window so the status quo is maintained and more *Pokemon* merchandise can be sold. I may have been under the spell of wanting to catch all the Pokemon in my youth, but *The First Movie* didn't leave me ecstatic to see the second, third, fourth or fifth movie that would also grace American cinemas.

PORCO ROSSO

DIRECTOR: Hayao Miyazaki | SCREENWRITER: Hayao Miyazaki | CAST: Michael Keaton, Cary Elwes, Susan Egan, Brad Garrett | GENRE: Adventure (Animated) | RUNNING TIME: 94 min | MPAA RATING: PG

CLASSIFICATION: BEST

Hayao Miyazaki's animated movies tend to exist in a space that is relatively out of time and with magical elements, but *Porco Rosso* (1992) is more grounded in time and place. It is set after World War 1, around the east coast of the Adriatic Sea where airborne pirates run rampant. There are no wizards, mythical creatures or grand fantasy elements present. The only exception is that the titular hero happens to be mysteriously cursed with a pig face.

Where did the curse come from and who gave it to him? Porco doesn't know and never dwells too long on such an unfortunate aspect of his appearance. He's far too busy taking on rescue missions to make some cash for his fighter plane. That is when he's not lounging in the sun with the paper on his face, the radio playing and his cigarette burning. After a long day of sleeping and besting air pirates in combat, he takes a breather at the local club/tavern where all pilots call a truce and enjoy the singing of Madame Gina. Porco loves her and is willing to fight a cocky American pilot who wants to steal her away.

Porco's plane is damaged at one point, and he needs a mechanic. He reluctantly accepts the help of the Flo, a feisty young female mechanic. She makes for a tremendous spunky companion that accompanies Porco on his flights and proves to be a great addition to his loner lifestyle. Miyazaki is a master of creating likable and capable women and Flo being no exception. She not only knows her way around every inch of a plane, but can successfully talk down a gang of pirates ready to turn Porco into bacon. Flo is smart enough to know that these men are so bent on their honor to settle their differences in the air that she can distract any pilot from committing a crime on land.

The animation, per usual for Studio Ghibli, is gorgeous. The sight of planes swooping through the air in the colorful sky, firing machine guns at one another, is exciting and beautiful. Miyazaki loves airplanes so much that he adds in an extraordinary amount of detail to them. Take a look at a brief shot in Porco's plane where he converses with Flo in the other seat. You can see the faintest reflection of Flo's face in a piece of glass that is moving as naturally as she is.

Most of the movie is pure fun, except one emotional flashback of Porco's pre-pig past. I was dreading this moment that would slow down the picture and demystify the appeal of Porco, but it's a surprisingly moving moment. Before his curse, Porco becomes lost in the clouds and loses a fellow pilot in a skirmish. He watches as his comrade's plane ascends higher into the blue, entering a cloud stream. On closer examination, he's entering into a massive fleet of all the pilots that were shot down in the line of duty. This vision, accompanied by Joe Hisaishi's echoing and gentle choir, is one of the most hauntingly beautiful moments in an otherwise action-packed tale.

As one of Miyazaki's early productions of Studio Ghibli, a lot of elements are carried over from *Porco* into his other films. Miyazaki's love of aircrafts can be seen in every little detail he adds to the planes, later capitalizing on his infatuation with the animated biopic *The Wind Rises* (2013). He would draw transforming pigs once more in *Spirited Away* (2001), where adults morph into gluttonous beasts. And he would continue to make his stories more dramatic and grown up as with *Princess Mononoke* (1997), his first animated fantasy that didn't skimp on war and violence.

Porco Rosso showcases that while Miyazaki still had a light sense of fun and adventure, he was growing with making his animated features more mature. His film features adult characters dealing with more adult themes of romance and honor. This could make it one of his lesser films for not being as kid-friendly, but the striking maturity still comes bundled with the same amount of charm and energy as that of *My Neighbor Totoro* or *Kiki's Delivery Service*. How could you not have fun with a pig piloting a plane?

THE PRINCE OF EGYPT

DIRECTOR: Brenda Chapman, Steve Hickner, Simon Wells | SCREENWRITER: Philip LaZebnik | CAST: Val Kilmer, Ralph Fiennes, Michelle Pfeiffer, Sandra Bullock, Jeff Goldblum, Danny Glover, Patrick Stewart, Helen Mirren, Steve Martin, Martin Short | GENRE: Adventure (Animated) | RUNNING TIME: 98 min | MPAA RATING: PG

CLASSIFICATION: BEST

Not to be outdone by Disney's musical grip on the 1990s, DreamWorks decided to pursue an animated musical that was a little more daring and biblical. When Jeffrey Katzenberg was a chairman at Disney, he pitched the idea of an animated version of The Ten Commandments, but was turned down by Michael Eisner. But when he would later pitch the idea to Steven Spielberg during the formation of DreamWorks, The Ten Commandments seemed to be the perfect idea for the studio to pursue. Founder David Geffen was also on board, but warned Katzenberg that this is not to be a fairytale and that they must be aggressive in this world. These stipulations were strictly adhered to, making *The Prince of Egypt* (1998) one of the most dramatic and epic animated pictures of the decade.

The story of Exodus begins with great music to set the tone for Ancient Egypt. It's a dark and epic song of newborn Hebrews being slaughtered as Yocheved quietly brings her baby to the river. She places him in a basket and lets the waves carry him off, but not before giving him one last tender lullaby to bid farewell. From this opening, we know this will not be the typical Disney musical production. It will be one of considerable danger on an epic scale, but also an emotional somberness and complexity. This story will not be handled with easy comedy and toe-tapping melodies, but with a dignity and power that echoed the expensive Biblical films of old Hollywood.

The film follows the Hebrew baby that grows up to become Moses (Val Kilmer), charting his discovery in the Nile to his founding of The Ten Commandments. In between, we see more aspects of his rise to leadership. We see the bond grow over chariot races between him and his brother Rameses (Ralph Fiennes), the son of the Pharaoh (Patrick Stewart) that takes in Moses. Rameses is made regent and Moses, his chief architect, but Moses discovers that he doesn't belong with the Egyptians. He accepts god and urges his brother to let his people go, his refusal leading to God's wrath. And so the story proceeds with high drama and music, leading up to the fantastically iconic parting of the Red Sea, looking far more amazing than it ever did in live-action depictions.

DreamWorks spared no expense for the animation on such a project. They combined traditional hand-drawn animation and computer-generated imagery to create a sense of great depth and stylish designs true to the era. Notice how angular the Egyptians appear in contrast with the roundedness of the Hebrews, yet both move and behave as very natural human characters, never exploding with expression and exaggeration. While you're looking at them, be sure to keep an eye on the backgrounds which showcase how vast and grand the land of Egypt appeared. One of my favorite shots to examine is when Pharaoh speaks privately with Moses; look at how much is included behind them from the massive monument to a full city to the sparkling waters to the pyramids far off in the distance. The scenes are so spectacular for a film that cost $70 million to make, whereas a live-action film would most likely cost twice or three times as much for the same scale.

Striving to distance themselves from the typical Disney formula, the studio took every precaution to make sure they weren't tarnishing religion for some of the attractive golden box office returns of animated movies at the time. The filmmakers mapped the story out ahead of time before production, and religious leaders were consulted to ensure the film would not be a mockery of theology. The devotion to the material and desire to make a lavish animated musical turned out to be one of the most magnificent and relevant early works of the DreamWorks studio. It carries a respect and sternness for such a legendary and spiritual tale, but also makes it entertaining with impressive animation and winning musical numbers that enhance the story rather than distract from it. Even the additions of Martin Short and Steve Martin do not overstep the boundaries of decency as high priests that provide a pinch of comic relief. Directors Brenda Chapman, Steve Hickner, and Simon Wells were not only successful in making an appropriate animated religious film, but a genuinely entertaining one as well.

PRINCESS MONONOKE

DIRECTOR: Hayao Miyazaki | SCREENWRITER: Hayao Miyazaki | CAST: Billy Crudup, Claire Danes, Minnie Driver, Billy Bob Thornton, Gillian Anderson | GENRE: Adventure (Animated) | RUNNING TIME: 134 min | MPAA RATING: PG-13

CLASSIFICATION: BEST

Hayao Miyazaki's Studio Ghibli was best known for their child-friendly and adventurous animated films, but he shook the cage of his studio's conventions with *Princess Mononoke* (1997). Unlike his other pictures, which were usually gentle and charming, *Mononoke* was violent, somber and dense with its themes of nature, environmentalism and the ethereal. The family audience that I saw the film with opening weekend probably wasn't expecting to see decapitation and amputation so sudden and shocking it evoked snickering and wincing.

The story takes place in ancient Japan where man is currently at war with the gods of the forest. The gods exist within oversized animals; boars are so giant they could bulldoze through walls of stone and wolves so enormous they could take your arm off with one bite. When the gods become angered and injured, they are infected by a demon spirit that spreads through their body in the form of inky worms. If the worms touch human flesh, they will curse their victim with a spreading infection. This tragic fate befalls Prince Ashitaka, a young warrior that is ejected from his village for being marked with the curse of the gods.

As he searches the forests for a cure, he runs across great violence and deception. He attracts Jigo, an agent for the emperor that is a schemer, but of what is not made clear right away. Ashitaka trusts him for the night as he seems to know about his people, the forest and which thieves would try to kill him in his sleep. Ashitaka continues on his own and stumbles upon a war between the iron-harvesting village led by Lady Eboshi and the forest gods led by their only human ally of Princess Mononoke. He meets with both of them, hears their plights and desperately seeks a means of peace before all sides are obliterated in the brutal battle of man versus nature.

For featuring so many intense scenes of war, *Princess Mononoke* still has the remarkable Ghibli tenderness in its quieter scenes. Ashitaka meets the spirit of the forest, an elk-like being, moving slowly with grace, that he watches from a distant in meditative silence. Also present in the woods is the cute little Kodamas, tiny sprites with abstract faces that tilt and rattle like bobblehead dolls. Lady Eboshi leads Ashitaka to her secret garden, revealing the lepers she has taken in with charitable kindness. These slower moments display that there's more complexity to this war than Ashitaka once thought, making him all the more conflicted and frustrated in trying to find a solution.

Joe Hisaishi composed the score, as he had done for nearly every Ghibli production, but this is by far his best work for the studio. It is one of the few soundtracks I have ever rushed out to buy after seeing the movie and still find it to be some of the most beautiful orchestral music ever composed for a film. I always get chills listening to the deep drums, foreboding chimes and beautiful violins that paint the pictures many tones of a grand fantasy and epic adventure.

For the English distributor of Disney, *Mononoke* came as a bit of a shocking divergence from the usual Ghibli productions. When Disney decided to buy the rights to all of Miyazaki's films, I doubt they expected him to deliver something as epic and violent as this film, as much as the audience that was caught off guard. Miramax's chairman Harvey Weinstein seriously considered editing the picture for a larger release, but Ghibli was adamant about keeping the film uncut when they sent Harvey a katana with the message "No cuts." The communication was received, and *Princess Mononoke* was released with a PG-13 rating from the MPAA.

The film was intended to be Miyazaki's last film, and it would've been a great film to cap his legacy. He helped with much of the traditional animation, drawing more frames than most productions would expect of a director. It became one of Japan's highest grossing films and would win the Japanese Academy Award for Best Picture. Among all the Studio Ghibli films, I consider it his most impressive achievement for a masterpiece so magical, beautiful and human.

PRIVATE PARTS

DIRECTOR: Betty Thomas | SCREENWRITER: Len Blum, Michael Kalesniko | CAST: Howard Stern, Robin Quivers, Mary McCormack, Paul Giamatti | GENRE: Comedy | RUNNING TIME: 109 min | MPAA RATING: R

CLASSIFICATION: WEIRD

There's nobody better than Howard Stern to lead his biopic of *Private Parts* (1997). Stern's genuine appeal as a successful radio personality is his honesty, and this film features him bearing more of his soul than most people know. He is aware others look down on him as a filthy shock jock, especially when he makes a stage appearance in his goofy and juvenile Fartman costume. But as the film's title implies, there's much more to him beyond the provocative language and bodily functions.

Stern begins his story at the very beginning when he was inspired early on by his father running a radio station. He grows up, graduates from Boston University and takes on the job of a DJ at various radio stations. He slowly moves up the chain to be a program director, but always feels awkward and unsure of himself on the air. But when working in Connecticut, something unusual happens; Stern lets his guard down and explodes onto the radio with talk and humor that knows no boundaries. The social awkwardness begins to vanish as he finds himself quitting more jobs than being fired from them. By the time he goes on air at a radio station in Washington D.C., he discovers he's not alone with his unique voice as he encourages Robin Quivers (played by herself) to riff along with him rather than just read the news. More fantastic stuff happens as chemistry is born for a new format of radio.

Despite the wishes of the station, Stern begins to experiment with outrageous stunts nobody has ever tried on the radio, testing the waters of both the interest in his listeners and the anger in his employers. One of his most notable bits involves giving a female listener an orgasm over the phone by having her straddle a subwoofer while he makes deep base sounds into his microphone. Such a stunt would get him fired, but the increase in ratings prevent him from being sacked. People are interested in Stern, and he knows it as he exercises his power to assemble his comedic troupe to include Fred Norris, a DJ he met at a previous job.

Sparks begin to fly with radio management when Stern's

popularity leads him to a gig at WNBC in New York. The station has no idea what they've bought, quickly realizing that Stern's vulgar approach needs to change. A program director that Stern dubs Pig Vomit (Paul Giamatti) believes the shocking radio personality can be tamed if he takes him under his wing. He comes on slow by intricately walking Howard through the process of saying the station name with the southern drawl of *"W Annnn B C."* Stern comes on fast by using this exercise as a framework for an on-air bit where he pretends to gargle Pig Vomit's sperm to get the pronunciation just right. Their battle over on-air content continues over several bits where Stern will bring in a female guest to get naked in the studio and then get around the censors to say cock and pussy for a gameshow.

Howard is brutally honest in the portrayal of himself, almost to a disturbing degree. He doesn't hide any of the awkwardness with his wife (Mary McCormack) when they have a miscarriage, and he jokes about it on the air. She is furious with him, and it won't be the last time as Stern's raunchy honesty continues. It's astonishing how she didn't divorce him during any of his acts on the radio, especially after he gets a massage from a naked guest and jokes that his wife died. He will later let Robin take the fall after a bit goes too far and is seen as a real jerk for not leaving with her when she was fired.

Director Betty Thomas does a fantastic job of turning Stern's provocative legacy into a real human story and not just a reel of his radio show's most significant bits. She directs Stern to be seen as a more flawed man with more than a few warts and roadblocks on his path to becoming the self-proclaimed King of All Media. Few actors would be willing to showcase themselves in such a creepy and immature light, but this is the appeal of both Stern and his radio show. He lets everything hang out in the open for everyone to see. Every mistake, every bad joke, every tasteless ribbing and every vulgar statement comes flowing out onto the screen. Most people would keep a tight lid on the shortcomings of their life, but Stern flips off the cover, dumps the contents into the street and invites onlookers to have a look.

PROBLEM CHILD

DIRECTOR: Dennis Dugan | SCREENWRITER: Scott Alexander, Larry Karaszewski | CAST: John Ritter, Michael Richards, Gilbert Gottfried, Jack Warden | GENRE: Comedy | RUNNING TIME: 81 min | MPAA RATING: PG

CLASSIFICATION: WORST

Problem Child (1990) went through a bizarre evolution of a been-there-done-that horror movie to a don't-want-to-be-here kid comedy. It was initially conceived to be a dark picture akin to The Omen for being based on a true story about parents who sued an adoption agency for not informing them about the adoptive child's mental issues that resulted in returns. Writers Scott Alexander and Larry Karaszewski wanted to turn the story into a more sophisticated comedy of adult leanings, similar to *Kindergarten Cop*. The studio, however, wanted to warp their script into a film more for the children than the adults. The result was a film so bad that Alexander broke down in tears at one of the screenings where 70% of the test audience walked out.

The redheaded 7-year-old Junior (Michael Oliver) is made out to be the most sinister of trouble-makers. He's been kicked out of multiple foster homes and orphanages, still laughing and smiling about his reign of hijinks. Adoption agent Igor (Gilbert Gottfried) does his best to sell Junior's innocence, only for the smart-mouthed kid to cackle, curse, and torment any adult in range of his abusive and destructive nature. The next unlucky foster parent dumb enough to fall for his cuteness is doomed.

Don't feel too bad for the adopting yuppie Ben (John Ritter), however, as he's a dolt of a first parent that knows nothing of discipline. He wants to be the sensitive and understanding parent, much to the chagrin of his conservative father/boss Big Ben (Jack Warden). When he first meets Junior in his new room that he has set on fire, Big Ben is quick to call him the devil. Ritter thinks he's overreacting, but a follow-up scene with Junior launching the cat at Big Ben and sending him tumbling down the stairs suggests otherwise.

The entire film is a showcase for how nasty Junior can be, and he tests the limits of a PG rating. He goes on a camping trip and urinates on the fire. He attends the birthday party of the neighbor's daughter Lucy and destroys the magic show, bringing a more sour tone to the use of the song "It's My Party." He plays on the Little League team and decides to cheat by bashing all the bullies in the groin with his baseball bat. Ben is such a pushover for punishment that when he discovers Junior had been returned thirty times, he takes pity on him and decides to stick with his adoption. That's noble, but maybe Junior should be given a psychiatric evaluation. You know, before a scene where Ben considers smothering Junior to death.

And it gets worse. It turns out Junior has been corresponding with serial killer Martin Beck (Michael Richards). Martin escapes from prison and meets up with Junior, under the impression that the person he had been writing to was an adult. How hilarious, especially when Martin decides to kidnap Junior and his step-mom for ransom.

With his nagging wife and destructive step-son gone, this should be a blessing for Ben, and even he seems to think so. It isn't until he looks at Junior's drawings of dad that he starts to think that maybe his son isn't a monster. No, he is a monster. Most kids don't crash cars into sporting goods stores or have serial killer pen pals. And most parents are not so forgiving or unstable as Ben, shifting between having the patience of a saint and the rage of a demon. One moment he's trying to be gentle with Junior, the next he's a frantic mess of a man who wants to get the kid out of his hair before he does something violent. He doesn't deserve to be a parent, and Junior doesn't deserve to be adopted for how he loves that negative attention.

The film was a severe rash that never went away. It was a big enough box office success to warrant a sequel of *Problem Child 2* (1991) and an animated TV series. I'm not sure who wanted to see more of Junior's destructive and mean nature, but apparently, somebody did. Junior was such an unlikable snot that critics couldn't stand with his bad behavior and sinister smile. Even the poster features Junior smiling at his accomplishment of shoving a cat into a working dryer, a marketing stunt that brought protest down on the film from animal protest groups. And while nothing like that occurs in the movie, Junior does splinter a cat's legs which probably pissed off the protesters even more. So I at least know one group who didn't like the movie.

PSYCHO

DIRECTOR: Gus Van Sant | SCREENWRITER: Joseph Stefano | CAST: Vince Vaughn, Julianne Moore, Viggo Mortensen, William H. Macy, Anne Heche | GENRE: Horror | RUNNING TIME: 104 min | MPAA RATING: R

CLASSIFICATION: WORST

Gus Van Sant's *Psycho* (1998) is a film experiment gone wrong. It is a shot-for-shot remake of Alfred Hitchcock's classic horror picture, minus the black-and-white. The script is almost entirely the same, with all the familiar characters, dialogue and plot developments. It is the most faithful remake in the regard of simplistic replication. But perhaps the experiment is how remaining highly faithful to the source material does not make a great movie. It's certainly the result.

What is there to say about the plot? It replicates the 1960 film with questionable changes. For example, when we first see Marion Crane (Anne Heche) presented the money she plans to run off with, Heche tries to put some extra acting into her role with subtle facial twitches to showcase the thoughts about fleeing with the cash more apparent. And, yet, in the scene where she catches a glance of her employers in traffic, there's less desperation on her face. It's almost as if Van Sant is trying to create polar opposite scenes in the expressions of his characters. Of course, this is more glaring in the scene when Marion is awakened by a highway patrolman that has a voice that sounds deeper as if to enhance how scary it is that a sunglasses-wearing cop is staring her down. It's not massively overblown, but feels, like every other addition to Hitchcock's original, unneeded.

The voyeur scene, where Norman Bates (Vince Vaughn) spies on Marion from behind a wall and masturbates, was creepy in the original film, but more for the suggestion. The more obvious implication by Van Sant features Norman's head jiggling, his face reaching orgasm and the splashy sound of him finishing his ejaculation. What was once disturbing and creepy is now silly and off-putting, inspiring both a laugh for the sound effect and a groan for its inclusion.

And, of course, there's the famous scene in the shower, this time with more blood and visibly red. Though darkness still obscures the killer's face with the hair, it's much more compelling in black and white with the face entirely covered in black shadow. The insistence of showing the redness of the blood adds nothing. It is one of the most iconic scenes in horror movie history and, while Van Sant doesn't tarnish it, he doesn't add anything of value that wasn't already present.

Casting the visual comparisons aside, the actors do not work here. Anne Heche feels as though she's struggling to nail all the conflicting emotions of Marion, her acting appearing as though she's walking on eggshells not to miss a beat. Vince Vaughn's Norman is not weird enough because Vaughn himself doesn't look at all odd. All you need to do is compare the ending smile of Anthony Perkins to that of Vaughn's; Perkins appears strangely odd and unpredictable, while Vaughn looks as though he's trying too hard to look like a serial killer.

I could go on with the comparisons, but the bottom line is that the film is a pointless idea of a remake. It is a film that will only be of use to film scholars to compare and contrast. The film may have some merit on the level of being a don't-do-this example, but a failed experiment is still a failure of a movie. While rewatching the film after many years, the simple thoughts again echoed in my head: I could be watching Hitchcock's *Psycho* right now.

PULP FICTION

DIRECTOR: Quentin Tarantino | SCREENWRITER: Quentin Tarantino | CAST: John Travolta, Samuel L. Jackson, Uma Thurman, Harvey Keitel, Tim Roth, Amanda Plummer, Maria de Medeiros, Ving Rhames, Eric Stoltz, Rosanna Arquette, Christopher Walken, Bruce Willis | GENRE: Drama | RUNNING TIME: 154 min | MPAA RATING: R

CLASSIFICATION: BEST

John Travolta and Samuel L. Jackson are driving to retrieve a stolen briefcase from some punks that have ripped off their boss, but they're not talking about the suitcase on the drive over. They're talking about hash bars, McDonald's burgers in France and foot massages. They continue this conversation after they exit the car and walk up to the apartment door, only breaking from their conversation when Jackson states, *"Let's get into character."* But even when they burst into the apartment and corner the thieves, Jackson still finds himself thinking about hamburgers as he asks for a bite of their breakfast.

That's the power of Quentin Tarantino's writing in *Pulp Fiction* (1994), where side dialogue is anything but boring or pointless. He creates real characters that have more going on in their lives than discussing who to rob, who to help or who to kill. We never see exactly what is inside the briefcase nor is it ever adequately explained why it was stolen, though there are plenty of theories. That's not the point of Tarantino's film which tries to find the interesting dialogue in scenes of gun violence, dancing, drug overdose and gimp suits.

This is why the non-linear and distracted nature of the script works so well. We remember the film better through its unforgettable scenes and characters than the overall story. When Jules (Travolta) takes out his boss' wife Mia Wallace (Uma Thurman) for a good time at a 1950s diner, they're not talking about Mr. Wallace; they're talking about $5 milkshakes before hitting the dance floor. When prizefighter Butch (Bruce Willis) returns to his motel room after killing a man in the ring, he's not talking to his girlfriend Fabienne (Maria de Medeiros) about the fight; they speak of pot bellies while they cuddle. Tarantino doesn't waste our time by restating things characters already knows and chooses instead to reveal about these people by how they speak and what they speak about.

This is a film that doesn't stop. There's a scene where Mia overdoses, and there's a frantic race for Vincent to save her life, but without dramatic music or sharp editing. He rushes her over to his drug dealer Lance (Eric Stoltz), and they stab her in the heart with a needle of adrenaline. She returns to life, the needle still dangling from her chest, and Lance's girlfriend Jody (Rosanna Arquette) says that was trippy. The transition from the darkness of death to the humor of recovery transitions seamlessly because Tarantino allows the scenes to play out naturally in tone. He doesn't invite us to laugh Mia's shock for being revived; we just do.

Even the scenes that come with surprises still keep the dialogue going. After Vincent (Jackson) and Jules are driving after finishing a job, Jules turns to the backseat to ask the other passenger a question about spirituality, only for his gun to go off in the passenger's face. Vincent is peeved, and Jules is in dazed apology for making a mistake. The violence isn't meant to be overly shocking because we don't focus on the blood as the scene quickly shifts towards how to clean up the car. This leads to a scene where Tarantino angrily complains about being involved with their mistake and Harvey Keitel details how to handle the situation. A lesser film would try to ramp up the tension and wouldn't find the humor in Keitel's professional manner so easily.

If Tarantino's *Reservoir Dogs* caused a quake in the independent movie scene, *Pulp Fiction* was a volcanic explosion for the new wave of indie cinema. The insightful dialogue, colorful characters, and unique story structures most likely inspired the likes of *Things to Do in Denver When You're Dead*, *The Boondocks Saints* and *Lock, Stock and Two Smoking Barrels*, just to name a few. Tarantino's name quickly became synonymous with the best filmmakers, despite having only directed two films at this point in his career. Past all the hype that surrounded the picture, *Pulp Fiction* remains a timeless film for its unforgettable iconic moments where characters are always talking, always quotable and still fun to watch.

QUIZ SHOW

DIRECTOR: Robert Redford | SCREENWRITER: Paul Attanasio | CAST: John Turturro, Rob Morrow, Ralph Fiennes, David Paymer, Paul Scofield | GENRE: Drama | RUNNING TIME: 133 min | MPAA RATING: PG-13

CLASSIFICATION: BEST

What is the big appeal of a televised trivia show? Is it the contestant, the questions or the money? I've noticed it's usually the contestant that holds the viewership, eager to tune in once more to see how long a champion can climb that ladder and raise his prize money earnings. But when the viewers are not as interested in seeing the same contestant week after week, new talent is required. And getting that new intellectual hero proves to be a significant shift in television where ratings trump genuine smarts.

Quiz Show (1994) aims for the controversy of the 1950s game show *Twenty One* supplying answers to contestants and rigging the games. During this era, these games were tough and required real smarts to win that big cash prize. An intelligent person could become a star on television for knowing all about science, playwrights, and history. But in the realm of television, anything can be staged. NBC executives took note of how Herbert Stempel (John Turturro), a nervous Jew, became a household name for winning several weeks on the program, but became concerned when ratings dipped, and his appeal began to fade. They needed a new hero contestant to replace him, leading to the staging of Herbert's defeat in which he will have to take a dive.

His replacement is Charles Van Doren (Ralph Fiennes), an intellectual WASP from an elite literary family. The executives want him to win as people love him for his irresistible charm and handsome appearance. Enticed by fame and fortune, Charles accepts their offer. They supply him with the right answers and supply Stempel with the wrong answers.

In their first television duel of trivia, we feel tension when we watch the game show, but not the same thought by the television audience. The American public is wondering whether or not Stempel will take the dive or shock the executives by giving the correct answer. He's asked to answer *On the Waterfront* for the question of which film won the 1955 Academy Award for Best Picture. He knows the answer is *Marty* as it's his favorite film. It's painful for him to throw the game, but he does. He'll later testify on the scandal of the show being rigged. The case becomes of great interest to congressional investigator Richard Goodwin (Rob Morrow). He wants to take down the network for fixing the show, but would instead not throw Charles under the bus. Goodwin knows Charles' family and, like the rest of America just likes the guy too much to watch him go down in a scandal.

Robert Redford directs this picture, and he doesn't shy away from making the film as historical as it is entertaining. He isn't afraid of referring to the NBC network that ran the show, the TV producer Dan Enright who instigated the scandal, the game host Jack Barry who played ball and the Geritol sponsor that promised to cure what ails you. The screenplay by Paul Attanasio picks its targets well and knows how to paint those that were in on the rigging, those that innocently played along and those that did nothing. We see Charles take the fall for cheating on the show, but watch as everyone else involved steps away from his side. Few of those realized how scandalous their actions were until they were finally caught.

Quiz Show is a downfall picture not so much of people, but another layer of honesty with the American public. It represents a time when game shows held a fascination and genuine appeal for the smart guy who answered questions correctly. Now we question what is real on television more than ever before. After all, when ratings are on the line, you can't afford to be real with a reality show.

RESERVOIR DOGS

DIRECTOR: Quentin Tarantino | SCREENWRITER: Quentin Tarantino | CAST: Harvey Keitel, Tim Roth, Chris Penn, Steve Buscemi, Lawrence Tierney, Michael Madsen | GENRE: Action | RUNNING TIME: 100 min | MPAA RATING: R

CLASSIFICATION: BEST

Reservoir Dogs (1992) is a heist movie that showcases everything except the heist. We see the planning, the backstories, the getaway and the brutal aftermath, all of which are far more entertaining than the heist itself would have been. Director Quentin Tarantino assumes we've already seen that movie and decides to pull back and show the more exciting side of the characters involved in the crime.

The film jumps around to the scenes with the best dialogue. Before the heist, the robbers share a meal where they discuss sex and tipping the bill. After the heist, two of the robbers drive back to their base of operations, one of them bleeding badly from the gut and the other trying to assure him he won't die. Back at the hideout, the remaining robbers discuss what to do next and who might have ratted them out. Through a series of flashbacks, we slowly learn all about the characters, including the rat of the group, as the events gradually build towards a climax more explosive and intense than the robbery.

The robbers are played by a stellar cast, referring to each other only by their code names by the heist organizer Joe Cabot (Lawrence Tierney). Harvey Keitel dominates the screen as Mr. White, equal parts controlling and emotional in how he booms with nearly every scene. Michael Madsen is an intimidating force as Mr. Blonde, a man calm enough to enjoy soda before cutting up his victims. Steve Buscemi is nervously contradicting as Mr. Pink, so uneasy he questions why he has to be Mr. Pink as it sounds too close to Mr. Pussy. Tim Roth can comfortably hold a conversation as Mr. Orange, but can still blubber like a baby when shot in the gut. The rest of the supporting cast fits their small roles well, even the usually overbearing Quentin Tarantino, who reserves his patch of dialogue for the opening scene.

Tarantino shoots his picture out of order to explore many different angles and gain a unique perspective of the characters. Jumping around the events leading up to the heist, we get to learn more about the rat of the group, listening to him rehearsing a story to tell in passing before transitioning into him saying it among thieves. Cutting back to the warehouse, Mr. Blonde proceeds to torture a captured cop all by himself to the tune of "Stuck In The Middle With You" while he dances with a knife. Though the director turns the camera away when Mr. Blonde cuts off the cop's ear, the camera mostly stays on Mr. Blonde, following him out to the car for a temporary break in the music to grab some gasoline for dousing the cop. While Tarantino doesn't showcase the exact moment of the heist, he does go for the explosive aftermath when Mr. White violently shoots up two pursuing cops. The rat is present in this scene and looks on with despair.

Reservoir Dogs featured the young Quentin Tarantino at his best for working with so little. Shot on a budget of $1.5 million, the film would not only make its money back, but it would receive multiple festival awards, make a profit at the box office and be regarded as one of the greatest independent films of all-time. It would also launch the career of Tarantino and lead to him directing *Pulp Fiction* (1994), considered one of the greatest movies of all-time. That's not too shabby for a guy who was working as a video store clerk before he became a director.

ROCKY V

DIRECTOR: John G. Avildsen | SCREENWRITER: Sylvester Stallone | CAST: Sylvester Stallone, Talia Shire, Burt Young, Sage Stallone, Tommy Morrison, Burgess Meredith | GENRE: Drama | RUNNING TIME: 104 min | MPAA RATING: PG-13

CLASSIFICATION: WORST

Of all the movies in the *Rocky* series, Sylvester Stallone seems to most regret *Rocky V* (1990). In an interview with The Sun, he admits he made the movie out of greed. When asked in an interview with Jonathan Ross about how he'd rate each *Rocky* film on a scale from one to ten, Stallone rated *Rocky V* as a zero. Why so low? Perhaps he regrets handing over his usual director's chair back to John G. Avildsen (who helmed the first *Rocky* film), or maybe he regrets changing out the original ending in which Rocky would die after a fight. Whatever the reasons, it's clear that *Rocky V* was not the best way to end the series that was in dire need of a merciful sendoff.

To its credit, the movie attempts to recapture some of the old glory of the first *Rocky* picture by not loading the film up with the usual corny flash of the sequels. Rocky (Stallone) is now crippled with brain damage and cannot continue boxing. His inability to compete makes him all the more eager to retire finally. Boxing promoter George Washington Duke (Richard Gant) challenges Rocky to fight Union Cane at a press conference, but those days are behind him. Rocky decides to spend more time with his son, Robert, played by Stallone's real son Sage Stallone. They bond well, even though his son seems more interested in art and drawing huge boobs.

Rocky soon loses all his fortune on a tax issue, and he is sent back to the dirty streets of Philadelphia where he once trained. He sells all his assets, moves into the townhouse in the old neighborhood and shifts focus from being a boxer to running Mickey's old gym for training boxers. It's amazing how hard this film tries to tear down all the overblown fame and glory from the previous movie, but this teardown is just too over-the-top. It begs the question why *Rocky V* didn't just skip ahead past all these clunky explanations for going back to his roots. It would make more sense considering how much older Stallone aged between pictures and how awkward it is that this film picks up from following minutes of *Rocky IV*.

The drama of the film concerns who Rocky will train. Tommy Gunn (Tommy Morrison) seems to be just the underdog product Rocky needs to keep himself occupied, but he ignores his son's bully problem at school by not only refusing to train him, but also cast him aside so Tommy can stay with the townhome. It isn't until Rocky eventually loses Tommy to being signed by George Washington Duke that he realizes he should be there for his son. Although considering the only knowledge Rocky can offer is how to punch real good, maybe Robert was better off training on his own.

All *Rocky* movies end with a grand showdown, and this one is by far the worst for not being a sanctioned boxing match. When Tommy is furious Rocky won't fight him in the ring, he suggests they compete in the street. In a way, this would be a victory for Rocky in that he can prove to Tommy that he's the better boxer without having Duke make a penny off of their match. But the fight is only interesting from that mind game perspective of Rocky proving himself and not for the same underdog rise we see in previous *Rocky* pictures. By the end of the film, Rocky is still poor and is probably even more destitute when he punches Duke after the promoter states he'll sue for assault.

This is a film that is misguided and pigheaded about Rocky's appeal. It tries to remove the franchise from its popcorn entertainment route, but turns the inspiring sports figure into an athlete that is going down for the count. It's such an anti-Rocky movie that the film's original ending of Rocky dying in the street fight feels more fitting. Stallone would eventually carry the character over into the more appealing sports films of *Rocky Balboa* (2006) where he makes a comeback and *Creed* (2015) where he trains the son of Apollo Creed. Those movies took the character to a far better place of finding contentment and purpose with the character, rather than kicking him to the curb on the streets of Philadelphia.

RUSHMORE

DIRECTOR: Wes Anderson | SCREENWRITER: Wes Anderson, Owen Wilson | CAST: Jason Schwartzman, Olivia Williams, Bill Murray, Seymour Cassel, Mason Gamble | GENRE: Comedy | RUNNING TIME: 93 min | MPAA RATING: R

CLASSIFICATION: BEST

Wes Anderson's *Rushmore* (1998) is a whimsically amusing and sometimes cynical tale of an unconventional love triangle between a struggling student, a depressed industrialist, and a knowledgeable teacher. They occupy a familiar and aged world that is sophisticated enough for discussions of Latin, blunt enough for revenge of cutting car brakes and creative enough for a school play about war with elaborate and loud special effects. It isn't every romantic comedy where a child actor wields a flamethrower on a high school stage.

Max Fischer (Jason Schwartzman) may only be 15 years old, but he's accomplished quite a bit in his time at Rushmore Academy. He has founded and devoted himself to dozens of extracurricular groups, from beekeeping to debating to his successful stage acting troupe. He also happens to be one of the worst students on an academic level, easily angering the frustrated headmaster Dr. Guggenheim (Brian Cox). Max has the potential to be an excellent student, as it's established that he was able to get into Rushmore after producing a one-act play about Watergate. He just needs to get those grades up and maybe cut down on all his clubs.

Two figures enter his life as new inspirations. The rich and dreary millionaire Herman Blume (Bill Murray) delivers a dry sermon at Rushmore about taking dead aim at the rich ones, brought about by his failing marriage and spoiled children. His words spark a fascination with Max, relatively poor himself, and the two become friends. Their new relationship is put to the ultimate test where they both fall for the beautiful new first-grade teacher Rosemary Cross (Olivia Williams). And the games are on for Ms. Cross' love, both of them figuring they can easily topple her current boyfriend of the meek Dr. Flynn (Luke Wilson). While Max puts everything he has into attaining her affection, going so far as to break ground on an aquarium for her on a baseball field, Herman finds her an easy enough woman to woo behind Max's back. For Max's limited sexual appeal as a student, that's just not fair for a boy who claims he was in love with her first.

The schemes of Schwartzman and Murray have a twisted and silly charm. Their pranks range from the dirty pool of filling a room full of bees to the cartoonish of staging a tree to fall and crush on cue. Even before the battle begins for Cross, Murray's violent urges spark in amusing scenes where he attempts to strangle his bratty kids and smack a basketball out of the hands of kids in passing. All the while Murray plays the role with a controlled bitterness and nihilism, maintaining a mute expression of resentment as he runs over Max's bike.

The characters never become lost within these silly scenes and a likable level of humanity is always present. Max is an egotistical student, far too ambitious and adult for his own good, finally realizing the error of his ways when kicked out of Rushmore and shunned by Ms. Cross. Herman falls deep into bouts of depression when his personal life becomes more lonely, coming to the sad realization that his best friend is a 15-year-old kid. Ms. Cross is an understanding woman, but also not afraid to confront and attack a desperate Max. Even Max's single father of a barber is such a kind and patient soul that it's almost out of mercy that Max leaves him out of the spotlight and lies about his profession as that of a brain surgeon.

There's a sweetness and a rustic charm to the way Anderson shot *Rushmore* in a manner that feels as relatable as it does fantastical. His shots make great use of depth and detail where the camera can focus on a central character, but reveal some beauty in the space they occupy. The dialogue is very adult at times for a cast primarily of kids under the age of eighteen, but has a particular childlike wonderment for the mesmerizing cinematography of Robert Yeoman and the retro music of Mark Mothersbaugh. There's a playful spirit throughout which can shift from the simple pleasures of chatting at the barber shop to the over-the-top production of Max's magnum opus of a school play, complete with wounded soldiers, miniature helicopters and explosive trails of napalm. In the opinion of the dry groundskeeper Mr. Littlejeans, *"best play ever, man."* Anderson, too, has created one of the best movies ever – sometimes somber, sometimes ridiculous, always beautiful.

SAVING PRIVATE RYAN

DIRECTOR: Steven Spielberg | SCREENWRITER: Robert Rodat | CAST: Tom Hanks, Edward Burns, Matt Damon, Tom Sizemore | GENRE: Action | RUNNING TIME: 169 min | MPAA RATING: R

CLASSIFICATION: BEST

Steven Spielberg's depiction of the battle of Omaha Beach in *Saving Private Ryan* (1998) is one of the most tragic, brutal and compelling scenes of any war picture. There are no major heroes in such a bloody offensive; just a lucky few who didn't die. The rest of the young soldiers were either blown to bits, shot between the eyes or hopelessly holding their guts inside as they slowly drift away. War is horrible, and Spielberg makes sure that his war picture makes this clear by zooming in on all its ugliness and inhumanity rather than turn in another film of simple heroism and PG-13 action.

A few days after the horrific D-Day event, eight soldiers are assigned to rescue Private James Ryan from enemy territory as he was declared missing in action. He was one of four brothers that went off to war, the other three dying in combat. This is a publicity stunt. Ryan's return will boost the spirits and create a great story to tell about how Ryan's mother will get to see one of her boys again. Captain Miller (Tom Hanks) is assigned to lead his men on a rescue mission through French territory they doubt is worth it or even possible. The German soldiers continue to shoot at them, and they find themselves questioning the mission.

There is lots of action and lots gruesome violence in this picture, but it's not meant to get our testosterone pumping or patriotism soaring. Yes, Spielberg shoots these scenes with lots of explosions, guns and high body counts, but he also sticks with it. Once the soldiers find cover on the beach, the camera watches the able soldiers readying bigger guns, but also focuses close on the wounded ones screaming as medics furiously try to save their lives. We're not meant to enjoy these scenes of war and Spielberg doesn't give us the comfort of cutting away when things get too grisly.

It can't be stated enough how well Spielberg has shot these scenes of war. Rather than stage them as grand and operatic, he makes them dirty, loud and hard to follow. The camera shakes and whips around the soldiers as bullets zing past them and explosions shake the ground beneath them. We feel as disoriented as they do for fighting their way up the beach with Germans mowing down advancing forces. There are many memorable shots of horror, blood and all.

And then there's that moment when the camera zooms in on Captain Miller. The footage slows down, and the sound drops. He watches in stunned silence as flaming soldiers flee their boat set aflame. One soldier huddles for cover from the gunfire, reduced to tears. Another soldier loses an arm and stumbles around in the line of fire, picking his arm up off the ground. He's disillusioned by what just happened, under some faint notion that his arm can be saved. Most of what I remembered after first seeing the film were scenes of wounded soldiers on the ground, screaming or crying out in pain, a chilling reminder that nobody could be prepared for such an onslaught.

If the action were shot poorly, *Saving Private Ryan* could have been in bad taste, but Spielberg makes sure we feel more than adrenaline in these violent scenes. He foregoes placing unneeded personalities on the characters. We don't need them. We know enough about these characters through their actions and how they act on the battlefield, making the tough choices of where to shoot, who to save and which call to make. There's a draining nature of the war that grows on the audience as it goes on. In an iconic moment where Hanks shoots at a tank with his pistol, his face is tired and battered by the time the tank finally explodes. This is a film that not only leaves unforgettable images in the mind, but feelings that stick with you long after the final shot.

THE SCARLET LETTER

DIRECTOR: Roland Joffé | SCREENWRITER: Douglas Day Stewart | CAST: Demi Moore, Gary Oldman, Robert Duvall, Robert Prosky, Edward Hardwicke, Joan Plowright | GENRE: Drama | RUNNING TIME: 135 min | MPAA RATING: R

CLASSIFICATION: WORST

Roland Joffé's *The Scarlet Letter* (1995) retools so much of Nathaniel Hawthorne's original novel that it's surprising he didn't change the title as well. It's as if the screenwriter Douglas Day Stewart was given of mission of punching up Hawthorne's story to be more erotic and driven by action, ignoring most if not all of the themes or moods of the book. If you know someone who gets all bent out of shape when the movies tarnish their source material of novels by changing the story, this one will make their brain explode with its bad choices in retooling.

Where to begin? Let's start with the story. Hester Prynne (Demi Moore) is the new Puritan of the Massachusetts Bay colony. Her husband hasn't arrived yet, and she is found to be pregnant. Unwilling to name the true father, she is condemned to wear a scarlet letter on her body. She births her daughter of Pearl, and the father is revealed to be Reverend Arthur Dimmesdale (Gary Oldman). Hester's husband becomes involved, and the novel ends with Dimmesdale confessing his sins right before he dies. Adultery is part of the story, but both Joffé and Stewart took that one aspect and ran wild with it as a concept for transforming the book into something that would play more like a Harlequin romance.

One of the most significant changes from the book is the actual act of adultery. The novel takes place after Hester and Dimmesdale have engaged in a sexual romp, but that's a scene too juicy for the filmmakers to pass up. The film portrays their moment of sinful love in a barn atop a hill of beans with a watching slave girl. Before this ridiculous scene, Hester first meets Dimmesdale while spying on him in the nude, the shot showing all the skin with moody lighting. And there is a lot of masturbation between these scenes. Meanwhile, Hester's husband (Robert Duvall) hangs out with an Indian tribe, donning a dead deer on his body and dancing around a fire.

The film trades in all the novel's sense of guilt for melodrama, no thanks to the cast. Moore feels very out of place and is so unsure of herself she spent her own money to reshoot a scene where she didn't like the way her hair looked. Duvall is a joke for throwing himself into a role that requires him to be involved in the most unintentionally silly of scenes. Oldman brings a little bit of class to his role, but still suffers from being an unconvincing preacher.

Of course, the biggest offense here is the altered ending, changed from a somber conclusion to a happier and more action-packed one. Remember when I wrote Dimmesdale tragically dies at the end as a mess of sin and guilt? The movie trades in that ending for one where he saves Hester from the gallows and an Indian attack saves the day from either of them being killed by the angry colonists. Hester and Dimmesdale take off for Carolina and live happily ever after, forgetting all about Hester's scarlet letter and Dimmesdale's sins. I guess a more profound ending about grappling with morality and hypocrisy didn't test well.

The Scarlet Letter is about as trashy as movie adaptations come for revered novels. The worst part is that nobody involved with this film seemed to care. Demi Moore mentioned in interviews that it didn't matter how much was changed because nobody read the book anymore. I'll bet fans of the novel loved that statement. And I can only imagine the disappointment of those who enjoyed the movie and decided to read the book, discovering the far darker ending and that there's nothing all that sexy about the story. Hawthorne must be spinning like a jet turbine in his grave for such a soap-opera adaptation of his work.

SCHINDLER'S LIST

DIRECTOR: Steven Spielberg | SCREENWRITER: Steven Zaillian | CAST: Liam Neeson, Ben Kingsley, Ralph Fiennes, Caroline Goodall, Jonathan Sagall, Embeth Davidtz | GENRE: Drama | RUNNING TIME: 197 min | MPAA RATING: R

CLASSIFICATION: BEST

Steven Spielberg took a risk making a film as bold and heartbreaking as *Schindler's List* (1993). Most people only knew him as the stellar director of genre pictures and not exactly a strong choice for directing a film about the Holocaust. Fearing he wasn't quite ready for such a project, he tried passing it off to more credible directors that included Roman Polanski, Sydney Pollack, and Martin Scorsese. But Spielberg would eventually come around to realizing that directing such a film would be a grand opportunity to not only prove himself as a mature filmmaker, but make it a personal and unflinching film for his family and religion. He was ready to make his most important and acclaimed movie ever made.

Based on the novel by Thomas Keneally, the film is set in the Polish city of Kraków where World War II has presented an opportunity for Oskar Schindler (Liam Neeson). The Germans have forced the Jewish communities of Kraków into the ghetto, allowing Schindler to take advantage of hiring a cheap workforce of Jews. Schindler sets up two factories: one for pots and pans and another for shell casings. They hire Jews, and they are manufacturing for the Nazis, but are not efficient enough to be of much use to them. Everyone working for Schindler, including his accountant Itzahak Stern (Ben Kingsley), knew that what he is doing is factory to con the Nazis out of using Jews for labor camps. He immerses himself so thoroughly in tune with the Nazis that the ruthless party wouldn't even consider him cheating them.

One Nazi focussed on during this con is Commandant Amon Goeth (Ralph Fiennes), a man so natural with killing Jews he picks them off for target practice off the balcony of a ski chalet. He represents the worst of humanity. If he weren't a Nazi soldier, he'd be a serial killer. His strategy is more about mind games with the Jews, wiping out any hope there is for survival. He'll leave a Jew alive long enough to let a smaller glimmer of hope peek through before shattering it with a bullet. It's one of Fiennes' most chilling performances.

Spielberg's focus feels razor sharp here in making us focus on the horrors of this atrocity. This is evident in the film's single burst of color with the red jacket of a little girl. Schindler watches her from afar as she ambles around the massacre of Jews. We're drawn to her as much as Schindler not just because of the color, but because it's a little girl of pure nature that had yet to be corrupted by the world around her. When she dies, so does an innocence of the future, her red coat still noticeable on her corpse among the other dead bodies.

The finale of the film features the most moving of scenes where Schindler is congratulated by the Jews that saved him and gifted a ring with the Hebrew words for *"he who saves one life, saves the world entire."* Schindler is shaken by this gift and still beats himself up for not saving more. He looks around at everything that he spent money on, now only seeing the lives that could have been saved. His car could've been worth ten more lives, a piece of gold two more. He breaks down into tears in one of the most heartbreaking scenes in movie history.

Schindler's List has been considered a cultural milestone of a picture for depicting a crucial aspect of history with great evil and absolute good. The evil is the devaluing of life, evident from Spielberg's decision to shoot the picture in black-and-white and his refusal to detail the specifics of the Nazi raids and concentration camps. The atrocities don't deserve to be dismissed with dry exposition. The good is in Schindler, but never made clear until the very end when he fully comprehends what he has done. He saved the lives of many Jews that would live on and extend their legacy. He was responsible for life continuing, a feat which did not seem possible during the darkest days of World War II. As the most humanitarian of all of Spielberg's pictures, it's not surprising that it won so many awards, including the Academy Award for Best Picture. But it was so much more than that. As Spielberg's childhood rabbi Albert Lewis describes it best, it was *"Steven's gift to his mother, to his people, and in a sense to himself. Now he is a full human being."*

SCHIZOPOLIS

DIRECTOR: Steven Soderbergh | SCREENWRITER: Steven Soderbergh | CAST: Steven Soderbergh, Betsy Brantley, David Jensen | GENRE: Comedy | RUNNING TIME: 96 min | MPAA RATING: R

CLASSIFICATION: WEIRD

Steven Soderbergh's *Schizopolis* (1996) is the boldest of film experiments for featuring such a direct approach to its strangeness that may or may not be a joke. It begins and ends with Soderbergh standing before a curtain and announcing the movie. To prepare us for the journey, he states that his film is the best made and must be seen multiple times if you find it confusing. He sounds full of himself, but is he? Is there something more hidden beneath such an abstract plot that can be unearthed from multiple viewings? I've watched the film three times and still feel as though I have miles to go before finding all its many meanings.

The film is separated into three acts that intersect one another, and all connect towards the end. I think.

The first section follows Fletcher Munson (Steven Soderbergh), an office worker that works for Mr. Schwitters (Mike Malone), an obvious parody of L. Ron Hubbard as a leader in the religion of Eventualism. Fletcher finds himself more interested in the meaning of what people say rather than what they're saying. His language has degraded to the point where he arrives home to greet his wife by literally saying *"generic greeting"* to which she responds *"generic greeting returned."*

The second arc focuses on Fletcher's doppelganger of a dentist. Also played by Soderbergh, this character is known as Dr. Korchek and is having an affair with Fletcher's wife. But Korchek, I think, might even be Fletcher; *"Oh my god. I'm having an affair with my wife!"* Between the two personalities, Korchek is a more pleasant man as he can hold a conversation better with Fletcher's wife, even with his corny dentist humor; *"You don't have to floss all your teeth, just the ones you want to keep."* But then Korchek finds himself infatuated with another woman who looks exactly like Fletcher's wife and is referred to as Attractive Woman Number 2. The dialogue at this point begins to degrade once more, this time into commands of three.

The third and final chapter is reserved entirely for Fletcher's wife. One would think that her perspective of encountering the two identical men would bring some logic and understanding to what's going on here. But Soderbergh teases us once more by making Fletcher and Korchek speak Japanese, Italian or French with cultural stereotypes in their delivery. And in case all that wasn't confusing enough, there's the ever-present wildcard element of the insane exterminator Elmo Oxygen (David Jensen), running around town with his babbling language (*"Nose army!"*) and perverted desire to show his penis.

The film is so aloof and abundant with its themes that it dares the viewer to try to figure it out. The most obvious one is the theme of how meaningless conversations have become that words don't matter, made apparent by Fletcher's random talk of addressing others without much of a response. Then there's the whole loss of identity as Fletcher and Korchek struggle to figure out who is the correct version of themselves or if they're the same person. There's also a denial of being, as though Fletcher and his wife are holding something significant back that prevents them from going wild. There are many ways to interpret such a film, and I think that's what pleases Soderbergh the most. It's as though he opened the box to an elaborate puzzle and then dumped it on the floor. Then dropped in another one. Then another one. And then a Rubik's cube for good measure. He doesn't care if we solve it and seems delighted that we'd even try.

Schizopolis is Soderbergh's most underrated film for going virtually unnoticed upon its release and being the strangest of productions. It was made for a mere $250,000 over the course of nine months as a passion project. Soderbergh employed friends and relatives to help, as well as his ex-wife Betsy to play the role of Fletcher's wife, which says all sorts of odd things about that relationship. Its initial premiere at the Cannes Film Festival brought a negative response, prompting the ironic addition of Soderbergh addressing the audience and then answering questions at the end of the film that nobody asked. It has garnered a cult status over the years for its audacity, large enough to warrant being a part of the Criterion Collection.

So what does it all mean? Further study is needed, but I have a hunch I'll figure it all out by the eighth viewing or so (or never). Try it at home and see if your brain doesn't melt trying to decipher this baffling picture.

SCREAM

DIRECTOR: Wes Craven | SCREENWRITER: Kevin Williamson | CAST: David Arquette, Neve Campbell, Courteney Cox, Matthew Lillard, Rose McGowan, Skeet Ulrich, Drew Barrymore | GENRE: Horror | RUNNING TIME: 111 min | MPAA RATING: R

CLASSIFICATION: WEIRD

Wes Craven directed *Scream* (1996) as both a bright jab of the slasher genre and a celebration of its tropes. The unlucky teenagers of this story criticize horror movies, but don't realize they're in one themselves. The amusing logic of this setup is perfectly conveyed during a party where Jamie Kennedy lays out the rules of horror movies. Rule #1: Never leave the others and say you'll be right back because you won't be back. After stating this rule, Matthew Lillard asks Kennedy if he wants a beer and makes an exaggerated face as he humorously says he'll be right back. He laughs now, but won't be cracking jokes when knives are being shoved into stomachs.

It's easy enough to balk at the logic of horror movies as most audiences shout for fleeing victims to go that way or not to go upstairs, but *Scream* is a movie with characters aware of these mistakes and finds themselves still meeting their end at the hands of the killer. Perhaps horror audiences are not as smart as they think when talking back towards the screen. Most of these teenagers, however, are not so astute, as in the opening scene where Drew Barrymore is questioned by the killer about her knowledge of horror movies for the life of her boyfriend. The attacker asks her who was the killer in the first *Friday the 13th* movie and she answers it was Jason. Wrong answer: Jason's mother was the killer in the first movie and he didn't start killing teenagers until *Part 2*. As a result, her boyfriend is killed, and the masked killer soon pursues her inside the house via the very tropes she was mocking a few moments ago.

The prospect of a killer on the prowl doesn't terrify the teenagers so much as arousing fascination amid their partying lifestyle. The high school students are less fearful of the recent string of murders and more ecstatic for school being suspended. A few of them are not as enthused. Sidney (Neve Campbell) is reminded of her mother's death as she was murdered one year ago by her father. Now being threatened by the masked killer, Sidney figures her father is the murderer on the loose, especially when the threatening phone calls she receives are traced to his phone. But, of course, the mystery is not so simply solved. Anybody in town could be the killer, from the pushy TV reporter Gale (Courtney Cox) to Sydney's mysterious boyfriend Billy (Skeet Ulrich) to the inept school principal (Henry Winkler).

The mystery doesn't matter though, as it's little more than a series of twists, resolving itself as more of a whodunit surprise than a terrifying conclusion. What's fascinating about the scenario is that the characters are aware they're inside a horror movie more or less. As such, they try to avoid the mistakes that every dopey horror victim makes. Sidney is relatively rejective of her boyfriend Billy wanting to have sex. A smart move as most killings in slasher pictures happens when a couple is in the act. If the teens are this knowledgeable of horror logic, how do they still end up slaughtered? Easy: they're teenagers. And while teens can walk around with a pompous knowledge of slasher movie logic, they're still human and bound by the same desires, hormones and exuberance that usually leads to bloody ends.

Scream was written by first-time screenwriter Kevin Williamson with both affection and knowing satire of slasher pictures that Craven picked up on. While the characters continue to refer to the likes of *Halloween* and *Friday the 13th*, their slaughtering is brutal and bloody. So violent was Craven's vision that he had to submit the film eight times to the MPAA before they would finally grant him an R rating as opposed to the box office poison of NC-17. Though *Scream* continued as a franchise of lesser sequels, the popularity of the first film led to a revitalization in the horror genre to be blockbusters once more, leading to a resurgence of such films as *I Know What You Did Last Summer* (1997) and *Urban Legend* (1998). Those films were not as bright, but at least *Scream* proved that there was potential for violent teen slasher pictures to be knowing, giving a smart wink before the sharp stab.

SEVEN

DIRECTOR: David Fincher | SCREENWRITER: Andrew Kevin Walker | CAST: Brad Pitt, Morgan Freeman, Gwyneth Paltrow, John C. McGinley, Kevin Spacey | GENRE: Horror | RUNNING TIME: 127 min | MPAA RATING: R

CLASSIFICATION: BEST

First-time screenwriter Andrew Kevin Walker said that he hated trying to find work in New York City, but admitted that such a negative experience inspired him to write *Seven* (1995). Though not explicitly set in New York, the story takes place in a city that seems dirty, busy and always rainy. A series of murders have occurred. A fat man has been forced to eat to death. An attorney has a pound of flesh removed. Both murder scenes have been left with intentional clues of "gluttony" and "greed." The killer is basing his victims and his murders on the seven deadly sins in the darkest and gruesome of presentations.

Investigating this case is the detective duo of Mills (Brad Pitt) and Somerset (Morgan Freeman). Mills is an overly ambitious detective who has intentionally plucked his wife Tracy (Gwyneth Paltrow) out of their upstate home and placed them in a grimy apartment of the depressing city. Somerset is an old cop who has seen it all and hopes his career of seeing the nasty side of humanity is coming to a close. They continue to track murder after murder that continues with each sin. A drug dealer has been tied to bed for a whole year with the words "sloth" etched into the wall along with a series of photos that showcase how the killer has been planning these deaths for quite some time.

What's unique about Seven is that it is not a traditional murder mystery, favoring more character than plot. The murders are not meant to be as invitingly intriguing as they are in a BBC drama, but brutal and ugly where the sights and smells overpower the initial thoughts of who did it. The case itself is not meant to be the allure either, as the killer confesses before all the bodies are found, strolling into the police station while colored in blood.

The real meat of this movie is the character of the detectives and trying to figure them out more than the murders. Somerset is seen as the veteran detective of a mysteriously lonely lifestyle while Mills is the hothead detective who still has a lot to learn. They sound like the typical odd couple of a duo that has to learn from each other, but both Pitt and Freeman bring some great dimension to such simple roles. They deliver performances that make the film seem more engaging past familiar tropes. Gwyneth Paltrow also does an astounding job for what looks like a nothing role, but is later revealed to be a substantial emotional core of the picture's humanity.

We also get to know more about the killer when the third act reveals him. He carries a smugness to his face and psychotic nature to his complex mentality. He must have a strong desire for such murders given that he commits them as far out as a year and as recently as a few days ago. There's no fear when he is arrested or questioned by the police, only the voice of a man who sounds intelligently calculative and believes himself to be righteous in his actions. He is the very embodiment of evil, going about his crimes so calculative that you're afraid to hear what he'll say next.

The film all leads up to the unforgettable and unnerving head-in-a-box scene. It's an emotionally draining moment; Pitt is a sniveling mess, Freeman is fearful, and the killer admires his final kill. This scene was initially rejected by New Line Cinema, but they accidentally sent this version to director David Fincher, and it remained in the film. Fincher became attracted to such a project for being more about focusing on humanity's darkness than feeling like just another police procedural. New Line still wanted the head-in-a-box scene cut, but Fincher refused to bend. He wanted his film to be as grim, dark and unsettling as possible. It remains one of his strongest works for being just that.

THE SHAWSHANK REDEMPTION

DIRECTOR: Frank Darabont | SCREENWRITER: Frank Darabont | CAST: Tim Robbins, Morgan Freeman, Bob Gunton, William Sadler, Clancy Brown, Gil Bellows, James Whitmore | GENRE: Drama | RUNNING TIME: 142 min | MPAA RATING: R

CLASSIFICATION: BEST

There was an oddly uplifting spirit and unique perspective to the prison setting of *The Shawshank Redemption* (1994). True, the Shawshank Prison is no picnic with its corrupt leadership, constant threat of violence from the guards and the painful isolation of it all. What makes it so enduring is the struggle of two prisoners to find something more within their cage. From their view, we see a warmth, calm and charm that is rarely seen in prison pictures. If you're going to be spending an extended period locked away, you might as well get comfortable with your cellmates.

The convicted murderer Andy (Bill Paxton) is our main character, but his story is told to us through fellow inmate Red (Morgan Freeman) in an introspective narration. We know enough about Red as a long-time prisoner who can get anything that anybody needs, but we know him best through his storytelling abilities as the film's central narrator. Freeman's voice and delivery could make the life of a cockroach seem epic, and his character builds up Andy as though he were a mythical hero of the prison. Andy doesn't strike Red as the type of guy who could make it in prison, but he soon proves everybody wrong. Red regales us with tales of how the unlikely prisoner broke into the warden's office and played a sweet song over the prison speakers. Every prisoner remembers that brief moment of musical pleasure more than the beating that Andy received when the guards busted in to stop him.

Because the whole story is told from Red's perspective, there is an intriguing air of mystery to Andy. We're not so much watching what Andy does as we are listening to Red's interpretation. This presentation builds Andy up as more of a legend, questioning how much of Andy's story is true and how much of Red's tale is embellished. After all, Red's initial perceptions of Andy being a pushover inmate are proved false. How much else could he be wrong about? The most revealing moments occur when Andy and Red find themselves talking about everything from the outside world to what they're in for. It is then that we begin to learn just a little bit of Andy's redemption philosophy: *"Get busy living, or get busy dying."*

 The Shawshank Redemption could be considered one of the first major successes of home video and cable viewings trumping a theatrical release. When first released into theaters in 1994, it did very poor business, most likely because there wasn't much interest in a prison drama that was over two hours long. But thanks to its low box office, the TNT network was easily able to acquire the television rights in 1997 for a cheap deal and began airing the movie regularly. While the film cultivated a new audience on television, it also became a hit on home video as a best seller and favorite rental from video stores.

 The film was based on a novella by Stephen King and directed by Frank Darabont, who would later direct other King adaptations including *The Green Mile* (1999) and *The Mist* (2007). Darabont's direction is mesmerizing as a slow burn where we experience the prison more through its passive days of isolation in another world than high moments of drama. As Red describes it best, *"Old life blown away in the blink of an eye. Nothing left but all the time in the world to think about it."* And there's plenty to think about behind those bars.

SHORT CUTS

DIRECTOR: Robert Altman | SCREENWRITER: Robert Altman, Frank Barhydt | CAST: Andie MacDowell, Bruce Davison, Julianne Moore, Matthew Modine, Jennifer Jason Leigh, Robert Downey Jr., Tim Robbins, Lily Tomlin, Tom Waits, Frances McDormand, Jack Lemmon, Huey Lewis | GENRE: Drama | RUNNING TIME: 188 min | MPAA RATING: R

CLASSIFICATION: BEST

Robert Altman quickly followed up *The Player* (1992), an offbeat picture about Hollywood's upper class, with *Short Cuts* (1993), a movie about Hollywood's middle class. Based on the short stories of Raymond Carver, Altman's film follows the lives of those who work odd jobs of pool cleaners, birthday cake decorators, and voices for phone-sex. It's an ensemble picture where several stories from around the city cross paths, but with an uncomfortable and warm sense of humanity that only Altman could deliver so well.

Lily Tomlin's character hits a 7-year-old kid with her car. The boy is still conscious, and Tomlin offers to take the boy to the hospital, but he refuses as he thinks he's okay and shouldn't talk to strangers. The boy returns home to his mom (Andie MacDowell) that tries to care for him, but her carelessness in letting him sleep after such an incident frustrates her husband (Bruce Davison). Their son is now in the hospital in a coma, a day before his eighth birthday. The couple has forgotten about the expensive birthday cake they've ordered when the baker (Lyle Lovett) calls to let them know it's ready. They don't want it. Lovett's character is furious they decline the cake and continues to call back and harass the couple for leaving him stuck with such an expensive dessert.

The film presents a series of characters who don't know the full story and sometimes choose not to, stewing in their isolation of unease. The baker doesn't know the birthday boy is in the hospital, believing the parents are just jerks. Tomlin doesn't know either, making her less concerned about what happened to the kid. There's a constant questioning of how life would be different if these people would take a moment to understand others.

There are more sad stories. Three men on a fishing trip find a dead body, reasoning that reporting it would ruin their trip. A cocky cop (Tim Robbins) uses his badge as an excuse for his behavior and cheats on his wife (Madeline Stowe). And, in one of the most surreal arcs, a pool cleaner (Chris Penn) endures his wife (Jennifer Jason Leigh) working as a phone-sex worker while staying with the kids at home. It is so bizarre and uncomfortable watching her talk about what a man should do with his penis over the phone while she changes a diaper; Penn watches from a distance and is disgusted because she never talks to him that way.

There's a lot of drinking in this movie, and it's understandable. These are characters so frightened and trapped within their lives that there doesn't seem to be an exit from all the sadness and guilt. And, yet, they're also good people who haven't given up yet. They persevere because they still have some hope left in them, as well as love to give others. It's the reason to stick with these stories, for the moments when Tomlin's husband (Tom Waits) is sweet when off the bottle and the 7-year-old boy's disappearing grandparent (Jack Lemmon) comes to terms with himself.

In the tradition of Altman's other pictures of large casts, this is a film that leads its characters and the audience down an unpredictable road. Most movies about Los Angeles try to portray it as either a scummy hole or a glamorous dream world. *Short Cuts* finds that sweet spot in the middle of people who find themselves unable to have control over their lives, but still have enough heart to keep on going. The film may sound like a chore to get through with a running time of three hours, but there are so many compelling stories present that never outstay their welcome. No bad movie is too short, and no good movie is too long. And *Short Cuts* is one of Altman's best for being so beautiful, engaging and all-encompassing of what makes a film so powerful with characters you care about and stories worth telling.

SHOWGIRLS

DIRECTOR: Paul Verhoeven | SCREENWRITER: Joe Eszterhas | CAST: Elizabeth Berkley, Kyle MacLachlan, Gina Gershon, Glenn Plummer, Robert Davi, Alan Rachins, Gina Ravera | GENRE: Drama | RUNNING TIME: 131 min | MPAA RATING: NC-17

CLASSIFICATION: WEIRD

Showgirls (1995) was marketed as a big-budget erotic movie, but written by someone who doesn't understand eroticism. Joe Eszterhas was one of the most profitable screenwriters in Hollywood, which says something when most of his scripts are about evil people who hate each other. Look past all its exposed breasts, and g-strings and all that Eszterhas and director Paul Verhoeven can serve up are the sleaziest of soap operas. It's trashy cinema, but the most delicious and rich of exploitation for both its cast, content and overblown budget.

Listen to this plot and tell me if you can guess which film it is ripping off. Nomi (Elizabeth Berkley) drifts into Las Vegas with aspirations of being a stripper, setting the bar fairly low for her future. She starts off by working at the small and shady Cheetah's Topless Club, where she soon attracts the eye of Stardust entertainment manager Zack Carey (Kyle Maclachlan) and his Stardust stripper star girlfriend Cristal Connors (Gina Gershon). Cristol hates Nomi, but can't wait to humiliate her by getting her an audition at Stardust, where she is forced to ice her nipples to get them hard for a show. Nomi still gets the job, and there's a battle for the mantle of the top stripper in games of prostitution, seduction, rape, and violence.

Did you guess the film? If you said *All About Eve*, you're right. If you said *A Star is Born*, you're also right. And if you said any low-rent sleazy smut, you're still right. In fact, it's a combination of all that, with the added elements of eating dog food and slipping on monkey poop for that extra trashy aroma. Throw in some eating of that monkey poop, and you have yourself a John Waters movie.

This film is in that very rare category of being so bad it's funny; probably the most famous of its kind. It's easy enough to see why with how intentionally and unintentionally silly this farce comes off as. For example, in a scene where a dancer has an injury with her knee, the choreographer has to squeeze her knee and hear her scream before he states, *"It's her knee!"* The dialogue is a laugh-riot of bad lines you can't help but snicker at. My favorites include *"How do you like your breasts?", "Man, everybody got AIDS and shit!"* and *"She looks better than a ten-inch dick, and you know it!"* Even throwaway lines somehow find a way to be over-the-top ridiculous, as when one character asks if somebody wants a knuckle sandwich, to which someone replies, *"Can I have mine anally, please?"* The stripping dance numbers are genuinely fun, but, much like everything in this film, they're overproduced routines where characters emerge from volcanos and perform sexual dance moves that seem to break the laws of gravity.

The NC-17 rating was considered a kiss of death for not being favored at larger movie theater chains, but *Showgirls* touted this rating as a positive for marketing purposes. While the film didn't exactly turn a huge profit, it did gross enough to be the most profitable NC-17 movie ever made. It's nowhere near as erotic, poignant or mature as other films with this rating, but it's remarkable that such a film was even made. It's a kamikaze project that's just nuts enough to be an admirable piece of garbage cinema, worthy of the cult status it accumulated over time. *Showgirls* is one hell of a show, even if it wasn't the one Verhoeven set out to make. He intended to make his film about the morality and reality of strippers being savaged in Vegas. Unfortunately, most couldn't stop laughing at strippers talking about their favorite brand of dog food to eat.

THE SILENCE OF THE LAMBS

DIRECTOR: Jonathan Demme | SCREENWRITER: Ted Tally | CAST: Jodie Foster, Anthony Hopkins, Scott Glenn, Ted Levine | GENRE: Horror | RUNNING TIME: 118 min | MPAA RATING: R

CLASSIFICATION: BEST

Though Anthony Hopkins spends most of his time behind bars or restrained in *Silence of the Lambs* (1991), he steals the show as Hannibal Lecter, one of the most memorable of movie villains in cinema history. He's vicious, witty, frightening, intelligent and always has something interesting to say. He's the type of person you wouldn't mind having an in-depth conversation with over dinner, so long as you're not on the menu with a side of fava beans and a nice Chianti.

What makes him such a great villain is that we can find a parallel between him and the more lawful Clarice Starling (Jodie Foster). As society doesn't accept Lecter for his serial killer nature, so too is Clarice not as respected by the FBI for being a woman. They both have troubled childhoods, questionable backgrounds, a need they want to be met and are willing to work together to achieve their goals. Clarice wants help with her case of tracking down the serial killer Buffalo Bill (Ted Levine), a reclusive man that prefers skinning women and believes that Lecter can provide some insight. Lecter agrees to aid her if she both reveals more about herself and helps him transfer to a prison that is much easier to escape from than his underground and isolated cell.

Lecter's presence is always an unnerving pleasure. One moment he could be chewing off someone's face, the next becoming entranced by classical music. When Clarice first meets Lecter, he is standing directly in the middle of his closed room with a firm posture and an odd smile behind the glass. His subtle movements and deviously concealing tone hold the eyes and ears, anxious to see what he'll do or say next. His relationship with Clarice during their discussions are fantastic in how Clarice attempts to maintain her allure while Lecter finds himself aroused by her curiosity and tenacity. Lecter jokes that people are going to think they're a couple by how often they speak. It's not an altogether silly notion considering how much the two identify with one another and find common ground. You know, outside of eating people.

Though not as iconic as Hopkins, Ted Levine does an admirable job as the frightful Buffalo Bill. His moments are perhaps more memorable for their simplicity as he tucks his penis when he dances in the nude or literally talks down to his victims about forcing them to use lotion. He's terrifying, but from a more base level with his creepy basement of horrors, slurring speech and disturbing indoor activities. Lecter is a far more frightening figure in how calculative and violent he can be in plain sight of law enforcement.

There are several touches from director Jonathan Demme that sell the disturbing nature well. Clarice meets Lecter and Bill the same way by descending stairs into the underground, visiting them in their very lairs of stewing thoughts. Lecter's display of a victim's brutalized body suspended in the air is echoed later in the symbol of an eagle on a cake. The editing is gripping as in the intense scene that cuts between Bill's real home and what the cops believe to be Bill's home in an investigation. The sequence in Bill's basement as he tracks Clarice with night vision goggles is beautifully punctuated with the sounds of heavy breathing, screaming victims, and barking dogs.

Silence of the Lambs is a bit of a surprising film for the acclaim it received as a dark, grotesque and uneasy thriller. It won several Academy Awards, including Best Actor (Hopkins), Best Actress (Foster), Best Director (Demme) and Best Picture. Hopkins would reprise the role of Lecter twice more for *Hannibal* (2001) and *Red Dragon* (2002), but wasn't as compelling for being as psychologically perplexing or frightening as he was in *Lambs*. It's scarier to listen to Hopkins talk about eating flesh than watching him serve up grilled brains for dinner.

A SIMPLE PLAN

DIRECTOR: Sam Raimi | SCREENWRITER: Scott B. Smith | CAST: Bill Paxton, Billy Bob Thornton, Bridget Fonda | GENRE: Drama | RUNNING TIME: 121 min | MPAA RATING: R

CLASSIFICATION: BEST

Three men stumble onto a plane crash in the snowy woods of rural Minnesota. Inside the plane are a dead pilot and roughly $4 million in cash. Faced with economic hardships, the trio decides to snatch the money before the cops discover the plane. What follows next is anything but simple in *A Simple Plan* (1998) as its crime story unfolds with greed, paranoia, and murder most Midwestern. Similar tales have been told before on screen, but not with such expert craftsmanship by director Sam Raimi.

The most prominent member of the money-stashing trio is Hank (Bill Paxton), a man who has the coziest of perfect lives. He has a stable job at a feed mill, a stellar social status, a librarian wife who loves him and their first child on the way. The money isn't so much for him as it is his lonely brother Jacob (Billy Bob Thornton), his drunk friend Lou (Brent Briscoe) and his pregnant wife Sarah (Bridget Fonda), who would prefer not to clip coupons for their groceries. Together, they decide to hide the money until the investigation of the crash has ended and then divide it among themselves. Simple enough, but not when the characters are emotional, fearful and desperate for their dreams to come true.

Hank, being the most educated of the lot, tries hopelessly to control all parties. Jacob becomes uneasy very quickly with Hank, questioning if his brother talked to the cops about the plane not long after they discover the money. Lou poses to be the most dangerous of the three as he blabbers in his drunken stupor that could let anything slip out around cops. As time passes, the money becomes an agonizing strain as the collective wait to either spend the money or spend time behind bars. This leads the characters making many wrong decisions that would seem outside of their nature, as when Sarah starts making logical decisions about returning some of the money, so it looks as though nobody took all of it. And, of course, things will get bloody when millions of dollars are involved.

Raimi does an astounding job at placing the audience within the setting and the situation. He firmly establishes the Midwest flavor of smoky bars, snowy woodlands and the chilling isolation of cold rural nights. We don't watch the plight of these men from afar, but get up close and personal with their mindset. As their secret crimes begin to mount, so does their uneasiness for the consequences of actions they wouldn't usually have taken if money wasn't on the line.

This is the type of story that is perfect for the right cast, and there is a lot of fantastic talent on screen. Bill Paxton does a great job as an everyman who seems sure of himself until something goes awry and the frustration builds on his face. Thornton is in his element as a wildcard for a crime who is just a little too pensive to trust fully. He's played this type of character before, but he eases into it well, as does the rest of the cast that never attempts to chew the scenery. They don't need to when their performances capture the immediate emotional triggers of such a tense situation.

If the Coen Brothers' *Fargo* was a darkly-comedic midwestern noir, *A Simple Plan* was the real deal of drama and bloodshed in the snowy woods of Minnesota. Its story does away with a lot of the fat that a more mainstream production would have favored with trying to whip up extra plotlines or character revelations. There's a precise focus on these characters and their descent into evil as the money weighs down their morality, threatening to cave in with greed and murder. For being so expertly written with conflict and heartbreak, it's a perfect film from Sam Raimi that shouldn't be overlooked in his full resume of *Evil Dead* and *Spider-Man* movies.

SISTER ACT

DIRECTOR: Emile Ardolino | SCREENWRITER: Joseph Howard | CAST: Whoopi Goldberg, Maggie Smith, Harvey Keitel | GENRE: Comedy | RUNNING TIME: 100 min | MPAA RATING: PG

CLASSIFICATION: WEIRD

Sister Act (1992) is a comedy premise so wild and original that it's incredible it was greenlit. Whoopi Goldberg plays Reno lounge singer Deloris Wilson. She's in love with casino boss/mobster Vince LaRocca (Harvey Keitel), but makes the mistake of walking in on him as he is murdering his chauffeur. She probably wishes she walked in on him with another woman as Vince promptly orders for Deloris to be executed for witnessing his crime. To live to testify against him, Deloris goes into the witness protection program that stashes her in a San Francisco convent under the new title of Sister Mary Clarence. And the plot practically writes itself from there.

As a lounge singer, the nuns quickly gravitate towards her singing experience with great interest. All except for the mother superior, played by professional old lady Maggie Smith, who is wary of this outsider. This goes double when she finds Deloris ditches for a bar the first chance she gets. To straightener her out, Smith places her in the convent's dismal choir group. As the trailer implies, it won't be long before Deloris shakes up the stuffy nuns and teaches them how to sing their hearts out and dance their butts off. The nuns are all typical tropes of women in need of a little bounce in their step. There's the jovial fat nun, the quiet nun and the older nun with deadpan delivery. She helps all of them come out of their shells, as well as how to add rock and gospel to a traditional hymn.

In addition to some great music, there's a lot of funny lines and real chemistry between Goldberg and her co-stars. It's hilarious watching Deloris try to convince everyone besides the knowing mother superior that she is a nun and not an impostor. When the pope comes to town, the other sisters gush that this is better than ice cream and springtime. Deloris mistakenly blurts out that this is better than sex, only to quickly retract; *"No, I mean - I've heard."* Admittedly, that joke doesn't sound hilarious on paper, and that's true for most of the humorous dialogue. But Goldberg's genuine spirit and ease of character hold this ship afloat.

It's a good thing that she's strong enough to lead a movie such as this as she doesn't have much help from the director or screenwriter. Director Emile Ardolino, best known for *Dirty Dancing* (1983), was at a point in his career of directing lukewarm feel-good comedies of *Chances Are* (1989) and *Three Men and a Baby* (1990) and maintains his somewhat distant approach to the actors and comedy. Screenwriter Paul Rudnick had been writing uncredited on several 1990s comedies and wanted his name changed with *Sister Act*, as his script was retooled so much he wanted to be disassociated with the production by having his screen credit changed to Joseph Howard.

Despite the people behind the camera, the film was a surprise hit, mostly due to Goldberg carrying the picture almost entirely. The film would gross $231 million worldwide and would receive a sequel of *Sister Act 2: Back in the Habit* (1993), where Deloris would take her musical skills to a high school. The film was also turned into a Broadway musical production. It's incredible how *Sister Act* came so far with a screenwriter that didn't want the credit. Maybe it had something to do with Bette Midler being the original choice for the lead. She turned down the role because she thought her fans didn't want to see her as a nun. It's hard to say if she'd make such a script work, but Whoopi did such a fantastic job with her seductive voice and dance, wearing that habit well.

SLING BLADE

DIRECTOR: Billy Bob Thornton | SCREENWRITER: Billy Bob Thornton | CAST: Billy Bob Thornton, Dwight Yoakam, J. T. Walsh, John Ritter, Lucas Black, Natalie Canerday, Robert Duvall | GENRE: Drama | RUNNING TIME: 135 min | MPAA RATING: R

CLASSIFICATION: BEST

Billy Bob Thornton's portrayal of the mentally challenged Karl Childers is such a striking performance that the camera holds on him consistently for his opening scene. It's hard to take your eyes off such a character with his back hunched, jaw jutted, hands ringing and eyes squinting. He delivers a monologue about why he was imprisoned with a raspy southern voice that makes you hang on his every word, occasionally punctuated with a comforting *"mmm hmm."* He's too simple to be a killer and too serious to be insane. There's more to this man than his one-note face reveals, making Karl an enigma for his inner thoughts and how Thornton was able to disappear in such a role.

Karl has recently been released from prison for murder and tries to rebuild his life in his southern community. Skilled with his hands, he takes a job as a mechanic and rents a room from a local family. His best friend is Frank, a little boy with a plucky spirit, a loving mother, and an abusive step-father. Karl likes talking to Frank, but there's concern under his one-note voice. He believes a boy should have a childhood free of darker thoughts and troubling adults. Karl never gets overly emotional about it externally, but it's of great concern the way he continually speaks of what a boy should and shouldn't have to experience.

Both Karl and Frank don't understand why Frank's mother Linda (Natalie Canerday) would stay with such a horrible man as Doyle (Dwight Yoakam). When he's not lounging on the couch with a beer in hand, he's beating Linda and saying awful things to Frank. There's nothing to like about Doyle. *"I'd like to kill that son-of-a-bitch. I hate him,"* says Frank. *"You ought not talk that way. You just a boy,"* says Karl. Karl is aware that something has to be done about Doyle, but isn't smart enough to form an intricate strategy. All he knows is that a sacrifice needs to be made if anything is to change for the better.

The sweetest aspect about Karl is that he seems to be willing to learn and understand for as hard as it is for him to change. Linda's boss, Vaughn (John Ritter), confesses to Karl that he is gay. Karl initially laughs at Vaughn as he has been raised religiously not to accept homosexuals. Over time, however, he grows to see the goodness in others; *"The Bible says two men ought not lay together. But I don't reckon the Good Lord would send anybody like you to Hades."* He speaks simply and literally about his job as a repairman, boiling down complex jobs into simple fixes and talking openly with his co-worker over french fries. He relays his darker memories to Frank, realizing his childhood was messed up and that the boy shouldn't have to experience such a tough life. He doesn't understand the whole Bible, but reckons he understands a good deal of it more than most, for better or worse.

Writer/director Billy Bob Thornton has not only created an original and memorable character with Karl, but also a unique film to place him within. He finds just the right way to stage shots to focus on the simple Karl, his most memorable scene being his testimony in a dark room beside a single lit lamp. The soundtrack perfectly capitalizes on Karl's inner emotions with soft piano for Karl's talks with Frank, transient twinkles for when he's lost in thought and intense, brooding guitars when confronting his demons. There's a lot to love about the film, but it ultimately comes back to Thornton's performance for disappearing into the role of a man with a weird walk, pure speech and a mind both rattled and gentle.

SONATINE

DIRECTOR: Takeshi Kitano | SCREENWRITER: Takeshi Kitano | CAST: Beat Takeshi, Aya Kokumai, Tetsu Watanabe | GENRE: Drama | RUNNING TIME: 94 min | MPAA RATING: R

CLASSIFICATION: BEST

Sonatine (1993) is an unconventional yakuza film in that its tone is that of boredom. It entertains the idea that not all mobsters are as charismatic or gritty as the movies portray them. Perhaps they're just simple people who sometimes shoot each other over turf wars, approaching their jobs with the same weariness of a desk clerk. When violence does break out in this Japanese gang, it's met more with a sigh than a scream.

Takeshi "Beat" Kitano sells this somberness with his stellar direction, on-point writing, and understated performance. I could never take my eyes off him as yakuza enforcer Murakawa, the way he approaches every situation with a peculiar passivity. Nothing astounds this man in his line of work, even when being ambushed at a bar with guns blazing. People die on both sides, and that's just part of the game, he most likely reasons. Death has become so common to him that even drowning one of his enemies holds no significant satisfaction. He's only slightly interested in seeing exactly how long it takes for his victim to die when being forced underwater, more out of dull curiosity than disturbed passion.

The only moments where Murakawa seems to enjoy himself comes in small doses when his men establish a headquarters at a beach house after their last space was bombed during a mission of allegiance. With nothing much to do near the beach, Murakawa entertains himself and his men with goofy pranks and childish games. He delights more in watching his associates fall into holes in the sand than shooting his enemies. When assembling paper dolls to use in mini-wrestling matches, he is smiling and laughing. When he lays waste to an entire room of mobsters with an automatic weapon, he is stone-faced and not the least bit aroused or excited.

Later in the picture, Murakawa rescues the beautiful Miyuki from being raped. Despite Miyuki being genuinely attracted to the harsh lifestyle of gangsters, Murakawa is unphased by her interest in him and no passion is restored to his life through meeting her. The two are caught in a rainstorm, and Miyuki removes her wet shirt to reveal her bare breasts. Murakawa smiles merely about how liberating it is not to wear clothing. Nothing more comes from their relationship besides trading smiles over beer and games on the beach. Even when Murakawa lets Miyuki try firing his automatic rifle, he is utterly unamused by the sight of a beautiful woman firing a gun.

Kitano's script is devoid of witty dialogue and profound character passages, favoring a more believable plot of gangsters grown weary. Very little of the exchanges between the gangsters is that of who to trust or who to shoot next. Most of their time is spent staring off into space amid drinks and cigarettes, desperately trying to have fun. They entertain a game of Russian Roulette where Murakawa isn't the least bit tense, either out of his tiredness for violence or knowing that he secretly didn't load any bullets. When night falls, the yakuza either share drinks while they dance or have a game of war with fireworks. These moments are serene and sweet, a stark contrast to the sporadic graphic violence that occurs quickly, bloodily and of a casual nature.

Sonatine was a failure in Japan, and the studio was reluctant to pursue an international release as they believed it to be too Japanese for international audiences. But when screened at film festivals, the film's popularity grew, and Kitano became an iconic figure of Japanese cinema. The film received numerous awards, including the Japanese Academy Award for Music thanks to composer Joe Hisaishi, best known for his scores on such animated pictures as *My Neighbor Totoro* and *Spirited Away*.

The title of *Sonatine* refers to the musical term sonatina, meaning a little sonata. Kitano chose this title as he recalls after learning piano sonatinas is when the learner must decide what style of piano they wish to play. This applies to Murakawa as a yakuza that has mastered the art of torture, fistfights and gunning down uncooperative people. He doesn't want to go anywhere specific with his life at this point, his dreams now that of his death. There is no fear of the end, however, as he waits for it with a cigarette in hand and no expression on his face. Kitano says far more about his character and the nihilistic nature of violence by just saying nothing, leaving the audience to ponder what is going through that tired head of his before a bullet reaches it first.

SOUTH PARK: BIGGER, LONGER AND UNCUT

DIRECTOR: Trey Parker | SCREENWRITER: Trey Parker, Matt Stone, Pam Brady | CAST: Trey Parker, Matt Stone, Mary Kay Bergman, Isaac Hayes, George Clooney, Eric Idle, Mike Judge | GENRE: Comedy (Animated) | RUNNING TIME: 81 min | MPAA RATING: R

CLASSIFICATION: BEST

Matt Stone and Trey Parker's *South Park* animated series was noteworthy in the media for being crude, vulgar and offensive with its cheap-looking animation and profanity-laced scripts. But that's only the superficial level, as the show itself was rather blunt and smart with its scathing humor of topical subjects. *South Park: Bigger, Longer and Uncut* (1999) adhered close to the format established by Stone and Parker. They decided they wanted their movie to touch on a subject they knew they would be scrutinized themselves for: the hysteria of film influencing children. And they would do so in a picture where they would set a record for the most profanity in any animated movie, including one musical sequence where the F-word is spoken 31 times. In hindsight, MPAA president Jack Valenti regretted letting the movie skate by with an R rating.

The film follows the familiar child foursome of Stan, Kyle, Cartman and Kenny (all voiced by Parker and Stone). On a winter morning, they're ecstatic to see their favorite television program, Terrance & Phillip, adapted for the big screen. It's a Canadian movie (Canadians are portrayed with egg-shaped faces and square bodies) where the titular leads open the picture with a barrage of farts, cursing, and accusations of having sex with uncles. The kids all laugh while the adults leave in a huff (*"Well, what do you expect - they're Canadian"*). The real controversy begins when they start repeating what they've heard in the movie and attempt to light their farts on fire, an act that kills Kenny. A running joke on the TV show was that Kenny would die every episode in some grotesque manner. The movie stays true to this formula, but breaks tradition by following Kenny as he descends into hell.

South Park walks a fine line between witty satire and gleeful juvenility as it drums up the hysteria on censorship and scapegoats until a war is launched between America and Canada. Diplomacy breaks down as America literally gives Canada the finger and begins to laugh hysterically at their pronouncing of "about." Canada launches an attack on America, but does so by bombing the entire Baldwin family. Trey and Stone continue to aim for more figures throughout the carnage of paranoia, savaging any celebrity along the way that they deem ripe for the comedic onslaught. In the same scene, Brooke Shields is slapped, and Conan O'Brien commits suicide.

There's a hilarious subplot that takes place in hell where Satan and Saddam Hussein are experiencing relationship issues. Satan isn't quite feeling like the prince of darkness while Hussein continues to find sexual humor in everything, progressively taking control of Satan's manhood. Their ultimate plan is to ascend to Earth, but Satan is more concerned with his relationship as he confides his issues with Kenny. Think about this for a minute: the soul of a boy in hell is acting as a counselor for Satan's love life. It's not every animated film that presents such strange concepts.

The many memorable musical numbers were composed by long-time composer Marc Shaiman, and they're as catchy as they are foul-mouthed. The propaganda song "Blame Canada" was nominated for the Academy Award for Best Original Song. Matt and Trey were invited to the awards ceremony for this nomination and, figuring they'd lose, decided to take acid and come in dresses of previous female award nominees. Appalled that they lost to Phil Collins, the duo would later produce an episode that mocked Collins and displayed him with his Academy Award shoved up his ass. If Matt and Trey didn't take the loss lightly, they at least found the perfect avenue to vent their harsh criticisms.

Bigger, Longer & Uncut was a genius slice of satire that took sharp aim at the response they knew their vulgar humor would receive. To merely dismiss it as juvenile entertainment for all its farts and profanity would be to not only miss the point but play directly into the hands of Matt and Trey's arguments about pop culture sensationalism. That type of direction may make the movie appear unfairly bulletproof in its idea, but *South Park* never played itself fair, timid or safe. It can make a point about the first amendment while still calling Kyle's mom a bitch in Broadway fashion.

SPACE JAM

DIRECTOR: Joe Pytka | SCREENWRITER: Leo Benvenuti, Steve Rudnick, Timothy Harris, Herschel Weingrod | CAST: Michael Jordan, Billy West, Wayne Knight, Theresa Randle, Danny DeVito | GENRE: Comedy | RUNNING TIME: 88 min | MPAA RATING: PG

CLASSIFICATION: WEIRD

There is no other film I can think of from the 1990s that better encapsulates the pop culture vibe of the decade than *Space Jam* (1996). Michael Jordan appears as himself during his mid-90s sporting career when he switched from basketball to baseball and back again. NBA superstars Charles Barkley, Larry Bird, Patrick Ewing, Shawn Bradley, Larry Johnson and Muggsy Bogues all make cameos as themselves as well. The Looney Tunes appear as sly and amusing as they always were, but now with an edgier 90s kick of sports. The soundtrack was a who's who of 90s cool from the likes of Busta Rhymes, Coolio, LL Cool J and Method Man, all singing on one track no less.

It's a premise so ridiculous that even the movie's director Joe Pytka, known for directing commercials with Michael Jordan and *Looney Tunes* at the time, was amazed at how such a silly idea came to be. The classic *Looney Tunes* characters, in all their hand-drawn glory, occupy a world beneath our own, yet exist as a franchise to humans. They are visited by some strange aliens from Moron Mountain, an intergalactic amusement park with a not-so-subtle jab at Disney's Magic Mountain. The aliens, known as Nerdlucks, have been tasked with capturing the Looney Tunes and enslaving them for their evil corporate master Mr. Swackhammer (Danny DeVito). The Looney Tunes laugh at the Nerdlucks' demands as they are not much bigger than Tweety. The Tunes agree to be enslaved if the pint-sized invaders can beat them in a game of basketball.

Using some strange and unexplained magic, the Nerdlucks absorb the powers of the NBA's top players to become beefier and stronger, in addition to being better at basketball. Fearing the Looney Tunes might need some help in this game for their lives, they kidnap Michael Jordan, aptly playing himself, and beg him to both play and coach on their team. The only capable toon that specializes in basketball is Lola Bunny, a powerful romantic interest for Bugs Bunny created explicitly for this picture. Lola may be an excuse to add some sex appeal to the otherwise sexually aloof toons, but she serves a purpose of grounding both the team and Bugs' manic antics.

Not to be outdone by the cartoon characters, the live-action actors can hold their own with natural grace. Michael Jordan is perfectly cast as himself, never succumbing to the lunacy of the crazy characters surrounding him. Up until one laughably lousy moment when he embraces cartoon logic to win the big game, Jordan never ventures far out of his typical personality and for a good reason. You don't want to try to be funny around someone as silly and witty as Bugs Bunny, one who can remark to Jordan's admission of being a baseball player with *"Right, and I'm a Shakespearean actor."* Bill Murray also could've gone off the rails with his personality among toons, but sticks mostly to his guns by drawing from his public persona and his usual brand of comedic delivery. Wayne Knight, as a sports publicist, is as stumbling and babbling as he ever was, but never upstaging the masters of slapstick.

During an era when Disney was king, *Space Jam* managed not only to be divergent, but also as biting as one would expect from the Looney Tunes. There are several satirical shots at Disney, pop culture and even the actors. Daffy Duck takes a shot at *The Mighty Ducks* when deciding on a team name (*"What kind of a Mickey Mouse organization would name their team the Ducks?"*). When Bill Murray enters into the big game, Mr. Swackhammer blurts out in shock *"I didn't know Dan Aykroyd was in this picture!"* The game itself turns into a chaotic series of gags and references, as when Elmer Fudd and Yosemite Sam don *Pulp Fiction* attire to shoot guns at the Nerdlucks.

Space Jam is more admirable for its elements than a movie as a whole. The premise of Looney Tunes playing a basketball game for their lives, amid the most blatant of commercial endorsement, is absurd. But it's hard not to laugh at Bugs' classic antics, admire the spirit of the actors that poke fun at themselves or sing along to the catchiest of soundtracks. If the infectious enthusiasm of Quad City DJ doesn't pump you up to "Slam Jam," I can't help you.

SPEED

DIRECTOR: Jan de Bont | SCREENWRITER: Graham Yost | CAST: Keanu Reeves, Dennis Hopper, Sandra Bullock, Joe Morton, Alan Ruck, Jeff Daniels | GENRE: Action | RUNNING TIME: 116 min | MPAA RATING: R

CLASSIFICATION: BEST

Speed (1994) is a simple concept for an action picture that has the intensity come standard with its premise. A bomb is attached to a bus, activated once it reaches 50 miles per hour. If the bus goes under 50 mph, it will explode. This leads to the bus smashing through city streets and forced to take alternative and action-packed routes to keep the vehicle moving. All it will take is one gridlocked road to make this bus out of service forever.

Before the bus, however, we have an elevator of a high rise tower. Passengers are trapped between floors, and they'll fall to their deaths if a terrorist is not paid $3 million to prevent him from blowing up the emergency brakes keeping the elevator from falling. Keanu Reeves and Jeff Daniels are the bomb experts called in to stop the bomber played by Dennis Hopper. Hopper's character was once a cop and is smart enough to be one step ahead of the authorities. He delights so much in the failure of the police department that the money may only be a secondary goal. He'll probably use it to buy more bombs anyway. What a vicious cycle.

His elevator scheme foiled, his new target of the bus proves to be a grander plot and a better location for a thrilling action picture of bombs and hostages. The bomb-on-the-bus angle is genuinely sinister if you consider L.A. traffic and is also way too fantastical if you consider actual L.A. traffic. Reeves boards the bus to stop the bus, but a small-time crook fires off his gun and kills the driver. What was the criminal doing on the bus and why did he shoot the driver? No time to explain! The bus is going to explode, and Sandra Bullock needs to drive while Reeves checks out the bomb. And for the rest of the movie, the bus will have to maintain its high speed while speeding through the wrong lane of traffic and jumping large gaps in the road. A real bus probably wouldn't clear a 50-foot jump over a gap, but they do in an action movie too fast-paced to question such logic.

This is a kitchen sink film that tosses as much as it can at the screen, staying true to its title by never slowing down or dialing back on ideas. Reeves tries everything in his power to save the hostages, including getting under the bus to disarm the bomb and calling in a speeding flatbed to catch up for passengers to disembark. Jeff Daniels frantically tries to uncover the identity of the terrorists while Dennis Hopper cackles over the phone to give hints as he has too much fun watching the news footage.

For an action film involving a bus, it's incredibly fun, even if it looks hilarious when the bus catapults into the air, as seen in the movie and on the poster. The bus edges around traffic, narrowly avoiding other cars and people. The vehicle at one point smashes into a baby carriage, and our hearts stop for a minute before we realize it was a homeless person's carriage of cans. Of course, the bus will finally stop, and it will explode...when it collides with a plane! And just when you think the movie is over, there's ANOTHER chase on a subway train where Reeves and Hopper will battle on top of one of the train cars.

Speed is an action film that makes the smart call of being so fast, so explosive and so over-the-top that it transcends its simple premise for tension and thrills. The stunts are fantastic, the energy is high, and the casting is exceptional with Reeves maintaining focus, Bullock running high on desperation to survive and Hopper having too much fun as the villain. It is so much more than just the movie with an exploding bus. It's also the movie with an elevator hostage situation and a subway fight with a decapitation, sandwiched in between the exploding bus.

SPICE WORLD

DIRECTOR: Bob Spiers | SCREENWRITER: Kim Fuller, Jamie Curtis | CAST: Victoria Adams, Emma Bunton, Melanie Chisholm, Geri Halliwell, Melanie Brown, Richard E. Grant, Alan Cumming, George Wendt, Claire Rushbrook, Mark McKinney, Roger Moore | GENRE: Comedy | RUNNING TIME: 93 min | MPAA RATING: PG-13

CLASSIFICATION: WEIRD

If *A Hard Day's Night* proved that The Beatles had the skills to be just as strong as movie stars as they were as rock stars, *Spice World* (1998) is proof that the 1990s pop band of the Spice Girls was a flash in the pan. But, wow, was it fun watching these girls burn to a crisp in their first and only movie.

To be fair, I was never a fan of the Spice Girls past the passing singing of "Wannabe" on the radio. I couldn't differentiate or understand the different personalities of Posh Spice, Scary Spice, Baby Spice, Sporty Spice or Ginger Spice. To be fair, I couldn't tell members apart of any ensemble bands at the time, as I easily mixed up the members of Backstreet Boys with N'Sync. The Spice Girls, despite being armed with this movie deal, still blended with those other pop groups that were more notable for their names and clothing than their musical talents. They're best distinguished by their material attributes, but these girls can't be that distinct when one of them is deciding on an outfit with her choices being the little Gucci dress, the little Gucci dress OR the little Gucci dress.

The movie's plot is nothing all that interesting, focusing on a day in the life of the Spice Girls. They sing, perform and chill out. When not on stage, they chat about how terrible it is to be famous. Uh huh. Making this struggle real are the sinister forces of a trashy newspaper editor (Barry Humphries), a hounding paparazzi figure (Richard O'Brien) and their uptight managers trying to push back screenwriters that want to write a movie about the Spice Girls. Who would want to watch a film like that?

The girls spend most of their time on a double-decker bus that has been reformatted to apparently look like the TARDIS on the inside with every home comfort except a bathroom. They will later have to pee in the woods. All the singing and dancing for the cameras is putting a damper on their desire to spend time with their pregnant friend Nicola (Naoko Mori), who will predictably have to be rushed to the hospital at the most inopportune time. Enough is enough, and they eventually storm out of talks for record deals so they can have some fun and get into trouble before their big concert. These antics include the aforementioned birth scene, making a photojournalist reform his ways and trying to convince a policeman not to arrest them.

Unlike *A Hard Day's Night* which found fun stuff to do with the talented Beatles, *Spice World* tries to find time-filler scenes for the girls in between singing, surprisingly more faithful to The Beatles cartoon show. The girls at one point have to race across London, making a ridiculous jump with their bus over the River Thames. There's a bomb on the bus which seems to be brought up once for a scare and then forgotten about until the very end of the movie. Cameos featured include Roger Moore as an eccentric record executive and Meat Loaf as the driver. And just when it seems the movie has used up all its lame tricks, the fourth-wall is broken at the end of the film where the Spice Girls attempt to speak directly to the audience. One of them points out *"those two in the back row snogging."* It's strange to think who would be making out during such a bizarre movie.

The only worth in going back to watch Spice World was for it being a snapshot of late-90s pop, where all you needed to be a music sensation was the right face, the right clothes and a lot of theatrics to cover up your singing. In that respect, I think I get the appeal of the Spice Girls. If they could become a pop sensation and garner their own movie, you too could spice up your life as well.

STAR TREK VI: THE UNDISCOVERED COUNTRY

DIRECTOR: Nicholas Meyer | SCREENWRITER: Nicholas Meyer, Denny Martin Flinn | CAST: William Shatner, Leonard Nimoy, DeForest Kelley, James Doohan, Walter Koenig, George Takei, Nichelle Nichols, Kim Cattrall, David Warner, Christopher Plummer | GENRE: Science Fiction | RUNNING TIME: 110 min | MPAA RATING: PG

CLASSIFICATION: BEST

Star Trek was always at its best when the stories were political parables. For this reason, *The Undiscovered Country* (1991) is one of the finest of *Star Trek* movies for playing on the end of the Cold War. Nicholas Meyer (*Star Trek II: The Wrath of Kahn*) returns to direct and co-write an engaging story based on Leonard Nimoy's suggestion of using the Berlin Wall as a reflective element of the times. It's a great recovery from the series' primary stumble of *Star Trek V: The Final Frontier* and a far better script than the original idea of shooting a prequel movie where Kirk met Spock. The original cast deserved one more great *Trek* picture and Meyer sends them off on a high note before being replaced by *Star Trek: The Next Generation*.

The homeworld of the Klingon Empire is dying after the loss of their moon, leading the warring race to enter peace talks with their rivals of Starfleet. Setting aside the long-standing feud, Starfleet sends the Enterprise-A to escort Klingon Chancellor Gorkon (David Warner) to Earth for negotiations. But Captain Kirk (William Shatner) takes issue with obliging the Klingons. His son was previously murdered by them about three movies ago. With a little coaching from the emotion-controlling Vulcan friend Spock (Leonard Nimoy), Kirk swallows his pride and escorts the Klingon Chancellor Gorkon and his right-hand man Chang (Christopher Plummer) to Earth with the most awkward of dinners en route. The dinner seems to be going well as Gorkon quotes Hamlet on the future of his race, but things quickly turn awkward when the Klingons call the humans racist, and Kirk begins quoting Hitler. Not exactly the greatest start to a long relationship.

And that relationship gets worse when a deliberate sabotage turns relations sour as the Klingons are attacked by both the Starship Enterprise and two mysterious figures in Starfleet Federation uniforms. Kirk and McCoy (DeForest Kelley) attempt to save the life of the injured chancellor, but fail and are placed under arrest by the

Klingon Empire. While the two of them are sentenced to life imprisonment on an ice asteroid, Spock takes control of the Enterprise to investigate the incident in hopes of unraveling the conspirator behind this act of manipulating galactic politics.

The film does feature some great action sequences, from exciting starship combat to zero-gravity phaser battles, but it's the script by Nicholas Meyer and Denny Martin Finn that makes *The Undiscovered Country* so strong. In classic Trek fashion, characters speak mostly in references to the past. Speaking in such dialogue makes this a future that's very much aware of history and culture that is more familiar than alien. The central plot is an intriguing whodunit of which crew member betrayed Starfleet and who is working with who to make sure peace talks do not go according to plan. This type of storytelling makes the movie more relatable so that the viewer doesn't have to be aware of the galactic politics of Klingons, Romulans and Federation officers; they just need to figure out who made a bloody footprint at the scene of the crime.

The familiar cast is present once more, but with some interesting changes. Sulu (George Takei) has graduated off the Enterprise and has become the captain of his own starship that teams up with the Enterprise to take down the attacking Klingon warships. In his place as the new helmsman is Valeris (Kim Cattrall), a young and intelligent Vulcan protégé of Spock. Kirk's dilemma of coming to terms with the Klingons murdering his son and impending doom of the Klingon Empire make him a more conflicted captain than before. Spock makes for a pretty good detective as well, though it's probably not as tough to extract information with the old Vulcan mind-melding technique.

The Undiscovered Country was the last *Star Trek* movie to feature the entire original cast, only a few sticking around for guest appearances in the following movie *Star Trek: Generations*. The very title of the picture refers to death in Shakespeare, but the movie appears to suggest this phrase relates to the future. In this case, it's a little of both. The original *Star Trek* crew would never reassemble on the big screen again, but the legacy of *Trek* would continue onward for years to come.

STAR TREK: FIRST CONTACT

DIRECTOR: Jonathan Frakes | SCREENWRITER: Ronald D. Moore, Brannon Braga | CAST: Patrick Stewart, Jonathan Frakes, Brent Spiner, LeVar Burton, Michael Dorn, Gates McFadden, Marina Sirtis, Alfre Woodard, James Cromwell, Alice Krige | GENRE: Science Fiction | RUNNING TIME: 111 min | MPAA RATING: PG-13

CLASSIFICATION: BEST

With the shackles of crafting a torch-passing *Trek* movie finally broken, screenwriters Ronald D. Moore and Brannon Braga were able to create a real *Star Trek: The Next Generation* movie with *First Contact* (1996). They lift the most popular of villains of the TV series, The Borg, a collective of cyborgs that absorb any organic and inorganic material into their hive-mind colony, bent on overtaking all living creatures. In one of the most shocking moments of the show, Captain Picard (Patrick Stewart) was once transformed into a member of the Borg and later saved by his crew. But those terrible memories of having his body violated by machines have come back to haunt him when the Borg attack Starfleet once more.

This time the Borg have a more cunning plan. They have traveled back in time to the moment when Earth finally makes the first contact with the Vulcans, opening up the door for Starfleet to send humans across galaxies. Their goal is to prevent the first contact and rewrite history by turning all humans into members of the Borg. The crew of the Enterprise have fortunately followed the Borg through time and are the only ones who can save history.

Two missions are mounted to preserve the future. One involves an away team, sent to Earth to ensure that the first use of a warp drive occurs on schedule so that the Vulcans can discover humanity. Commander Riker (Jonathan Frakes) is ecstatic to meet the man who invented warp drive, but is slightly underwhelmed to find out that the legendary Zefram Cochrane (James Cromwell) was a drunk with motion sickness.

While they try to aid Cochrane in the experiment he is reluctant to pursue, Picard stays on the Enterprise to quell the infesting Borg. The collective of cybernetic zombies quickly begin to take control of the ship, capturing deck after deck as they forcibly absorb more crew members into their order. Though acting mostly as one, this particular group is led by a Borg Queen (Alice Krige), who sexually convinces Data to shirk his humanity for a more comfortable life among cyborgs.

 The original script called for Picard to be on the away team, but Patrick Stewart argued against this as he knew his character had a bigger bone to pick with the Borg. This leads to some rather powerful scenes as the usually collected Picard begins to boom with frustration, anxiety, and bloodlust. The only one who can ground him is the addition of the 21st century Lily Sloane (Alfre Woodard) who may not understand 24th-century strategy, but is smart enough to recognize a Captain Ahab when she spots one as consumed for revenge as Picard.

 There's a solid mix of tones with the two missions. The away mission is a fairly light race for space travel with the fearful Cochrane enlightening the Enterprise crew with his love of Steppenwolf's "Magic Carpet Ride." Cromwell has some great dialogue as he slowly begins to accept his role as a trailblazer when he can hardly stand to look at the path. On the other end of the spectrum, the mission of defending the ship is a rip-roaring action picture with horror elements. The Borg have a terrifying presence as they adapt to weapons and increase their numbers with each human injected with robotic parts. Crew members will crawl through air ducts to escape the Borg, as the enemy pounds on doors and slowly stalks their prey.

 Jonathan Frakes stepped up as the director of this picture and proved that he knew how to direct this great cast with more urgency and energy than mild tension amid technobabble. It is the most exciting of *The Next Generation* pictures for giving the crew members more to do than push buttons on a deck that shakes and sparks. Here they are running and gunning in between questioning history, artificial intelligence, and revenge, landing performances as varied as their phaser frequencies. So much of this picture is on point that I didn't even mind the odd note of ending with Cochrane blasting "Oobie Doobie" on a jukebox for Vulcans.

STAR TREK: GENERATIONS

DIRECTOR: David Carson | SCREENWRITER: Ronald D. Moore, Brannon Braga | CAST: Patrick Stewart, William Shatner, Malcolm McDowell, Jonathan Frakes, Brent Spiner, Whoopi Goldberg | GENRE: Science Fiction | RUNNING TIME: 118 min | MPAA RATING: PG

CLASSIFICATION: WEIRD

Generations (1994) plays more like a *Star Trek* crossover special than a theatrical passing of the baton. The original cast from the past six *Star Trek* movies were ready to move on, and the cast of TV's *Star Trek: The Next Generation* had recently wrapped production on their show. It was time for the old guard to be replaced by the new team that had been given seven seasons of prep on television. They were indeed ready for the big screen, but this movie may not have been prepared for them.

Not all of the old crew is present here as only William Shatner, James Doohan and Walter Koenig reprise the roles of Captain Kirk, Scotty, and Chekov. Leonard Nimoy and DeForest Kelley were asked to return as Spock and Bones, but turned down the offer, and it's easy to see why with such reduced roles. Kirk is on the maiden voyage of the latest Enterprise, but encounters an alien energy wave known as the Nexus that plucks him out of time. Thus ends the old generation.

Fast forward to the future with the new Starship Enterprise D, helmed by Captain Jean-Luc Picard (Patrick Stewart). More dignified and steadfast in his leadership, he finds himself crippled emotionally when he receives word of his family members dying in a fire. But the tears will have to wait as he faces off against the villainous Soran (Malcolm McDowell), a survivor of the Nexus that desperately wants to go back. Since spaceships cannot enter this thin energy wave without being obliterated, Soran's evil scheme is to blow up a star to direct the path of the Nexus towards a planet. On this planet, he plans to stand on a cliff and jump into the Nexus, just as the planet is obliterated.

What's so special about the Nexus is that it's the ultimate MacGuffin. Inside this mysterious ribbon exists a universe where time has no meaning, and anything is possible. Through its flexible logic, you can also leave the Nexus at any time and arrive at any point in your own universe. The script forgets to put limits on the Nexus, preventing the nerdier audience from questioning why Picard wouldn't embrace the Nexus and then travel back to the time before Soran had a chance to plan his attack. Of course, Picard decides to come back just a few minutes before the Nexus swallowed him so he can fight with Soran on a cliff.

The rest of the Enterprise D crew don't have much to do, but still have their moments. The android Data (Brent Spiner) places a chip for emotions in his brain, allowing him to emote in some over-the-top line readings, including the movie's punctuating expletive. Commander William Riker (Jonathan Frakes) is given control of the Enterprise during a ship-to-ship battle with the Klingons, though he ultimately crashes what's left of it. The telepath/bartender Guinan (Whoopi Goldberg) seems to have the most knowledge of the Nexus, but doesn't play much of a role in this plot besides stating exposition.

The movie works best when it focuses more on the relationships between the characters and less on the clunky plot. There's a tender scene when Picard is inside the Nexus and is treated to a vision of a Christmas with the wife and children he never had. Slowly, Picard comes to realize that this life isn't real and learns to let go. On paper, this scene is corny, especially when factoring in the poor logic of the Nexus that is divulged by Gainan on a carousel. But the lighting of the Christmas-festooned home, the somberly sweet score by Dennis McCarthy and the committed acting of Patrick Stewart sold the emotion of what appeared to be an excuse for some Dickens in *Trek*.

What *Generations* ultimately leads up to is the imagery of seeing Captain Kirk and Captain Picard meet each other while in the Nexus, a prospect that was probably enough for most Trekkies to salivate over. I'm not sure how many fans imagined these two would be sharing the screen while making eggs or riding on horses in a *Star Trek* movie. A most illogical use of these two actors that are far too likable for such a silly story.

STAR TREK: INSURRECTION

DIRECTOR: Jonathan Frakes | SCREENWRITER: Michael Piller | CAST: Patrick Stewart, Jonathan Frakes, Brent Spiner, LeVar Burton, Michael Dorn, Gates McFadden, Marina Sirtis, F. Murray Abraham | GENRE: Science Fiction | RUNNING TIME: 103 min | MPAA RATING: PG

CLASSIFICATION: WORST

Insurrection (1998) plays like a familiar two-parter script of the *Star Trek: The Next Generation* series in that it's light in tone, more straightforward in action and takes place on a planet that bears a striking resemblance to California. All that's lacking is a competent script and sufficient allegory to pull it past its cheapness. But when that fails, the audience is left with an odd *Star Trek* movie where Patrick Stewart dances to samba and sings Gilbert & Sullivan songs.

The crew of the Enterprise is put in a tight spot when they decide to resolve a hostage situation with their old android crew member Data (Brent Spiner), who has malfunctioned during a secret mission involving the Ba'ku (who essentially appear as regular humans with goofy costumes). The Starfleet Federation has advised against the involvement of the Enterprise, but Captain Picard (Patrick Stewart) has to help his android pal. When they become involved, the Enterprise discovers a secret operation by the Federation to move the Ba'ku off their planet so that they may harvest a youth-regenerating formula. Picard, knowing this action to be immoral, plans to go to war against Federation Admiral Dougherty and his conspiring partners of Ba'ku's rival species, the Son'a, led by a stretchy-faced F. Murray Abraham.

Aside from the Federation breaking their Prime Directive and colluding with a blood feud, Dougherty's secret operation is more morally perplexing than it is evil. The population of the Ba'ku is about 600 occupying the planet, and the remaining dying Son'a want to take back control of this world. The Son'a have apparently banished centuries ago because they embraced technology and wanted to take power. Were the Ba'ku in the right for keeping their planet clean of tech or were the Son'a delivered a death sentence for their desire to grow and learn? And what of the billions of people Dougherty planned to save with this planet's youth radiation? What happened to Spock's dying words of the needs of the many outweigh the needs of the few?

These are moral questions that are batted around, but never seriously considered as the Son'a merely want revenge and seek to poison the planet. Tampering with the Ba'ku is against the Prime Directive, and Picard aims to abide by these rules established by Starfleet, even though the Prime Directive was more or less a guideline in early *Star Trek*. The movie finds a clunky means of concluding that Picard is in the right and that the secret Federation operation is evil.

With such a flimsy premise, the movie attempts to find funny and action-oriented things for the crew to do. Picard falls in love with one of the Ba'ku women, but only as much as he'd fancy any other alien lady he has run across in the past. Some of the youthful gas from the planet begins to seep into the Enterprise, and it isn't long before Riker and Troi are going at it like they're in their twenties and Picard starts to dance like a fool. The Enterprise races to come within contact range of the Federation to inform them of this secret and illegal operation, leading to a ship-to-ship chase of firing lasers and torpedoes. Picard helps the people of Ba'ku flee from capturing robots, but the most exciting part of this sequence is when Worf fires a bazooka that shoots purple energy. Data was a heavy robotic character in the previous *Star Trek* movie, but he now appears to double as a floatation device, as he states when he falls in the water, and some part of his lower torso can be heard inflating.

This isn't so much a *Star Trek* movie as it is a silly homage to the TV series. The production values are surprisingly cheap, including the starship sequences which were entirely rendered with computer animation for the first time in a *Trek* movie (and it shows). The attempts at finding humor in the more quieter moments of the film come off as awkward and even more bizarre in the louder moments when Picard and Worf must distract a renegade Data by lulling him into singing musicals. I never knew that Enterprise transport ships came standard with karaoke. This is not *Star Trek* at its finest, cheaply going where it has already been before.

STAR WARS: EPISODE I - THE PHANTOM MENACE

DIRECTOR: George Lucas | SCREENWRITER: George Lucas | CAST: Liam Neeson, Ewan McGregor, Natalie Portman, Jake Lloyd, Ian McDiarmid, Anthony Daniels, Kenny Baker, Pernilla August, Frank Oz | GENRE: Science Fiction | RUNNING TIME: 133 min | MPAA RATING: PG

CLASSIFICATION: WORST

The Phantom Menace (1999) was almost doomed to disappoint from the level of hype surrounding its release. It was the first new *Star Wars* movie in sixteen years, and everyone wanted to see it. When the first trailer debuted six months before the movie would premiere, fans were so thrilled to see it that they would often pay for a film they didn't want to see just to see the trailer in the theater once more. All this excitement was in service of a movie that would turn out to be the most underwhelming of the *Star Wars* series.

The story was an idea of George Lucas that had apparently been rattling around in his brain for many years. He opted to hold off on the production of a prequel trilogy until special effects technology could match his vision. By the late 1990s, the technology had improved to allow Lucas to craft visually believable characters of robots and aliens, rendered entirely through computer animation. The visual effects all look stunning in this picture with a high amount of detail for the time, but it's clear that Lucas put more effort into the movie's look than its substance.

Set several decades before the events of the first Star Wars movie, The Phantom Menace finds a young Obi-Wan Kenobi (Ewan McGregor) acting as an apprentice of Jedi Knight Qui-Gon Jinn (Liam Neeson). Their services are required to settle a trade dispute between the planet of Naboo and the Confederate armada. It isn't too long before they're caught up in a battle to rescue Queen Amadala (Natalie Portman) from being captured by an army of robot soldiers. Along the way, they pick up the annoying slapstick sidekick of Jar Jar Binks, a computer-animated character. He's a weak comic relief character with his odd speech that reeks of black stereotypes, made all the more depressing that Lucas stated during production that this role was the key to making the movie work.

A pitstop is made on Tatooine where the Jedi discover a young Anakin Skywalker (Jake Lloyd), the boy who would grow up to become the evil Darth Vader. But before he was building Death Stars to blow up planets, he was making a pod-racer to race in competitions for money. A slave of junk dealers, Anakin is aided by Qui-Gon to bargain his way out of slavery by winning a race. Anakin is of particular interest to Qui-Gon as he believes this young boy to be the chosen one who will bring balance to the force. We know Anakin will eventually become a villain, as does a council of Jedis that see something dangerous in him, but Qui-Gon and Obi-Wan believe the opposite.

But after an exciting pod race sequence, Anakin's story is tossed aside so that our characters can resolve the issue of Naboo's war over trade disputes. Obi-Wan and Qui-Gon do battle with the horned Darth Maul, a face-painted Sith lord with a double-sided lightsaber. Padame leads a group of blaster-wielding soldiers into her palace to retake her throne. Anakin unwittingly pilots a starship to destroy the Trade Federation Fleet, which can't be too hard to defeat given that a child could do it. Jar Jar Binks leads his race of Gungans in a land battle with Trade Federation robots, somehow managing to beat a few with his absent-minded luck.

While all this action is very epic with some fantastic special effects, they're all in the service of plots and characters without much investment. We already know what will happen to Anakin and Obi-Wan, but the movie doesn't display anything surprising about these characters, aside from Anakin being the creator of the droid C3PO. There are new elements added to the *Star Wars* mythos, but aspects that should probably have remained unexplored. I could do without knowing about how the Force power in a Jedi is measured in "midichlorian" counts. There's nothing all that interesting about the Trade Federation either, organized by rejected animatronics of *Teenage Mutant Ninja Turtles* and enforced by inept robots so flimsy and dumb they make Stormtroopers appear as crack shot marines.

George Lucas was technically right in how Jar Jar was the key to this film, as the failing of making a likable CGI character became the mediocre centerpiece in a profoundly flawed production. All the technology in the world can't save a script that is crap. Or, as Jar Jar would call it, *"icky icky goo."*

STARSHIP TROOPERS

DIRECTOR: Paul Verhoeven | SCREENWRITER: Edward Neumeier | CAST: Casper Van Dien, Dina Meyer, Denise Richards, Jake Busey, Neil Patrick Harris, Patrick Muldoon, Clancy Brown, Michael Ironside | GENRE: Science Fiction | RUNNING TIME: 129 min | MPAA RATING: R

CLASSIFICATION: WEIRD

While Paul Verhoeven started working on a movie entitled Bug Hunt at Outpost Nine, there were a few similarities between the script and the novel *Starship Troopers* by Robert A. Heinlein. Preparations were made to buy the license of the book, but Verhoeven was not interested in reshaping his movie to reflect Heinlein's story. Verhoeven only made it two chapters into the book before he dropped it for being too boring, depressing and right-wing. Instead of adhering to the book's message and tone, Verhoeven only retroactively added elements of the book in name only and favored more of a fascist parody for right-wing science fiction military drama.

Starship Troopers (1997) makes itself known as a smartly savage satire right from its opening scene, depicting an ad for joining the space marine corps. There is the distinct aroma of propaganda as soldiers let the kids play with their weapons and pass out bullets as take-home presents. The footage then shifts to the news of a murderer being sentenced to the death penalty, his execution to be screened live on television at 6 pm. Cut to newsreel footage featuring kids stomping on bugs, the announcer urging everyone to *"do their part"* in the war effort. Verhoeven does a marvelous job at conceiving a world that may be prepared to handle the threat of these human-killing bug aliens, but can't do much else.

In this goofy and gory conflict, the movie follows a collective of young people that serve different areas of the space military forces. Johnny Rico (Casper Van Diem) is the brave young soldier who isn't much interested in questioning why this society requires military service to earn citizenship. There are only two things on his mind: sex and revenge on the bugs that killed his family. He's attracted to the lovely Carmen (Denise Richards), but an urgent need for young military leadership separates them in the war on alien bugs. Rico is stationed in infantry while Carmen becomes a starship pilot. They both meet new people they partner up within their unit; Rico falls for the playful Dizzy (Dina Meyer), and Rico's rival Zander (Patrick

Muldoon) works alongside Carmen. In a more poignant military drama, Rico would end up with Dizzy and Carmen would end up with Zander. But this movie is entirely a subversion and does away with such expectations. Violently.

Verhoeven loads up the picture with as many of his iconic campy elements as he does state-of-the-art special effects. A group shower with the troops is a shameless scene for nudity. The cast only agreed to this scene if Verhoeven would film it as naked as the rest of his actors, which he had no problem accepting. The transitions of Earth commercials and propaganda are wonderfully absurd in how human death is treated somber whereas alien deaths are treated as comical reels. And there is loads of blood and gore in this war where humans are chopped, slashed, decapitated, incinerated and have their brains sucked out through a straw by the nasty bugs. Even the starship crews are not immune from gruesome ends; a malfunctioning door crushes one unlucky captain.

It's important to note that this sci-fi epic is a satire. For being portrayed so thoroughly as a fascist society of Nazi leanings, the film has come under fire for celebrating fascism more than mocking it. It's an understandable concern; the movie is so well made, features impressive special effects (which won an Academy Award), boasts an energetic cast and blazes with intense enough action that it's easy to lose sight of the parody at play. If you for some reason find yourself viewing the film more as a pro-military production, consider Verhoeven's words about the world he created: *"Everyone is beautiful, everything is shiny, everything has big guns and fancy ships, but it's only good for killing fucking bugs!"*

STAY TUNED

DIRECTOR: Peter Hyams, Chuck Jones | SCREENWRITER: Jim Jennewain, Tom S. Parker | CAST: John Ritter, Pam Dawber, Jeffrey Jones, Eugene Levy | GENRE: Comedy | RUNNING TIME: 88 min | MPAA RATING: PG-13

CLASSIFICATION: WEIRD

Television isn't just bad for your eyes in *Stay Tuned* (1992), but will send you to hell. That's what happens when you buy a satellite dish from the devil Mr. Spike (Jeffrey Jones) who sells the unwitting couch potato of Roy Knable (John Ritter) on a satellite package offering the most immersive of experiences. While fighting with his wife Helen (Pam Dawber), the two of them are zapped by the satellite and transported inside hell's television program system, Hell Vision. If they can survive for 24 hours in the various TV worlds that are all designed to kill them, they can return home.

While Roy and Helen try to solve their marital issues while not being damned for eternity, there is a power struggle going on in hell as well. Spike is in control of the television-trapping scheme, armed with his soul-zapping remote control that he keeps up his sleeve with a handy holding device to zip out when needed. There's a young upstart of an executive Pierce (Erik King) vying for the position, but Spike finds the shrimpy Crowley (Eugene Levy) more fun to send into the programs to fight for his life. You don't have to be a genius to see that good things are in store for Pierce's future, especially when Spike becomes too preoccupied with entering the television programs to kill the Knables personally.

The movie has a lot of fun with dark parodies of television programs that come in the form of new worlds to venture through with great gags. The most meta of these involves Ritter ending up on the set of his old sitcom, *Three's Company*, resulting in him screaming in terror before exiting the show. Sometimes the rules of the programs become a little convoluted, as with an animated world where Roy and Helen are transformed into cartoon mice pursued by a cat that wants to eat them. If cartoon characters can do anything and never truly die, wouldn't it make sense to ride out the 24 hours in this world where it's easiest to defend yourself? Still, it's a fun sequence and features a brief cameo by legendary animator Chuck Jones, who also directed the animation for this film.

Much like *The Naked Gun* and *Hot Shots* movies, this is a film that packs in so many hilarious parodies they trump the lukewarm plots of Roy and Helen patching their marriage, their children trying to free them, Spike trying to kill them and Crowley trying to help them. The jokes are not quite as biting as they should be, however, and most of them come packaged as MAD Magazine bits with a darkly violent edge. Some of them include Three Men and Rosemary's Baby, Autopsies of the Rich and Famous, Saturday Nite Dead and Driving Over Miss Daisy. They're straightforward bits, but presented so quickly that we never linger on them long enough to become annoyed with the joke. This creates a zippy energy where Ritter can quickly transition from being a Captain of the Starship Enterprise on *Star Trek* ("Holy Shatner!") to a colorfully dressed Prince in a music video.

Stay Tuned was such a chaotically wild film with its satire that it never found a proper audience. It was too weird for most adults and way too violent for kids, leading to a dismal box office and mixed reviews from critics that did not receive preview screenings. But for being a mixtape of dark parodies, it's skillfully directed with cleverness in the concept and passion in the production. And there's just something so amusing about a big-budget mockery of famous television series and movies, with the glee to make a quick joke of an exercise program called The Exorcist; *"Cool down. Shake it out. O.K., now vomit."*

STOP! OR MY MOM WILL SHOOT

DIRECTOR: Roger Spottiswoode | SCREENWRITER: Blake Snyder, William Osborne, William Davies | CAST: Sylvester Stallone, Estelle Getty, JoBeth Williams, Roger Rees | GENRE: Comedy | RUNNING TIME: 87 min | MPAA RATING: PG-13

CLASSIFICATION: WORST

When Sylvester Stallone isn't tracking down criminals as typical tough cop Joe in *Stop! Or My Mom Will Shoot* (1992), he spends most of his time whining at his elderly mother played by Estelle Getty. *"Mom, what're you doing here?" "Mom, I don't like eggs." "Mommy, I don't want to be changed!"* That last line was from a dream sequence in which Stallone appears dressed in a diaper. Is it any surprise that Stallone considers this the worst movie he has ever starred in?

I can't imagine Estelle Getty being all that pleased with the picture either. She only agreed to be in the movie if there were no guns, a promise made by producers that lied to get her to sign on. She must have been peeved to star in a movie where the plot of illegal gun dealing involves her buying a gun, aiming a gun and washing a gun while she sings *"This is the way we wash our gun."*

It was probably more insulting that Getty, a usually spry and witty woman on TV's *The Golden Girls*, was reduced to the role of the inept mother Tutti. She's an entirely oblivious character that at least a modicum of Stallone's whining holds merit. This is a woman who is portrayed as using detergent to wash her son's firearm and then decides to replace it by buying a gun off the street. She believes her son will be happy that she bought him a brand new gun, completely ignorant of gun laws and obvious street criminals.

Tutti, in her oblivious nature, while buying a gun, stumbles onto a murder. The murder and the gun become valuable clues in an insurance fraud case. As Joe works on the case, Tutti is along for the ride as the nosey and irritating mother. This leads to many tired gags of Getty continually hovering, and Stallone is profusely pleading for her to stop. While Stallone tries to coax a suicidal jumper off a ledge, Getty embarrasses him from below with a megaphone. The jumper decides against ending his life after seeing how bad Stallone has it with his mother. It could be an amusing scene, but it's bereft of all comedy from the atrocious direction and the unshakable fact that the whole movie is going to play out in this watered-down sitcom manner.

It's not that Stallone isn't funny, as he proved in *Oscar* (1991). We know that Getty is amusing, having played Sophia on *The Golden Girls* for seven seasons. But neither can be funny when given such one-dimensional characters as the easily embarrassed cop and the stereotypically out-of-touch elderly mother. Was it that funny to watch Getty hold a gun towards her son and state *"Go ahead! Make your bed"* in a tasteless joking manner? One of the three writers or three producers must have found it hilarious.

Why would Stallone subject himself to such a painfully unfunny comedy? He argues that he only took this role because he had heard that Arnold Schwarzenegger was interested in the project, but Arnold was faking it to play a trick on Stallone to accept. Dirty pool, Arnold! You may have bested Stallone, but the audience still had to suffer from a script that should have died before any star was attached.

THE STRAIGHT STORY

DIRECTOR: David Lynch | SCREENWRITER: John Roach, Mary Sweeney | CAST: Richard Farnsworth, Sissy Spacek, Harry Dean Stanton | GENRE: Drama | RUNNING TIME: 112 min | MPAA RATING: G

CLASSIFICATION: BEST

David Lynch's films are usually known for being surreal, horrific and graphic with sex and violence. But *The Straight Story* (1999) is his most unconventional and surprising of films for featuring almost none of these elements. It was a biographical picture that was written not by him, but screenwriters John Roach and Mary Sweeney. It was released by Walt Disney Pictures, and it was rated G by the MPAA, his only film to receive such a wholesome rating. Take that in for a moment; David Lynch directed a Disney film that was rated G.

The film is based on the true story of Alvin Straight, played in the picture by an old Richard Farnsworth that still has a bit of kick left in him. At the age of 73, he resides in Laurens, Iowa with stuttering daughter Rosie (Sissy Spacek). Alvin is saddened to learn that his brother (Harry Dean Stanton) in Mt. Zion, Wisconsin is dying and wants to see him. He doesn't own a car, and Rosie isn't a good driver. Still determined, he sets off on his 300-mile journey by riding a ride-on lawnmower for the entire trip. The townsfolk think he is crazy and that he won't make it very far. Their correct in that his mower breaks down, but he buys another one and keeps on going with a trailer in tow.

There are a lot of stops along the way with many odd looks and colorful characters questioning his quest. He'll meet a runaway girl, and they'll chat a little over a campfire for the night. He'll pass by some bikers and smile at them as they either smile back or stare in confusion at an old man driving a lawnmower on a long stretch of road. He'll make a pitstop in a town where he can have his mower repaired and share a drink with the locals. Through it all, Alvin opens up to strangers a little more by revealing secrets he has kept and wisdom he has gained. He mentions being a soldier in the war, telling others of how braving miles of cornfields is no big deal after such an experience, only later to talk about war stories he seems to have told few about. He'll later chat with some young people who ask what the worst part of getting old is. Alvin has the most perfect and thoughtful answer; *"Remembering when you were young."*

The Straight Story is a genuine surprise of a film as both a road trip story and a David Lynch movie. Alvin's journey seems as though it could have been drummed up for extra drama and comedy, but it's surprisingly subtle and easy-going with its simple adventure. There's a bit of anticipation with a David Lynch film as we wait for some gruesome moment of horror, a sly bit of melodramatic satire or a vision of another dimension. None of that is present here. It's just a warm and charming tale of one man trying to visit his brother many miles away. There's no need for additional elements of sentimentality, comical detours or elongated passages about getting old. Lynch and Farnsworth can convey this without much dialogue. By the time Alvin reaches his brother, there isn't much he has to say to him. What more could he say? You hear his simple, matter-of-fact talk and know that he's not a poet, but his smile and determination says everything you need to know about the man.

STRANGE DAYS

DIRECTOR: Kathryn Bigelow | SCREENWRITER: James Cameron, Jay Cocks | CAST: Ralph Fiennes, Angela Bassett, Juliette Lewis, Tom Sizemore, Vincent D'Onofrio, Michael Wincott | GENRE: Science Fiction | RUNNING TIME: 145 min | MPAA RATING: R

CLASSIFICATION: WEIRD

Strange Days (1995) takes place in the not-at-all-distant future of 1999, two days before the end of the millennium. It is a believable vision where Los Angeles is ripe with the street violence of gangs fighting cops and the video medium of the moment is MiniDiscs (remember those?). The only breakthrough technology in this world is a squid-like device that can record what you see through your vision, but it has been outlawed for apparent reasons.

Lenny Nero (Ralph Fiennes) deals these recordings like a drug dealer. He takes in his product from those that stage or acquires MiniDiscs of other people's visions. His usual spots for dealing includes nightclubs of punks and hotels of scummy clientele. The sex sells better than the snuff, as Lenny isn't much interested in selling the opening footage of a heist that ends with a criminal diving a roof.

The virtual sex videos are a far easier sell for Lenny's discreet clients as the ultimate form of prostitution; no worry of STDs, no hotel required, no fear of a prostitute ripping you off and no wife the wiser. Lenny, however, prefers only one MiniDisc to view on his off hours; a memory of his sunnier days with his wife Faith (Juliette Lewis). There is sex in the video, but it is a more intimate viewing where Lenny feels vulnerable and appreciative that there was a happier time in his life; a time when Lenny wasn't a dealing MiniDiscs and Faith wasn't a mess of a singer hooked up with an abusive music mogul.

A mystery is afoot as a prostitute runs from two violent LAPD officers pursuing her for a crime she witnessed with her recording device. She is eventually murdered, but what's creepy is that the murder was recorded onto a MiniDisc that Lenny receives from one of his contacts. He watches helplessly from the killer's point of view as Iris is slowly raped and slaughtered. Who could have recorded such a brutal video and why did they do it? The plot only thickens once Lenny discovers the MiniDisc the murderer was after. It is a revealing video of police brutality that could shake the already chaotic war in the streets.

Though the setting is futuristic, the story is a reasonably old-fashioned one of film noir with thriller elements. Lenny's mission of uncovering the mystery behind the recorded murders follows a typical thriller course, complete with car chases, shootouts, battles on balconies and an explosive moment where a limo is set on fire and drives off a pier. And the ending on New Year's Eve is one of the most ludicrous of finales that ends with everybody cheering and celebrating when they were a few moments ago brutally being each other in the streets.

Where the film succeeds is its technical side for a world that is brilliantly conceived by director Kathryn Bigelow. The first-person footage of the MiniDiscs is expertly shot, placing the viewer directly inside the visions of robbers, murderers, witnesses and even those that have their brains scrambled. Most of these scenes appear as long unbroken shots where hands are visible, and reflections can be seen in mirrors, almost as if Bigelow is a magician trying to show us there are no visible wires. The story by her former husband, James Cameron, is also smart about the technology, if not original with its plot. Cameron's dialogue is laced with technobabble that sounds less as though he's just inserting words he read in a few computer manuals or technothrillers.

Aside from the futuristic landscape, the film is held together by some excellent performances. It was remarkable to watch the usually refined Ralph Fiennes play a scummy guy with long hair and tacky clothing. Angela Bassett provides the perfect supporting role as the limo driver Mace that once had a thing for Lenny, reluctantly aiding him with a gun at the ready. Tom Sizemore provides some charismatic support as the private investigator Max and Michael Wincott practically melts into the background of the scummy nightclub as the robe-wearing abuser Philo Gant.

Strange Days was the result of blending Cameron's love of high-tech excitement with Bigelow's inspiration of the 1992 Los Angeles riots. It also carries with it many heavy themes of racism, rape, voyeurism, and sexism, but these feel more peppered than punctuated in the plot. Still, for being as scattershot as it was, the film is a neat cyberpunk time capsule that was more daring and thoughtful than most movies of the era that didn't treat science fiction with such ambition.

STREET FIGHTER

DIRECTOR: Steven E. de Souza | SCREENWRITER: Steven E. de Souza | CAST: Jean-Claude Van Damme, Raúl Juliá, Ming-Na Wen, Damian Chapa, Kylie Minogue, Wes Studi | GENRE: Action | RUNNING TIME: 102 min | MPAA RATING: PG-13

CLASSIFICATION: WEIRD

As movies based on video games began to take off, Capcom did not want to wait to get in on this train with *Street Fighter* (1994). They entered into a movie deal with Steven E. de Souza, forcing him to conceive a screenplay practically overnight and shoot it within a few months to be ready in time for Christmas 1994. Despite Souza's ambition and affinity for the franchise, the company probably should have waited until Christmas 1995 for what turned out to be a film more goofy and convoluted than adventurous and straightforward.

M. Bison (Raúl Juliá) is the ruthless dictator of the country of Shadaloo that has humanitarian workers of the Allied Nations held hostage for $20 billion. The Allied Nations send in Guile (Jean-Claude Van Damme), a beret-wearing hero with the right muscles for the job. He'll gain allies along the way in the form of the reporter Chun-Li, sumo wrestlers Honda and boxers Balrog. Bison isn't alone either. He has henchman just as ridiculous with the Russian bodybuilder Zangief, the break-dancer-turned-gun-for-hire Dee Jay, scientist-turned-witch-doctor Dhalsim and science-experiment-turned-monster Blanka. Fans of the video games will at least appreciate that these characters are identifiable from the costumes, but a layman will be seriously questioning why Dhalsim starts looking like a witch doctor and why Blanka's hair turns red. They'll also probably be wondering why Bison can fly and shoot electricity.

I would say a natural explanation for any of the nonsense is that it's staying true to the video games, but I don't think this is the case. It's a strange plot of Bison wanting to breed the perfect soldier, build his city called Bisonopolis (no, seriously, that's the name he chose) and, you know, rule the world. Whatever. From this flimsy story, we get lots of funny moments of slapstick and silly dialogue, both intentional and unintentional. The director knew what he was doing with having Zangief and Honda duke it out on a miniature model of Bisonopolis, complete with Godzilla sound effects. It's a corny bit of comedy, but I couldn't help but laugh. There are a few genuine moments of humor in this action-packed farce, the best being Zangief's reaction to a television monitor displaying a runaway truck headed straight for his position; *"Quick - change the channel!"* But for as much as I love those silly scenes, the film never establishes a firm tone with all its characters and events, appearing more like a chaotic dogpile of ideas good and bad. For as many cool fights with real martial arts, there are just as many that feel cheap and not entertaining, even when trying to be comical.

The film was as much a mess behind the scenes as it was on camera. Raúl Juliá was stricken with cancer at the time and had to have his fight scenes drastically reduced; he appeared very thin and pale for the screen as well. Van Damme had drug problems, causing production to stall when waiting for him on set and then dealing with him slurring lines on camera. The film had a tough time gaining its PG-13 rating, as the first cut was violent enough to warrant an R, but de Souza states that the second cut came back with a G rating. Tricky thing, that PG-13.

Steven E. de Souza had stated that his goal for Street Fighter was to deliver a cross between *Star Wars*, *James Bond*, and a war picture. Those elements didn't exactly blend well together and made the film more ambitious than it should have been. *Street Fighter* is often noted as one of the worst video game movies ever made, but considering its competition of the time with *Super Mario Bros.* (1993) and *Double Dragon* (1994), it's an easy recommendation for a bad film being so audacious and silly that it's good. The film does have some significant claims to fame with it being the last film of Raúl Juliá (earning him a posthumous nomination for Best Supporting Actor from the Saturn Awards) and spawning a music video of Van Damme dancing to M.C. Hammer's single "Straight to my Feet." You can take those as positives or negatives, but the film has an adorable energy that I couldn't help but fall for its insanity.

SUDDEN DEATH

DIRECTOR: Peter Hyams | SCREENWRITER: Gene Quintano | CAST: Jean-Claude Van Damme, Powers Boothe, Raymond J. Barry, Dorian Harewood | GENRE: Action | RUNNING TIME: 110 min | MPAA RATING: PG-13

CLASSIFICATION: WEIRD

Sudden Death (1995) is *Die Hard* on ice with Jean-Claude Van Damme. What, you need more than that? That short description isn't enough to make you want to close this book and watch this movie right this second? Fine, read on, but I doubt there's any possible way to build up the scene where Van Damme gets into a slugfest with the mascot character of the Pittsburgh Penguins.

Van Damme plays French-Canadian Darren McCord, a firefighter that failed to save a little girl from a house fire. He resigns, divorces and becomes the fire marshall of the Pittsburgh Civic Arena. The story picks up with him working the night of a big game between Pittsburgh and Chicago, with his young children of Emily (Whittni Wright) and Tyler (Ross Malinger) in attendance. The United States Vice President (Raymond J. Barry) is also attending the game, making him a primary target for terrorists led by Joshua Foss (Powers Boothe), a former CIA operative turned terrorist psychopath. When Foss takes hostage a skybox full of people, including McCord's kids, it's time for the firefighter to show that he can fight more than fires. And, of course, there are bombs rigged all around the stadium. You gotta have bombs in a movie like this.

Foss wants money and sets up the rules for his deadly game. Millions of dollars must be placed in his special bank account. If the amount doesn't increase throughout the hockey game, he kills a hostage at the end of each period or match or whenever. If the game ends and the total sum is not deposited, he'll blow up the stadium. True to the title, the game will go into sudden death, and McCord buys himself a few extra minutes. But if the bombs were timed for the end of the game, how would they know not to explode if there was sudden death? Whatever.

Sudden Death is built on the most ludicrous of action movie plotting to be a fun film, despite the dark tone of Powers Boothe murdering hostages. Forget about the precise timing of the bombs and the fact that nobody in the stadium is asking why the Vice President can't be seen from his skybox. What matters is that Van

Damme gets to show off more of his fighting skills on terrorists and that a few bombs blow up.

While there are some fantastic sequences with the arena flooding and a helicopter smashing into the rink, nothing can top Van Damme's showdown with a terrorist dressed as the Pittsburgh Penguins mascot. They do battle in a kitchen where Van Damme makes excellent use of his set by defending himself with knives and deep-friers. It is such a surreal scene for being so goofy, but played so earnestly with its danger and violence. You haven't lived until you've seen Van Damme kill a costumed mascot by sending it through an automatic dishwasher.

Van Damme seemed to land this role as opposed to the other top-rated action stars of the era because it was apparently his turn. Arnold Schwarzenegger didn't want to overwork himself with his already busy shooting schedule, Sylvester Stallone didn't like the script and Bruce Willis was active with the next *Die Hard* picture and probably didn't want to repeat himself with a *Die Hard* clone after a *Die Hard* sequel. They probably didn't want to fight a penguin either. It's just as well as director Peter Hyams, who previously worked with Van Damme on *Timecop*, delivers a surprisingly fun action picture for being so ridiculously campy, making for one of Van Damme's most genuinely enjoyable action pictures.

SUPER MARIO BROS.

DIRECTOR: Rocky Morton, Annabel Jankel | SCREENWRITER: Blake Snyder, William Osborne, William Davies | CAST: Bob Hoskins, John Leguizamo, Dennis Hopper, Samantha Mathis, Fisher Stevens, Fiona Shaw, Richard Edson | GENRE: Science Fiction | RUNNING TIME: 104 min | MPAA RATING: PG

CLASSIFICATION: WORST

As the first movie directly based off a video game property, there was a lot of pressure for adapting the highly-successful Mario franchise for the big screen. Nintendo most likely thought they were making a smart move by releasing the production rights to a small studio outside of the usual big-name Hollywood companies that would probably muck up their property. It was just one of many mistakes made in *Super Mario Bros.* (1993), a picture that was such a confusing mess I doubt anyone involved had the slightest clue what this movie was supposed to be.

Bob Hoskins and John Leguizamo play the Mario Brothers of Mario and Luigi, a plumbing duo that finds themselves on hard times in modern day New York City. They're being driven out of business by a mafia-led construction company. Luigi finds himself attracted to the lovely archeologist, Daisy, in town to investigate dinosaur bones. What are dinosaur bones doing in New York? It turns out that the sewers of Brooklyn contain a portal to the mythical Dinosaur World.

This world, as detailed in the poorly-animated prologue, exists as another dimension where dinosaurs evolved to look more human and form a *Blade Runner* style city of smoke and neon. Daisy is captured and drug into Dinosaur World by its corrupt mayor King Koopa (Dennis Hopper), who has big plans for dominating his kingdom, pushing back evolution and merging dimensions. The ambitions of the Mario Brothers are less convoluted as they just want to save Daisy.

This film was an absolute disaster of conflicting ideas and general confusion. Multiple writers were tapped and couldn't decide if they were making a fantasy adventure, a charming kid comedy or an adult post-apocalyptic film. All of these ideas blended into a sloppy script that continued to be reworked during filming, as the directing duo of Rocky Morton and Annabel Jankel wanted something darker while screenwriter Ed Solomon wrote something sillier. Script changes were made on set to the point that the actors had no clue what type of film they were making. This sloppiness led to an angry Hopper that stopped reading the ever-changing script and Hoskins drank heavily between scenes. Leguizamo also drank which didn't bode well for the driving scenes, one of them ending with him slamming on the brakes too hard and breaking a door.

The only competent part of this production was the sets and special effects, albeit scattershot in their value to the story. The dimension of Dinosaur World is mostly confined to a city that looks surprisingly detailed for being built within an old cement factory. The devolved foot soldiers referred to as Goombas look silly with their small heads and giant suits, but they're also charming for looking so odd. There's also an elaborate animatronic for the small dinosaur Yoshi, though it pales in comparison to the far grander dinosaur effects of *Jurassic Park* that was released a few weeks later.

Super Mario Bros. set a negative first impression for movies based on video games. For not accurately representing the games or appealing to outsiders, it was a critical and financial disaster, a result that was practically written on the walls with its catastrophe of a production. The film has gained a cult status over time for apparently just existing at all. Unless you want to see Hopper look like Max Headroom, watch Hoskins stick his face into a big pair of boobs or hear Leguizamo trying to sound Italian, there's no reason to watch this messy film that never delivers anything concrete enough to be funny or exciting. It does, however, add one new bit of trivia to Mario lore: the last names of the Mario Brothers are in fact Mario, making their full names Mario Mario and Luigi Mario.

TALES FROM THE CRYPT PRESENTS: DEMON KNIGHT

DIRECTOR: Ernest Dickerson | SCREENWRITER: Mark Bishop, Ethan Reiff, Cyrus Voris | CAST: Billy Zane, William Sadler, Jada Pinkett Smith, Brenda Bakke, C. C. H. Pounder, Thomas Haden Church | GENRE: Horror | RUNNING TIME: 92 min | MPAA RATING: R

CLASSIFICATION: WEIRD

With the recent success of the *Tales from the Crypt* horror anthology TV series, there was undoubtedly a bit of pressure for this movie. There had already been a *Tales from the Crypt* movie before the show that maintained an anthology premise, but this new film is one contained tale of terror. And while I was initially dismayed to discover that *Tales from the Crypt Presents: Demon Knight* (1995) would only be one horror story, I was pleased to see it was an excellent choice of a single episode of the show, blown up for the big screen with better effects and a more substantial cast.

True to the series, the film begins with a prologue from the Cryptkeeper, a creepy puppet of a ghoul voiced by the reprising voice actor John Kassir. He is in the middle of directing a movie and is peeved that his actors are *"hacks"* and lets loose with the puns. Worth noting is how much creepier it is to see the Cryptkeeper in a full body shot as he darts towards the actors on set. He finally notices the camera, greeting the audience with a *"hello, kiddies"* and goes into his usual introduction of another tale of frights.

Demon Knight takes place in the deserts of New Mexico where the drifter Frank Brayker (William Sadler) is being chased by some mysterious figure known as The Collector (Billy Zane). One car crash later, Frank finds his way to a church turned boarding house where he rents a room. Along with a fake ID, Frank is carrying an ancient key-shaped relic that looks as though it were plucked right out of an *Indiana Jones* movie. The Collector wants it so badly that he fools law enforcement into making Frank return it. When things don't go his way, The Collector decides to drop the act, summon his undead army and stage an assault on the boarding house.

Inside the house is one of the most amazing casts assembled for a horror film. A young Jada Pinkett Smith plays the housemaid Jeryline, bitter about doing all the chores and escorting people to their rooms. Thomas Haden Church plays Roach, a sexist and deceptive man with a wild shirt and long hair, eager to sell out his friends if he can survive the night. Charles Fleischer is the pensive and sweet Wally that just can't hold down a job. Horror staple Dick Miller plays a fairly significant role as Uncle Willy and brings his usual charm to the picture. William Sadler does a great job as the gun-toting Frank, and it's impossible to take your eyes off Billy Zane having way too much fun in the role of a demonic killer.

The plot is a relatively ridiculous tale of ancient curses and blood magic with origins relating to Jesus Christ, but that's par for the course with *Crypt*. The horror effects range from the fantastic (Zane smashes his fist so hard through the face of a cop he rips off his head) to the campily cheap (cartoonish lightning launches demons into the air). The performances by Zane and Pinkett are rather stellar as they steal the show. Pinkett's grit is engaging (*"If I hadn't made a place for her she'd be behind bars... or dead."*) and Zane's devilish charisma is a pleasure on the screen (*"Humans! You're not worth the flesh you're printed on!"*). The only major issue I have with the film is that it feels more like an episode of the show than a movie. It features the same opening titles, the Cryptkeeper prologue, the same font for the opening credits at the beginning of the story and the cast, despite being notable, feels like a typical lineup for the series. But for mostly being a more extended episode, it's one of the best of the series.

TANK GIRL

DIRECTOR: Rachel Talalay | SCREENWRITER: Tedi Sarafian | CAST: Lori Petty, Ice-T, Naomi Watts, Malcolm McDowell | GENRE: Science Fiction | RUNNING TIME: 104 min | MPAA RATING: R

CLASSIFICATION: WORST

The 1990s was starting to see a rise in action pictures based on comic books, but studios were still mostly clueless about how to make the transition from page to screen. *Tank Girl* (1995) was the most unlucky of casualties in this sub-genre. Based on the British comic series by Alan Martin and Jamie Hewlett, it was a project that became of great interest for director Rachel Talalay who had become obsessed with the comic and sought out the rights. She hired on a fantastic production designer of Catherine Hardwicke that did her best to work with Martin and Hewlett to respect their work. Even the Stan Winston workshop offered to work on the film at a reduced rate since they were fans of the comic as well. So much talent came together for this project that it's surprising to see it crash and burn so badly to the point where they might as well just show a slideshow of the comic book. Surprisingly enough, the film does just that when it starts to run out of money.

Lori Petty plays Rebecca "Tank Girl" Buck, the eccentric and punkish survivor of the apocalypse in the year 2033. In the eleven years since a comet struck Earth, she operates an independent water well with her boyfriend. This independence angers the greedy Kesslee (Malcolm McDowell) of the Water & Power corporation that wants to run a monopoly on the water. Rather than buy Rebecca out, Kesslee sends assassins to capture her and kill her boyfriend. Enslaved by the Water & Power Corporation, Rebecca makes her escape with Jet Girl (Naomi Watts) in a tank, while also befriending the kangaroo mutants known as the Rippers. It's weird enough that the Rippers look like creatures better suited for *The Island of Dr. Moreau*, but even more bizarre to think that one of them, under all that makeup, is Ice-T. Teaming up with the Ripper, Rebecca leads an assault on Kesslee's empire, armed with a tank and the lamest of humor.

The acting is surprisingly bad. Lori Petty get aggravating real quick as the hero and narrator that tries way too hard to make this post-apocalyptic setting funny. Malcolm McDowell struggles to be a furious villain by smashing as many things as possible in his fits of rage, unable to sound menacing with his evil scheme to turn people into the water. Naomi Watts, in one of her earliest roles, is surprisingly ineffective as a character that might have been present in a lesbian relationship with Rebecca, but this is never fully taken advantage of.

The production values on *Tank Girl* were so cheap that they apparently couldn't afford to establish shots or transitions. In their place are illustrations of these locations, annoyingly packaged with pans, zooms and quick-cuts to either make the movie more action-packed or to create the illusion of realistic buildings. They do neither. Perhaps they intended to remind the audience that *Tank Girl* was a far superior comic book than its film adaptation.

The film is jam-packed with confusion in nearly every aspect of its production. The movie stops for a musical number in which Rebecca sings along with a kicking chorus line that feels like it's from another movie. The film will later take a break so the Rippers can perform a dance number in a bowling alley. Animated sequences are randomly edited into the footage, apparently meant to fill in the gaps for scenes that were not filmed. Though these animated scenes are quite eye-catching and much more fun than the live-action movie, they do little to bridge the clunky story, becoming more akin to the scribbled-on doodles of Bakshi's *Cool World*.

There is also a significant lacking element of sexuality to the picture that was left on the cutting room floor. In a post-sex scene between Rebecca and a Ripper, the Ripper's penis was built to be visible, but never made it into the film. Other sexual elements edited out included Rebecca's bedroom of dildos and a scene where she makes an enemy slip on a condom.

For being so edited and unfinished, *Tank Girl* feels like a repressed teenager struggling to break out of its shell and hardly making a crack. If only the studio had made an effort to add in a little money and leave a few more scenes, this could have been a genuine surprise of a comic book movie that touched on more rebellious and sexual themes than most action pictures dared to showcase. The film does have the energy of a sugared-up kid, but, as with any sugar high, that enthusiasm wears off fast.

TEENAGE MUTANT NINJA TURTLES

DIRECTOR: Steve Barron | SCREENWRITER: Todd W. Langen, Bobby Herbeck | CAST: Judith Hoag, Elias Koteas, Corey Feldman, Kevin Clash | GENRE: Action | RUNNING TIME: 93 min | MPAA RATING: PG

CLASSIFICATION: WEIRD

Based off the hit cartoon series of the late 80s, *Teenage Mutant Ninja Turtles* (1990) begins with a lot of anticipation for the titular heroes. They're only seen from the shadows in an opening scene where they stop a gang that tried to steal the purse of reporter April O'Neil (Judith Hoag). One of their weapons knocks out a streetlight, scuffling can be heard in the darkness, and the gangsters are already tied up for when the cops arrive. Down in the sewers, their voices can be heard; the title pops up on screen and the Turtles finally jump into the frame. And for being assembled by Jim Henson's Creature Shop, they're not too shabby for bringing the silly concept of anthropomorphic turtles to the big screen with animatronics.

In a surprising shift from the usually colorful and silly cartoon series, *Teenage Mutant Ninja Turtles* is much darker in tone and setting, despite staying true to the protagonists' California accents and affinity for pizza. After all, you can't be too chipper if your home is a sewer devoid of light and clean water. New York City is portrayed as a grimy and corrupt metropolis, gripped by the crime wave of the secretive cult known as the Foot Clan. The Clan is led by the ruthless and armored warrior Shredder, luring in youth for his secret crime wave with promises of arcade games, skateboards, and cigarettes, their choice of regular or menthol. When the Turtles encounter the Foot Clan with jokes and all, their battles are filmed to be more intense and dramatic, despite the lack of blood for Turtles that wield swords and a sai. Credit Steve Barron for making these bloodless fights as exciting as any action film out there.

The Turtles were raised in the sewers by their rat master Splinter, instructing them on the finer points of ninjitsu, but mostly the part about not being seen. He will, however, inspire them enough to communicate with his spirit over a campfire with ninja magic or whatever. Leonardo (Brian Tochi) tries to act as the leader, but finds it difficult to manage them. In particular, Raphael (Josh Pais) discovers himself cold and distant from his family, preferring to disguise himself and go out to see movies on his own. Donatello

(Corey Feldman) and Michelangelo (Robbie Rist), also known as the purple and orange Turtles, just laugh and enjoy the simpler things in life, enjoying the moonlight shining into the sewers as they await the pizza guy. The favorite food of the Turtles is pizza, leading to the obvious commercial tie-in of Domino's Pizza. Oddly enough, it was Pizza Hut that was engaged in a $20 million marketing campaign with the film, including a commercial placed at the beginning of the VHS tape.

The writing here is surprisingly sharp for a film aimed at kids with talking turtles. It's mostly due to their delivery which makes the quieter moments more easy-going with the humor. When the Turtles find themselves compromised, they hide out at a country house with the cocky hockey punk Casey Jones (Elias Koteas), where he trades alphabetical insults with Donatello while they work on a car. Not all the deeper emotions work of revenge and loss, but most are sold surprisingly well with the competent costumes that work in darkness and daylight. There's rarely a moment where they appear as cheap puppets, incredibly believable in scenes of action and simple banter.

The film had a massive disconnect with adult critics who savaged the film for having no personality and featuring shameless product placement. As a kid, I found the film mesmerizing for treating characters I'd only known through toys and cartoons as action stars, in a film that portrayed them just as dark as they were comical. I still adore the movie with a big grin on my face with every viewing. I am, however, willing admit it comes from a bias of being a 1990s kid who dug seeing my favorite cartoon characters in a live-action film that felt strangely adult for a moment when Ralph curses the city with a loud *"DAMN!"*. Maybe I was hypnotized by the marketing, but it's hard to deny how awesome it felt to charge out of the theater quoting and cheering *"God, I love being a turtle!"*

TEENAGE MUTANT NINJA TURTLES II: THE SECRET OF THE OOZE

DIRECTOR: Michael Pressman | SCREENWRITER: Todd W. Langen | CAST: Paige Turco, David Warner, Ernie Reyes, Jr. | GENRE: Action | RUNNING TIME: 96 min | MPAA RATING: PG

CLASSIFICATION: WEIRD

There's an absolute silliness that must be accepted to enjoy *Teenage Mutant Ninja Turtles II: The Secret of the Ooze* (1991). It must be accepted that radioactive ooze can mutate animals into bipedal mutants in just a few hours. The sewers of New York City can hold an undiscovered subway ruin that is a livable paradise for the four Turtles. A battle that spills into a rap concert doesn't lead to chaos, but an impromptu song by Vanilla Ice about Ninja Turtles. The fans of the *Ninja Turtles* cartoon that dominated the late-80s/early-90s were well versed in this spirit. Being one of those Turtle-loving kids, my entertainment expectations were thoroughly met.

Far from the darker aspects of the previous movie, *The Secret of the Ooze* is lighter and more colorful than its grimmer predecessor. In the opening scene, the Ninja Turtles are not concealed in darkness, but fully visible in an open and empty mall where they battle with masked criminals. Aiming for more cartoonish violence, the titular heroes do battle more with yo-yos and sausage links than their weapons of swords and nunchucks. They've become less raw warriors and more Jackie Chan jokesters.

Their costumes have been improved by the Jim Henson's Creature Shop, allowing for more expressive faces and more visual slapstick. We can make out who is feeling bitter, silly, inquisitive or crushed more from their faces than the lighting. There are no shadows to hide in this time as their new home of an abandoned subway station appears very bright and warm. The night scene of a rusted junkyard is very well-lit, so not a single Turtle becomes lost in the chaos. Even the mysterious lab that concocts a dangerous ooze is seen by both the audience and the Turtles more as an elaborate video arcade (*"Where do you put the quarter?"*).

The Turtles' nemesis of Shredder returns from the grave, somehow surviving being crushed in a trash compactor at the end of the last movie. He gets the old gang back together of his masked Foot Clan, but realizes he's going to need a little something extra to fight the Turtles this time around. Fight mutants with mutants, he reasons. His Foot Clan steals a supply of the same ooze that turned the Turtles into teenage mutants and uses it on a wolf and snapping turtle, dubbed Tokka and Rahzar. It doesn't entirely go according to plan since the two mutants are more toddler than teenager, childishly banging metal and calling Shredder their mama in between their mindless snarls. Shredder is understandably upset as these mutants don't present much of a threat to the Turtles. It isn't until Shredder morphs into the giant and more blade-heavy Super Shredder that the Turtles find themselves facing a significant threat, though still an easy one to dispose of with some falling debris.

With the threat not as grave, the heroes are allowed to have a little more fun, as opposed to the previous picture which found them brooding and feuding between laughs. They bond comfortably with their human pal April O'Neil (this time played by Paige Turco), who graciously lets them stay at her apartment until they can find a new home. She comes home with pizza, and they instantly start joking and roughhousing with each other, big smiles all around the room as they talk about finding a new place to stay and play indoor football with a pizza slice. There's a chummy element of family to any scene they occupy, even if they're mostly speaking in California slang and churning out movie references.

Additional characters are added more as snarky and plucky additions, matching the more cartoonish tone. The Turtles befriend an amateur martial artist/professional pizza delivery boy Keno (Ernie Reyes, Jr.), a young adult that gets to experience the amazement of Ninja Turtles with more significant interest than that of April. The prim and authentically English Professor Perry (David Warner) is forced against his will to create some mutants for Shredder and tries to convince the audience that there is some science behind all this nonsense.

For not being as tonally sophisticated as its predecessor, *The Secret of the Ooze* features some stable comedic energy and neat physical stunts with the familiar foursome that never takes itself too seriously. After all, how dark can you make a story about pizza-consuming turtles that fight a man made of blades with his bumbling baby-mutant henchmen?

TEENAGE MUTANT NINJA TURTLES III

DIRECTOR: Stuart Gillard | SCREENWRITER: Stuart Gillard | CAST: Elias Koteas, Paige Turco, Vivian Wu, Sab Shimono, Stuart Wilson | GENRE: Action | RUNNING TIME: 96 min | MPAA RATING: PG

CLASSIFICATION: WORST

The Teenage Mutant Ninja Turtles degraded poorly with this sequel. In particular, the special effects of the Turtles themselves went through the harshest of degradations. In *Teenage Mutant Ninja Turtles III* (1993), the iconic four seems to have lost their visual allure when taken out of the hands of Jim Henson's Creature Shop and into the cheaper craftsmanship of the All Effects Company. This is most apparent with the Turtles' rat master Splinter that has been reduced from a full-bodied animatronic to a hand puppet.

Also in disrepair was the script. Turtles fans were anxious for what familiar villain from the cartoon series would grace the screen, having been let down by the previous movie filling in the roles of Bebop and Rocksteady with original creations Tokka and Rahzar. Non-fans were just hoping not to be bored by a picture with anthropomorphic teen-speak turtles. Neither were appeased with a time-travel story that features no memorable characters from the cartoon or memorable characters in general.

The color-coded Turtles (Leonardo, Donatello, Michelangelo, and Raphael) still dwell in the sewers of New York City with their human link April O'Neil (reprised once more by Paige Turco), still visiting them from time to time. While stopping by to pass out some presents she picked up from a flea market, one item she unwittingly acquires is a magical Japanese scepter. The mystical item has the power to swap the holder of the scepter with another person in time. So when a 14th-century Japanese prince holds the scepter and recites the secret words to activate its magic, he takes April's place in the 1990s. The Turtles take it upon themselves to rescue April from the past by traveling back in time with the scepter as well, swapping places (and clothes) with four samurais from the past.

With the Turtles traveling back in time to an era better suited for their ninja training, they do little more than crack lame pop-culture jokes while masquerading in samurai garb. When meeting the evil Samurai Lord Noringa, their reaction to his appearance is to spout *"Hey, look, it's Wayne Newton!"* One Turtle falls over and asks for help with *"Help! I'm a turtle, and I can't get up!"* They catch a glance of April's exposed legs and give her a *"Shwing!"* In between all their anachronisms, the Turtles will occasionally ride some horses, swing some swords, scale some walls, rescue April from a cage suspended in the air and defeat the other villain Walker (Stuart Wilson), a forgettably bland English trader who delivers standard sneers and double-crosses. Meanwhile, in present-day 1993, the four samurais are easily amused by TV hockey and the corny music of Baltimora.

Despite being a rather simplistic premise, the mechanics of the story are ridiculously convoluted. According to Donatello's "calculations," the scepter only allows you to be out of your current spot in time for 60 hours before traveling back is impossible and the turtles become "turtle soup" as Donny puts it. Some of the Turtles question this logic with jokes about if the scepter can only be used on certain days or if it can make wrong turns and send them to "Godzilla-land." But they make solid points about the holes of this concept. How do they know the scepter would transport them back to the exact time and place as April? I guess they figured the coordinates would have to be accurate if there is to be any sort of rescue adventure.

The writer/director Stuart Gillard was best known at the time as a TV director on such programs as *90210* and *Bordertown*. Though his script has all the signs of a TV show on its last legs of creative ideas, his eye for Feudal Japan is surprisingly not too shabby. The costumes, sets, and lighting are all pleasant to the eye and somewhat true to the era. Squint and you can almost see a director trying to make a competent samurai picture. I guess you'd also have to plug your ears as well to get over the annoying dialogue.

The previous *Turtles* movies had a certain charm with the titular heroes that had genuine wit and a sense of character. With Gillard's script, however, they have been reduced to vehicles of quips working overtime, trying desperately to spout every line of dialogue as a one-liner. Their comedic antics had diminished, making them appear as old hipsters falling back on their same old tricks for a scenario that doesn't suit them. The Turtles were once an ensemble that kids could enjoy for all their silly sentiments and favor of pizza, feeling as though the characters were created just for them. *Turtles III* makes them appear as lame parents cracking dad jokes.

TERMINATOR 2: JUDGEMENT DAY

DIRECTOR: James Cameron | SCREENWRITER: James Cameron | CAST: Arnold Schwarzenegger, Linda Hamilton, Robert Patrick, Edward Furlong | GENRE: Action | RUNNING TIME: 137 min | MPAA RATING: R

CLASSIFICATION: BEST

While James Cameron's *The Terminator* was a dark and neo-noirish chase of a woman fleeing a stalking killer robot from the future, his follow-up feature is an entirely different movie. It is louder, grander, flashier and heavier on the violence. But much more than big action and the most advanced of special effects of the era are on display in *Terminator 2: Judgement Day* (1991).

Arnold Schwarzenegger returns in the role of another T-800 robot with a beefy body, but this time he has a much different mission for traveling back in time. He's come looking for both the imprisoned Sarah Connor (Linda Hamilton) and her son John Connor (Edward Furlong), the boy who would grow up to become the leader of the resistance against the robot uprising. Sarah spends her days in a mental ward, screaming about the impending apocalypse as she continues to have vivid and horrific nightmares of nukes wiping out humanity. John, now adopted and nearly a teenager, lives a life of hacking into ATMs and blowing the cash at the arcade.

But the T-800 does not want to kill them, as was his original mission in the previous movie. Reprogrammed by the human resistance of the future, he's come to protect the recluse John from another Terminator that's been sent to kill him. This new Terminator is an upgraded model known as the T-1000 (Robert Patrick), a smaller and less muscular threat, but just as dangerous for its self-healing body composed of liquid metal. Mere bullets and explosions will not be enough to counter this danger that can reconstruct its figure with ease.

John realizes how mighty the loyal T-800 can be at breaking out his mom and preventing the robot uprising, but also how ineffective the big guy is at human interaction. While John is initially impressed that his new robotic friend can stand up to anyone who threatens him, he quickly realizes that this strength cannot go unchecked. John instructs the T-800 that he cannot kill anyone. Not an easy task for someone as beefy and gun-toting as Schwarzenegger, but he complies and comically finds loopholes in Connor's instructions. He shoots a guard in the leg, reasoning that he'll still live. He picks up a minigun as he marches towards a swarm of cops, assuring John that he'll be careful not to kill anybody. The T-800 can still blow up cars and shoot at people while not being an inhuman killing machine. Whoever said Schwarzenegger couldn't be a positive role model?

The T-1000, on the other hand, has no qualms about murder, using his liquid-metal body to form sharp knives that slice through those in his way like butter. He's so determined to ensure the death of both John and Sarah that he's willing to pursue them on foot when they make a getaway in a car. He can transform himself into anybody, leading to some shocking scenes of questioning who to trust. And the moments when this machine is smashed, burned, ripped and blown into separate pieces are some astonishingly gross and amazing scenes of top-notch special effects with great detail.

Look closely at the scene where the T-1000 turns himself into a blob of liquid to ooze inside a helicopter, and you can see the reflection of the stunned pilot on his mercury-like surface. There's not enough praise in the world to bestow on Industrial Light and Magic for their remarkable contributions to creating one of the most memorable and dangerous movie villains of all-time.

Everything in *Terminator 2* is at full throttle. The acting is strong all around, from the enthusiastic Edward Furlong to the silently vicious Robert Patrick to the insanely overreacting Linda Hamilton. The father-son dynamic between Furlong and Schwarzenegger is incredibly amusing as Furlong attempts to be a guide for morality while Schwarzenegger hopelessly tries to put on a human smile. Their genuine levity helps balance out the more violent and gritty action sequences, all of which are fantastically staged with big guns, exploding cars, close-quarters combat and lots of energy. The fight to save mankind from murderous robots has never looked so good, felt so intense or portrayed with such fun. There's so much to enjoy with this movie that the plot holes and time paradoxes are minor quibbles in an otherwise robust and perfect action picture.

THELMA & LOUISE

DIRECTOR: Ridley Scott | SCREENWRITER: Callie Khouri | CAST: Susan Sarandon, Geena Davis, Harvey Keitel, Brad Pitt | GENRE: Drama | RUNNING TIME: 129 min | MPAA RATING: R

CLASSIFICATION: BEST

Ridley Scott's *Thelma & Louise* (1991) plays like a female rendition of *Easy Rider* with the same amount of passion, action, and grit. It plays out as an almost mythical tale of a rebellious duo that dared to challenge the world in their 1956 T-Bird. And it ends with one of the most memorable, tragic and poignant endings to a car chase ever filmed.

Before they hit the road, we learn enough about the titular pair and why they decided to raise hell. Thelma (Geena Davis) is a wife looked down on by her rug salesman of a husband that expects her to fall in line with household chores. Louis (Susan Sarandon) is a waitress with a loser boyfriend in a band going nowhere with both his career and their relationship. For the weekend, they go off on a road trip where they can let their inhibitions run wild. They stop at a bar where Thelma, eager to go nuts, slams some drinks and flirts with an urban cowboy. Flirtation soon turns into an attempted rape by the stranger. Louise comes to the rescue and shoots the man dead. The road trip to get away from the men in their lives quickly turns into an escape from lawmen after their lives.

Their adventure has its share of detours both sweet and violent. They hook up at one point with J.D. (Brad Pitt), a charming young drifter that is far more successful at coming on to Thelma. It's not too tough for a man who looks ripped and sexy without a shirt on while he regales the women with tales of robbery. They'll also run into state troopers they'll have to hold at gunpoint while they shoot out their radio and make their escape.

There's a police hunt on for the women, and the only cop who seems sympathetic to bring them in is Detective Hal Slocumb (Harvey Keitel). He knows that these women are desperate and wants to prevent the situation from escalating further, hoping to bring them in safely. But as the road trip of Thelma and Louise progresses, they find themselves more accustomed to this lifestyle. They feel freer and in control than they ever did before. They're able to pull over a trucker that insults them, force him to apologize at gunpoint and then blow up his rig. You don't get that kind of thrill from cleaning the kitchen or serving coffee.

Both Davis and Sarandon are phenomenal in this film. They perform a unique balancing act of characters that are desperately seeking to escape and bitter enough to take violent revenge on the world they feel has wronged them. This type of material could have become too silly or too mean-spirited, but the script by Callie Khouri (who won an Academy Award for this screenplay) writes this scenario to be believable enough, and Ridley Scott's direction makes the film as much an atmospheric road movie as it is an exciting chase.

As one might expect, the film became a massive hit with the female audience, presenting a film that portrays women of high power, emotion, and appetites for thrills. It's a film that has been hailed by feminists as everything from a neo-feminist road movie to the last great film about women. The appeal is easy to spot; there weren't very many female revenge pictures at the time, and very few were this complexly presented with personality and enthusiasm.

The film has gone down in history for its iconic final shot of the two women plunging their car off the Grand Canyon. Despite the grim conclusion to their tale, it's a happy ending for two women who lived fast and died free. The film ends on the unforgettable shot of the T-Bird accelerating into the air one last time, holding on the shot before fading out. We don't need to see the crash as we know how it will end. For Thelma and Louise, everything ends at that moment as they kiss and accelerate. A fiery explosion adds nothing more to their tale of sisterhood and revenge.

THERE'S SOMETHING ABOUT MARY

DIRECTOR: Peter Farrelly, Bobby Farrelly | SCREENWRITER: Ed Decter, John J. Strauss, Peter Farrelly, Bobby Farrelly | CAST: Cameron Diaz, Matt Dillon, Ben Stiller, Lee Evans, Chris Elliott | GENRE: Comedy | RUNNING TIME: 119 min | MPAA RATING: R

CLASSIFICATION: BEST

The Farrelly Brothers have such a daring nature to always go one step further with their comedies, and *There's Something About Mary* (1998) is their most ambitious of vulgar comedies. It's funny enough that Ben Stiller's character of Ted masturbates before his date with the mysterious Mary (Cameron Diaz) and doesn't realize ejaculate is left on his ear. But it's even more uproarious that Mary would mistake it for hair gel and use it for a ridiculous updo.

Ted first met Mary in high school, as the movie opens with a pimply-faced Stiller and a long-haired Diaz. He hit things off pretty well with her when he comes to the aid of her mentally challenged brother Warren. They were to go to the prom together, but when zipping himself up in her parent's bathroom, his penis and testicles become lodged in his zipper. Again, the Farrelly Brothers relish this bit for all its worth as character after character comes into the bathroom and reacts horrifyingly at the sight, briefly shown in one of the film's grossest and most hilarious moments. A cop that enters the bathroom assures him that everything will be okay when they quickly zip downward. Cut to Ted being rushed out of the house in a stretcher; *"We got a bleeder!"*

Years later, Ted is an adult and still struggling to work up the courage to talk to Mary that hasn't seen in years. He decides to take some advice from his pal Dom (Chris Elliott) and hires private investigator Pat Healy (Matt Dillon) to stalk and dig up some information on Mary. In Pat's investigation, he discovers that Mary is living in Miami as an orthopedic surgeon. Her best friend is Magda (Lin Shaye), a middle-aged sunbather that prefers her skin to have the appearance and texture of beef jerky.

As Pat's investigation continues, he lies to Ted about Mary, telling him that she's become incredibly fat with age. But she still looks as hot as she ever did, leading to him pursuing Mary's love. He's not alone though. Mary's longtime co-worker, Tucker (Lee Evans), has been pretending for the longest time to win Mary's affection by posing as an English cripple. It's deceptive, but he probably has a better shot than being honest as an American pizza delivery guy. Dom also has a thing for Mary, and an NFL quarterback is playing himself is fighting for her as well.

The premise sounds like an old-fashioned screwball romantic comedy, but the execution is deliciously 100% vulgar and uproarious. To try to get on Mary's good side, Pat notices that Mary's roommate has a dog that only barks at bad people. He feeds the dog a sedative and comes over to her place so he can pet the content dog on his lap. Only when Mary goes to the kitchen to get him a drink does Pat notice the dog isn't breathing and begins to perform CPR. The little dog body inflates and deflates with each puff and will eventually catch on fire when he tries to shock it back to life with electricity. The dog will later attack Ted in a scene that ends with the dog jumping out the window and spending the rest of the movie in a cast. Another amusing bit involves a singing narrator who appears to exist outside of the story until the final shot where someone decides to assassinate him.

There's Something About Mary is a success of comedy where the hilarious bits trump the solid story. It's impressive how furious this film is to go for a laugh, even with the more disgusting moments of slapstick. Ted goes on a date with Mary at the beach, only for him to get a fishing lure caught in his lip, shown in a close-up with graphic detail. The jokes sometimes double up on each other with admirable absurdity; Ted accidentally stumbles into a gay hangout at a rest stop that lands him a spot on a criminal television program, Dom witnesses this episode on TV while someone is giving him fellatio in a perfect reveal. The comedy of the Farrelly Brothers was pretty hit or miss throughout the 1990s with *Dumb and Dumber* and *Kingpin*, but this was their grand slam where so many jokes evoke the biggest laughs I entirely forgot what the movie was about when I came back to rewatch it after so many years. I never forgot how much I laughed at Ted's zipper scene and still smile at it today for all its ridiculousness of the money shot and the delivery of Keith David asking the probing question; *"Is it the franks or the beans?"*

TIMECOP

DIRECTOR: Peter Hyams | SCREENWRITER: Mark Verheiden | CAST: Jean-Claude Van Damme, Ron Silver, Mia Sara | GENRE: Science Fiction | RUNNING TIME: 98 min | MPAA RATING: R

CLASSIFICATION: WEIRD

Time travel is a messy element in science fiction, and *Timecop* (1994) will make your brain melt in confusion if you think too long and hard about its perplexing notions. It is the year 1994 and scientists have finally figured out how to travel through time. Now comes the hard part of making sure it doesn't fall into the wrong hands with someone changing the present or the future for the worst. We don't know who initially would do this, but why take chances? The US government establishes a time travel protection team, The Time Enforcement Commission (TEC), to keep our timeline safe from tampering.

It's a good idea, but the film shoots itself in the foot with its silly logic. A rule of time travel established in the movie is that you can go into the past, but you can't go into the future as that part of history hasn't happened yet. But if you travel to the future and then have to return to the present, wouldn't you technically be traveling into the future? And, for that matter, how do you determine what is the exact time to re-enter the present/future without creating a paradox? These are questions a more intelligent film would have resolved, but this is apparently built more as a Jean-Claude Van Damme action vehicle than smart science fiction.

Van Damme plays TEC officer Max Walker with the pathos of a cop. He once had a loving wife, but she was murdered by some unknown punks that blew up their house. Skip ahead to the year 2004 and Max is now a veteran officer of the TEC. He uncovers a corruption scheme of time travel to 1929 when a former time cop tries to fix the stock market for Senator McComb to acquire funds for a presidential campaign. To investigate the corrupt senator, Walker works alongside his new partner to travel to 1994 and find out what McComb is up to. And the film gets messier from there with the blending of a buddy cop formula, a political conspiracy, an intricate plot across centuries and time paradoxes where the TEC is shut down, and Walker has a child.

The film was directed by Peter Hyams and the sets hold a

striking resemblance to his previous sci-fi film *Outland* (1981). While a lot of the future sci-fi tech looks a little cheap and silly, the time-traveling special effects are neat with reality-distorting portals that look like the ripples of a puddle in the air. There's also some fantastic uses of this effect, from falling off a building into a portal and Van Damme exiting a portal in the middle of the street, where he is nearly run over by a truck speeding towards him. The film's single greatest special effect, however, is the surprising climax when Van Damme shoves the villain into another version of himself, creating a paradox that contorts their bodies together in a grotesque display of merging flesh that melts into a puddle. Nasty things, those time paradoxes.

While Van Damme doesn't showcase his best fighting abilities in this picture, he does show off a lot of his muscular body. There's a sex scene with his character's wife, shot with plenty of erotic closeups, beautiful lighting, and smooth music to make love by. The action scenes also feature some skin. In the film's single silliest and most iconic moment, Van Damme, in his underwear, narrowly avoids being electrocuted by a conductive floor by doing the splits between kitchen counters. Not many beefy action stars could perform such a feat. Van Damme's splits were so impressive that he would later perform them for a 2013 car commercial, doing the splits between two moving trucks.

Timecop could technically be considered a comic book movie for being written by Mike Richardson, the founder of Dark Horse Comics, who also produced a tie-in comic book for the film upon its theatrical release. It could also be considered Van Damme's most massive blockbuster success for a film that made $100 million worldwide. While the film does handle the concept of time travel poorly for not thinking about the bigger picture, it's strangely unique for being a misfire of an ambitious sci-fi plot. The daringness makes it worth watching. That, and seeing Jean-Claude Van Damme in his tighty whities.

TITANIC

DIRECTOR: James Cameron | SCREENWRITER: James Cameron | CAST: Leonardo DiCaprio, Kate Winslet, Billy Zane, Kathy Bates, Frances Fisher, Victor Garber, Bernard Hill, Jonathan Hyde, Danny Nucci, David Warner, Bill Paxton, Gloria Stuart | GENRE: Drama | RUNNING TIME: 195 min | MPAA RATING: PG-13

CLASSIFICATION: WEIRD

Oh, how I wanted to loathe *Titanic* (1997) for its unbelievable lasting hype. It stayed in theaters for many months, shattered box office records and its theme song "My Heart Will Go On" sung by Celine Dion became just as big of a hit. I recall despising that song at my elementary school talent show where 90% of the musical acts were renditions of the song in the form of solos and duets. Forget my heart; my brain couldn't go on after the sixth version sung off-key.

But it's not fair to just judge a movie based on hype, especially one that is deserving of such praise. James Cameron approaches this romance on the sinking ship with the same amount of grand scale, dazzling special effects and exciting action sequences as he does for any of his movies. What's most shocking is that he stages a love story around it that is surprisingly engaging albeit melodramatic. Rose (Kate Winslet) is a 17-year-old passenger that finds her life doomed to be passionless when her poor mother marries her off to the wealthy snob, Cal Hockley (Billy Zane). She'd much rather hook up with the rebellious and adventurous Jack Dawson (Leonardo DiCaprio). Jack and Rose dart away from Cal's servant, Lovejoy (David Warner), and go exploring around all the nooks and crannies of the ship. They venture through the ship's busy engine room, dance a jig in the lively steerage and have a steamy romp inside a stored car.

But the film is more all-encompassing for steering away from Jack and Rose for moments that focus more on the ship. We meet the ship's captain (Bernard Hill), designer (Victor Garber) and managing director (Jonathan Hyde) to get a better understanding of what was going on behind the scenes of the Titanic workings by the time that nasty iceberg hits them. The ship was apparently trying to break the trans-Atlantic speed record, but didn't have the ease to turn fast enough if they encountered an obstacle. The Titanic strains to make the turn to avoid the iceberg, but cannot escape it.

For the second act, the film transforms from a soap-opera love story into a high-energy disaster picture. Cameron spared no expense in showcasing the sinking of the Titanic with flooded interiors and a sliding deck that forces passengers into the freezing waters. There's a lot of tension and action with people toting guns as they get desperate to leave the ship and take revenge. The orchestra plays their last song while the captain prepares the somber duty of going down with his ship. It's an unforgettable sequence, especially for the shot of one unlucky passenger who falls off the back of the sinking ship, smacking into the propeller on his way down. It's tragic and exhilarating at the same time.

Cameron had a love for the material with his bookended segments of modern day scientists investigating the ruins of the Titanic with an old Rose telling her story about the ship. From this opening and closing, it becomes clear that Cameron's love story was just something to place on top of his meticulous obsession with recapturing how such a massive boat sank on that fateful night to remember. I can't imagine he put much thought into the choice of having Rose give Lovejoy the middle finger.

As much as I want to despise the picture for being more appealing to teenage girls at the time, I've grown to like the movie more over time. There's a reason it stuck around in theaters for so long and became one of the highest grossing films of all-time. It stays with you in a handful of scenes, whether it's the flooding ballroom, the steamy sex scene, Kate Winslet's exposed breast or the propeller guy. The romance still feels hokey, but the technical aspects hold up well for such an expensive film. The hype for *Titanic* as a romance may have gone down in years, but its appeal of an exciting spectacle will go on, much longer than Celine Dion and her heart she won't shut up about.

TOMBSTONE

DIRECTOR: George P. Cosmatos | SCREENWRITER: Kevin Jarre | CAST: Kurt Russell, Val Kilmer, Michael Biehn, Powers Boothe, Robert Burke, Dana Delany, Sam Elliott, Stephen Lang, Joanna Pacula, Bill Paxton, Jason Priestley, Michael Rooker, Jon Tenney, Billy Zane, Charlton Heston | GENRE: Western | RUNNING TIME: 130 min | MPAA RATING: R

CLASSIFICATION: BEST

You won't find a more badass ensemble of men in the 1990s than in the all-star western *Tombstone* (1993). Here is a film that is overflowing with classic machismo for the Old West with an expert cast in their finest of roles. Kurt Russell is a furious force as Wyatt Earp, Val Kilmer as a keenly calm Doc Holliday, Sam Elliott as a thoughtful Virgil Earp, Bill Paxton as an eccentric Morgan Earp and Powers Boothe as the smug and drunk outlaw Curly Bill. And there are some surprising supporting roles by the likes of Stephen Lang, Charlton Heston, Thomas Haden Church, Michael Rooker, Billy Bob Thornton and Billy Zane. All that's missing is a quick cameo by Clint Eastwood, and you have the best western ensemble picture ever made.

The film centers on Wyatt settling down with his wife and brothers in the town of Tombstone, Arizona. He's looking to put aside his old life of gunslinging as a peace officer and make an honest living. Unfortunately, Tombstone is not the place for Wyatt to escape his troubles. For one thing, Doc Holliday is in town, and he's a bit of a casual and antagonizing gunslinger, despite his handicap of worsening tuberculosis. The Earp family attempt to stay out of trouble, but trouble finds them when Curly Bill and his Cowboys come to town and shoot the marshal. Unable to accept the lawlessness where Bill is allowed to shoot up the town in an opium-fueled haze, the Earps slowly begin to take charge of Tombstone's law enforcement. The war is soon on between the outlaws and the Earps with many gunfights, tough talk and deaths both tragic and gritty.

Tombstone doesn't do much to avoid the typical tropes of old Westerns nor does it add anything to the legend of Wyatt Earp that wasn't already known in other pictures. But for not reinventing the genre, director George P. Cosmatos stages all of it to be as exciting and entertaining as any western of familiar characters and convention. Nearly every character has a force all their own in this picture, whether its Powers Boothe as the cackling outlaw with a devilish mustache or Billy Bob Thornton in the small role of the unlucky troublemaker Johnny Tyler.

There are plenty of amazing scenes in Tombstone and not just the shootouts at the O.K. Corral or across the plains on horseback, fantastic as those scenes may be. Russell and Kilmer have a fantastic chemistry with the unshakable friendship of Wyatt, and Doc. Russell's performance has a lot of power for both his determination to do the right thing and his romantic love affair with Dana Delany playing the beautiful Josephine. But it's Kilmer's performance that was a real standout for how this sick man is at death's door, but is still a committed enough gunslinger to get a few good shots. There was a lot of effort that Kilmer put into this role, getting comfortable with his accent, mustache, and gun-drawing that he could sling a line like *"I'm your huckleberry"* with an ease of antagonism and wit.

Cosmatos was brought into the picture as a second director after the previous helmer of Kevin Jarre became overwhelmed with the production. Cosmatos was a smart pick for his meticulous devotion to detail in his story with everything from the events surrounding the legendary western figures to the scenery they occupied to the guns they brandished. He demanded so much authenticity to the point that he has been quoted for boasting that all the mustaches and lightning were real. The mustaches I accept, but the lightning is a little hard to buy with the perfect timing during some of the more chilling moments. But, damn, do I want to believe they're real.

TOTAL RECALL

DIRECTOR: Paul Verhoeven | SCREENWRITER: Ronald Shusett, Dan O'Bannon, Gary Goldman | CAST: Arnold Schwarzenegger, Rachel Ticotin, Sharon Stone, Michael Ironside, Ronny Cox | GENRE: Science Fiction | RUNNING TIME: 113 min | MPAA RATING: R

CLASSIFICATION: BEST

Arnold Schwarzenegger's large size usually makes him the big guy in charge of an action picture where he gets to fire the biggest guns and rack up the most extensive body count. *Total Recall* (1990) places him in a much different setting where he isn't entirely in control of what is happening to him. He isn't sure if what he's experiencing is reality or virtual reality, finding himself confused about who to trust and what to believe. His plight makes the non-stop action, gritty violence, giddy humor and science fiction decoration all the more pleasing in a picture that has as much brains as it does firepower.

Schwarzenegger plays Quaid, a buff construction worker of the future that takes an interest in Recall implants. Through implanted memories, the Recall agency can make one believe they have taken a grand vacation without actually having it. It sounds dangerous and Quaid is warned about it by his co-worker, but finds himself intrigued to pursue a virtual vacation. The implanted memories can additionally be tailor-made to enact any fantasy the customer chooses to experience. In Quaid's case, he picks the secret agent package of a daring spy on a mission to Mars who falls in love with a woman of his choice.

But when the memories are implanted, Quaid makes a violent escape from the facility and can't figure out why. His pal tries to turn him in, and his wife tries to murder him. Another version of himself contacts Quaid and gives him instructions on what to do, from pulling a tracking beacon out of his sinuses to getting his ass to Mars. Is all this real or is Quaid in a simulation? A man visits him at one point to inform him he is in a simulation and that it's gone awry, offering a pill to terminate the program. The presence of sweat on the man's forehead makes Quaid refuse, but keeps him wondering.

While Quaid ponders these weighty questions, he is always on the run from gun-toting bad guys as he shuffles through the underworld of a Mars colony. This is a remarkable microcosm of an enclosed society where the rich live in deluxe suites while the poor dwell in scummy bars. Quaid visits once such bar where he runs into all sorts of odd characters with mutations that range from melted faces to three breasts. The most critical and weird mutant he seeks is Kuato, a freaky looking figure that resides as a parasite of sorts on another human's stomach. He reveals to Quaid, through mindreading no less, that an alien artifact holds the key to defeating the evil Mars governor Cohaagen (Ronny Cox), who runs the business of providing air to the Mars colony with an iron fist.

There's a lot of intense violence in the stylish Mars enclosure. Why would guards in an all oxygen environment carry machine guns? That's easy: so they can accidentally shatter glass sending bodies flying out into the unbreathable Mars environment and experience the most horrific and over-the-top deaths. Those that are sucked out into Mars have their eyes bug out, and their throats swell up in the most disgusting and comical of special effects puppetry. When characters are shot, gushers of blood spew forth from their explosive wounds. One unlucky fellow has both his arms torn off in an elevator accident. Is all this excessive violence necessary? It is in a thrilling Schwarzenegger action picture.

Total Recall is the type of movie that manages to balance so many surprising elements of high-concept science fiction and brutal action. It's a high-energy thrill ride with plenty of gun chases, car chases and the fate of many lives hanging in the balance. It's a treat for the eyes with its rich production values of amazing sets and detailed mutants. And it manages to be as thought-provoking as the best science fiction tales, questioning one's own reality and identity. The ending has the guts to leave itself reasonably open-ended, refusing to acknowledge if Quaid's journey was real. It doesn't matter if it was all a dream or his reality, as the journey itself was such a wild experience. But it's still fun to debate anyway.

TOY STORY

DIRECTOR: John Lasseter | SCREENWRITER: Joss Whedon, Andrew Stanton, Joel Cohen, Alec Sokolow | CAST: Tom Hanks, Tim Allen, Don Rickles, Jim Varney, Wallace Shawn, John Ratzenberger, Annie Potts | GENRE: Adventure (Animated) | RUNNING TIME: 81 min | MPAA RATING: G

CLASSIFICATION: BEST

Similar to Disney's development of *Snow White and the Seven Dwarfs* in 1937, Pixar's *Toy Story* (1995) erupted as an entirely new realm of animation filmmaking. Computer generated imagery had been a contributor to hand-drawn and live-action films in the past, but this was the first time the medium would hold its own as a feature-length production and usher in a new age of animated movies. Kids adored it for just being a fun and exciting film, but adults may have dug it more for its breakthrough technology that was able to conceive an entire world from the perspective of toys.

The toys of Andy's room, when not being played with, are sentient characters that only move and speak on their own when Andy has left the room. After an active playtime, the toys dust themselves off and find stuff to do before Andy comes back. Mr. Potato Head (Don Rickles) picks his facial features up off the floor, grumbling about how he is only meant for ages three and up after Andy's baby sister plays with him. Slinky Dog (Jim Varney) attempts to set up a game of checkers under the bed. But Andy's favorite toy Woody (Tom Hanks) has much on his mind as the leader of the toys. Andy will be moving soon, and the toys are worried about being left behind. The early birthday party further complicates matters for Andy's toys, as a day of possible new toys which breeds fear among the ranks.

From these opening scenes, we gain a sense of the order and routine for the toys, but also see a grander sense of the computer-rendered world when the toy army men are sent downstairs to run recon on the party. There's weight when the small figures haul a walkie-talkie out of the bedroom. There's depth when they scale down to the first floor. There's texture when close-ups reveal peeled plastic on their helmets. All of this establishes the believability of this CGI world.

And there's plenty to see of this world as Woody, and Andy's new favorite toy Buzz Lightyear (Tim Allen) find themselves out of the house and struggling to make it back home. They are stranded at a gas station where they are nearly crushed into the pavement by an approaching truck. They sneak into the science fiction themed Pizza Planet eatery/arcade, concealing themselves inside food containers and darting behind rows of arcade machines. They stumble into the house of Sid, a sadistic boy that fancies destroying toys, his room a mess of power tools, rock posters, and cereal bowls. And their climactic high-speed chase through a suburban street has a massive amount of detail and scale, from the traffic to the passing houses.

Toy Story was a much different type of animated film for Disney at the time in that it was a buddy picture with no musical numbers. The humor is sharp and bright, making the necessary toy puns and references when appropriate for the story rather than when the whim strikes the writers. There's a lot to like about the characters from Woody's paranoia of not being the best to Buzz's comedic misunderstandings of believing he is a space ranger. Even the supporting characters have a surprising amount of range in bringing a voice and personality to familiar toys. I can no longer look at a Mr. Potato Head without hearing Don Rickles' grumpy attitude.

The movie has become a crucial milestone in animated films for its breakthrough animation and an intelligent script that perfectly taps into the imaginative fascination with toys. The film launched not only the creative studio of Pixar, but brought about a new era of filmmaking as several studios jumped onto the trend of computer-animated features. Better technology followed, but *Toy Story* stood the test of time for being a genuinely entertaining and engaging film rather than just being the first of its kind. Its inspiration will last to infinity and beyond.

TRAINSPOTTING

DIRECTOR: Danny Boyle | SCREENWRITER: John Hodge | CAST: Ewan McGregor, Ewen Bremner, Jonny Lee Miller, Kevin McKidd, Robert Carlyle, Kelly Macdonald | GENRE: Drama | RUNNING TIME: 93 min | MPAA RATING: R

CLASSIFICATION: BEST

Rarely does a film about drugs make you feel an all-encompassing experience of the highs and lows of heroin. *Trainspotting* (1996) begins with probably the most noteworthy and iconic rantings of an addict about choosing what to do with your life. *"Choose Life. Choose a job. Choose a career. Choose a family. Choose a fucking big television, choose washing machines, cars, compact disc players and electrical tin openers."* And so on. This opening monologue perfectly sets the tone for a film that urges us to consider everything in a movie that is not pro or anti-drug. All that's present is the craziness and camaraderie between those that are hooked on drugs, leaving it up to the viewer to decide how wild and depressing these lives indeed are.

Based on the novel by Irvine Welsh, the story follows Renton (Ewan McGregor), a man about Scotland that finds its filthiest corners for the most intoxicating of drugs. He surrounds himself with other users. Spud (Ewen Bremner) is too tweaked to land a job or avoid prison. Sick Boy (Jonny Lee Miller) is a more business-oriented addict for favoring a career in pimping and drug dealing. Tommy (Kevin McKidd) is someone who just can't kick the habit of drugs, but Franco (Robert Carlyle) is too proud to be an aggressive drunk.

Their lives are dirty and unpredictable, flowing from place to place in search of their next score. They exist outside the realm of ordinary people, ignoring all responsibilities and typical concerns with no significant attachments. Renton will attempt to detox himself after having violent diarrhea, locking himself in a room until he has cleaned up. He will get off drugs, but won't stay away for long. How could he when presented with one of the only major thrills in his life? Renton knows that his life will turn dirty and depressing once more, but those blissful few moments of experiencing the ultimate pleasures of intoxication seem worth it.

Renton's odd group is seen as both quirky and immoral. Sure, they have their strange moments of drug-induced babbling about if Iggy Pop is dead, but they also attack bystanders and steal money.

One of their worst offenses is when Sick Boy ignores his infant daughter that dies of neglect. Even this event, seen with the disturbing imagery of the baby's corpse, doesn't stop their consistent quest for highs. But the dead child is so unshakable that Renton will later hallucinate the dead baby crawling up to the ceiling and twisting its head around.

The film refuses to be pinned down as one type of film, as chaotic as Renton's opening rant. There are moments where it's stylish and intense, appearing as a slickly-directed heist picture at times. The highs come in the form of wickedly frenetic pleasure while the lows are downright disturbing and ugly, from the dead baby to the worst toilet in Scotland. The lives of these users are a whirlwind of emotions dark and euphoric. It's a film that asks if such people can get off drugs and seems to suggest they never will. They all seem to come back to drugs, even if a few of them die along the way. Renton vows at the end of the film to go straight, but he would return to the lifestyle once more in *T2: Trainspotting* (2017).

There was an extreme amount of effort put into such an offbeat film. Director Danny Boyle made the most of his limited budget by achieving some astonishing shots within Glasgow, even though the story takes place in Edinburgh. Ewan McGregor researched his role with books and interviews with addicts to the point that he almost considered injecting himself with heroin to gain the full experience. Robert Carlyle intelligently played Franco as a violent man with closeted homosexual urges, a theory that the novel's original author Irvine Welsh later confirmed. All of this works to make Trainspotting a film about drug addicts where they are not seen as merely silly dopes or depressed victims. They exist in a purgatory of no consistency, their freedom out of their grasp to choose. They don't want it. As Renton continues, *"I chose not to choose life. I chose somethin' else. And the reasons? There are no reasons. Who needs reasons when you've got heroin?"*

TROLL 2

DIRECTOR: Drake Floyd | SCREENWRITER: Drake Floyd | CAST: Michael Stephenson, George Hardy, Margo Prey, Connie McFarland, Deborah Reed, Jason Wright | GENRE: Horror | RUNNING TIME: 94 min | MPAA RATING: PG-13

CLASSIFICATION: WORST

Troll 2 (1990) holds a special place in the pantheon of bad movies. It belongs on the finest of terrible movie pedestals, placed alongside the likes of *Plan 9 From Outer Space* and *The Room*. It was initially written as Goblin, but adopted the title of Troll 2 to have the selling point of being a sequel, though the original *Troll* wasn't worth much. The story was conceived by Rosella Drudi more out of her frustrations with vegetarians than anything all that scary. Despite filming in Utah, the majority of the crew were Italians that did not speak English well, including the director Claudio Fragasso (pseudonym Drake Floyd). This meant that a lot of the strange dialogue, spoken by mostly non-actors, comes off as poorly written and acted. I wouldn't blame the actors as they have stated that Fragasso demanded they speak the lines as awkwardly as possible. Fragasso would later deny this and call his actors dogs. Now that's the perfect recipe for a bad movie.

The Waits family are going to be leaving behind their suburban lifestyle for a trip to a rural farming community. The town they're traveling to is Nilbog, which is goblin spelled backward, revealed in the silliest of scenes where the Waits son spots the reflection of a Nilbog street sign. The son is Joshua, a typical boy who seems to easily entertain his parents in the car with his rendition of Row Row Row Your Boat. Joshua is later visited by the ghost of his grandpa who informs him of Nilbog's vegetarian trolls that want to eat humans. Of course, vegetarian goblins can't eat meat. They need to transform tourists into plants by poisoning their food and drinks. It's up to Joshua to stop his family from eating or drinking anything in Nilbog. One of his many solutions is to urinate all over dinner.

The entire film is wall-to-wall scenes of surreal weirdness with poor choices in dialogue and actions. Joshua's father reacts to the urination at the dinner table with the strangest of lectures; *"You can't piss on hospitality! I WON'T ALLOW IT!"* The teenage sister, Holly, invites her boyfriend, Elliott, on the trip and they share the strangest of conversations. He says he needs to release his lower instincts, to which she kicks him in the groin and tells him to release them in the bathroom, leading to this unbelievable exchange:

Elliott: Are you nuts? You tryin' to turn me into a homo?
Holly: Wouldn't be too hard. If my father discovers you here, he'd cut off your little nuts and eat them.

Some of Holly's friends tag along to act as fodder for the goblins. The glasses-wearing Arnold encounters the goblins and receives a pike to the chest. He later discovers the plot of the goblins, made possible by some sort of magical stone, and proceeds to deliver hilarious line readings of *"Oh my god!"*

The goblins, once they reveal their true ugly form, are the silliest of movie monsters. They appear as the cheapest of Halloween costumes with plain burlap sack suits and rubber masks that look like depictions of melted cartoon characters. Even the one goblin with a working mouth that delivers the final line of terror can't be scary, even when eating up the goop of someone else's mother and offering their children a bite.

Troll 2 is a bad movie so unfathomably awful it must be seen to be believed. Certain scenes defy all explanation and line readings are so terrible you can't help but quote them. There are too many silly misfires to count, from the sex scene that involves corn turning into popcorn to the showdown where a Bologna sandwich saves the day. So strange was this film that it warranted a documentary, *Best Worst Movie* (2009), further detailing the troubled production and the aftermath that followed. I would recommend it as a film that was so bad it's good, but I can't in good conscience do so when the director employed a mental patient who was massively high during filming. Now that makes a *bad* movie.

A TROLL IN CENTRAL PARK

DIRECTOR: Don Bluth, Gary Goldman | SCREENWRITER: Stu Krieger | CAST: Dom DeLuise, Phillip Glasser, Tawny Sunshine Glover, Cloris Leachman, Charles Nelson Reilly | GENRE: Fantasy (Animated) | RUNNING TIME: 76 min | MPAA RATING: G

CLASSIFICATION: WORST

Don Bluth's career as an animation director was heading into a downward spiral of incoherence in the 1990s. *Rock-a-Doodle* (1991) and *Thumbelina* (1994) were such confusing displays of colorful animation that it's highly unlikely anyone over the age of twelve would have interest in such pictures. With *A Troll in Central Park* (1994), I lowered that bar to ages four and up, which in retrospect might be an insult to four-year-olds. There's nothing wrong with making a movie for kids that young, but only if it is something they can carry with them in their memories as they grow older. I doubt any of the intended audience could remember this dim film twenty years later.

Even describing the movie makes it sound as if it were more a fever dream than an animated feature. The magical troll Stanley (Dom DeLuise) is shunned by the dark Kingdom of Trolls for having a green thumb, both literally and figuratively. And magically as well, as he can spawn sentient flowers with the mere touch of his appendage. The bad trolls, who literally have to refer to themselves as such to remind us that they're evil, despise Stanley's flower-creation powers as plants are forbidden in the kingdom. He is promptly kicked out and banished to Central Park under a bridge, where he can spend his days making flowers that dance.

While enjoying his exile, Stanley runs across young kid Gus and his toddler sister Rosie. They've run away from home as their parents are too busy to take them to Central Park, but don't seem to miss mom and dad too much as Stanley entertains them with his magic without rules. Not only can Stanley breathe literal life into plants, but he can additionally enlarge a toy boat so that the kids can travel down a river. Oh, and he can make the boat fly as well through the power of believing in dreams and lousy screenwriting.

No real conflict occurs until well into the third act when the evil troll queen Gnorga (Cloris Leachman) decides to kidnap the children and turn Gus into a troll. Don't worry, kids; Stanley easily bests the nasty troll, reforms Gus and is soon revived after being turned into stone. There's nothing too dangerous here, parents. There's nothing all that interesting either as incredibly forgettable musical numbers crowd the screen.

Despite running a brisk 76 minutes, the majority of this picture is animation filler. It is technically competent and high in quality, but devoid of almost all narrative and character. There's an overly extended sequence in which Rosie cries, and the flowers attempt to cheer her up with a song and dance, as Rosie suckles on a bottle in the background. The song is not memorable, the dance is nothing special, and I doubt that Rosie's bottle was all that enjoyable either by the expression on her face.

A Troll in Central Park is so innocuous and bereft of conflict to an insulting degree. Some have discredited the movie as only being fun for the youngest of children, but don't those children deserve a more competent story that doesn't talk down to them? It's no wonder that it was such a monumental failure at the box office (an embarrassing $71,368), a result of Warner Brothers' lacking promotion from such low confidence in the movie. When compared against Disney's animated features of the era, blazing new trails in technology and storytelling, *A Troll in Central Park* wasn't only outside of Disney's league; it wasn't in the same solar system.

TRUE LIES

DIRECTOR: James Cameron | SCREENWRITER: James Cameron | CAST: Arnold Schwarzenegger, Jamie Lee Curtis, Tom Arnold, Bill Paxton, Art Malik, Tia Carrere | GENRE: Action | RUNNING TIME: 141 min | MPAA RATING: R

CLASSIFICATION: WEIRD

James Cameron's *True Lies* (1994) is the director's most unapologetically goofy, bloody, sexy, intense, macho and politically incorrect of action pictures. One could easily write it off as just another excuse for action shlock where Arnold Schwarzenegger shoots up bad guys and spouts some snappy one-liners. To do that, however, you'd have to write off the audacity of the stunt work, which features Schwarzenegger riding a horse through a high-rise hotel and saving his daughter while hovering in a Harrier jet. It's not every action movie you see scenes that outlandish.

Schwarzenegger plays Harry, computer salesman to his wife Helen (Jamie Lee Curtis) and expert spy to the US government. It's hard to buy Schwarzenegger as a computer salesman with thick glasses, but who cares? All of this is just an excuse for some silly antics amid a terrorist nuke plot that is itself an excuse for action. Harry is paired up with his smart-mouthed partner Gib, played by Tom Arnold with the right amount of comedic slapstick and backtalk during missions. As Harry goes undercover at a dinner party, Gib provides humorous commentary through his earpiece on Harry's dance with the exotic Juno (Tia Carrere) and his explosive shootout.

This is easily one of Tom Arnold's strongest roles in how he evokes comedy so effortlessly in scenes of action. He follows a terrorist on foot, taking cover behind a lamppost as he is shot at with an automatic weapon. Miraculously, Arnold is not hit and does a quick check of his body, more relieved that no bullet hit his testicles than anything else. It's a quick gag, and there are dozens more that come as fast as the bullets.

Jamie Lee Curtis wears thick glasses as Harry's husband, Helen, but movie logic dictates they won't be on for long. She is secretly having an affair of sorts with a used car salesman (Bill Paxton) that happens to be involved with terrorists. Work and home collide, eventually leading to a scene where Curtis pretends to be a hotel room stripper and Schwarzenegger the client. What was the point of this scene? Simple: To watch Curtis be both sexy and klutzy with her striptease while Schwarzenegger makes odd expressions with a disguise that's straight out of *Home Alone*. Paxton's character also gets his moment in another series of events that lead up to him pissing himself and blubbering to Schwarzenegger about sparing his life and his tiny dick.

The central plot of nuclear missiles going off in America takes a backseat to the chemistry, dialogue and incredible action. Even the characters don't seem as concerned when Harry and Helen share a kiss during a nuclear explosion in the background. The plot does little more than service more neat sequences, as when a terrorist group holds Harry's daughter Dana hostage as the leader arms a nuclear warhead. All you need to know is that the warhead can only be activated with a key and that Dana ran away with it onto a ledge, leading to a Harrier jet sequence. More action scenes leading up to this event, including the classic moment where Schwarzenegger, under truth serum, divulges his plans to his captors about how he'll slaughter them when he breaks his handcuffs. He does not disappoint.

And *True Lies* as a whole does not disappoint. Cameron has put as much effort into the comical chemistry of the characters as he did the grand-scale explosions. The dialogue between the low-key Schwarzenegger, the smart-mouthed Arnold, and the clumsily-frantic Curtis is all perfectly silly and amusing. The action is massive with lots of amazing stunts involving plenty of guns, cars, and jets. And it's a priceless moment to see Schwarzenegger pursuing terrorists on a horse, radioing for support with *"Can you hurry up? My horse is getting tired."* *True Lies* makes good on its action promises and then some.

TRUE ROMANCE

DIRECTOR: Tony Scott | SCREENWRITER: Quentin Tarantino | CAST: Christian Slater, Patricia Arquette, Dennis Hopper, Val Kilmer, Gary Oldman, Brad Pitt, Christopher Walken | GENRE: Comedy | RUNNING TIME: 118 min | MPAA RATING: R

CLASSIFICATION: BEST

Before Quentin Tarantino turned movies upside down with *Pulp Fiction*, he penned a cool and chaotic genre mixture with the always-buzzing direction of Tony Scott. If Tarantino's directed films were a subversion of genre pictures, this one is a playground of his favorites, playing more as a mixtape than an original composition. This makes the world of *True Romance* (1993) a fantastical wonderland of familiar material, punched up with the right amount of fantasy and fun to be a gleefully fun picture of love, guns, hookers, and drugs.

The film is written as the ultimate dream of a pop culture geek. Christian Slater plays Clarence, a guy who works in a comic book shop, marathons kung fu movies and is astounded to meet a blonde in the movie theater who digs the same type of films he does. The blonde is Alabama Whitman (Patricia Arquette), a prostitute that will sleep with him for free because she likes Clarence that much. To be fair, Slater does have a powerful enough charisma to pull off such appeal. Alabama's pimp is Drexl, played by Gary Oldman in his most wild of roles of a dreadlocked crazy.

The plot gets crazier. A vision of Elvis tells Clarence to kill Drexl. He does so and takes back what he assumes are Alabama's belongings. What he picks up is a hefty amount of cocaine. Clarence and Alabama try to sell it, but, of course, the cocaine dealing proves to be a challenging venture. And the film spins itself a tangled web of other characters including film producers, mafia bosses and gun-toting cops.

The film features perhaps one of the greatest supporting casts of the decade in some of the best scenes made for them. The most notable of exchanges occur between Christopher Walken as a mafia boss and Dennis Hopper as a security guard, in what is referred to as the Sicilian scene. Hopper is being interrogated by Walken and is sure he is going to die. Rather than finally tell his assaulters what they want to hear, Hopper breaks into a story about how Sicilians are all ancestors of black people. Laughs are had before guns are fired.

Tarantino based this dialogue on a real conversation he heard from a black guy that had been living in his house at one time. Other supporting players worth noting are Brad Pitt as a stoner, Val Kilmer as the vision of Elvis and James Gandolfini as a violent rapist that gets his head smashed with the top of a toilet.

Through scene after scene of fantastic character performances amid preposterous plotting, *True Romance* is one bizarrely intoxicating film. While it carries Tony Scott's unique direction of machismo, the film ultimately feels more like a Quentin Tarantino movie for his script that pops with charisma. You can even see shades of his previous film, *Reservoir Dogs*, in the film's climactic shootout where there is a lot of shouting, betrayal and few left alive. It's a star-studded feast of violence, character, and strangeness that only Tarantino plucks from a film geek's dreams and Scott places on the screen with high energy and insanity.

THE TRUMAN SHOW

DIRECTOR: Peter Weir | SCREENWRITER: Andrew Niccol | CAST: Jim Carrey, Laura Linney, Noah Emmerich, Natascha McElhone, Holland Taylor, Ed Harris | GENRE: Drama | RUNNING TIME: 103 min | MPAA RATING: PG

CLASSIFICATION: BEST

Truman Burbank (Jim Carrey) lives an ideal life in Seahaven. He resides in a sunny and gorgeous neighborhood with his wife Meryl (Laura Linney) and works as an executive at an insurance company. Life seems sweet. Almost too sweet. He's never left Seahaven, fearing to venture over water from his childhood fear when his father drowned. But it appears as though everyone seems to be preventing him from going.

What Truman doesn't know is that his entire life has been part of television. Born in an enclosed space, Seahaven is an artificial environment with hidden cameras filming all his exploits for TV, 24 hours a day. Every person in his life is an actor, coached over their earpieces about how to approach Truman, what to say to him and how to push the product placement. His wife always comes home with some new kitchen product she correctly positions for the camera. His best friend from childhood, Marlon (Noah Emmerich), becomes someone that Truman can confide in with all his paranoia about his life being controlled by some outside force. Louis knows the truth, and it's not easy for him to lie to someone who trusts him so well.

Watching all of this from the massive control room in the sky (the moon to be accurate) is the show's creator and director, Christof (Ed Harris). He directs everything for the show including the dialogue, camera shots, music cues and even the weather. He has been watching Truman since his birth on this thirty-year show and has grown far too fond of this person he has never met in person. He's not so much concerned with the program as he is for Truman, preferring to keep him in a tidy box of a town where he can manipulate everything to give him a comfy life.

This story is a premise straight out of *The Twilight Zone* that could have turned into a dark and terrifying picture for Truman realizing hundreds controlled every single aspect of his life and seen by billions. But director Peter Weir manages to make this film somewhat sweet and touching for a story about a man who lived a lie. The slow peeling back of the curtain comes with as much curious wonderment as it does heartbreaking desperation.

Truman starts poking around the corners that many did not suspect him to venture. His wife leaves promptly in the morning for surgery, but Truman has never seen her in an operating room. He follows her into the hospital and finds that everything is preventing him from finding the operating room, from hordes of wheelchair-bound patients blocking his path to equipment-pushing nurses. He'll later start toying with the routine of predictable patterns and try every possible means of unexpectedly leaving Seahaven. Broken buses, gridlocked roads, and forest fires are used to keep Truman contained. And when Truman starts learning that everyone is in on this staging of his life, there's a sad sense of madness for not being able to trust your wife who will try to redirect tough conversations with a new drink product.

The Truman Show is a film of big ideas and prophetic speculation. It carries heavy themes of spirituality, made very blatant with the emotional reveal of Truman discovering the physical border of Seahaven and Christof speaking down to him as a voice from above. The idea of a reality show with an artificial environment became quite common on television soon after the film's theatrical release and the prospect of 24-hour reality programs is all the more possible in the internet age of live streaming. The film is a mesmerizing voyeur experience; every shot inside Seahaven seems to be from a camera concealed or hidden behind something as evident in the borders of the frame. It's an astounding film that provokes enough big thoughts to earn its triumphant ending, cheers and all.

TWIN PEAKS: FIRE WALK WITH ME

DIRECTOR: David Lynch | SCREENWRITER: David Lynch, Robert Engels | CAST: Sheryl Lee, Moira Kelly, David Bowie, Chris Isaak, Harry Dean Stanton, Ray Wise, Kyle MacLachlan | GENRE: Horror | RUNNING TIME: 134 min | MPAA RATING: R

CLASSIFICATION: WEIRD

David Lynch's *Twin Peaks* is some of the most surreally intoxicating television ever conceived. The easiest way to describe the show is that of a murder mystery, but even that doesn't begin to scratch the surface of the show's unusual nature. American audiences became obsessed with finding out who killed Laura Palmer as much as who shot J.R. on *Dallas*. With the second season-ending the series on a cliffhanger after being canceled, fans wanted more. Imagine their disappointment when the *Twin Peaks* movie, *Fire Walk With Me* (1992), turned out to be a prequel.

Taking place a few days before the series begins, the story mostly follows Laura Palmer (Sheryl Lee) and the show of events that led to her death. We view her prim and proper side at school and home, but also her dark desires when running off to a scummy bar for drugs and sex. She is haunted during this time by an evil spirit that creeps into her dreams and rapes her, making her home a house of nightmares. Even though fans of the series already know what will happen to this character, there's enough brooding and foreshadowing to build the anticipation for her eventual demise. And when that moment finally arrives, it's more twisted than I had initially thought it would be.

Having already known who killed Laura Palmer and what happens to individual characters, there's a sense of familiarity so that Lynch can glaze over the specifics of this story. There isn't much of an explanation about Bob being the spirit of evil or the weird backward-speaking occupants of the red room. Even if you're familiar with them, Lynch provides no easy answers in his filmmaking loaded with cryptic symbolism and strange worlds.

Several members of the original cast reprise their roles. Kyle MacLachlan returns as the overly chipper and paranoid FBI agent Dale Cooper, before being assigned to Laura's murder. David Lynch himself slips back into the role of FBI Chief Gordon Cole, a deaf man that shouts all his orders about the overlapping events that lead towards Laura's death. But most of the supporting characters fall to the wayside as guest spots, be they newcomers of FBI Agent Sam (Kiefer Sutherland) or series regulars as The Log Lady (Catherine E. Coulson). There's even a special guest appearance by David Bowie as a field agent gone missing that seems to know too much.

While the TV series featured many tones, *Fire Walk With Me* reserves itself entirely to the horror angle. There's a sense of overwhelming dread that washes over the characters, even in the quietest of moments. Laura shares a frightening experience of a dream where she is continuously speeding into oblivion. Laura's father, Leland (Ray Wise), begins to have dark thoughts when encountering a hooker that resembles his daughter. Laura later indulges her vices at a seedy club with loud music, portrayed as a vile and depraved outing for the good girl who wants to let loose with strangers. When Laura meets her end, it is a dark and brutal death intensified with screams, flashing lights and a shocking amount of pain for all involved.

Fire Walk With Me was considered a significant failure for its low box office gross, scathing reviews from critics and a savage booing from its premiere at the 1992 Cannes Film Festival. Among those at Cannes, filmmaker Quentin Tarantino was hugely disappointed by the picture, writing Lynch off as someone who had *"disappeared so far up his own ass."* Despite the lackluster box office and press that followed, *Fire Walk With Me* has gained a small cult following among devoted fans of both Lynch and *Twin Peaks*. As with all of Lynch's films, it's a beautiful puzzle to piece together while still getting under your skin with genuine terror. It is a world so surreal and layered that it's easy enough to see why Lynch wanted to return to it so badly.

UNFORGIVEN

DIRECTOR: Clint Eastwood | SCREENWRITER: David Webb Peoples | CAST: Clint Eastwood, Gene Hackman, Morgan Freeman, Richard Harris | GENRE: Western | RUNNING TIME: 131 min | MPAA RATING: R

CLASSIFICATION: BEST

In the late 1980s/early 1990s, westerns were not a favorite genre. During an age of significant special effects and independent efforts, films about cowboys and dusty plains seemed too old-fashioned for cinemas. But then western star Clint Eastwood stepped in with *Unforgiven* (1992) to save the genre with an original script and modern style that reflected an era of significant change, proving that westerns could still be relevant to the right story.

In the same way that westerns were a rarity of the late 20th century, so were the gunslingers of the 1880s. Times were changing, and men who were once cold-blooded killers are finding themselves at more conflicting points in their later years. William Munny (Eastwood) is one such figure who is trying to reform. He's a hog farmer now, but not very good at it. He has two kids and a dead wife. His money is running low. And then the Schofield Kid (Jaimz Woolvett) comes to his farm to hire him for a bounty hunting gig. There's a thousand dollar reward for shooting two drunken cowboys that cut up a Wyoming prostitute and Schofield will split it with Munny.

Munny and Schofield are not great bounty hunters. Schofield's vision is so bad he can't land a shot. Munny is so old that mounting a horse has proven to be more difficult with age. They hire the additional help of Munny's old pal, Ned Logan (Morgan Freeman), who will also receive a cut of the reward. The trio will team up to combat the cowboys and the corrupt Sheriff Little Bill Daggett (Gene Hackman) of Big Whiskey, Wyoming. Daggett doesn't allow guns in his town and savagely beats down any visitors caught with one.

Eastwood's direction gives us not only a sense of these characters but the era they occupy by following some of the smaller roles. We get to know Big Whiskey's brothel owner Skinny Dubois (Anthony James) that only wants compensation for his damaged prostitutes. He views Delilah (Anna Thompson) more for how much she's worth. To madam Strawberry Alice (Frances Fisher), she's worth enough to pay a high bounty on her assaulters. Also in town is

English Bob (Richard Harris), a famous gunfighter made all the more known by following journalist W.W. Beauchamp (Saul Rubinek). The gunslinger lore is so intriguing for Beauchamp that he'll soon gravitate towards Munny to hear his story.

Though Munny will eventually turn into the ruthless gunslinger once more, the movie is not primarily about his mission or recapturing the thrill of his youth. It is more about a man trying to become a better person and a lingering fear that this will never happen. When tragedy strikes, he becomes more of an avenging figure, but not a hero entirely sure of himself. He confesses to Ned at one point that he thinks back to some of his past kills with a sense of regret. Ned suggests that he's changed since then, but Munny still feels as though he hasn't done enough to make up for his dark past. On the surface, he likes to think of himself as an enlightened person with a farm and kids, but how many fathers leave their kids behind to kill for money?

Eastwood's film was both a fitting tribute to westerns (dedicating the picture to the recently deceased directors of Sergio Leone and Don Siegel) and a revival of the genre. It was a significant box office success and would win the Academy Awards for Best Director and Best Picture. It could be argued its success led to a string of new western films that included *Tombstone* (1993), *Wyatt Earp* (1994) and *The Quick and the Dead* (1995). Most of those 1990s westerns, however, stuck close to the convention. *Unforgiven* stood out from the pack for Eastwood's desire to not only make a great western but one that deconstructs the genre to find something a little more than spurs and shootouts.

THE USUAL SUSPECTS

DIRECTOR: Bryan Singer | SCREENWRITER: Christopher McQuarrie | CAST: Kevin Spacey, Stephen Baldwin, Gabriel Byrne, Chazz Palminteri, Kevin Pollak, Pete Postlethwaite, Suzy Amis, Benicio del Toro, Giancarlo Esposito | GENRE: Thriller | RUNNING TIME: 106 min | MPAA RATING: R

CLASSIFICATION: BEST

Who is Keyser Söze? He's referred to by name as the man responsible for an explosion and a bloodbath that took place on a docked ship. He is a legend spoken of like a Turkish crime lord who voluntarily shot his family held hostage. This myth sets up the mystery of *The Usual Suspects* (1995), but also the high surprise in one of the most eye-widening twists of any crime film.

There are only two survivors from the boat incident. A Hungarian mobster with severe burns is in the hospital and keeps repeating his name. The club-footed and uneasy Roger "Verbal" Kin (Kevin Spacey) is in better condition, questioned by U.S. Customs Agent Dave Kujan (Chazz Palminteri). Verbal recounts and narrates his flashbacks for the Kujan, revealing the whole story of what led up to such an explosive event. But perhaps it isn't the entire story.

Six weeks ago, he explains that he was one in a group of four other criminals (Gabriel Byrne, Stephen Baldwin, Benicio Del Toro and Kevin Pollak) that banded together during a police lineup for a hijacking crime. They bond together well, cracking each other up as they go through the motions of the lineup, stepping forward and saying what they've been told to read with giggles and smirks. Their leader is Keaton (Byrne), a former cop; they complete a jewel heist that leads them to another heist in California. It is there that they meet the shrewd lawyer Mr. Kobayashi (Pete Postlethwaite), informing them that he works for Söze and has a job for them. There's a shipment of $91 million of cocaine that he wants. If they're lucky, they can split the money amongst themselves. Or, instead, cut it with whoever survives such a dangerous heist.

Verbal's recount of the events that led to the boat heist plays out with the slow burn of a mysterious noir. Detail after detail unravels as Verbal builds up the heist, and Kujan fiercely pieces it together. Though every actor present is in top form, Spacey steals the show for a multilayered performance with some of the best lines. When describing Söze, Verbal speaks of him so romantically for being a man he supposedly hadn't met; *"That was his power. The greatest trick the Devil ever pulled was convincing the world he didn't exist."* At his lowest and most pathetic when questioned about why he didn't stop Söze, Spacey becomes a whimpering mess; *"How do you shoot the devil in the back? What if you miss?"*

Bryan Singer, who would go on to direct the *X-Men* movies, directed this film as what he called a blend of *Double Indemnity* meets *Rashomon*. It plays with a high replay value for a crime picture that is slick and layered with deception and action. It's such a skillful and intriguing film that it's astonishing to think that Singer had considered the title and the poster before having a script. And though he draws from several familiar sources, including a *Citizen Kane* like climax for the big reveal of Söze, he weaves them so well to form an original crime plot all his own. I'll never look at coffee cups the same way again.

VEGAS VACATION

DIRECTOR: Stephen Kessler | SCREENWRITER: Elisa Bell | CAST: Chevy Chase, Beverly D'Angelo, Ethan Embry, Marisol Nichols, Randy Quaid | GENRE: Comedy | RUNNING TIME: 93 min | MPAA RATING: PG

CLASSIFICATION: WORST

The *National Lampoon's Vacation* movie series came to a somewhat disappointing ending at the theater with this fourth and pitiful installment of *Vegas Vacation* (1997). Many of the familiar elements were removed. It was the first of the series to receive a family-friendly PG rating. John Hughes was absent as the screenwriter for the first time in the history of the series. Even National Lampoon took their name off the title. How much more clear could it be made that the Griswold family has grown too old for the same old shtick?

The setting of Las Vegas doesn't leave much room for the hapless Griswold family to get into trouble. Clark and Ellen decide to take a family trip to Nevada where they plan to renew their vows, with children Rusty and Audrey in tow. What hi-jinks could be had in the city of sin feels strangely limited from the usual Griswold adventures? Clark accidentally causes a leak in the Hoover Dam and gambles away all of his life savings. Ellen catches the eye of Wayne Newton, and their relationship only goes so far as a few throwaway jokes for a celebrity inclusion. Rusty acquires a fake ID to hit the tables while Audrey takes in the wonderment of exotic dancing.

All of these arcs could be amusing, but they're all filtered through timid direction, relying mostly on the situation of the comedy and not the character. One of the first physical gags involves Audrey being trapped and crushed by the sunroof of a limo. It's a surprisingly mean-spirited bit in that it goes on way too long where Audrey pleads for help, and nearby people believe she is just partying hard.

As comedy backup, Cousin Eddie (Randy Quaid) returns to be the pestering dolt towards Clark but does little more than expected. He takes Clark to an all-you-can-eat buffet where he proceeds to steal rolls and eat like a pig. Quaid remains true to his character, but there's that smart stupidity missing from his scenes to make him a more chaotic force. Clark and Eddie later venture to a cheaper casino with such games as Pick a Number and Coin Toss, a lame satire on games of chance. Nothing particularly funny happens during this scene as it's mostly about watching how much Clark sucks at rigged games just as much as Eddie and how quickly he becomes addicted. Again, this sequence proceeds way past its expiration date. And what does it say of the hapless Griswolds when their victory is winning enough money to ride off in their new luxury cars?

All the crass, biting and offensive humor of the previous *Vacation* pictures had been watered down to a National Lampoon picture built for families. I think the message is made most evident with the returning gag of the Ferrari woman flirting at Clark, except this time she has a child. The shot is more depressing than amusing, the way a symbol of provocative perversion has been brought down a peg with age. Considering the long-running National Lampoon magazine stopped publishing one year later, it was a sign of the times that the once button-pushing comedy factory of the era was no longer viable. It would have to come to a close sometime, but I didn't expect in the form of a sellout commercial for Las Vegas, a premise that National Lampoon would have gleefully mocked in their golden age.

VERY BAD THINGS

DIRECTOR: Peter Berg | SCREENWRITER: Peter Berg | CAST: Cameron Diaz, Jon Favreau, Daniel Stern, Jeremy Piven, Christian Slater | GENRE: Comedy | RUNNING TIME: 100 min | MPAA RATING: R

CLASSIFICATION: WORST

Was there ever a more fitting title for such a disgusting movie? The black comedy of *Very Bad Things* (1998) requires one to laugh at a scenario better suited for a dark drama or even a horror picture. But the more I think about it; this plot probably wouldn't sit well in either of those genres.

A bachelor party goes wrong when Jeremy Piven accidentally murders an Asian hooker in the bathroom of a hotel room. The group, composed of Piven, Jon Favreau, Leland Orser, Christian Slater and Daniel Stern, panic at such a discovery with a bathroom coated in hooker blood. A black security guard comes investigating the noise, discovers the blood and is murdered by Slater out of desperation. The group decides to form a pact of silence, chop up the bodies and bury them in the desert. Are you laughing yet? How about when the party argues over keeping the body chunks separate as per Jewish law? Or when they bicker if there are Jews in Asia? Or when they debate if the black or the Asian body parts should be classified first?

For the rest of the movie leading up to the wedding, the plot relies on watching these men squirm and sweat over the anxiety of being caught by authorities or having one of them squeal. What I suppose is intended to be the comical aspect of all this is how life only gets worse for these people as they begin to kill each other off. One of them is convinced to blab which results in another ramming a car into the snitch. Said victim's wife might know what they did, so the group has to kill her as well. On and on the deaths continue to mount, supposedly funny for the frequency and offensive nature. The deaths themselves are not entertaining, nor is the aftermath that follows, which brings about more guilt and more killing in this cycle of violence.

Favreau's fiancee (Cameron Diaz), mere days from her wedding, hears of what went down in Vegas. A reasonable person would go to the police, but this is not a movie about rational people. She is so committed to her wedding day that she advises Favereau to kill off the rest of his friends to tie up any loose ends. Even the dog becomes a target. I'm surprised the dog came before the kids involved, but, then again, movie logic dictates dogs are more likely to die than kids.

Worse than the premise of *Very Bad Things* are the characters that occupy this agonizing hell of an existence. Everyone is either filled with wicked thoughts, acidic views or is just a blubbering mess of weakness and guilt. Slater is a lunatic of a psychopath who hardly bats an eye when killing his friends. Favreau is the meek man about to be married, groveling with his future wife to not make him kill anyone else. Diaz is so consumed by her wedding that she hates every person on the planet that is not her. The only character I felt even a little bit of sympathy towards was Stern's character; he is still a manic mess but has a chaotic family to at least justify his slapstick stumblings and constant sweating.

Not only are the violent acts devoid of humor, but scenes that seem as though they should contain something funny appear noticeably lazy. When the bachelor party arrives in Las Vegas, nothing memorable or amusing happens to them before they kill two people. A smarter dark comedy might find something more hilarious to evoke from a Jewish funeral, but the movie retreats to slapstick as some of the characters fall into the casket. It's such a shame that the capable direction of first-time director Peter Berg and an all-star cast is in service of a screwball plot that is equal parts lame as it is blindly toxic.

Very Bad Things confuses dark charm with sour cynicism. There's a terrible emptiness in the movie's finale in which Cameron Diaz collapses in the street, crying out in frustration at the direction of her life. If the film seriously wants the audience to find such an agonizingly nihilistic conclusion funny, they might as well slap a clown nose on Diaz or set her scene against silly music. The movie reaches a point long before this moment where laughter is so empty, and I questioned what the hell I was watching. It undoubtedly wasn't a comedy, even on the terms of a dark comedy. This picture is an ugly comedy, the type of humor that wants to be putrid and spiteful of humanity, begging the audience to laugh at the cruelty of it all. *Very Bad Things* indeed.

WAG THE DOG

DIRECTOR: Barry Levinson | SCREENWRITER: Hilary Henkin, David Mamet | CAST: Dustin Hoffman, Robert De Niro, Anne Heche, Denis Leary, William H. Macy | GENRE: Comedy | RUNNING TIME: 97 min | MPAA RATING: R

CLASSIFICATION: BEST

When the President of the United States is in trouble, the President's staff calls its #1 spin doctor, Conrad Brean (Robert De Niro). As the central orchestrator in *Wag the Dog* (1998), he is presented with his biggest challenge yet: the current US President is discovered to have been making sexual advances towards another woman during his re-election campaign. This is Brean's toughest assignment ever, but he has just the solution to avert a PR nightmare: staging a war.

To accomplish such a feat, he taps Hollywood producer Stanley Motss (Dustin Hoffman), looking like an uncanny version of real-life producer Robert Evans, to produce a war. Stanley says this plan out loud to stress how crazy this sounds. But the more Stanley thinks about it; the idea begins to interest him. He starts bouncing thoughts off of Brean and soon he's in a room spitballing ideas with his assembled crew of Fad King (Denis Leary) and musician Johnny Dean (Willie Nelson). Their conversations lead into all sorts of wild areas for staging a war with Albania, a country they don't know a whole lot about; *"Jim Belushi is Albanian!?"*

Motss proceeds with creating this war as he would any other movie production. He hires an actress (Kirsten Dunst) to play an orphan and run around a studio. Special effects are added in post to create the look of a ravaged Albanian village, the sounds of warring devastation in the background and a cute dog digitally inserted under her arm. Will the public believe such footage? Considering most Americans don't know that much about Albania, they buy it and the public shifts their focus from scandal to war. The CIA discovers their scheme and announces the war is over, but Motts comes up with a new story about a soldier left behind enemy lines. A new media catchphrase is created ("discarded like an old shoe"), another theme song performed ("Good Old Shoe") and another actor hired for the role of the rescued soldier, this time played by a prison convict (Woody Harrelson).

Wag the Dog is a film all about absurdist media tactics that continue to spin for the benefit of politics. It's a brilliant script more infatuated with the mechanics of the machine than the people running it. Brean proves himself to Motts as the man working with the White House not with words, but by ordering over the phone for the live presidential spokesman to speak his exact words on television. The media blitz moves along at a progressive rate, focusing on every little detail to sell the country a lie. A unique addition to the discarded shoe soldier story features Motts and Brean tossing tied shoes into a tree as a symbol of patriotism.

It's not until the very end that Motts finally realizes what he's created and how little he'll be rewarded for his work. The success of the President's reelection is attributed in the media to the lackluster campaign ads and not Motts' war staging. He doesn't feel disgusted but cheated by what he's done. He rants to Brean about how there is no Academy Award for producing and that he wants to blow the lid off this scheme to be recognized for his talents. He won't get far.

The deception of *Wag the Dog* continues to build bigger and crazier as the story goes on. Brean and Motts at one point find themselves stranded when their plane crashes and one of their actors is shot dead. But there is never a moment when the public learns the truth, and everyone is busted. There are snags in the plan, but Motts seems to roll with the punches and Brean has no significant worries as he can always slink back into the shadows. It's hilarious what they try to do in a darkly satirical manner. It's chilling that they get away with it.

WAYNE'S WORLD

DIRECTOR: Penelope Spheeris | SCREENWRITER: Mike Myers, Bonnie Turner, Terry Turner | CAST: Mike Myers, Dana Carvey, Rob Lowe | GENRE: Comedy | RUNNING TIME: 95 min | MPAA RATING: PG-13

CLASSIFICATION: BEST

There were plenty of *Saturday Night Live* skits that found their way to the big screen in the 1990s, but none were as full of energy and wit than *Wayne's World* (1992). It's a movie that could have gone the easy route of portraying the leads as brain-dead "yeah, right" losers who find themselves humiliated at every turn of their rock and roll lifestyle. But the basement dwelling duo of Wayne (Mike Myers) and Garth (Dana Carvey) are given enough smarts and dignity in between their grovellings of *"we're not worthy"* and horny gestures of *"Shwing!"*

Seen from outside the public access television show they produce themselves, Wayne and Garth are two hapless dorks that are too goofy to hold a job, but too sweet to be dangerous. Their evenings after taping are spent hanging out at the local donut shop, attending concerts for local rock bands and stargazing close to an airport runway to experience the thrill of planes landing so close to their eardrums.

Life is as sweet, and it's about to get sweeter when their television antics gain the attention of TV producer Ben, played with smarts and smarminess by Rob Lowe. His initial scheme is to use Wayne's World as a commercial platform for an arcade franchise, but his villain goals shift to stealing away Wayne's new girlfriend Cassandra Wong (Tia Carrere) with a record deal for her band. It's up to Wayne and Garth to save their show and Cassandra from the evil TV producer. Or unmask a *Scooby Doo* villain. Or whichever ending they prefer.

Wayne's movie world is a little odd, but always inviting. Myers directly addresses the camera with a smile, happy to divulge the ins and outs of his lifestyle. He introduces us to several weird and lovable characters, such as his creepy stalker ex-girlfriend Stacy (Lara Flynn Boyle) and the quietly psychopathic donut shop manager Glen (Ed O'Neill), who is just one lousy customer away from turning that smile into something dangerous. Cameos are also given a comical makeover when Alice Cooper meets Wayne and Garth backstage and breaks into a conversation about the history of Milwaukee.

Every scene is approached as a new avenue for comedy, both simple and sophisticated. In one of the most genius scenes, Wayne and Garth discuss the offensive nature of product placement while promptly holding brand-name products up to the screen with a knowing wink. Notice how they got all those products out of the way and then never shamelessly promote for the rest of the movie. Other bits are as simple as Wayne and Garth playing street hockey, talking about their futures when they're not shouting *"Car!"* to disperse from the oncoming traffic.

The smart comedy of *Wayne's World* left a significant impact on pop culture. The use of Queen's "Bohemian Rhapsody" in the car scene pushed the then 17-year-old song up on the Billboard charts and gave Queen a much-needed boost in popularity after the recent passing of Freddie Mercury. The one-word catchphrases of *"Schwing,"* *"Schyea"* and *"Not!"* became iconic battle cries of party monsters. The movie's popularity was enough to push for a quick sequel in 1994 which, while not as high in premise, retains much of the same glee with the characters and cameos (especially with a surprise cameo Charlton Heston). Unlike a lot of party/slacker movies from this era with the dimmest of characters and thinnest of plots, *Wayne's World* was one of the rare pictures worthy of partying on. And what a party it was.

WE'RE BACK! A DINOSAUR STORY

DIRECTOR: Dick Zondag, Ralph Zondag, Phil Nibbelink, Simon Wells | SCREENWRITER: John Patrick Shanley | CAST: John Goodman, Rhea Perlman, Jay Leno, Charles Fleischer, Walter Cronkite, Julia Child, Yeardley Smith, Martin Short | GENRE: Adventure | RUNNING TIME: 72 min | MPAA RATING: G

CLASSIFICATION: WORST

After Steven Spielberg wowed audiences with *Jurassic Park* (1993), all eyes were on his animation studio Amblimation to see what they could do with the more kid-friendly dinosaur tale *We're Back! A Dinosaur's Story* (1993). Based on the children's book by Hudson Talbott, it was in production for four years while the studio was working on additional projects. The result suggests they should have spent five years on the film and not so much of it on the promotion with Pizza Hut.

It's clear that more effort went into the animation and ad campaign - which included a giant inflatable character for the Macy's Thanksgiving Day parade - than any of the "story" present in this picture. Try to follow this plot if you can: Dinosaurs are plucked from their natural environment by the time-traveling inventor Captain Neweyes (Walter Cronkite) and fed his Brain Grain cereal that transforms them from mindless beasts into cuddly figures. Don't bother questioning Neweyes' alien companion Vorb (Jay Leno) as there's no time for that with this convoluted plot.

With all this technology, Neweyes' ultimate goal is to fulfill the dreams of children and bring real dinosaurs to them. He drops the dinos off in New York City, instructing them to head to the Museum of Natural History and not to be distracted by the evil circus master Professor Screweyes. Why doesn't Neweyes just drop the dinosaurs off right on the doorstep of the museum? Simple: If he did, the dinosaurs wouldn't have a wacky adventure where they disguise themselves as parade floats or end up caged for a circus.

The dinosaurs enlist the aid of two kids, Louie (Joey Shea) and Cecilia (Yeardley Smith), to help them find their way through New York City. Both have planned to run away from home and join the circus, leaving them open to free agents for the dinosaurs. The kids help their giant friends appear as floats in a parade and rescue them from the evils of Screweyes' Brain Drain, cereal that reverts the dinosaurs into violent creatures once more. It's a premise both scary and confusing for the kids.

It's baffling how Spielberg went from producing an animated dinosaur movie with real heart and adventure, *The Land Before Time*, to another animated dinosaur movie with no ideas. Most of its visuals and story elements come lifted from better movies, including Spielberg's *Close Encounters of the Third Kind* for Neweyes' spaceship and Disney's *Pinocchio* for the warping transformations of runaway children. When the script and animation are not ripping off better movies, it's often missing grand opportunities for excitement. Couldn't the dinosaurs do more on their quest than sing a ho-hum song, tumble through the streets in a car chase and then frighten children when they become brainless?

Captain Neweyes was originally going to be voiced by John Malkovich, but he dropped out of the project for how much he hated the script. He remained silent about the movie for years until he revealed in an interview how the production was more about the bottom line than the artistry to create something unique. He stated that film such as this *"just make you sick."* I share his nausea.

There are, however, two positive traits to this convoluted story with forgettable animation. The voice cast features top talent (John Goodman, Julia Child, Martin Short) and the running time is only 72 minutes. Though given how little material there is present in the script, stretched out with needless plots and too many characters, the movie may feel longer than it is.

WES CRAVEN'S NEW NIGHTMARE

DIRECTOR: Wes Craven | SCREENWRITER: Wes Craven | CAST: Robert Englund, Heather Langenkamp, Miko Hughes, John Saxon | GENRE: Horror | RUNNING TIME: 112 min | MPAA RATING: R

CLASSIFICATION: WEIRD

Director Wes Craven was determined with *New Nightmare* (1994) to bring the bloody legacy of Freddy Krueger back to its darker roots rather than just churn out *A Nightmare on Elm Street 7*. Craven was depressed that the horror icon he had developed, an evil spirit that attacks teenagers in their dreams with a glove of finger-blades, had turned into a cartoonish joke. By the sixth entry, *Freddy's Dead: The Final Nightmare* (1991), the once-terrifying figure that lurked in the shadows was now murdering with Nintendo's Power Glove accessory. To undo the damage, Craven returned to the series with a more cerebral and meta approach that not only explores the concept of Kruger but the moral questioning of horror movies in general.

Heather Langenkamp, the actress who played Nancy in the original *A Nightmare on Elm Street*, returns playing herself. Her life outside of the movies is that of a wife to her special effects wizard of a husband and mother to her young son afflicted with sleep problems. She just can't stay away from the horror movies as she's invited onto talk shows for her role, performs public bits with Freddy Krueger star Robert Englund (playing himself) and is approached by Wes Craven (also playing himself) about a new *Nightmare on Elm Street* movie. But the films begin to turn into a reality as visions of Krueger start to assault Heather by kidnapping her child's mind, attacking her husband and haunting her dreams.

Englund additionally reprises his role as the killer Freddy Krueger, but more terrifying and menacing than he was in previous sequels. He appears darker and bloodier in the shadows as opposed to looking rubbery and goofy in brighter lighting. His kills don't come packaged with silly themes or gimmicks, as he lets his claws do the talking more than his sense of humor. His kills are downright terrifying; one unlucky babysitter gets the claws to the gut and is drug up the walls and onto the ceiling. It's also probably the most intimidating of landscapes for Freddy's dream world, as when he drags Heather into his version of hell with gothic structures and giant flames. Even Freddy's outfit feels a little more mature with him donning a long black coat alongside his fedora and Christmas-colored sweater. The jacket makes him look more like he means business.

Craven admits in the film that Krueger is an unstoppable force, reasoning that the only way to stop Freddy is to make another movie about him. This is literal for this film's meta-world where Freddy is a real nightmare figure that haunts those who worked on the films, but there is perhaps some truth to Craven's statement about the movie monster. He couldn't have been happy with leaving the *Nightmare* legacy on such a funny note of Dream Demons and the Power Glove. This is a more fitting and cerebral end to Craven's creation.

But, of course, this would not be Freddy's last film. He would return in 2003 as his old cartoonish self for *Freddy vs. Jason*, putting to bed that lingering question of who would in a fight, eluded to in *Jason Goes To Hell* (1993). Freddy would be given a darker makeover in the 2010 reboot where Jackie Earle Haley would play Kruger, looking somehow more silly as an accurate depiction of a burn victim. Oh well. At least Craven was able to wedge in one last thoughtful and intriguing interpretation of the dream killer.

WHAT DREAMS MAY COME

DIRECTOR: Vincent Ward | SCREENWRITER: Ronald Bass | CAST: Robin Williams, Cuba Gooding Jr., Annabella Sciorra, Max von Sydow | GENRE: Drama | RUNNING TIME: 113 min | MPAA RATING: PG-13

CLASSIFICATION: WEIRD

I will never witness a more thought-provoking and grand depiction of the afterlife than the one present in *What Dreams May Come* (1998). It's a tale that entertains the idea that heaven is not a grounded vision of clouds and gates, but an amalgamation of our memories. In the case of Chris (Robin Williams), he remembers his wife's art as he enters the world of a moving painting he can control. Birds can swoop through a sky of swirling blue and flowers can be crushed into oil paint in your hand. It is easily the most dazzling vision of heaven, formed from the most original theories of consciousness.

The film approaches the subject of death with a somber and fascinating realization. Chris had led a great life before his untimely death. He met his wife Annie (Annabella Sciorra) while vacationing in Switzerland when their boats collide and their hearts connect. They fall madly in love, marry each other and have two children. They lose both kids in a car crash, and life turns dark. Annie suffers mentally from the experience, but Chris soldiers her on through life for as long as he is able. His happiness in the next world is well-earned, but it's a little empty without Annie.

The rules (or lack of rules) are revealed to Chris by his guide Albert (Cuba Gooding, Jr.), continually assuring him that the afterlife is what you make of it. Vast vistas of various colors can be created with a mere thought, partially controlled by Albert to give the world a little bit of surprise. Walking can turn into flying; paint can turn into coffee and walls can transform into doors. There are a handful of rules to the afterlife, but the movie quickly displays that they can be broken. Albert is baffled when a tree forms in this realm that was not willed into it, existing as that of a painting Annie created after Chris' death. Suicide disqualifies souls from a creative world as they are transported to their hell, where they do not realize they are dead. When Annie commits suicide, Chris will not accept her fate and makes the tough choice of journeying to hell to get her back.

On his travels, he meets various guides which seem familiar, plucked from identities Chris has associated from his own life. Every world he visits also carries a familiarity, causing Chris to recall memories that flesh out more of his story. Since he controls nearly every aspect of this world, a more prominent question to consider is that this struggle is all an invention of his own mind. Perhaps he is not saving his wife's soul, but merely preserving the association of her identity, as he wants to remember for eternity. Maybe there is no heaven or hell, only manifestations to give his consciousness a place to live and breathe. But now I'm getting too far down the rabbit hole.

Such questions, however, are far more intriguing than the plot which tries too hard to weave a happy ending for Chris and Annie. They're both genuinely likable and relatable characters I certainly wanted to root for, but perhaps not for a finale mushier than the world made out of paint. The movie has such grand ideas of the perceptions on death which causes the resolve more simplistic and hokey than it needed to be, lacking in the movie's more clever ideas and visuals. I had some hope when I spotted the Alternative Ending on the DVD, but those hopes were quickly dashed upon the realization that it was the same ending with a much worse epilogue.

Despite stumbling over itself as it crosses the finish line, there's still much to ponder and marvel at in *What Dreams May Come*, especially its stunning computer-animated worlds that won the Academy Award for Best Visual Effects. It may be a tad too cornball in its depictions of the great unknown, but the terrific performances and gorgeous cinematography make the afterlife a little more inviting and believable for its sublime wonderment. It beats the clouds and harps any day of the week.

WHAT'S EATING GILBERT GRAPE

DIRECTOR: Lasse Hallström | SCREENWRITER: Peter Hedges | CAST: Johnny Depp, Juliette Lewis, Mary Steenburgen, Leonardo DiCaprio, John C. Reilly | GENRE: Drama | RUNNING TIME: 118 min | MPAA RATING: PG-13

CLASSIFICATION: BEST

What's Eating Gilbert Grape (1994) is a film that could have gone wrong quickly with a dramatic script calling for a mentally disabled boy and a 500-pound woman. Thankfully, a very young Leonardo DiCaprio perfectly conveyed the mannerisms of someone with retardation, taking care not to make the character too dumb or too intelligent. Darlene Cates does well as a 500-pound woman considering, well, that's how much she weighs. But past the portrayals of obesity and mental disabilities, this is a film that feels real for a rural family where every day is stressful with such handicaps.

The Grape family live in the small town of Endora, Iowa where there isn't much to do. Arnie Grape (DiCaprio) likes to climb the water tower, but can't remember how to get down. Arnie's massive mama Bonnie (Cates) spends her days on the couch, unable to get over the death of her husband. Arnie is mostly cared for by his brother Gilbert (Johnny Depp), the 21-year-old responsible for most of his family. Gilbert's life is tough, though not as rough considering the small town. He's a generally sweet guy that does a good job fixing up the house and taking care of Arnie. Whereas the Grape sisters of Ellen and Amy become easily frustrated with Arnie's antics, Gilbert does his best to keep them in line and force his "nobody touches Arnie" policy.

But when the traveling Becky (Juliette Lewis) stops into town, Gilbert is conflicted about his duties to his family and his romance with this new girl. Their relationship forces Gilbert to break the routine and bring about feelings of guilt and frustration for him and his family. It's painful that Gilbert would leave Arnie to freeze in the bathtub alone to go off on a date, but how often would he get a chance like this? This doesn't bode well for when Gilbert finally introduces Becky to the family, making for a tension-filled visit.

There are many great moments of conflicting emotions that cover so many complexities. Take the scene at the dinner table when the family is discussing what to serve at a party. Bonnie starts questioning the preparation of bacon while Arnie keeps chiming in about wanting to eat hot dogs like a child eager to make a point. Gilbert tells Ellen not to speak with her mouthful of food, and she tells him that he's not her dad. Arnie laughs and repeats. Gilbert tells him dad is dead. Arnie laughs more and begins repeating "dad's dead" continuously. He can't control his emotions, and the dinner explodes into a whirlwind of erupting feelings.

What's Eating Gilbert Grape is a film of both drama and tragedy, but not pity. We don't look down on the likes of Arnie, Bonnie or even Gilbert as lesser folk, but people with sensitive issues trying to get by. There is a heart in the picture, but it is never overly sentimental by refusing to go for the easy tears. Plenty is going on in town with the arrival of a new supermarket forcing out the old one, but there are far more significant concerns in the Grape household. The film succeeds because it is character driven by the strongest of casts. Depp commands the screen in a demanding role of a boy burdened with too much and believed he could take it all on before he starts to crack. Cates, for her first movie role, does a fantastic job as an overweight woman who has more to her character than her weight. Of course, DiCaprio became a breakout star and nominated for numerous awards, including the Academy Award for Best Supporting Actor. They deliver fantastic performances in a film that requires delicate and demanding control, ultimately providing a warm and real world that is as joyous as it is troubling.

WILD AT HEART

DIRECTOR: David Lynch | SCREENWRITER: David Lynch | CAST: Nicolas Cage, Laura Dern, Willem Dafoe, Crispin Glover, Diane Ladd, Isabella Rossellini, Harry Dean Stanton | GENRE: Drama | RUNNING TIME: 124 min | MPAA RATING: R

CLASSIFICATION: WEIRD

David Lynch establishes the ominous tones of *Wild at Heart* (1990) right from the first scene. Sailor Ripley (Nicolas Cage) descends the stairs at a party when a hitman attacks him. Cage bests him and proceeds to violently smash the man's head until blood is spilling out onto the marble floor. Having confirmed his kill, he staggers up, lights a cigarette and gazes up at horrified onlookers with an expression of a cool rebel. Everything you need to know about the film is in this scene: surprise, horror, romance, coolness and violence, all stirred with that oddly uneven Lynch-ian assembly.

Sailor is in love with the beautifully trashy Lula (Laura Dern). They're a pair made for each other with their rebellious enthusiasm. She picks him up from prison and buys him a snakeskin jacket that he views as a sign of individuality. They shack up in a motel where they have sex for hours and then go out dancing at a club. Sailor steals the mic and begins singing Elvis. No, he not only sings Elvis, but he also speaks like Elvis so regularly that he may believe himself to be the reincarnation of the celebrity.

Pursuing them is Lula's mother, Marietta (Diane Ladd), hateful of their relationship after Sailor refused her sexual advances. She puts out a hit on Sailor with the strangest of people, quickly turning her into a mess of regret for her bad decisions. Word gets around to Sailor's old friend Perdita (Isabella Rossellini), who he visits in Big Tuna, Texas. Perdita conspires with the sinister Peru (Willem Dafoe), a man with the mustache of the devil and the teeth of a circus freak. Peru invites Sailor on a robbery but plans to kill him during the heist. And as if that weren't enough tension, Lula has some serious misgivings about her lifestyle when she discovers a shocking development in her life.

The film features many familiar Lynch traits of bouncing between melodrama, humor (light and dark), musical sequences, grotesque violence and surreal horror. The heist goes from being an intense ticking-clock of a crime to a hilarious bit of dark slapstick with an accidental head explosion and a shot-off hand that is taken by a dog. Throughout the picture is the ever-present hallucinatory imagery of *The Wizard of Oz*, where Lula starts seeing the Wicked Witch and Sailor is visited by the Good Witch. Lynch fans will notice a few familiar faces from Blue Velvet and *Twin Peaks*. The most peculiar of the cast is Sheryl Lee being cast as the Good Witch. She played the dead girl Laura Palmer in *Twin Peaks*, representing a sense of innocence and good that was lost to evil. Lynch must genuinely believe Sheryl is an angel to cast her in such otherworldly roles.

Wild at Heart was not an audience pleaser. A test screening found multiple people leaving during a horrific torture scene. Lynch refused to remove this scene, even after a second testing saw even more people leaving. It would debut at the Cannes Film Festival where it won the Palme d'Or prize, provoking a polarizing audience reaction of cheers and boos.

Lynch has described the film as finding love in hell. For all the violence, darkness and ugliness that he includes in the script, it ultimately ends with a happy and fantastical ending where everything turns out okay for the conflicted protagonists. Some think it to be ironic as Lynch was always a director that found satire in the dramatic convention, but he assures it is intended to be a straight happy ending. And after all that odd chaos, why not end on a positive note? That is if you consider Nicolas Cage singing "Love Me Tender" over the credits to be happy.

WILD WILD WEST

DIRECTOR: Barry Sonnenfeld | SCREENWRITER: S. S. Wilson, Brent Maddock, Jeffrey Price, Peter S. Seaman | CAST: Will Smith, Kevin Kline, Kenneth Branagh, Salma Hayek | GENRE: Action | RUNNING TIME: 106 min | MPAA RATING: PG-13

CLASSIFICATION: WORST

The most memorable aspect of the dismal action-comedy *Wild Wild West* (1999) was the ridiculous theme song sung by Will Smith. It says something about a 1990s adaptation of a classic TV western when the lyrics *"wicky-wild-wild, wicky-wild-wild"* are present in the movie's theme. The rest is forgettable, or at least it should be. I can't imagine anyone speaking highly of a blockbuster where Will Smith appears in lousy drag, Kenneth Branagh seems with no legs, and the special effects artists were forced to create a gigantic robotic spider for a western setting.

The duo of Will Smith and Kevin Kline are federal agents West and Gordon, tasked by President Grant to investigate the recent disappearance of scientists. Salma Hayek tags along as the daughter of one of the scientists and the obligatory corset-wearing love interest. In their investigation, they discover that the man behind these kidnappings is the mad Dr. Arliss Loveless (Kenneth Branagh). I describe him as crazy because you'd have to be looney to have the idea of creating giant steam-powered metal spiders. These machines are slow, clunky and can be easily bested by tripping one of their many wobbly legs, an easy feat for the setting of Monument Valley. The AT-ST walkers from *Return of the Jedi* appear stable and robust by comparison.

Smith and Kline don't exactly have the best chemistry as their buddy status remains as artificial as the giant spider. Kline is supposed to be a master of disguise, but he's no Ethan Hunt as he mostly disguises himself as a woman in the most unconvincing of costumes and makeup. The movie would rather the audience laugh at his disguises than believe them to be capable. Since he sucks in that department, Kline's character also has the abilities to be a genius inventor for conveniently moving the plot along. Some inventions are as practical as a chainmail vest. Others are as preposterous as a projection device that can reveal what a murdered man last saw. He's mastered that enigma of tapping into the human brain, but somehow hasn't perfected the fine art of dressing up as a woman.

Smith, in his typical comedic fashion, hangs around to crack jokes, as when he mistakenly slaps a woman's breasts and says that's how his African ancestors communicated. He is confronted by a lynch mob for his actions and continues to stammer with improv, desperate to find something funny in such an awkward scenario. The director leaves it to Will Smith to hang himself for this scene with uncomfortable wording. Another scene where he appears to be left out to dry is when he dresses in drag to be a belly-dancer that distracts the villain. How hilarious.

Salma Hayek's character? Just breasts and ass. There is one scene where Smith and Kline have a conversation entirely about her boobs and her ass behind her back. The less said about her, the better, considering she ends up with nobody. And then there is Kenneth Branagh, awkwardly cast as the literal mustache-twirler Loveless. In the original TV series, Loveless was a dwarf, but I suppose being a legless villain would have to suffice. Branagh puts on his thickest of southern accents either out of fear of revealing his English accent or realizing he was playing a cartoon character. His character fluctuates between being a ruthless gun-toting killer to an over-the-top presenter that pops out of an exploding head of Abe Lincoln. Nothing much to see here.

There are several questions about why such a bafflingly incoherent movie as *Wild Wild West* made it through production. For instance, why the inclusion of a giant mechanical spider, present in the movie poster, the action climax and the final shot of the sunset? So the story goes, producer Jon Peters wanted a giant spider to appear in a *Superman* movie that was never made. Peters' wishes were finally granted with *Wild Wild West*. I'm not sure if it was his genuine vision for his giant spider to be a mechanical monstrosity roaming the western plains, but he probably took what he could get.

WING COMMANDER

DIRECTOR: Chris Roberts | SCREENWRITER: Kevin Droney | CAST: Freddie Prinze, Jr., Saffron Burrows, Matthew Lillard, Tchéky Karyo, Jürgen Prochnow, David Warner | GENRE: Science Fiction | RUNNING TIME: 100 min | MPAA RATING: PG-13

CLASSIFICATION: WORST

Wing Commander (1999) is a historical bad video game movie for featuring actors and dialogue worse than that in the video game. The game Wing Commander IV featured filmed sequences with actors Mark Hamill and Malcolm McDowell that had enough talent to stand out when video games with cutscenes were usually rampant with bad acting. They weren't exactly A-listers and didn't deliver particularly memorable performances, but they were far more refined and capable than the likes of Freddie Prinze Jr. and Matthew Lillard shouting *"WOO"* amid space dogfights.

The very premise of *Wing Commander* is silly in that it wants to be a submarine movie in outer space. In a zero-gravity environment of endless black, the marines of the Terran Confederation still shout phrases of *"Torpedoes incoming! Brace yourself!"* or *"Hard to port!"* The movie seems to entirely forget that it takes place in space as in one scene where a bulldozer pushes a downed spacecraft out of the hangar bay, tumbling downward into space. The sound is also present in space as the crew silence themselves when sonar reads a destroyer vessel above them that rattles the hull. There's sci-fi pulp, and then there's sci-fi junk that wants nothing to do with science, rarely asking if the action of a submarine picture may not work as well in space.

Such laughable logic could be forgivable if the plot weren't so disposable. It's a battle of generic looking humans versus the cat-like Kilrathi aliens that want to destroy the universe. Or are they more like turtles with their hunched armor? Or goats with their long beards? They apparently appeared more like cats in the video games, but they seemed to have been given a makeover for the movie. The game's creator Chris Roberts, who directs this picture as well, was not entirely pleased with the designs of the Kilrathi in the video games and just as displeased with the movie version. We may never see Roberts' vision of how the Kilrathi should genuinely appear.

Fighting these odd creatures is a band of noble young human heroes. At least most of them are if you consider Blair (Freddie

Prinze, Jr.) a half-breed, as he is referred. He is half-Pilgrim, a breed of humans that have developed a gene specifically for space travel. Regular humans don't like the Pilgrims very much for their gung-ho desire for travel, but they seem to tolerate them for taking humans to the stars. Prinze is likable enough as a *Top Gun* style pilot and seems to generate some electricity when paired with the always cackling Matthew Lillard, appropriately named Maniac. Additional actors seem to be taking their roles seriously as well, including the ever refined David Werner.

But they are all trapped in a hokey script that can't decide if it wants to be a science fiction adventure or a navy military drama. Characters appear dressed in classic navy uniforms but are battling against ridiculous looking aliens in space. The heroes pilot starfighters that shoot down enemy starships, but the fighters appear as clunky World War II aircrafts without any practicality for space flight. Even the space helmets resemble World War II era attire, the only separating feature being an odd-looking eyepiece for targeting or something.

Without any exciting story pulling the fight of humans versus Kilrathi, *Wing Commander* ultimately becomes a dull sci-fi picture of pointless battles, forgettable dialogue and banal visuals that are more laughably ugly than thrillingly immersive. The only moment of genuine drama occurs when one pilot doesn't quite land her starfighter on the hangar of a spaceship. It's too bad the scene is ruined by the sheer cheapness of the entire production. I can't decide what was more laughable in that scene: The juvenile exchange of *"Just ease it in, girl"* and *"I love it when you talk dirty"* or the fact that the pilot lands with a crash on the outside of the hangar where there is no gravity.

ABOUT THE AUTHOR

Mark McPherson has written as a film critic for MovieSpoon.com and TwinCitiesGeek.com and has a Bachelor of Science in Media Arts and Animation. He lives and works in St. Louis Park, Minnesota.

MadnessMark.com

OTHER BOOKS BY THE AUTHOR

Pixels to Premieres: A History of Video Game Movies

The Great Animated Movies

Printed in Great Britain
by Amazon